Schumann's Virtuosity

ALEXANDER STEFANIAK

Schumann's Virtuosity

Criticism, Composition, and Performance in Nineteenth-Century Germany

INDIANA UNIVERSITY PRESS

Bloomington & Indianapolis

This book is a publication of

Indiana University Press
Office of Scholarly Publishing
Herman B Wells Library 350
1320 East 10th Street
Bloomington, Indiana 47405 USA

iupress.indiana.edu

Publication of this book was supported by the AMS 75 PAYS Endowment of the American Musicological Society, funded in part by the National Endowment for the Humanities and the Andrew W. Mellon Foundation.

Manufactured in the United States of America

Library of Congress Cataloging-in-Publication Data

Names: Stefaniak, Alexander, 1983– author.
Title: Schumann's virtuosity : criticism, composition, and performance in nineteenth-century Germany / Alexander Stefaniak.
Description: Bloomington ; Indianapolis : Indiana University Press, 2016. | Includes bibliographical references and index.
Identifiers: LCCN 2016021002 (print) | LCCN 2016021399 (ebook) | ISBN 9780253021991 (cloth : alkaline paper) | ISBN 9780253022097 (ebook)
Subjects: LCSH: Schumann, Robert, 1810–1856—Influence. | Virtuosity in musical performance—Germany—History—19th century. | Music—Germany—19th century—Philosophy and aesthetics.
Classification: LCC ML410.S4 S83 2016 (print) | LCC ML410.S4 (ebook) | DDC 780.92—dc23
LC record available at https://lccn.loc.gov/2016021002

1 2 3 4 5   21 20 19 18 17 16

For Eliana, a poetic virtuoso

Contents

Acknowledgments

Perhaps the most rewarding aspect of writing this book has been meeting and working with many generous, kind people who have helped the project along at various stages. I especially owe thanks to several archivists who shared sources from their collections, guided me through their holdings, and extended their hospitality during my research trips: in particular, Thomas Synofzik and Hrosvith Dahmen of the Robert Schumann Haus in Zwickau, Matthias Wendt of the Robert-Schumann-Forschungsstelle in Düsseldorf, and the staff of the music reading room at the Bayerische Staatsbibliothek in Munich.

Numerous friends and colleagues in musicology and other disciplines gave freely of their expertise and provided moral support. Ralph Locke, Bill Marvin, and Holly Watkins were instrumental in shaping this book's methodological pluralism. At Washington University in Saint Louis, Ben Duane, Denise Gill, and Paul Steinbeck read several of chapters, and the university's Eighteenth-Century Interdisciplinary Salon (led by Tili Boon Cuillé) workshopped chapters 1 and 4. Brad Short of Gaylord Music Library tirelessly acquired resources important for my work. Other friends and colleagues in Saint Louis and elsewhere commented on sections of the book or answered specific queries: Jonathan Bellman, Julie Hedges Brown, Todd Decker, Matt Erlin, Catherine Keane, Caroline Kita, Jonathan Kregor, Karen Leistra-Jones, Att and Robert McDowell, Laurie McManus, Craig Monson, Dolores Pesce, Robert Snarrenberg, Hanne Spence, Marie Sumner Lott, Lynne Tatlock, and Kira Thurman. All shortcomings, of course, remain my own.

Some individuals and institutions granted me permission to quote extensively from sources to which they hold rights. Claudia Macdonald allowed me to draw a music example from her edition of Schumann's F-Major Piano Concerto; Hofmeister Verlag—to draw a music example from their edition of Schumann's "Sehnsuchtwalzer" Variations; and Thomas Synofzik—to publish my translation of Schumann's epilogue to his "Ein Opus II" essay. A version of chapter 4 has appeared in *Journal of Musicology* 33, no. 4 (2016).

Raina Polivka and her colleagues at Indiana University Press have steered this book steadily through review and production. Janice Frisch, Naz Pantaloni, and my anonymous readers were especially helpful in the earlier stages, and David Miller and Mary Ribesky oversaw production. Eileen Allen prepared the index. Washington University PhD student Joseph Jakubowski engraved the music examples—no small feat, given the complex piano textures—and Karen Olson proofread them with an eagle eye.

Finally, my family has been at my side from the beginning of this project. My parents, Martha and Carl, and my brother, Andy, have always supported my musical and scholarly endeavors and were ever ready to hear more about nineteenth-century virtuosity and the writing process. My wife, Eliana Haig, was behind this book in ways big and small, sharing every day her ready humor, infectious curiosity, unsinkable confidence, and musician's ear.

Schumann's Virtuosity

Introduction:
The Virtuosity Discourse

In 1843, Robert Schumann published a review that captures, in miniature, the range and urgency of the issues that virtuosity raised for him. The essay covered violinist Antonio Bazzini's May 14 concert at the Leipzig Gewandhaus. Its opening does not bode well for the Italian star: Schumann seems to announce himself as a staunch antivirtuosity critic. He describes a horde of virtuosos glutting the concert scene and suggests a sweepingly negative view of their work:

> The public has lately begun to notice a surplus of virtuosos, and so has this journal (as it has often made known). Their recently arisen desire to travel to America seems to indicate that the virtuosos themselves feel this, and there are many of their enemies who harbor the silent wish that, for Heaven's sake, they will all stay over there. For, all things considered, the newer virtuosity has contributed but little to the benefit of art.[1]

And yet, in his next breath, Schumann claims that Bazzini himself stood apart from this multitude. "But when virtuosity confronts us in as delightful a form as the above-mentioned young Italian," he wrote, "we gladly listen to it for hours." The rest of the review suggests diverse ways in which Bazzini, for Schumann, redeemed virtuosity. Schumann praises Bazzini's compositions, specifically his Concertino in E, Op. 14: "The natural flow of the whole . . . the really enchanting luster and euphony of individual passages . . . most virtuosos have barely any idea of these things." He describes Bazzini's stage presence, his "strong, youthful face" that provided a welcome contrast to "world-weary, pale virtuoso figures." He acknowledges Bazzini's nationality and distanced him from stereotypes of Italian frivolity, calling him "an Italian through and through, but in the best sense." Schumann also surely recognized that, on this occasion, Bazzini was lending his star power to an orchestra that had become an exemplar of serious programming under Felix Mendelssohn's baton. At times, Schumann did worry that Bazzini stumbled off this pedestal and delighted the crowd with merely physical stunt-artistry. Schumann chided him for programming his *Fantaisie dramatique* on themes from Donizetti's *Lucia di Lammermoor* and his Capriccio on themes from Bellini's *I Puritani*. "In both of the following pieces," he complained, "I saw unhappily that he was not ashamed of flattering the public. Here was not so much music but rather a piling up of violin artifice, in which, in any case, nobody can imitate Paganini." Mostly, though, Schumann commended Bazzini's virtuosity. In one striking passage, he suggested that the violinist embodied Romantic ideals about music's ethereal qualities, its transcendence of the sensuous world: "Sometimes when he played, it seemed that he came from the land of song—not a land that lies here or there, but that land from which everything unknown eternally beckons."[2]

This review represented one small episode in Schumann's lifelong effort to shape what I call the virtuosity discourse: a lively, at times acrimonious discussion in which musicians and writers debated the imagined distinctions between transcendent and superficial virtuosity. Participants ranged across Europe and included often-anthologized writers such as Schumann himself, François-Joseph Fétis, Eduard Hanslick, Heinrich Heine, Franz Liszt, A. B. Marx, and Richard Wagner, but also myriad anonymous reviewers of sheet music and concerts. In its most basic definition, virtuosity entailed an extraordinary display of physical skill from the performer—velocity, power, facility, even the ability to invent and execute radically new sounds.[3] As the Bazzini review illustrates, Schumann and his contemporaries examined virtuosity in various guises. In some cases, they viewed virtuosity in soloists' live performances or public images. In others, they considered how musical compositions scripted virtuosic display. Often, these works came from genres that conventionally promised flashy passagework and were designed to show off or train a performer, such as concertos, etudes, variation sets, and opera fantasies. In still other cases, writers emphasized broader musical practices or abstract aesthetic questions, such as trends in concert programming or ideas about how a performance should relate to a musical work. Schumann's review also illustrates that virtuosity could take on a variety of cultural and aesthetic meanings within these different contexts.

This discourse responded to bourgeoning public fascination with the feats and creations of virtuoso instrumentalists. During the early nineteenth century, star virtuosos gained new centrality in musical life, thanks partly to the growth of the public concert and mass markets for instruments and printed music. They captured audiences' imaginations and prompted lively journalistic accounts. For several writers, the heyday of virtuosity symbolically began in the late 1820s, when Nicolò Paganini began touring outside of Italy, and it reached an iconic height with Berlin "Lisztomania" in 1841. Hanslick's 1869 history of Viennese concert life described the years between 1830 and 1848 as his city's *Virtuosenzeit*, or "Age of Virtuosity."[4] The rage for virtuosity unfolded not only on the concert circuit but also in the drawing rooms of piano-owning, middle-class households. In the latter milieu, amateur musicians purchased showpieces en masse for recreational playing, sometimes enticed by famous performers.[5]

Instrumental virtuosity also attracted unprecedented critical scrutiny. Many musicians and writers lamented that the virtuosity craze—or at least some of its manifestations—was immersing audiences in superficial, mechanical display and that it was threatening music's status as an art form. When present-day scholars explore nineteenth-century responses to virtuosity, they often emphasize this anxiety. Recent studies have described a "backlash" or "battle" against virtuosity, a view of the virtuoso as a "threat from within"—even, in one book, "virtuosophobia."[6] These accounts chart vital currents in the virtuosity discourse, and I am not seeking to debunk them. Battle imagery captures the high-pitched rhetoric Schumann and other critics employed. It also acknowledges that many critics were denigrating individual musicians or entire traditions, sometimes aiming to purge musical life of what they considered unsavory elements. The opening of Schumann's Bazzini review, after all, advocates self-exile for a generation of virtuosos. Nevertheless, Schumann's response to Bazzini himself points to a different belief that musicians and writers advanced with equal fervor: that certain performances and showpieces could harness astonishing physical display to contemporary concepts of transcendence and seriousness. It is this multifaceted view of virtuosity that I want to explore through Schumann—the ambitions as well as the anxieties.

As Schumann and his contemporaries struggled to make these distinctions, the virtuosity discourse influenced manifold aspects of musical life. It affected the status of the performer (notably the belief that the ideal virtuoso was a reverent interpreter), the public images of individual virtuosos (such as in the Franz Liszt–Sigismond Thalberg rivalry), and the role of pyrotechnic display within showpieces themselves (works as different as Adolph Henselt's etudes and Johannes Brahms's concertos). The virtuosity discourse constructed enduring hierarchies: the exclusion of popular pianist-composers Henri Herz and Frédéric Kalkbrenner from the canon and the inclusion of Frédéric Chopin, for example, the long-ambivalent reception of Liszt's compositions, or Clara Wieck Schumann's enshrinement as a "priestess" of music.

On a larger scale, the virtuosity discourse helped cement ideologies crucial to the culture of serious music. A broad, diverse network of movements among many nineteenth-century writers, listeners, and musicians elevated music's standing among the arts and within society. Though this phenomenon is most often associated with German contexts, it in fact pervaded Europe. When individuals who counted themselves part of this art world evaluated virtuosity, they judged it against their larger beliefs about music's social and aesthetic significance. Schumann thus spent his career exploring a question that preoccupied many musicians and listeners of his generation: What could virtuosity mean for this culture of serious music, a culture Schumann idealized as a *Davidsbund* (a "League of David") locked in struggle with musical "Philistines"? When and how could resplendent technical display take on the transcendent qualities that he and his contemporaries believed music should embody?

Traces of Schumannian Virtuosity.
And, Schumann the Antivirtuoso?

Exploring how Schumann approached these questions will take us from one end of his career to another. Schumann was active as a pianist, writer, and composer from the late 1820s through the mid-1850s, a crucial stage of the virtuosity discourse. Scholarship over the past two or so decades has often concentrated on charting how Schumann integrated music and literature. Virtuosity, though, was equally central to his activities. The teenage Schumann who immersed himself in Jean Paul and wrote poetry was also an aspiring piano virtuoso who practiced etudes, variations, and concertos by bestselling pianist-composers such as Kalkbrenner, Ignaz Moscheles, and Johann Nepomuk Hummel. His idols included not only Schubert and Beethoven but also contemporary virtuosos. An 1830 trip to a Paganini concert fired his musical and literary imagination, and for decades he kept a program from an 1818 concert at which he sat behind Moscheles. Schumann performed in salons and on student-run concerts during his Gymnasium days, after matriculating at the University of Leipzig in 1828, and while spending a year at the University of Heidelberg.

The prospect of virtuoso stardom was what led Schumann to turn his avocation into a career. In Leipzig, he met the piano teacher Friedrich Wieck and began full-time studies with him in 1830. He studied alongside Friedrich's daughter, Clara, who was nine years Robert's junior and already establishing herself as a virtuoso pianist. She and Robert, of course, married in 1840. Robert watched Clara's career unfold almost from its beginning and saw her assume many roles: a pianist whose playing (according to German critics) emanated from her inner being or resonated with the listener's, a champion of young "Romantic" composers, an authoritative interpreter of the canon, and one half of an idealized composer–virtuoso partnership. Schumann wrote some of his first compositions as vehicles for his own performance, including the "Abegg" Variations, Op. 1, and his unfinished F-Major Piano Concerto.

Schumann, however, shaped the virtuosity discourse most influentially not as a performer but as a composer, critic, and collaborator. He began to complain of a hand injury as early as 1830 and by 1831 recognized that it had ended his piano prospects. In 1834, he and several colleagues founded a music journal, the *Neue Leipziger Zeitschrift für Musik*. The following year, he became the sole owner and editor of the journal, now renamed the *Neue Zeitschrift für Musik*. Schumann wrote on a variety of subjects for the *Zeitschrift*. Among these, he was the main reviewer of virtuosic piano music, contributing essays on concertos, variations, etudes, and other genres and covering the Leipzig concert scene. During the 1830s, Schumann mainly composed solo piano music and wrote several works in virtuosic genres: for example, two sets of Paganini transcriptions, Opp. 3 and 10, the Toccata Op. 7, the *Études symphoniques*, Op. 13, and the *Concert sans orchestre*, Op. 14. Schumann's activities also brought him into personal contact with a wide circle of virtuosos. Some were known mostly in Leipzig, such as Ludwig Schuncke and Ernestine von Fricken. Others were internationally renowned, including Chopin, Liszt, Thalberg, Mendelssohn, and English pianist-composer William Sterndale Bennett.

After his marriage, Schumann engaged with virtuosity within a more diverse field of compositional activities. No longer focused primarily on solo piano music, he published symphonies, chamber music, and theatrical works. He moved his family to Dresden in 1844 to provide a base for his operatic plans and, in order to devote his time fully to composition, sold the *Neue Zeitschrift* to critic Franz Brendel. Robert's collaboration with Clara became increasingly public and central to both spouses' careers and images. After several unfinished attempts at writing a concerto, he completed his Piano Concerto Op. 54 and his Introduction and Allegro Appassionato Op. 92, both of which Clara premiered. The Schumanns continued this collaboration in Düsseldorf, where Robert served as municipal music director from 1850 until he was institutionalized in 1854 (suffering, he and his contemporaries believed, from debilitating mental illness). Robert also codirected the 1853 Lower Rhine Music Festival, an event that sparked a relationship with the young violinist Joseph Joachim. In Düsseldorf, Schumann produced a string of concerted works for Clara and Joachim: his Introduction and Concert Allegro Op. 134, his violin Phantasie Op. 131, and his posthumous Violin Concerto. Early in the Düsseldorf years, he also composed his Cello Concerto Op. 129, a work that went unperformed during his lifetime.

Understanding Schumann's significance for the virtuosity discourse requires us to integrate a diverse body of sources. His showpieces range from pithy etudes to structurally enterprising concertos, his writings from descriptions of live performances to analyses of compositions. Many of these sources I newly discovered through my archival research. Others have been hiding in plain sight, long available to scholars but afforded scant attention. These new sources include:

- The *Fantaisies et finale*, an early version of the *Études symphoniques* that Schumann briefly considered ready for publication—essentially, a substantial piano work unknown to most performers and scholars.
- Schumann's unpublished epilogue to his often-anthologized "Ein Opus II" essay on Chopin. Long assumed lost, this piece of writing presents Schumann's fictional character Raro offering his thoughts on Chopin's "Là ci darem la mano" Variations, Op. 2.
- Reviews in which Schumann and other critics claimed that virtuosity could convey the sublime.
- Documents of Schumann's association with Leipzig salon hostess Henriette Voigt.
- Liszt's 1854 essay on Clara Schumann, a complex and contentious portrait of the Schumann partnership.

Still other sources are well-known but take on new significance when reexamined in this rich context: drafts that partially document the genesis of Schumann's Piano Concerto, for example, and his reviews of Liszt's 1840 Leipzig concerts.

This evidence opens a new window into Schumann's work. Much recent scholarship on virtuosity centers on performance, whether the activities of individual musicians or the aesthetics of performance and interpretation. Liszt often single-handedly emblematizes nineteenth-century virtuosity altogether. These accounts helpfully correct a historiographical tradition that has privileged musical scores and canonized composers. They have also shed new light on individuals and practices long considered marginal.[7] Scholars do almost unanimously recognize Schumann as an important thinker on virtuosity. Perhaps because Schumann had no performing career after 1831, though, none has explored his engagement with virtuosity on its own terms and probed its complexity, extent, and significance. When Schumann does make an appearance in scholarship on virtuosity, he usually receives brief mention as a foil to or outright opponent of popular performer-composers. In many cases, scholars cite him as an example of the critical scrutiny that confronted virtuosos. Dana Gooley, for example, argues that Liszt constantly reinvented his persona partly because he was "shaken to the core" by the "war against virtuosity" that critics such as Schumann and Fétis were waging. When Laure Schnapper explains the disrepute into which Herz's music fell, she includes Schumann among the many French and German critics who dismissed it as trivial.[8]

Schumann scholarship itself has yet to revise this view of the composer. Studies of Schumann's showpieces often invoke their seriousness as a foregone conclusion—a mark of quality that should be apparent to the reader—rather than investigating the composer's and his listeners' basic assumptions about virtuosity.[9] Leon Plantinga's still-standard book on Schumann's criticism includes only a small portion of his writings on virtuosity (understandably for such a wide-ranging study) and emphasizes ambivalent or negative responses.[10] Schumann's virtuosic works have received valuable studies that I draw upon, but these elucidate issues of form, genesis, and genre rather than the broader cultural and aesthetic questions virtuosity raised.

Beyond musicological scholarship, representations of Schumann in literature, film, and visual art often give the composer an antivirtuosity stance to symbolize his introversion and idealism. Roland Barthes's 1979 essay "Loving Schumann" calls the composer a "musician of solitary intimacy," a description that would seem to fit ill with flashy concertos and halls packed with applauding fans.[11] The Belgian symbolist artist Fernand Khnopff depicted this view of the composer in his 1883 painting, *En écoutant du Schumann* (Listening to Schumann). Here, a seated woman raptly listens to a pianist, her hand covering her face. Khnopff suppresses evidence of physical music-making, showing only a hint of the pianist's right arm. As the historian Peter Gay notes, the image captures a typically nineteenth-century, middle-class view of music as an inward-directed activity, and I would add that Khnopff specifically named Schumann as an emblem of this extreme interiority.[12] The 1947 Schumann biopic *Song of Love* sets up its own dichotomy between the Schumanns and virtuosity. Here, Clara Wieck (played by Katherine Hepburn) introduces concert audiences to Robert's music with the lyrical "Träumerei" from *Kinderszenen*. The historical Clara Wieck, by contrast, first publicly played Robert's music when she premiered his Toccata. When Hepburn's Clara hears Liszt perform his transcription of Robert's "Widmung," she insults her rival, telling him that his virtuosic elaborations have missed the song's simple, heartfelt essence. A more recent fictionalization of the Schumanns' lives, J. D. Landis's 2000 novel *Longing*, portrays Robert's hand injury not just as a career-altering catastrophe—which is certainly how the composer saw it in the 1830s—but as an idealistic act of resistance. The rise of popular virtuosos such as Franz Hünten and Henri Herz "was enough to tempt one to destroy his hand. . . .

He had confronted the Philistines and had slung the potent, smooth stone deep within his own brain." "Schumann," Landis writes, "had destroyed himself as a performer of music so that he might become its creator."[13]

Scholars and critics, though, have hinted that there is a more complex story to tell about Schumann and virtuosity. Gooley's essay on the "Battle against Instrumental Virtuosity" observes, "For Schumann, virtuosity must contribute to the animation of mind that makes music a poetic art." A century and a half before (and without Gooley's scholarly distance), the German critic Carl Koßmaly made a similar point. In an 1844 panoramic review of Schumann's piano music, Koßmaly wrote that Schumann had inherited a lamentable musical scene dominated by "a virtuosity that sees in itself the sole, ultimate aim of art, when, after all, virtuosity should be a means to serve . . . the soul and spiritual expression of music." He characterized Schuman as an exception, one of the musicians who strove for "nobler goals" in their compositions."[14] Both Gooley and Koßmaly raise and leave open the question of specifics—what strategies Schumann used to suggest that the music he composed or championed realized these ideals, and how they fit into the larger virtuosity discourse.

Visions of the Virtuoso

Schumann spent his career shaping several different strands of the virtuosity discourse. Like a fascination with virtuosic performance, the desiderata of Romantic aesthetics and the nineteenth-century German ideology of serious music were central to his intellectual framework and professional identity. Schumann, therefore, was constantly exploring questions of transcendence and superficiality in virtuosity. For him, transcendent virtuosity was always an open question—not a straightforward category but an ideal that was subject to negotiation and reinterpretation. His answers were highly context-dependent and evolved as he redefined his career, moved between musical venues, engaged with different aesthetic concepts, and encountered different performers. His approaches to virtuosity depended, for example, on whether he was writing lightweight showpieces for amateurs or warhorses for professionals, on whether he was listening to Chopin in the 1830s, Liszt in 1840, or Clara Schumann in the 1850s. They depended, too, on whether he was attempting to channel "poetic" interiority or sublime overload—and on whether he was an upstart composer of abstruse piano pieces or a composer of symphonic and chamber music at the height of his renown. In some of his writings, Schumann explored virtuosity as written into compositions, in others he responded to live performances, and in still others he considered composition and performance in conjunction or even opposition. At each turn of his career, he engaged his contemporaries in a different conversation about what it meant to be a virtuoso. Some of his contributions shaped influential, even central, episodes in the history of nineteenth-century virtuosity. Others remained meaningful mainly for the composer and his immediate circle.

Indeed, I use the phrase "virtuosity discourse" to stress an important aspect of my approach. Ideas about transcendent and superficial virtuosity, I would argue, do not necessarily translate into musical topoi or clearly defined stylistic categories. Instead, they represented aspirations and rhetorical strategies. Whether centered on the score or the performance, the virtuosity discourse offered a framework in which nineteenth-century musicians discussed and conceptualized the meaning of flashy pyrotechnics, compared musical styles, and developed strategies for presenting virtuosity.

Schumann and his contemporaries, after all, interpreted virtuosity in conflicting (at times self-complicating) ways. Such tensions and disagreements concerned not just the merits of specific showpieces and performers, but fundamental questions about virtuosity. When Schumann reviewed Chopin's "Là ci darem la mano" Variations in 1831, for example, he aligned himself with some critics who heard transcendent qualities in the work, diverged from others who panned it as unattractive and poorly wrought, and drew criticism for his own style of writing. Schumann's evaluations of Liszt and Thalberg fluctuated throughout his career and depended on whether he was studying their scores in the quiet of his study or being wowed by live performances. As we will see again and again, claims about virtuosity were by no means free of self-interest. Friedrich Wieck reviewed showpieces that his daughter-protégé was performing, and journals routinely touted showpieces to which their publishers owned rights.

My discussion keeps this contingency and pluralism in view. I am not attempting to show whether Schumann's or any other composer's showpieces fit any transhistorical categories of seriousness or transcendence.[15] Nor am I seeking to settle nineteenth-century debates about virtuosity—I would not presume to argue whether some composers' or performers' work was somehow "better" than others', or whether any of Schumann's or his contemporaries' critical judgments were more persuasive, accurate, or disinterested than others'. Rather, I seek to explore what aspects of specific works and performances Schumann and his contemporaries responded to, what shapes their arguments took, and what contemporary ideals their own virtuosity drew upon. For this reason, my discussion often involves written sources that document receptions or illuminate the intellectual and cultural arenas virtuosity entered.

As the reader might already have guessed, though, this book continually returns to the compositions Schumann wrote and reviewed. In this sense, it differs from more performance-centered scholarship on virtuosity. One reason for my focus is pragmatic, fitted to the nature of my sources. With only a brief performing career, Schumann did not leave behind a voluminous record of performance and reception comparable to Liszt's, Paganini's, or Clara Wieck Schumann's. Though he wrote rich, revelatory accounts of performances, he devoted much of his critical output to reviewing compositions.

Schumann's compositions made elaborate public statements about virtuosity. In many cases, the showpieces he wrote for specific performers (notably, but not exclusively, Clara Wieck Schumann) helped shape their public images. Critics also heard an elevated kind of virtuosity scripted into the compositions themselves. Many of these works give the soloist unconventionally styled passagework and deliver it in surprising contexts. Schumann's early Toccata, for example,

Example 0.1. Schumann, Toccata Op. 7. Coda.

peaks with an expansive coda excerpted in example 0.1. Amid the leaping octaves that emphasize each downbeat, Schumann suddenly seems to shift the barline one sixteenth-note forward. The resulting jolt injects new energy into the motoric double-note figuration. When the poet and music critic Ernst Ortlepp reviewed Clara Wieck's 1834 premiere of the work, he wrote, "We are convinced that what a Sebastian Bach, what a Beethoven, what a Paganini carried within himself also lies within Schumann."[16] His encomium ranks the then little-known composer alongside one icon of pathbreaking virtuosity and two emblems of compositional greatness. Schumann's 1853 Introduction and Concert Allegro Op. 134 dates from nearly the opposite end of his career. A single-movement work for piano and orchestra, the Concert Allegro culminates with the musical deus ex machina shown in example 0.2. As if called forth by the pianist's chords, a brass melody suddenly materializes and soars to a climax on the sweeping arpeggios. The work delivers its virtuosic peak as a surprise apotheosis. When the *Signale für die musikalische Welt* reviewed the published score in 1855, it advertised the piece's display of technique, praising the "extraordinary brilliance" and noting that "the excitement lies particularly in the passagework." The reviewer assured readers that Schumann had combined this appeal with a "dignified, inner artistic worth" and that the work would succeed with a "cultivated" audience. The *Signale* predicted that, like Mendelssohn's concertos, Schumann's showpiece would enter the repertoires of all piano virtuosos who were "worthy of respect."[17]

Schumann, then, invites us to use musical works as one form of evidence that reveals how nineteenth-century musicians and writers engaged with virtuosity. One form of evidence among many—accounts of performances by Clara, Henselt,

Example 0.2. Schumann, Introduction and Concert Allegro Op. 134. Coda.

Liszt, Joachim, Robert himself, and other virtuosos augment insights we can gain from works, forming a flexible context that embraces score and stage. Moreover, my discussions of compositions emphasize how showpieces package virtuosity: how they realize flourishes, climaxes, and transformations of passagework, and position them within musical processes. The Toccata, for example, presents its final burst of fireworks as a Beethovenian coda-peroration (see chapter 4), and Schumann designed the Concert Allegro to capture Clara Schumann's midcentury persona (see chapter 6). Considering virtuosic compositions from this perspective takes into account their function as performance vehicles, as works that allowed performers and listeners to experience virtuosic display along trajectories delimited by the composer.

Each chapter of this book explores a different view of virtuosity that Schumann tried out or wrote about, emphasizing those that illuminate larger currents in nineteenth-century music. The chapters proceed in loosely chronological order and trace the composer's changing views, circumstances, and relationships. Many subchapters focus on individual works, writings, or events, so that readers interested in specific topics will be able to locate focused discussions. The first part of this book concerns Schumann's piano decade and traces the way he positioned the music he reviewed and composed within (and sometimes against) the highly popular "brilliant" or postclassical style of piano virtuosity. Chapter 1 explores Schumann's critique of the pleasures that such showpieces provided. Chapter 2 analyzes his concept of the "poetic," and chapter 3 traces his involvement with amateur music-making and salons that cultivated "poetic" virtuosity. Chapter 4 shows how Schumann attempted to channel the sublime in virtuosity. The second part of this book explores how Schumann allied his work with the culture of the Austro-German canon and its guiding ideology, the work concept. The term "work concept" embraces a complex set of attitudes and practices, all of which centered self-consciously serious musical life on idealized musical works. Though Schumann was preoccupied with these issues from early in his career, most of the cases I consider here offer new insight into his activities during the 1840s and 1850s. Chapter 5 examines how Schumann navigated a tension that nineteenth-century writers perceived between the spectacle of virtuosity and the aesthetics of the musical work. Chapter 6 follows Robert's collaborations with Clara and Joachim, two virtuosos whose interpretations of canonic repertoire gained them reputations as "priests" of high art.[18]

Whereas musicians such as Liszt and Paganini tend to focus our attention on the international careers of touring stars, Schumann draws us into the German culture of serious music, a hotbed of controversy about virtuosity. This is not to deny that Schumann was part of the international—indeed, cosmopolitan—networks on which virtuoso performers and music circulated. Schumann played and reviewed showpieces by Paris-based pianist-composers, personally encountered international musical celebrities, toured Russia and the Netherlands with Clara (and contemplated an American tour shortly after their marriage), and entered debates that consumed musicians and critics across national boundaries. Nevertheless, he specifically illuminates how the virtuosity discourse unfolded in

German-speaking contexts. The great majority of the periodicals and writings I explore are German-language. Most of the events I explore occurred within German locales, whether in Leipzig salons or when Clara Schumann premiered Robert's Piano Concerto. The writers on whom Schumann based his understanding of the sublime and the poetic represented currents in German literature and aesthetics. And, Schumann occasionally presented virtuosity from a cultural nationalist perspective, such as in his critical writings or his involvement in the Lower Rhine Music Festival.

Schumann reveals that mid-nineteenth-century Germany underwent a multifaceted, contentious, ever-evolving project to cultivate virtuosos who embodied this culture's loftiest musical ambitions (and, of course, to stigmatize those who supposedly did not). His work also broadens our understanding of how musicians believed they were elevating virtuosity. First, it documents the diversity of strategies he and his contemporaries used. When scholars discuss nineteenth-century attempts to self-consciously elevate virtuosity, they usually stress manifestations of the work concept: virtuosos who interpreted canonic repertoire, writers who saw performance as a metaphysical merging of subjectivities between performer and composer, or showpieces that reflected thinking about the ideal composition.[19] Though Schumann engaged with these practices, he explored many other ways of presenting virtuosity as transcendent, some of which emerged from popular pianism rather than the canonic tradition. Second, the writings I consider by Schumann and other figures often focus on the immediate listening experience rather than on abstract aesthetics. Rich in vivid detail, they bring to life the effects that specific showpieces and performances produced onstage or in the drawing room, and they interpret these encounters by considering them alongside larger cultural and aesthetic issues. Finally, Schumann was a highly ambivalent critic. In his *Zeitschrift* articles, he invented fictional alter egos who would argue contrasting viewpoints, notably Florestan, Eusebius, and Raro. Even when writing in his own voice, he often allowed contrasting perspectives and arguments to coexist. Schumann, then, highlights some of the tensions and ambiguities in his and his contemporaries' thinking about virtuosity.

The Cultural Status of Virtuoso Display

But why did Schumann and his contemporaries believe it was so important to distinguish performers such as Bazzini and showpieces such as the Toccata and Concert Allegro from supposedly superficial instances of virtuosity? Scholars have uncovered an array of issues that informed the reception of nineteenth-century virtuosos, ranging from gender and nationalism to philosophies of the self and questions of authenticity in text and performance. All are deeply relevant, and my discussion will invoke many of them. For Schumann and many of his musical and literary colleagues, though, discussions about virtuosity often revolved around an anxiety intimately connected to their professional identities. For them, the virtuosity craze raised fundamental questions about music's status as an art form and the cultural prestige it could claim.

Composers and critics intimated this concern well before the 1800s. Eighteenth-century writers on opera, for example, often complained that star prima donnas and castrati transformed the genre from a carefully crafted synthesis of music and poetry into a spectacle with limited dramatic meaning. Benedetto Marcello's 1720 satirical treatise *Il teatro alla moda* caricatures self-serving singers who ran roughshod over the composer's and librettist's work. Marcello's virtuosos frivolously demanded changes to arias (or new arias altogether), pushed composers to include dramatically unmotivated coloratura, broke character during performances to cavort with fans, and obscured the meaning of the text with their acrobatics.[20]

Discussions about virtuosity took on new urgency, though, during the nineteenth century. When writers and musicians elevated music's social and aesthetic standing, they were responding not just to the intellectual tenets of Romantic aesthetics but also to more worldly factors, notably changes in musicians' career options. The decline of aristocratic and church patronage and the mushrooming of a mass market created both opportunity and instability. As Celia Applegate, David Gramit, and William Weber have shown, one wing of the music profession worked out a particularly ambitious—and, it turned out, enduring—solution to this perceived crisis.[21] They established themselves as cultivated professionals who commanded the respect of the educated (particularly the university-educated) middle class. Especially in Germany, this demographic held the levers of state arts patronage. Capturing this audience meant countering an eighteenth-century intellectual tradition that set music low on the hierarchy of the arts and instead embracing it as what E. T. A. Hoffmann called "the most Romantic of the arts."[22] It meant persuading listeners that music could embody or stimulate the interiority the middle class prized, that music engaged not just the body and the senses but the spirit and the intellect (that amalgamation the Germans termed *Geist*). It meant staking the claim that music possessed a richness of meaning equal to that of literature and could further one's *Bildung* (or intellectual and personal cultivation). And, it meant distancing the music profession from courtly entertainment on one hand and from lower-class, provincial musicians such as dance-band players on the other.

Scholars have traced the construction of serious music in numerous arenas. Its more concrete manifestations included the silencing of audiences during concerts, the burgeoning of music criticism by expert writers, and canon formation. Its ideological framework incorporated concepts such as the musical sublime, the notion of musical depth, and the category of absolute music. This revaluation of music, I would add, also gave critics a framework for identifying serious approaches to virtuosity and gave composer-performers a powerful incentive to court that distinction.

Schumann's own background encapsulated the confluence of the virtuosity craze and the culture of serious music. The widely read, university-educated son of a bookseller, Schumann befriended and played music with professors, scholars, jurists, and their families beginning in his Gymnasium days. (In 1840, he obtained a doctorate himself from the University of Jena.) Schumann thus emerged from and moved within the very demographic whose respect and patronage nineteenth-century musicians most eagerly sought. His music and writings themselves made a provocative claim that John Daverio aptly summarized: for Schumann, "music should aspire to the same intellectual substance as the lettered arts: poetry and philosophy."[23]

When Schumann and his contemporaries wrote about virtuosity, they often expressed anxiety that certain approaches to virtuosity compromised music's cultural status. Gustav Schilling's 1838 article, "Virtuos," for his music encyclopedia made the anxiety explicit (in reference, the article clarified, to both performances and compositions). "Only when virtuosity seeks its goal solely in the overcoming of technical difficulties," he wrote, "does it sink beneath all actual artistry and become hand-work [*Handwerkerey*]."[24] The virtuoso, Schilling feared, risked becoming a craftsman who worked with his hands rather than an "artist" who worked with his intellect and spirit.

Comparisons between circus performers and virtuosos proliferated in nineteenth-century writings. In an 1833 letter to Moscheles, Mendelssohn sneered at Henri Herz:

> But why should I listen to this or that variation set by Herz for the thirtieth time? It gives me less pleasure than rope dancers and acrobats; with these, one at least has the barbaric pleasure of always being afraid that they'll break their necks . . . whereas the piano-vaulters never once risk their lives but only our ears. . . . Even if I didn't always have the misfortune of having to hear it, the audience would desire it; but I also belong to the audience and desire just the opposite.[25]

In 1842, August Kahlert's essay, "Das Concertwesen der Gegenwart," for the *Neue Zeitschrift* made a similar point in a more public forum. "The tightrope walker does not stand any lower than a virtuoso," Kahlert claims, "who only has set the so-called unbelievable as his goal."[26] As David Gramit explains, these comparisons emphasized the physicality of virtuoso performance and translated a mind–body dichotomy into a statement about social status.[27] Mendelssohn, after all, was likening Herz to a plebian entertainer.

Similar concerns about prestige informed more philosophically elaborate articles about virtuosity, such as those the *Neue Zeitschrift* published during the 1840s. Schumann printed several articles, for example, by music critic, scholar, and choral conductor Eduard Krüger. These included his 1840 "Ueber Virtuosenunfug" (On Virtuoso Nonsense).[28] Gooley has shown that Krüger applied Hegel's concept of the self to the virtuosity discourse. In this scenario, the performer transcended his own ego by subordinating it to some greater entity, most often a musical work.[29] Krüger's most pressing concern, though, was not so much to advance a particular model of selfhood as to defend music altogether. Schooled in Hegelian philosophy, Krüger devoted many of his writings to refuting Hegel's assertion that music conveyed only inwardness and subjectivity and therefore lacked what Hegel called "content."[30] Krüger's essays on virtuosity served this larger project. Here, he specifically argued that a focus on a performer's personality and physical feats compromised music's status as a content-filled art form.

Reverently interpreting canonized masterworks, Krüger argued, was one way the virtuoso could avoid this pitfall. Such performers revealed a work's content and assumed a place within nineteenth-century *Kunstreligion*: "The little sufferings of the little ego vanish like the smoke of a sacrifice when the awareness of divine content animates the martyr."[31]

The virtuosity discourse addressed listeners as well as performers. Both Mendelssohn's and Krüger's elitism, for example, extended from the piano bench into the audience. Mendelssohn exuded scorn for Herz's devotees. Krüger's article unfolds as an exchange of letters in which a fictional Music Director attempts to educate a Dilettante who is all-too-easily seduced by star virtuosos. Becoming a better listener, for Krüger, meant embracing his canon-centric vision of virtuosity.

As we will see, Schumann himself always kept one eye on virtuosity's cultural status. So did his reviewers; the *Signale*, for example, commended the Concert Allegro by imagining its "cultivated" audience. We will see in chapter 1 that, when Schumann compared brilliant showpieces to cavorting aristocrats and fine luxury items, he was positioning them within current discourses about pleasurable cultural consumption. Attempting to identify or channel poetic interiority or the sublime was in part a strategy to redeem virtuosity from mere sensuous appeal and place it in more prestigious categories. For Schumann and other nineteenth-century musicians, the virtuosity discourse raised urgent, interrelated questions about their work and listeners, and it promised to enhance the cultural status of dazzling instrumental pyrotechnics.

Part I

Schumann and the Piano Virtuosity of the 1830s

During Robert Schumann's years as an aspiring piano virtuoso, one of the core showpieces in his repertoire was Johann Nepomuk Hummel's Piano Concerto No. 2 in A Minor, Op. 85. Schumann publicly performed the first movement at least once—while a university student in Leipzig, he returned to his home city of Zwickau to play it at an "Evening Concert" on April 28, 1829. The young pianist seems to have delighted in the work and played it masterfully. After Schumann moved to Heidelberg for his law studies, he played the Hummel for his friend Theodore Töpken, who recalled, "I was struck by the aplomb of his playing, by this consciously artistic rendering." In a letter to Hummel himself, Schumann boasted that he could perform "the A-minor concerto (there is only one) calmly, securely, and without technical mistakes."[1]

Hummel's concerto displays the pianist's skill in a kaleidoscopic range of virtuosic and consistently transparent textures. Example 1.1 provides two excerpts from the first movement's exposition. Flickering, single-line runs embellish the second theme, varying melodic contours as they recur and enlivening sustained notes. At the end of the exposition, the soloist showers listeners with double notes, arpeggios, and scalar figures. Over the regular stride of the accompaniment, right-hand patterns change every two to four measures. Several times the piano figuration works its way into the uppermost register, climbing toward increasingly bright sounds, only to descend and begin another ascent. Hummel uses stark contrasts to highlight these sections. In its last measures, the transition to the second theme slows and dwindles to a pianissimo. At measure 217 of the expositional close, two measures of alternating neighbor tones momentarily create a dense, closely voiced flurry of chords that the transparent passagework suddenly dispels.

Schumann's youthful performance vehicle exemplifies a style of piano music that contemporary writers often described as "brilliant" and that present-day scholars term "postclassical."[2] Soon after Hummel published the concerto in 1821, for example, a reviewer singled out both junctures as delightful and compelling.

Second theme:

Example 1.1. Johann Nepomuk Hummel, Piano Concerto No. 2, Op. 85. Movement 1.
Second theme and expositional close.

In the close of the exposition, he wrote, "fast parallel thirds create a highly brilliant image and plunge from the highest height of the soprano into the bass register with ecstatic speed." When the solo embellishes the second theme, it "appears to the ear in an entirely new, interesting form."[3]

Schumann engaged with postclassical virtuosity throughout his compositions and reviews: in various cases, such virtuosity adopted, transformed, or pointedly diverged from postclassical idioms. One important thread in chapters 1 through 4 will track this engagement during the late 1820s and 1830s, when Schumann was mostly composing solo piano music. Schumann's engagement with this style, moreover, extended across his career: the concertos we will encounter in chapters 5 and 6 also employ postclassical conventions.

Though postclassical piano showpieces displayed composers' individual styles, they shared an approach to piano texture. In Jim Samson's description:

> Its basic ingredients included a bravura right-hand figuration that took its impetus from the light-actioned Viennese and German pianos of the late eighteenth century and a melodic idiom . . . that was rooted either in Italian opera, in folk music, or in popular genres.[4]

Expositional close:

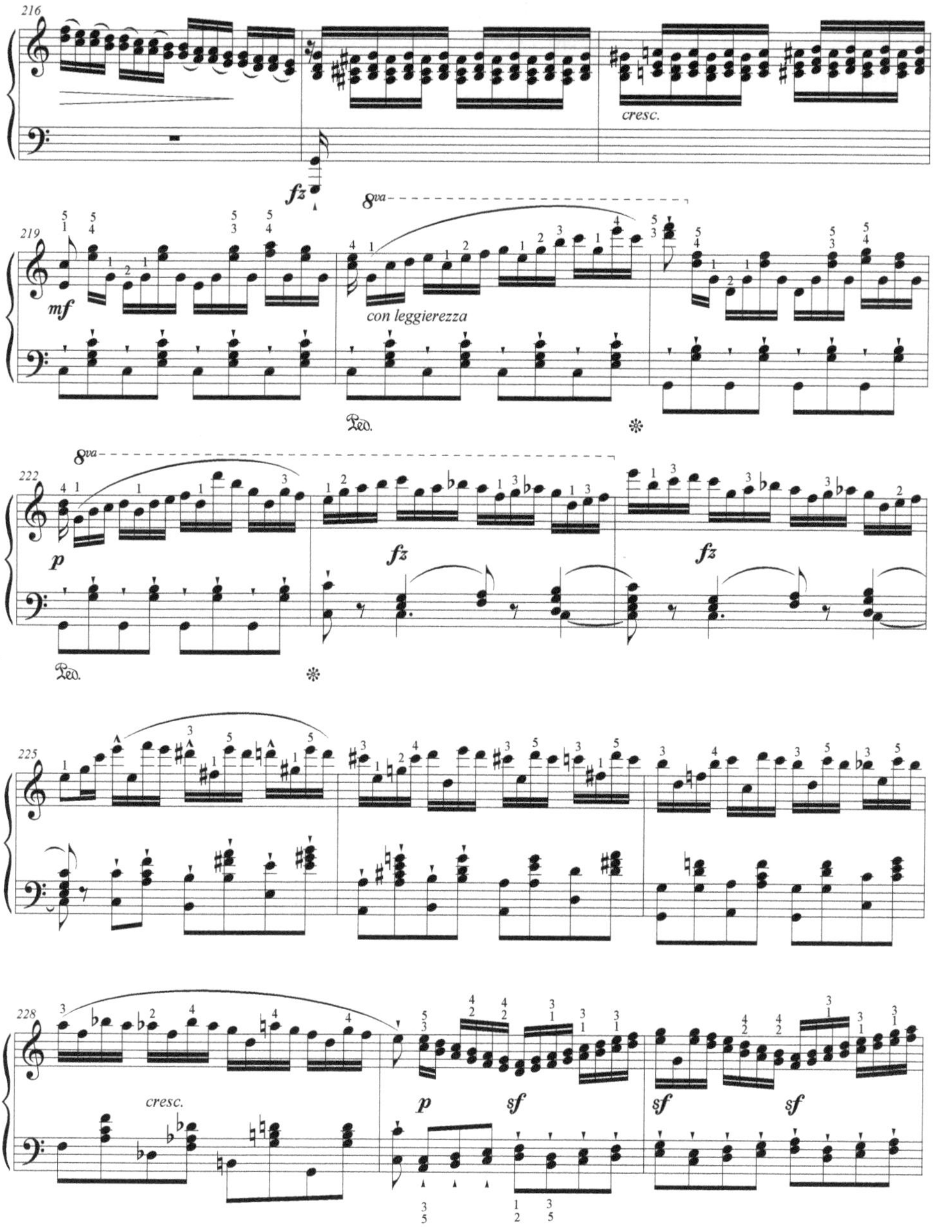

Example 1.1. (*continued*)

Showpieces like Hummel's feature transparent, glittering textures that highlight the attack of each individual tone. They often embellish simple melodies or harmonic schemes with ornate detail. In sections of constant passagework—virtuosic variations, for example, or the closes of concerto expositions and recapitulations—figuration unfolds in rhythmically foursquare, consistent patterns. The "brilliant" sound emerges when strings of pristinely audible notes and patterns fly by at high velocity and in regular succession, especially when they course through the piano's clarion upper octaves.[5]

Conventions other than texture shaped the way listeners encountered these sounds. The structures of postclassical concertos, for example, differed from those of Mozart and Beethoven, and the variation set and opera fantasy genres featured their own norms. Composers of postclassical showpieces also drew upon a conventional vocabulary of figurational patterns, musical topoi, and genre markers, some of which Samson has mapped: ideas based on scales, turns, double notes, and broken octaves, for example, and styles such as the march, prelude, pastoral, or bel canto aria.[6]

Postclassical virtuosity pervaded early and mid-nineteenth-century musical life. Compositions ranged from large-scale fantasies and concertos to compact etudes and rondos, and they graced the drawing rooms of amateur pianists as well as the concerts of professional virtuosos. The variation sets of Henri Herz, for example, consumed a large share of the Parisian sheet-music market and also appeared on Clara Wieck's concerts from the late 1820s through the mid-1830s.[7] Besides Herz and Hummel, composer-pianists who wrote in this tradition included Carl Czerny, Frédéric Kalkbrenner, Carl Maria von Weber, Franz Hünten, Theodore Döhler, and Henri Bertini. Postclassical virtuosity also informed early works by Frédéric Chopin, Franz Liszt, Sigismond Thalberg, and Ignaz Moscheles. Most of these composer-pianists had their heydays between the late 1810s and the 1830s (though some careers, like Herz's, continued well beyond): Schumann himself wrote that Moscheles's 1815 "Alexander" Variations evoked "a time when the word 'brilliant' gained momentum and legions of girls fell in love with Czerny."[8] Many composers of postclassical piano music were based in Vienna or Paris. The latter city, especially, offered a booming concert scene, a vibrant salon culture, and advantageous publishing opportunities. Star pianist-composers also trained in these cities, particularly at the Paris Conservatoire or in Carl Czerny's Vienna studio. These virtuosos and their music also enjoyed international dissemination and popularity. Like the Franco-Italian operas whose themes they borrowed for fantasies and variations, their showpieces sold well and influenced composers throughout Europe and North America. Many virtuosos completed training or established credentials outside Vienna or Paris and only later went to these cities, some for the rest of their careers (Chopin, for example), some for extended stays (Schumann's friend, the lesser-known virtuoso Ludwig Schuncke), and others for significant concert tours (Clara Wieck).

Schumann, who spent his career in Germany, was part of this cosmopolitan current. At the same time, he joined a generation of composers and performers who absorbed postclassical pianism but also developed strikingly original, idiosyncratic approaches to virtuosity that set them apart from their postclassical models and colleagues. For example, Liszt's 1826 *Étude en douze exercices*—composed shortly after he completed studies with Czerny—features figuration typical of postclassical etude collections. In his 1837 *Grandes études*, he extensively reworked these early exercises to create less transparent effects: massive sonorities that push the piano to its limit, figuration that demands vertical, aggressive gestures, and climaxes that arise from accumulating layers of texture. Chopin complicated postclassical figuration with intricate counterpoint possibly influenced by his study of Bach.[9] Though Thalberg's early opera fantasies burst with brilliant passagework, his signature "three-handed technique" embeds melodies within wide-ranging arpeggios, blending individual notes into resonant waves of texture that sustain a sweeping melody. In his writings and compositions, Schumann also reimagined the sound of piano virtuosity and the kinds of listening experience it could offer.

1 Florestan among the Revelers: Postclassical Virtuosity and Schumann's Critique of Pleasure

This chapter explores a debate that consumed Schumann as a critic during the 1830s and centered on popular, postclassical showpieces.[1] Though the discussion raised issues of compositional style, its fundamental concerns were affect and listening experience: the pleasures these pieces offered the listener (or listening player). Schumann and many other commentators agreed that these showpieces were designed to stimulate unflagging delectation and engagement. Whether they were commending or critiquing, they usually described this pleasure as sensuous in effect, and they stressed that it was effortlessly accessible to perceive, produced no strain on the listener, and appealed regardless of one's musical learnedness. "Accessible" here did not necessarily mean "easy to play"—the music required an advanced technique and, though writers did note when pieces were comfortable for the pianist, they emphasized the auditory experience. Throughout his reviews for the *Neue Zeitschrift für Musik*, Schumann waged an elaborate critique of this pleasure. Particularly in writings on Herz, Kalkbrenner, Döhler, and Thalberg, Schumann painted the delights they generated as frivolous and superficial, as shallow pleasures lamentably unredeemed by transcendent, inner qualities.

On the other hand, some largely unexplored sources from two powerful writers on virtuosity delivered a spirited defense of this aesthetic of pleasure. Both provide an important context for Schumann's critique: ideals and in some cases specific reviews to which he was responding. One was Gottfried Wilhelm Fink, editor of the *Allgemeine musikalische Zeitung*—the archrival of Schumann's *Neue Zeitschrift*.[2] Though the *Zeitung* was one of the most significant German-language music journals of its time, Fink's work has attracted little scholarly attention, and studies that do exist emphasize his tolerant tone and pleas for artistic pluralism.[3] Specifically exploring his discussions of pleasurable virtuosity, though, reveals his basic assumptions about virtuosity's aesthetic and social significance. The other writer was Carl Czerny, who produced a massive oeuvre of showpieces and wrote several pedagogical treatises. Scholars have already mined Czerny's writings for insight into compositional conventions and improvisation practices. My discussion here newly considers the effects that Czerny believed virtuosic improvisations and compositions should produce for the listener. It would be reductionist to treat Czerny's treatises as a key to all postclassical pianism. However, he was an influential teacher whose students included Liszt, Thalberg, and Döhler. He also wrote about genres and composers Schumann knew and reviewed, offering analyses and viewpoints that clarify those we find in the *Zeitschrift*.

Schumann's critique of pleasure became a central point of contention in the skirmishes between the *Neue Zeitschrift* and the *Allgemeine musikalische Zeitung*. Until Fink retired in 1841, one could read writers for the two papers sniping at one another in their essays. There were several causes for the rivalry. It started with personal enmity: when the *Zeitung* published Schumann's "Ein Opus II" essay on Chopin in 1831, Schumann believed Fink had mishandled his review (see chapter 2). The rivalry also hinged on larger issues, including Fink's relatively conservative perspective versus Schumann's belief that his *Davidsbund* was rebelling against an ossified older order, Fink's pragmatic, tolerant outlook versus Schumann's belief that contemporary music journals were not exacting enough, and Fink's critical stance toward what he called "Romanticism" versus Schumann's embrace of it.[4] In essays that described actual showpieces, though, both writers returned again and again to the issue of pleasure. Schumann or one of his reviewers would criticize a piece for primarily offering sensuous, pleasant experiences, and the *Zeitung* would retort that there was nothing wrong with that. In some cases, Fink argued that providing such experiences was in fact a laudable goal.

Schumann's role in this debate reveals several new dimensions of his engagement with virtuosity. At the simplest level, it helps us revise the canonized view of his criticism. Even when scholars have refrained from explicitly endorsing Schumann's judgments, they have often interpreted his writings as a quest for sheer musical quality. Leon Plantinga reveals the sophistication and nuance of Schumann's writings, for example, but still characterizes the *Zeitung–Zeitschrift* rivalry as "a case of high standards versus no standards." Similarly, Joachim Draheim has mapped Schumann's wide-ranging responses to Herz but contends that his more exasperated reviews were attacking "dull musical substance that is in no way commensurate with the technical demands."[5] Schumann did pan music that he considered badly written or hackneyed. In fact, however, many of his writings on popular showpieces were responding to an aesthetic that other critics presented as wholesome, philosophically and practically justified, and a sign of good compositional craftsmanship. Schumann applied his critique even to music he considered effective and original.

These sources also help us ground our discussion of postclassical virtuosity and Schumann's critique in the listening experience. Recent scholarship has often viewed the postclassical repertoire through an economic lens. Jim Samson notes, "This was music designed to be popular and happy to accept its commodity status," Laure Schnapper has revealed the symbiotic relationship between the practicalities of the sheet-music industry and the conventions of popular variation sets, and Holly Watkins has argued that Schumann himself developed his concept of the "poetic" to insulate musical meaning from erosion via commodification. (Watkins acknowledges that the compositions in which Schumann worked out these concepts inevitably entered the marketplace as commodities themselves.)[6] Samson has taken a different approach and charted postclassical piano music's tenuous relationship with the work concept. This repertoire, he argues, was based on a shared vocabulary of keyboard idioms rather than ideals about the individuality of musical works.[7]

By no means do the writings I consider here preclude these interpretations; even so, they offer a different view by emphasizing what it felt like to listen to brilliant, popular showpieces. These accounts, moreover, did not stop at description and interpreted listening experiences by placing them within larger cultural and aesthetic frameworks. Schumann, Fink, and other writers for their journals entered nineteenth-century German debates about pleasurable cultural consumption and the social position of music. For Schumann and his contemporaries, the aesthetic of pleasure raised a question fundamental to their identities as musicians: the cultural status that virtuosic showpieces and performances could and should attain.

Schumann's rhetoric about pleasure and superficiality, however heated, conceals a complex, at times ambivalent perspective. He did not argue that virtuosity should suppress its pleasurable or sensuous aspects. Rather, he and his listeners valorized kinds of pleasure that, in the nineteenth-century imagination, incorporated but ultimately transcended "mere" sensuous delight and reached a higher, even rarefied plane of cultural prestige. These included the bracing thrills of the sublime (such as I discuss in chapter 4) or the experience of hearing Clara Schumann at the Lower Rhine Music Festival (see chapter 6). Throughout the writings I present in this chapter, Schumann repeatedly describes one such delight, which he called the "poetic." Here, he defined the poetic negatively, as an antidote to superficiality, and only hinted at its characteristics. In chapters 2 and 3, we will see that "poetic" virtuosity, for Schumann, captured qualities of interiority and appealed especially to "cultivated" audiences. However, the boundary between superficial and poetic virtuosity—between sensuousness and interiority— was for Schumann a flexible, porous one. It was along this ambiguous border that many of his ideas about virtuosity developed.

Schumann and the Diversity of the Postclassical Repertoire

Like any stylistic categories and descriptors, "postclassical" and "brilliant" oversimplify aspects of this repertory even as they recognize important commonalities. The former term risks drawing a misleading lineage. As Samson's description recognizes, this music was just as rooted in nineteenth-century musical genres and instruments as in the "classical" style of Haydn and Mozart. "Brilliant style" is more descriptive than interpretive but highlights texture at the expense of equally important structural conventions

Both terms, however, capture features that were important to nineteenth-century commentators on this repertory. For them, postclassical pianist-composers did, to an extent, continue an eighteenth-century "classical" tradition. Schumann himself suggested that Hummel's Opus 125 Etudes emulated the "serenity, grace, ideality, and objectivity" that marked both "the Mozartian school" and "ancient artworks."[8] Professor and music critic Adolph Kullak generalized in his 1861 treatise *Die Ästhetik des Klavierspiels* that Hummel and his contemporaries combined an eighteenth-century style with a new emphasis on virtuosic display. (For Kullak, Hummel succeeded in writing "semiclassical" compositions, but other composers let the "Mozartian school" decline.)[9] The aesthetic of pleasure and accessibility resonates with eighteenth-century ideas that Mozart famously articulated in one his letters to his father: he assured Leopold that his Piano Concertos K. 413–415 would delight both connoisseurs and the uninitiated.[10] Writers who described accessible pleasure in nineteenth-century showpieces, though, connected it to current contexts rather than an older tradition.

Schumann recognized and experienced firsthand the diversity of the postclassical repertoire. I stress this richness to make an important qualification about my argument: the aesthetic of pleasure that Fink and Czerny valorized and that Schumann critiqued does not give us a grand, unifying theory for the postclassical tradition, the popular pianism it nourished, or Schumann's own writings. A repertory that stretched from Hummel to Thalberg cannot be reduced to a single credo. Like any musical works, these showpieces invite exploration from many different angles. Nor can we assume that the sources I consider here reveal unmediated the intentions of the pianist-composers. Rather, they document the public discussions that surrounded this music—critical discourses and aesthetic principles that composer-pianists were certainly aware of when they sat down to compose and perform but that they inevitably filtered through their individual goals, styles, and practices.

The postclassical tradition embraced composer-performers with various styles and career paths. Hummel studied with Mozart and eventually became a *Kapellmeister* in Weimar, whereas the much younger Herz mixed a touring career with piano manufacturing and a professorship at the Paris Conservatoire. Czerny remained based on Vienna, whereas Kalkbrenner toured extensively. Moscheles, one of Schumann's early idols, enjoyed an uncommonly wide-ranging career. Roughly the same generation as Hummel, he lived from 1794 to 1870. He toured as a pianist, conducted the London Philharmonic, gave "historical soirees" where he performed Bach and Scarlatti, and taught at the Leipzig Conservatory. In addition to piano showpieces like his "Alexander" Variations, he composed chamber and orchestral music and, by the 1830s, was writing concertos that Schumann believed were turning away from postclassical norms (see chapter 4).

Schumann immersed himself in postclassical piano music during his years as an aspiring virtuoso. At the age of eighteen, he played the first movement of Kalkbrenner's Concerto No. 1, Op. 61, on a Zwickau Gymnasium concert. He also performed the "Alexander" Variations on the Zwickau concert where he played the Hummel first movement and in Heidelberg on a January 24, 1830, concert for the Museum, a student-organized concert series. Schumann worked on Czerny's Toccata Op. 92, and relentlessly practiced Hummel's etudes during his studies with Friedrich Wieck.[11] Schumann also practiced (but never performed) Herz's *Variations sur la cavatine favorite de "La Violette" de Carafa*, Op. 48, and saw Clara

Wieck use it as a concert closer. Schumann looked to star postclassical virtuosos as models and potential mentors. Friedrich Wieck had promised Schumann's mother that he would teach her son to play "more ingeniously [*geistreicher*] and warmly than Moscheles and more magnificently than Hummel."[12] As Schumann grew frustrated with his lessons, he contemplated a year of study with Moscheles in Vienna or with Hummel in Weimar. Even after a hand injury ended his performing career around 1831, he sought Hummel's advice about his compositions, including *Papillons*, Op. 2, and his unfinished Piano Concerto in F Major. Schumann also based original compositions on the postclassical showpieces he played. To cite but two examples: Claudia Macdonald has shown that Schumann used the formal proportions of Herz's Concerto No. 1 in A Major, Op. 34, as a model for his F-Major concerto. Erika Reiman notes that the first movement of *Papillons* alludes to Weber's brilliant *Aufforderung zum Tanze*.[13]

Rather than making sweeping judgments, Schumann wrote about most of the music he encountered on a composer-by-composer or piece-by-piece basis. He took a dim view of Czerny's compositions, and one of his reviews reads, "If I had enemies, I would destroy them by only letting them hear Czerny's music." However, he wrote elsewhere that few would guess the composer of Czerny's Grosses Rondo, Op. 405, because of its "romantic tone."[14] Schumann took only a gently critical view of Hummel and described the Etudes as the old-fashioned work of an otherwise admired master. Even there, Schumann's fictional alter egos express differing opinions. Eusebius strikes a reverent tone, Florestan urges impetuous rebellion, and Raro grumbles that the younger men have been unduly influenced by Hummel's fame. Amid the satire Schumann lobbed at Herz's music, he credited the pianist-composer with improving a generation's piano technique, and he differentiated between Herz's later variation sets and his "earlier, fresh, and inventive ones."[15]

When Schumann did critique brilliant virtuoso showpieces, he positioned his remarks within a variety of conceptual frameworks. His reviews include jabs at some pianist-composers' perceived commercialism. "What does he want," he asked of Herz," but to amuse and become rich in addition?"[16] Schumann also invoked an ideology—increasingly dominant in the nineteenth century—that valorized composers' works over virtuosos' ephemeral performances. His 1836 review of Thalberg's Piano Concerto Op. 5, for example, lamented that the composer-pianist seemed bent on "enjoying the charming mortality of the virtuoso life at the cost of a posthumous fame which he would not be able to enjoy."[17] Another Thalberg review, this one of his Nocturne Op. 28 and Andante Op. 32, alludes to notions of musical depth by differentiating between surface decoration and compositional essence: "In order to get to the bottom of a composition, we must disrobe it of all adornments. Only then does it show whether it really is beautifully formed."[18]

Schumann's critique of pleasure, then, did not target or explain an entire tradition or even the whole outputs of individual composers. Instead, he analyzed and took aim at a particular quality that he and his contemporaries heard in many individual postclassical showpieces. This pleasure, they believed, was a key to the music's design and wide appeal.

Fink's *Zeitung* and the Value of Pleasure

Schumann's critique of pleasure confronted head-on the ideas his rival journal was promoting. Fink's writings about pleasure fulfilled the platform the *Allgemeine musikalische Zeitung* had adopted since its founding in 1798. The journal's title stressed its "general" scope, and it equally addressed readers searching for light piano music to purchase and devoted connoisseurs ready to read essays by Joseph Haydn and E. T. A. Hoffmann. The *Neue Zeitschrift*, by contrast, aggressively divided the public into Philistines and *Davidsbündler*.

A *Zeitung* review of Herz's Piano Concerto No. 2, Op. 74, exemplifies the qualities that Fink and his reviewers praised in brilliant showpieces. In this and other reviews, Fink was specifically discussing musical scores that a reader might purchase. However, he often evaluated these scores by imagining the effects they would produce in performance—some of his writings even immerse the reader in imaginary performances (or, perhaps, recall unspecified performances he or his reviewers had witnessed). Fink waxed poetic about "the pleasure Herz has brought to the masses," noting, "the bravura passages Herz writes ring, are easy to hear, have a fresh glimmer . . . and charm [listeners] to applause through clever closing passagework; the highest pleasure at which many players aim." Fink described the concerto as "well suited for many listeners and players, better than a more profound one, with which at the end they would not know how to begin."[19] An 1835 review of Kalkbrenner's *Variations brillantes sur une mazourka de Chopin*, Op. 120, described a similar listening experience. The work was "so brilliant, beautiful, and animatedly entertaining, that the player will bring joy and win acclaim with it."[20] In Fink's language, adjectives pile up, as if musical pleasures keep accumulating to coax a listener's delight.

From the time he assumed his editorship in 1827, Fink became a (sometimes ambivalent) spokesman for this aesthetic of pleasure. In an 1828 review of three fantasies by Czerny, he described their pleasurable effect and offered an explanation for the composer's popularity. One was his original *Grande fantaisie en forme de Sonate*, Op. 144, and two—from Czerny's Opus 131—were potpourris on Boieldieu's *La dame blanche*. In Fink's analysis, Czerny's music offered an antidote to the stresses of middle-class work and the recent deprivations of the Napoleonic Wars:

> The oppression of days not long passed felt by most, the burden still felt by some, has brought most people to seek light recreation that diverts the spirit from the serious side of life after their worrisome work; they prefer to be eased, as it were, by a pleasant stimulation of the senses so that for a short time they forget unpleasant reality without reflection of any kind.[21]

What these listeners wanted, Fink wrote, was effortless listening that spun out a parade of musical attractions:

> Patience is already exhausted by the unavoidable dealings of life; nothing is liked more than that which hurries superficially from one object to another, that which

leads picture after picture before the senses; that which is light-minded will be best received—only to be forgotten again. One flutters from one thing to another; novelty follows novelty, and must do so if it is not to lose its appeal.[22]

Fink did not unequivocally endorse Czerny. In some regards, the review positions him among critics who wanted to steer the public away from supposedly frivolous entertainments. Fink claimed that interest in "serious oratorios" and "simple lieder, full of content" had supposedly declined. "It is certainly true that artists corrupt the public," he wrote, "but the public also corrupts the artist." Unlike his later rival, Fink pledged to recognize the good qualities of every work he reviewed, writing "I declare myself an enemy of all harshness and ruthlessness."[23]

In other essays, Fink explicitly defended the pleasures of brilliant virtuosity. His 1833 article, "Bravourstücke für verschiedene Instrumente mit Orchesterbegleitung" (Bravura pieces for Diverse Instruments with Orchestral Accompaniment) opened with an essay on virtuosity in general. Fink again made a plea for critical tolerance and implied that he was defending virtuosity against puritanical, shortsighted critics. His argument continually returns to the sensuous pleasures of virtuosity. Comparing virtuosity to a pear tree, he wrote, "Its leaves and branches rustle in the wind of our time in a lovely way, and its fruits, when ripe, appeal to children." Fink argued that this pleasure had many positive effects. The constant search for new musical delights, he suggested, stimulated change and originality. He wrote, "Curiosity and the attraction of pleasure are like air and water: they decompose that which is solid and then shape anew and raise up, ennobled, that which would have remained underground." "Fleeting swirling," he concluded, "fosters non-ephemeral things better than sluggish obedience does."[24] Pleasure itself, Fink proposed, ultimately supported more self-consciously serious virtues and never lapsed into gluttony. "Change is life's best friend in all things called pleasure; here, he [change] remains the ruler, just as truth may remain the ruler in serious, good things. Pleasure, however, serves seriousness, who rightly loves it and knows how to differentiate it from greed."[25]

It is not exactly clear whom Fink was rebutting. By 1833, he and Schumann had already begun their relationship on a sour note, and Schumann's "Die Davidsbündler" articles for the Leipzig journal Der Komet were satirizing the Zeitung's style of criticism. Fink might also have been thinking of critics more powerful than the upstart Schumann. For example, Ludwig Rellstab of the journal Iris im Gebiete der Tonkunst often presented conservative, Berlin-based composers as bulwarks against the flood of popular piano pieces.

Regardless of his specific target, Fink's description and defense of kaleidoscopic musical pleasure were not unique to his Zeitung: they echo what some of his contemporaries were writing about the benefits, even the necessity, of pleasurable cultural consumption. Karin Wurst has unearthed similar viewpoints throughout late eighteenth and early nineteenth-century German writings on entertaining pastimes, especially the Viennese Journal des Luxus und der Mode, which ran from 1786 to 1827. Fink, in fact, compared the development of new showpieces to the pursuit of novelty in fashion, writing, "Bravura entirely resembles its close friend, fashion; it gladly changes; the fresh dress is always the best, even if it doesn't last."[26] The *Journal* commanded a wide readership thanks to seismic social changes that gathered steam in the eighteenth century and set the tone for middle-class life during the nineteenth: a burgeoning consumer revolution that produced an unprecedented quantity and variety of luxury items, and the regulation of middle-class life into a strenuous workday and largely sedentary evening leisure time. Within these currents, *Journal* writers presented what Wurst describes as a "popular philosophy" about the pleasures of literature, fashion, and the theater.[27] Just as Fink did in his Czerny essay, writers for the *Journal* described pleasurable entertainments as a way of liberating the enjoyer from the toil of middle-class life. Also like Fink, they described perpetual novelty, constant change, and ongoing innovation as the sources of this pleasure, and they distanced it from activities such as profound contemplation or strenuous study. An 1802 report on fashion and entertainment in the mercantile powerhouse city of Hamburg, for example, noted that these busy, modern individuals wanted above all to be "amused, vividly occupied, and surprised."[28] When the anonymous author described the city's operatic life, he noted that citizens sought "new splendor, unusual passages, striking, noisy choruses, new pranks, new operatic chaos." The reporter, like Fink, took a tolerant but gently condescending tone. Even if the operas are "full of errors, ten times more than usual," he observed, "that does not bother the Hamburger." "Haunted by monotony and discipline," Wurst summarizes, "the modern mind becomes addicted to the novelty and freedom . . . that modern forms of entertainment provide."[29]

Like Fink, writers for the *Journal* lauded such pleasure as not merely appealing but also beneficial. The Hamburg reporter, for example, noted that operagoers attended not out of boredom but to refresh themselves for renewed labors the next day. Many of his colleagues at the *Journal* stressed that proper self-care meant creating a varied lifestyle that included pleasurable entertainment. Like Fink, others argued that the search for new pleasures drove innovation in the arts. Still others noted that experiencing these pleasures was not merely a passive experience but refined the senses and enriched the imagination.[30]

Fink's writings on virtuosity did differ from the exact arguments in the *Journal*. Whereas the Hamburg reporter and other writers saw constant change and novelty occurring when consumers sampled the flow of new cultural products, Fink's Czerny essay imagined pleasurable variety happening within the space of a single composition. Nevertheless, Fink's writings about virtuosity bolstered a larger discourse that viewed accessible, sensory pleasures as an important component of middle-class culture, one that was compatible with more stereotypically serious pursuits and worth defending.

Generators of Pleasure

Fink's reviews and Czerny's treatises describe how composer-pianists could elicit these states of unflagging delectation. The two authors did write in different genres (music criticism and pedagogical treatises) and took different tones: whereas Fink stressed the listener's ease and delight, for example, Czerny admonished pianists and composers about the study and practice needed to master the art of pleasing an audience. Both, however, describe similar listening experiences and refer to many similar compositional strategies. These techniques are by no means recondite and might even strike an analyst as obvious. They invite us to understand how composers could use such simple means to generate and modulate a listener's pleasure.

As Fink's Czerny essay suggests, some of this accessible pleasure came from a frequently shifting flow of contrasting styles and figurational patterns. Czerny's treatises recommended that a composition or improvisation should keep listeners engaged and unwearied by alternating between lyrical (possibly borrowed, operatic) melodies, brilliant passagework, and other styles. (Czerny did not draw a firm line between improvisation and composition. Many of his recommendations are similar for both practices, and he suggests compositions as models for improvisation.) His 1836 *A Systematic Introduction to Improvisation on the Pianoforte*, Op. 200, gives the following advice for improvising a potpourri:

> In dealing with a large, very heterogeneous public, the majority will be entertained only by pleasant, familiar tunes, and their spirits sustained by piquant, glittering performance. . . . The unexpected entrance of a new theme can reawaken flagging attentiveness. By continual alternation of new images, as in the visual domain, such an improvisation can be spun out at length that would be tiresome and unfitting in every other kind of artistic performance.[31]

His 1848 *School of Practical Composition* similarly recommends:

> In the succession of themes, regard must be had to variety, and as connecting links, brilliant figures, elegant embellishments, together with melodic, harmonic, and even fugued passages must be introduced. But the chief aim of the composer must always be to remain tasteful and interesting, to stretch out no passage too much, and to preserve the most beautiful and animated ideas for the end.[32]

A good improviser, Czerny wrote, should anticipate the audience's desire for novelty and change. "With regard to arrangement [*Zusammenstellung*]," he counseled, "the performer must be guided by refined taste . . . particularly that fine discretion by means of which he can discern whether and how soon the attention of the listeners must be sharpened again through a new motive, in order to never let it cool down."[33]

Fink evocatively described the effects of such tasteful, engaging variety. In his 1836 review of Thalberg's Caprice Op. 15, he wrote that through its "beautiful richness of happy imagination, combined with a succession of ideas as clear as it is pleasant and brilliant individuality in the succession of details," the listener "will be held within—indeed, amiably lifted into—a most attractive suspense, which will not confuse itself with excessive strain."[34] In a January, 1831 review, Fink compared Herz's variation sets to a good conversationalist, able to maneuver in high society without boring or offending:

> Sometimes in his *Galanterie* there wafts a truly individual society-spirit [*Gesellschafts-Geist*] that charms us. . . . Flitting changeability combines with a quick wit that knows how to connect the most distant things finely and surprisingly. To the delicate, flirting passage a leaping one joins itself, which in a skillful realization strings a whimsical passage together with a graceful one; something

acrobatically bold, which makes a full somersault with a smiling face. All manner of hints and short sayings resound amidst this colorful alternation of graceful forms over which he, a good conversationalist, never lingers, which shows clearly that he is not wholly unfamiliar with the ways of higher circles.[35]

Fink wove a similar metaphor about Kalkbrenner's Rondo, "La Crainte et l'Espérance," Op. 131, writing, "He never oversteps the bounds of a spirited conversation in high society and does not want to allow the effort of lingering enlargement upon a seriously expanded topic."[36]

Within this framework of engaging variety, Czerny and Fink identified more specific means of generating pleasure. As Fink did in his review of Herz's Concerto No. 2, Czerny described brilliant figuration itself as a source of delight. His 1839 *Vollständige theoretisch-practische Pianoforte-Schule*, Op. 500, evokes the radiant clarity of such passagework. "Brilliant playing," he wrote, "must resemble beautifully ordered lighting, brought forth with many thousand lamps, but not the confusing flames of a firework."[37] His treatises often advised that "piquant," "rousing" virtuosity was particularly necessary at the end of showpieces—the longer the fantasy, the more "interesting or glittering" the conclusion should be.

Czerny also described lyrical themes themselves, especially borrowed operatic melodies, as generators of pleasure. Scholars have often explored the symbiotic relationship between Franco-Italian opera and nineteenth-century variations and fantasies. Schnapper has described the use of "current lyrical hits" as an important way in which composers ensured variations' marketability. Other scholars have considered how these works, particularly Liszt's opera fantasies, could summarize or reinterpret the dramatic content of their source operas.[38] Czerny, by contrast, stressed a listener's response to hearing a well-loved theme. His *School of Practical Composition* advises:

> The public in general experiences great delight on finding in a composition some pleasing melody with which it is already familiar and has already heard with rapture at the opera; for, most melodies acquire their popularity by the fine performance of a human voice and the charm of theatrical effect. Now, when such melodies are introduced in a spirited and brilliant manner, in a fantasia, and there developed or varied, the composer and the practiced player can be assured of success.[39]

Perhaps for this reason, Czerny's prescriptions for writing variations stipulated that the theme should remain consistently audible. Variations should follow the actual melodic contour of the theme or at least retain its leading motive or follow its harmonic scheme. Rondo finales of variation sets or fantasies should begin with a complete or nearly complete version of the theme.[40]

Schumann's sometime practice assignment and Clara Wieck's concert vehicle, Herz's "Violette" Variations, exemplifies the ever-changing lyrical and brilliant pleasures that Czerny and Fink described. Based on a theme from Michele Carafa's 1828 opéra comique *La Violette*, the showpiece was an intercontinental bestseller that remained popular from its 1829 composition well into the 1860s.[41] As shown in example 1.2, the contours of Carafa's theme remain clear and audible

Example 1.2. Henri Herz, *Variations sur la cavatine favorite de "La Violette" de Carafa*, Op. 48. Sequence of variations and finale.

Example 1.2. (*continued*)

throughout each variation: lyrical pleasure infuses the virtuosic display at every step. Herz keeps the textures transparent and harmonic and metric dissonance to a minimum, so that the markings *graziosamente*, *leggieramente*, and *egalamente* not only instruct the performer but also describe qualities scripted into the figuration. The larger trajectory of the variations illustrates Fink's observation that Herz could mix contrasting ideas and passages to create a tasteful, elegant assemblage. Even before the customary, penultimate slow variation, Herz intersperses variations that highlight the brilliant range of the piano with those that dial back the tempo or relegate rapid figuration to the left hand. The result is a gradual crescendo of dazzle that never loses its transparency and lyrical clarity. Herz was only one of the composers of variation sets whose work Schumann knew and whom Czerny recommended as a model for variation-set composition: one could draw examples from Kalkbrenner, Moscheles, Hummel, and other composers that use a similar approach to piano figuration and variation construction (but that, of course, differ in their details).

Czerny singled out his former student Thalberg as an exemplary composer of opera fantasies.[42] Thalberg (who lived from 1812 to 1871) was somewhat younger than Herz and, in several of his showpieces, developed pianistic effects that subverted postclassical transparency. However, his *Grande fantaisie et variations sur des motifs de l'opéra "Norma,"* Op. 12, features the frequent stylistic changes and brilliant textures that Czerny and Fink described as means of sustaining the listener's engagement and pleasure. (The piece, as we will see, was also the subject of one of Schumann's most complex essays about postclassical pleasure and one of Fink's rebuttals.) Example 1.3 excerpts the work. A fantasy on two themes from Bellini's opera, Thalberg's piece alternates lyrical operatic melodies (plus an original bel canto theme in the Introduction), zones of transparent passagework, and complex counterpoint. Thalberg's use of a learned style not generally associated with the opera fantasies genre showed off the training he had received in Vienna—in addition to piano lessons with Czerny, he studied counterpoint with Simon Sechter (who taught Schubert and went on to teach Bruckner). In all cases, though, Thalberg mitigated contrapuntal complexity with more accessible styles, creating a trajectory toward increasing brilliance and transparency organized around lyrical, operatic pleasures. His second variation on the chorus "Dell'aura tua profetica," for example, changes styles from phrase to phrase. Both sections of the rounded binary form realize their opening phrases with imitative counterpoint, but both simplify the texture after only four measures. The first refracts the theme through chromatic harmonies, and the second moves to a more straightforward presentation of the theme with an arpeggiated accompaniment. The following variation moves even farther from the learned style and breaks into transparent, brilliant figuration.

Thalberg's finale projects this fluctuation between learnedness, lyricism, and transparency onto a larger canvass. It is based largely on the theme "Padre, tu piangi?" from the opera's finale. Thalberg includes a stretto-driven fugal episode but, after only twenty measures, reverts to a more conventional, sonata-like development, with modulating sequences accompanied by flourishes in both hands.

Variations 2 and 3:

Example 1.3. Sigismond Thalberg, *Grande fantaisie et variations sur des motifs de l'opéra "Norma,"* Op. 12.

Thalberg offers a culminating display of contrapuntal engineering when he overlays "Dell'aura tua profetica" and "Padre, tu piangi?" He seems to promise that this combination will lead to a fully textured climax: the right hand moves toward a cadence, while the left adds a new layer of texture with a bass tremolo on a dominant pedal. At this moment, the finale bursts into a span of brilliant figuration, the "rousing, piquant" ending Czerny recommends. At the end of each sextuplet, glistening notes ring near the top of the keyboard, and the bass simplifies to create a rhythmically consistent, unobtrusive accompaniment. In the coda, the tempo increases to *più presto*. Brilliant sextuplets seem to hit walls of dissonance when brief chromatic digressions lead to diminished-seventh chords, only to cascade down the keyboard again in shimmering consonance. A dam of harmonic and textural complexity seems to break and release a last reserve of brilliance.[43]

Finale:

Example 1.3. (*continued*)

One could multiply examples of Thalberg's tasteful variety. His Introduction, for example, promises a B minor tonic but artfully withholds a confirming cadence with chromatic progressions and unresolved dominants. The tonal fog clears and the suspense dissipates when a dominant elaborated by four chromatically sliding voices resolves into an original, lyrical theme that reveals the tonic as B major.

Though Czerny and Fink wrote many of their reviews and treatises about opera-based fantasies and variation sets, the strategies they described applied to other, more wholly "original" genres. Fink found accessible pleasure in Kalkbrenner's original rondo as well as in Herz's variations. Concertos, as Fink wrote in his Herz review, could also embody these qualities. The contemporary piano concertos Schumann knew featured sharp formal divisions between thematic areas (the first and second theme groups of an exposition, for example) and passagework areas (transitions, and the closes of expositions or recapitulations, for example).[44] They thereby employed the alteration between singable lyricism and transparent brilliance that Czerny and Fink described as essential for maintaining an audience's pleasure. Expositions and recapitulations themselves conclude with expansive, kaleidoscopic displays of transparent figuration, a section of the concerto form I call the "culminating display."[45] As Claudia Macdonald has shown, such closes differ from those earlier concertos by Mozart and Beethoven. The latter unfold as two or three long crescendos that manipulate a consistent pattern of figuration—their harmonic backgrounds often outline and extend complete phrases. Postclassical culminating displays, by contrast, string together short, sharply individuated modules of contrasting figuration. Dominant–tonic vamps often drive these concatenations, by turns confirming and digressing from the local tonic.[46]

Schumann's youthful warhorse, Hummel's Concerto No. 2, contains typically postclassical culminating displays. As we saw in example 1.1, every two to four measures drive to a cadence in C major, and each module brings a new pattern of figuration.[47] Such passagework evokes the fluctuating pleasure Fink and Czerny described. Sections of the concerto end in a state of ever-changing brilliance, a steady flow of new textures that display different ways in which the piano can shimmer. Because of the repeated arrivals on tonic, this flow sounds as if it could continue indefinitely, limited only by the composer's invention and estimation of the audience's desire.

Schumann's Critique of Pleasure and His Rhetoric of Luxury, Aristocracy, and Femininity

Schumann's reviews of postclassical showpieces often read like satirical distortions of Fink's. His essay on two Bellini-based works—Thalberg's aforementioned "Norma" Fantasy, and Kalkbrenner's *Variations sur un thème de "La Straniera,"* Op. 123—deploys a complex of claims, images, and rhetorical stances that appear in varying combinations throughout his critique of pleasure. The review appeared in the *Neue Zeitschrift* on June 2, 1835.[48] Using his trademark narrative style of criticism, Schumann depicted Florestan commenting on these pieces at a high-society salon. The reader can imagine him- or herself standing apart from the games, flirting, and bantering, trying to hold a conversation with Florestan:

(Soirée at the Countess's)

Attaché: "What happy keys these fingers of yours play, Countess! Truly, if I were a piano, with every note would I call out to the player a different name of beauty and youth: Corinna for C, Desdemona for D, Eleonore for E, Fiormona for F—do you guess what I'm asking for?"

With good reason do we group the above compositions together. The sole difference between them lies in the additional "3" in the opus number. There are charming characters whom the wide world has polished smooth and shiny, like ice. One learns flattery from being flattered: giver and receiver drink the same draught of this sweet poison. Truly . . .

Countess: "*The Last Days of Pompeii?* Oh, I love that book. The blind woman is divine."

Artist: "Doesn't she remind you of Mignon?"

Countess: "Certainly. But does Bulwer understand German?"

Mother: "Hasn't he translated *Götz von Berlichingen?*"

. . . truly, I envy these composers, the way they can converse with the most charming ambassadresses without offending anyone through brilliant opinions, with what grace they understand how to pick up a glove. Actually, the younger of the above composers still has some ways to go before anyone grants him significance in the salons, which the older has long secured for himself: there, the former still sometimes cites Beethoven or Goethe and even speaks with more inspiration than is allowed in higher circles, while the latter quickly makes conquests with his old, knightly refinement. However, we do not wish that . . .

—Attaché: "You cannot solve the charade, Your Grace? I'll repeat it for you. I give you three syllables. The first is a well-known mineral that often finds itself in the last two, which repeat perfectly the name of a well-known mountain. All in all you love a great virtuoso . . ."[49]

Countess: "I have solved your charade through another with two syllables. Without the first, the second does not exist, and vice versa. The whole possesses rich grounds; only be careful not to approach where both syllables stop . . ."[50]

It is already striking 11 o'clock. Where could Eusebius have gotten to?

Florestan

Rogue, I saw you through the window sitting with a glass of wine while you rubbed your forehead and finally went after the Fidibus-becher [sticks with which to light a pipe] to prompt critical thoughts. But that is a curious style of reviewing . . .

Euseb[ius]

Schumann recognized the pleasurable qualities of Thalberg's and Kalk-brenner's music but derided them as superficial, describing sensuous surfaces that masked less wholesome qualities. Every key that the Countess touches radiates beauty and euphony. However, the pleasure the music provides is only "flattery," a "sweet poison": external satisfaction that covers a hollow or even baneful inner essence. Schumann invoked the elegance and brilliance Fink praised in his reviews, but he compares this "smoothness" and "shininess" to ice—glimmering in appearance but frigid and lifeless in essence. The review does differentiate between the two pieces. Schumann acknowledged the ambitious features of Thalberg's fantasy, perhaps its contrapuntal and tonal complexity. Kalkbrenner's work, as he hints, is more accessible and conventional. Its Introduction, for example, trumpets its tonic from the opening chords, and the showpiece unfolds a series of transparently textured variations. Nevertheless, Schumann's crack about the

"3" in Kalkbrenner's opus number hyperbolically skewers both pieces for their shared aesthetic.

Schumann embroidered this critique with images of luxury, aristocracy, and femininity. He compared the music to fine gloves, charming salon guests, "knightly refinement," and courtly etiquette. Whereas Fink invoked similar associations as selling points, Schumann presented them as backhanded compliments. Kalkbrenner's and Thalberg's stratagems for keeping their music accessible were, for him, limitations—manners that required tempering one's "brilliant opinions" for a listener's comfort. Florestan even implies that further success in these circles might require Thalberg to tone down his "inspired" qualities. Schumann also feminized Thalberg's and Kalkbrenner's music. Though men are present in the salon, the Attaché compares the piano keys to female literary characters, so that the very sounds of the music exude femininity. The Attaché and the pianist-composers themselves pay court to countesses and ambassadresses.

Schumann's 1837 review of Thalberg's Etudes, Op. 26 (book 1), named the "poetic" as an alternative to such supposed superficiality. In one short passage, Schumann encapsulated his critique of accessible pleasure and his aristocratic, feminizing characterization. He added that Chopin had transcended these qualities to reach "poetic states":

> They are all grateful, ingratiating, and fall well on the ears and fingers. Thalberg, who increasingly has the public rather than the artist in mind, can no longer write any differently. . . . Except for the first, which too much resembles an exercise for a student, I would call these salon etudes, Viennese etudes, etudes for countess pianists, on account of whose eyes one overlooks a wrong note; by contrast, masculine players and characters will spend less time with them. Such a goal naturally closes off poetic states, such as those the profound [*tiefsinnige*] Chopin has unveiled for us.[51]

The contrast between "artists" and the "public" may make it seem as if Schumann was criticizing Thalberg simply for writing for amateur pianists. However, his invocation of Chopin precludes this reading: Chopin's nocturnes, waltzes, and mazurkas were marketed mainly for domestic performance. The real contrast is between what Schumann described as the sensuous pleasures of Thalberg's etudes—"ingratiating" qualities that satisfied the ears and fingers—and the "poetic" ideal Chopin supposedly attained—one that inhabited inner depths, as the images of "profundity" and "unveiling" hinted.

Other writers for the *Neue Zeitschrift* employed similar rhetoric. One 1834 review critiqued Thalberg's *Grande fantaisie sur "I Capuletti e Montecchi,"* Op. 10. (The author only signed the review with the cipher "10.") Thalberg's work features strategies similar to the "Norma" Fantasy. He opens the first variation with intricate, four-voice part-writing and follows with a "brilliant" second variation. His finale switches between a fugato based on the main theme and quicksilver, dance-meter figuration. The reviewer interpreted this stylistic heterogeneity as a calculated attempt to please various groups within Thalberg's audiences. He essentially criticized Thalberg for following strategies similar to those Czerny and Fink recommended. "One sees very clearly how the composer wanted to make the variations pleasing for the connoisseur as well as the layperson," he wrote, "how he thinks to satisfy the former with pretty fugued or four-voice passages and, for the latter, to compensate for their boredom with brilliant and elegant passages." Like Schumann, "10" sought to deflate Thalberg's ambition by comparing his to more conventionally accessible virtuosity, writing, "His composition is nothing more than a new, more elegant version of a work by Herz or Czerny, one that has a hint of learnedness." The review likened the pleasing showpiece to articles of clothing meant to impress and charm: "Does he use the word 'fantasy' in the sense of French *gilets* [jackets] *de fantaisie* or *foulards* [scarves] *de fantaisie*? But I ask—is it sublime in nature to ground everything in ravishing *Phantasie* so that, like a [female] paramour, it adorns itself with different colors for each person?" In the review, "10" described an alternative that emanated from the composer's interior, responded to ethereal (indeed, divine) inspiration, and reached beyond fashion and the physical world itself:

> Mustn't music irresistibly come from within [*aus dem Innern*] the poet as well as from within the composer and, snatching him away from the world, make him a slave of God? Raised above all conventional and fashionable things, it bears no restraint other than that of the true art which nevertheless, when laid upon the master, becomes a magic ring in which others are held fast?[52]

These three essays on Thalberg stoked the rivalry between Schumann's and Fink's journals. An anonymous *Zeitung* writer (possibly Fink himself) rebutted "10" and Schumann in an 1835 review of Thalberg's Opp. 10 and 12. He agreed with their analyses but not their judgments: "Someone even found fault that this young man has obviously striven to make his works enjoyable for the knowing and the uninitiated. In such pieces of music, though, this is a word of praise, not blame."[53] Another anonymous review disputed Schumann's review of Thalberg's etudes. "If Thalberg is not profound enough for these," he writes, "he is preferred that much more by many others for that reason. All six [etudes] are pleasing, not hard for the listener to understand, attractively entertaining and brilliant . . . and united with a pretty melody." He characterized Schumann and his reviewers as a disproportionately vocal minority. The number of Thalberg's detractors, he writes, "is not as large as many would think who forget that it is the sickest children who scream the most."[54]

Schumann's critique of accessible pleasure extended beyond his writings on Thalberg. After all, these essays made their points by grouping Thalberg with Herz, Czerny, and Kalkbrenner. Schumann's remarks on Döhler's *Variations de bravoure sur la cavatine favorite de "Anna Bolena,"* Op. 17, reveal another case in which he applied this critique even to works that he considered effective and original. The review appeared in an essay on variation sets by Chopin, Kalkbrenner, Charles Mayer, Józef Nowakowsky, George Alexander Osborne, Charles Schuncke, and Ludwig Schuncke. The opening of the review compared the whole stack to fine articles of clothing and high-society etiquette. Each issue of the *Zeitschrift* included a motto on its front page, and this one used the first stanza of Heine's Prologue from his *Aus der Harzreise*:

> Black dress coats and silken stockings,
> White, polite collars,
> Polite conversation, embraces,
> Ah, if only they had hearts![55]

This verse, Schumann wrote, would make "the best review for most of the above variations." His comparison painted these showpieces not even as skin-deep but as worn over the skin, as governed by external convention rather than by the heart. "All," Schumann summarized, "stand far removed from any poetic sphere."[56]

His discussions of individual variation sets drew finer distinctions. Schumann qualified that Chopin's *Variations brillantes sur le rondeau favori de "Ludovic,"* Op. 12, was not banished from the "poetic sphere." He praised details of Döhler's "Anna Bolena" Variations: a cantabile passage for left hand alone that compresses melody and accompaniment, and the third variation, where the theme appears in octaves surrounded by sweeping arpeggios.[57] However, Schumann made clear that, for him, Döhler's aesthetic of pleasure relegated his showpiece to a lesser category. He did not exempt the "Anna Bolena" Variations from the sweeping generalization at the beginning of the review, and his discussion of the piece mingled tolerance with dismissiveness:

> These are brilliant variations on a theme by Donizetti, and one knows it all beforehand. . . . It is useless for music journals to try to open the eyes of the world to what they call "amiable" talents, such as Kalkbrenner, Bertini, etc. One can already see through glass; there we need no tiresome explainer. Puff! Paff! Down to the smallest "and" we know them and their fingers. Who could be angry with Herr Döhler that he wishes to win the greatest [possible] applause for himself[?][58]

Schumann's mention of "glass" evokes what he regarded as the obviousness of Döhler's objective and, like the "ice" in his soiree review, hints at the accessibility of the music and the transparency of its textures.

Like Fink and Czerny, Schumann discussed the aesthetic of accessible pleasure in genres other than variation sets and fantasies. He criticized the first movement of Kalkbrenner's Piano Concerto No. 4, Op. 127, for what he heard as its calculated heterogeneity. Example 1.4 excerpts the second theme and the expositional culminating display. Here, Kalkbrenner takes to an extreme the stylistic contrasts that Czerny and Fink described. The second theme aims for hyperexpressivity with its striking harmonic gestures, including unexpected flashes of modal mixture. The movement snaps back to brilliant, harmonically straightforward figuration once the culminating display begins, even changing the meter signature to emphasize the new affect. Macdonald has noted that Schumann attacked the second theme for an unconvincing attempt to emulate younger, "Romantic" composers. Schumann wrote, "One thinks only of the elegant Kalkbrenner, pistol to

Second theme:

Example 1.4. Frédéric Kalkbrenner, Piano Concerto No. 4, Op. 127. Second theme group and expositional culminating display.

Expositional culminating display:

Example 1.4. (*continued*)

his head, where he writes *con disperazione* in his piano part, or desperate near an abyss, when he writes for three trombones in the adagio. It doesn't work, it doesn't suit him; he has no talent for Romantic audaciousness."[59] I would add that Schumann interpreted this mixture as a calculated strategy to ensure the audience's comfort:

> We see . . . Kalkbrenner himself, however, standing at a crossroads, wondering whether he should continue on the old path with the laurels he has already acquired or whether he should struggle for new ones on the other. There the comfortable and the usual entice him, here the fiery shouts that the Romanticists experience. Entirely in his own conciliatory character, he does not throw himself too strongly into the new sphere, just as if he would first test what the audience thinks about it.[60]

Whether Kalkbrenner was delighting listeners in the salon or the concert hall, Schumann imagined him as an inauthentic, aristocratic virtuoso. His images stressed the externality of Kalkbrenner's changing affects and denied them an inner component. "Though he put on the most diabolical mask, one would recognize him by the kid gloves with which he held it."[61]

The Cultural Status of Pleasurable Virtuosity

It was not just Florestan's glass of wine and tobacco-fueled musings that led Schumann to imagine fine coats, kid gloves, sycophantic diplomats, and countess-pianists. Nor were they simply metaphors for superficiality. By invoking these images, Schumann wove a tangle of interrelated cultural meanings into his critique.

On one level, these images disparage the audiences (real or imagined) who sustained this music. Though the middle classes were the main consumers of sheet music and public concerts, popular virtuosos advertised their association with glittering high society. In Paris, for example, Liszt and Thalberg waged their rivalry in exclusive, aristocratic salons, and newspapers tantalized middle-class readers with accounts of virtuosos' performances in such circles. Liszt literally surrounded himself onstage with aristocratic women, who sat in the best seats and chatted with him during pauses.[62] Fink, as we have seen, likened Herz's and Kalkbrenner's compositions to the refined discourse of a gentleman. In his analysis, such showpieces were designed to bring the high-society salon into the drawing room.

Schumann's descriptions of countesses and high-society salons not only betray middle-class notions of aristocratic frivolity—they also reflect his German cultural nationalist outlook. Celia Applegate has recently revealed the composer-critic's immersion in midcentury nationalism and the degree to which it shaped, for example, his ideas about the social significance of music criticism.[63] German nationalists of Schumann's time envisioned what Applegate calls a "community of mind" or (quoting the philosopher Jakob Fries) a "national spiritual unity" constructed through vibrant participation in the public sphere: scholarship, literature, journalistic debate, and music, for example. This arena, they believed, was under threat from international commerce and the cosmopolitan aristocracy. They saw commerce and aristocracy as inherently superficial, as networks built on privilege and meretricious self-interest rather than more authentic, inner sources.

Schumann's critique of pleasure also hinted at German stereotypes about Parisian and Viennese shallowness. His review of Thalberg's Piano Concerto, for example, implied that Parisian audiences could corrupt the composer: "In his joy over the laurels that one wastefully hangs on excellent virtuosos there, he could in the end completely put the composer [in himself] to flight."[64] Schumann even speculated in a later review that Parisian living was hampering Chopin's productivity.

In addition, the feminizing imagery that runs throughout these reviews supported a larger nineteenth-century discourse in which critics (who were usually men) devalued music written primarily for women to perform in domestic settings.[65] Though professional, touring virtuosos were most often (but not exclusively) men, women represented the largest market for published piano music. Women played piano in a variety of settings, from solitary recreation to larger social events. For them, piano playing could potentially combine a passionate avocation, a means of socializing, a form of domestic service, and a display of accomplishment, class status, and even marriageability.[66]

This was true of repertoire geared toward less-advanced players as well as difficult fare that also appeared on professional concerts. Czerny recognized this range of abilities in his treatise *Briefe über den Unterricht auf dem Pianoforte*, which he structured as a series of letters written to a fictional young woman. Czerny promised that, after a few years of study, "Fräulein Cäcile" would be ready for Chopin etudes and Hummel concertos.[67] James Parakilas has aptly termed real-life women who could perform such repertoire "domestic virtuosos"—avid and accomplished pianists who were not encouraged to take their virtuosity outside the home or did not desire to.[68] (We will encounter one domestic virtuoso, Henriette Voigt, in chapter 3.) Friedrich Wieck's 1853 *Clavier und Gesang* also describes pianistically accomplished women and hints at the contexts in which they might display their virtuosity. His treatise presents several object lessons: fictional, satirical accounts of piano students who represent common pitfalls of learning the instrument. One introduces "Fatime," an eighteen-year-old whose aunt and mother want her to "get to know all the beautiful concert pieces by Döhler, Liszt, Dreyschock, Willmers, and Thalberg and practice them to perfection." Wieck skewered not the goal but the family's insistence on immediate gratification. Fatime's teacher tells Wieck that he wanted to start with etudes and scales, but "soon after the beginning, Mama wanted modern pieces for birthdays, name days, etc."[69] As a result, Fatime renders Thalberg's "Les Huguenots" Fantasy "boldly and not without capability" but "without touch . . . without tone, [and] without meter." Despite his emphasis on the gaps in Fatime's training, Wieck maintains that playing Thalberg and comparable showpieces would be an attainable goal for her, given the graduated instruction he and other pedagogues advocated.

National and gender stereotypes, however, do not wholly account for Schumann's critique. Schumann's view of Parisian musical life was not monochromatically negative. His review of Thalberg's concerto, for example, also acknowledged that working in Paris allowed a virtuoso to meet significant composers and literary figures. As we will see in chapter 2, Schumann attributed the "poetic" qualities of Ferdinand Hiller's Etudes Op. 15 to his immersion in the Parisian virtuoso scene. More broadly, as Applegate reminds us, Schumann shared with other midcentury German liberals a variety of cultural nationalism characterized by "soft boundaries and cosmopolitan awareness."[70] He saw no conflict between his investment in German musical life and his admiration and support for non-German musicians such as Chopin, Bennett, and Berlioz. Nor were Schumann and other *Zeitschrift* writers scornful of amateur or female music-making. They vociferously promoted music that had been designed for this very market, including Chopin's nocturnes and Mendelssohn's *Lieder ohne Worte*. We will see in chapter 3 that Schumann himself expressed admiring views about female amateurs, especially when it came to real individuals he actually knew. In short, describing heartless clothing and vapid attachés was not simply Schumann's knee-jerk reaction against music he regarded as foreign, feminine, and amateur.

Through his imagery and rhetoric, Schumann was also making a claim about postclassical pleasure that lay closer to his immediate, professional concerns as a composer, critic, and ex-virtuoso: his imagery called into question the cultural prestige this kind of virtuosity attained. Schumann thus drew upon and entered two intertwined nineteenth-century discourses about the cultural significance of the arts. First, eighteenth- and nineteenth-century German authors carried on an extensive debate about whether and to what extent the so-called fine arts—particularly literature—were luxury items. As Germanist Matt Erlin has shown, this question winds through a variety of texts, from Goethe's 1800 essay "Kunst und Handwerk" to Novalis's 1802 novel *Heinrich von Ofterdingen* (which Schumann read and excerpted in his *Mottosammlung*). These writings responded to the sweeping consumer revolution and to wide-ranging debates about the social and moral consequences of luxury consumption. Authors in various fields tried to insulate literature from the category of luxury, or at least to distance it from negative connotations of luxury and link it to more positive ones. Scholars have often read this discourse as an ideological critique of capitalism or as a middle-class effort to define itself against the aristocracy. Erlin, however, emphasizes that nineteenth-century writers were most concerned with defending the validity and prestige of literature as a profession, activity, and cultural product. In his words, writers attempted to "define their own creations in such a way as to protect them from . . . accusations of self-indulgent egotism, of providing empty sensual pleasures, of prostituting their talents for the sake of financial gain." Conversely, they invoked negative images of luxury to critique other artworks. These writers did display considerable ambivalence and struggled to draw these distinctions. Their cumulative effect, though, was to define (select) artworks as what Erlin terms "the luxury that is not a luxury" but rather an essential part of one's self-formation, or *Bildung*.[71]

Second, nineteenth-century music critics distanced music from the tradition of courtly entertainment and from an aristocracy they portrayed as cosmopolitan and effeminate. One can find such rhetoric, for example, in writings that presented the oratorio as a serious, elevated genre by contrasting it with court-sponsored opera. David Gramit has shown that this discourse did not merely signal a changing of the guard in musical patronage. It also represented an important way in which writers made the case that music (or at least certain categories of music) merited the respect of the educated middle class.[72]

Denigrating certain pieces as women's pastimes supported this bid for prestige: critics urged readers (men and women) to look down upon music whose intended audience supposedly thrilled to fashion and tended to frivolity. Nineteenth-century writers routinely assumed that women fixated on the pleasing details of artworks instead of on deeper, intellectual issues or larger, ambitious structures.[73] The fictional women who appear in Schumann's critique of pleasure were "girls" rather than adults, aristocratic mediocrities rather than musically cultivated bourgeois.

Schumann did not fit flush into these discourses about luxury and aristocracy. He did not discuss luxury or aristocracy in general terms or cite contemporary philosophical writings about them, and he invoked these ideas through imagery and implication rather than through rigorous, explicit argumentation. The aristocrats in his reviews occupied estates and salons, not princely courts. As an alternative to shallow luxury, Schumann emphasized not the project of character formation but qualities of interiority.

Nevertheless, Schumann's antiluxury, antiaristocratic rhetoric revolved around the question of cultural prestige. One of his early essays for the *Zeitschrift*, for example, invoked this connection amid a call to arms against the "Philistines." In Florestan's Shrovetide speech, delivered after an imaginary performance of Beethoven's Ninth, the character climbs atop a piano and begins, "Gathered *Davidsbündler*, that is, youths and men who should strike dead the

Philistines, musical and otherwise."[74] Throughout, Florestan vents his exasperation with Philistine responses to the Ninth: a pedantic cantor who protests that Beethoven does not prepare the dissonances of the "Schreckenfanfare," and self-satisfied concertgoers who try to explain and pass judgment on the work despite (Florestan alleges) their lack of music literacy. Florestan reaches his peak of annoyance when describing "a Silesian country nobleman" who writes to a music merchant:

> Dear Sir,
> I will soon have my music cabinet in order. You should see it, how splendid it is. Alabaster columns on the inside, a mirror with silk curtains, busts of composers— in short, marvelous. But to adorn it with the most exquisite thing, please send me the collected works of Beethoven, because I like this composer very much.

Florestan finishes, "I don't know what else I could say."[75] Schumann was not, of course, critiquing Beethoven's music itself, and it is hard to imagine him objecting that a music store stocked Beethoven editions. Rather, his target is the nobleman, who reduces Beethoven's oeuvre to the status of a luxury item, just one more piece of finery among curtains and cabinets that adorn his estate and just one more display of his refinement and wealth. His appreciation of Beethoven, Schumann hinted, stopped at superficial pleasure, at "liking the composer very much" and regarding his music as an "exquisite" accoutrement. The nobleman even betrays a hint of vanity when he wishes that the merchant could see the cabinet.

The Schumann reviews that we have been exploring brought this argument to bear on the aesthetic of pleasure. Rather than locating aristocratic and luxurious superficiality in a listener's attitude, he and his *Zeitschrift* writers found these qualities within the music and its effect. By aiming to stimulate sensuous pleasure, Schumann implied, Döhler's "Anna Bolena" Variations and other similarly designed pieces could not claim cultural prestige greater than articles of fine clothing. By tailoring their Bellini fantasies to ingratiate, Thalberg and Kalkbrenner gave them a place among fine gloves, opulent surroundings, and charming but inauthentic manners. Schumann maintained that these showpieces were not merely superficial in an affective sense but reached what he considered a lesser or even negligible cultural status. His imagery, indeed, obliquely raised the specter of *Handwerk*, a category from which self-consciously cultivated musicians recoiled and that Gustav Schilling (quoted in the Introduction) described as a particular risk of virtuosity. Schumann thereby viewed postclassical pleasure from a different corner of the discourse about the cultural status of virtuosic piano music than Fink did. While Fink and other writers emphasized the positive aspects of pleasurable cultural consumption, Schumann joined more alarmed critics who anxiously drew boundaries between certain categories of art and pleasurable luxuries (and who saw the latter category as a lesser one).

Pleasure Validated, and the Poetic Discovered

In the three chapters that follow, we will encounter alternatives Schumann developed to the pleasure he critiqued. To reiterate an important point I made at the outset of this chapter, though, Schumann saw the boundaries between the pleasurable and the poetic—and between transcendent virtuosity and the idioms of popular pianism—as porous. For him, "pleasurable" and "poetic" were not antithetical categories but overlapping, potentially compatible responses informed by a mixture of listening experience and musical analysis.

Schumann's writings on Thalberg illustrate this overlap. Despite his barbs against the Etudes and the "Norma" Fantasy, Schumann also showed that he appreciated the pleasurable style of Thalberg's showpieces. In 1839, for example, he reviewed the second book of the Etudes. Schumann did strike a condescending tone, joking that "if one criticizes Thalberg, one finds all German and foreign girl-dom at one's throat," and reminding readers, "Thalberg himself would be the first to deny that these compositions can be classed with those of Beethoven." And yet, in the middle of the review, he also exuded delight in the etudes' appealing qualities: "How he then overlays his melodies, doubles them, spins them out with new figuration, how he makes it, in his own way, often surprising, dazzling, and enrapturing."[76] For a moment, Schumann sounds like Fink, savoring the ever-changing pleasures of Thalberg's virtuosity.

More strikingly, Schumann also suggested that some of Thalberg's fantasies and variation sets combined sensuous pleasure with more interior, transcendent qualities. He made such a claim later that year in a review of Thalberg's signature work, his *Fantaisie sur des thèmes de "Moïse,"* Op. 33. Schumann cited many of the same characteristics that Fink and Czerny described as generators of pleasure and engagement. Unlike in his Döhler review, Schumann's tone here is admiring rather than dismissive. The mention of "inspiration" hints that this pleasurable virtuosity issued from an inner source rather than from superficial calculation:

> The Phantasie was written in a fortunate salon inspiration and gives the virtuoso all means and weapons for the conquest of the public, to which belong, for example: a gripping introduction full of suspense, virtuoso display-passages [*Kraftstellen*], charming Italian melodies, stimulating interludes and soft quiet parts—and now a coda befitting such a Phantasie. And when the Maestro rises from the piano, the public will barely be satisfied and invite him cheering to sit down again: and then the same stormy effect. Who does not gladly look on a public excited to enthusiasm?[77]

Schumann claimed that Thalberg at least partly redeemed virtuosity from the superficial style of his predecessors: "Let us therefore value such pieces for what they are. . . . Let us congratulate ourselves that, in place of complete barrenness and lack of content, such as shows itself in Gelinek and later in Czerny, a more artistically combined one, more full of ideas, has entered, and in this better style of salon music Thalberg may be regarded as the matador."[78] For Schumann, Thalberg's fantasy stimulated pleasure but also contained more incorporeal qualities—"ideas" and "content"—behind the passagework.

Though Schumann's review did not discuss Thalberg's "Moïse" Fantasy in concrete detail, he was surely aware that it departed from the style of his earlier "Norma" and "Capuletti" fantasies. Rather than spinning brilliant, transparent figuration, Thalberg blends individual notes into complex, sonorous textures that surround the melodies. Early in the fantasy, he introduces an original, nocturne-like theme and places it in a middle voice surround by octaves. The fantasy ends with a climactic apotheosis of the act 3 prayer, "Dal tuo stellato soglio," supported by Thalberg's "three-handed" texture. Thalberg delivers the lyrical pleasure Czerny described as essential but carries it on long, resonant waves of figuration instead of crystalline brilliance.

Schumann's personal experience with Thalberg surely shaped his opinion, too. When Schumann visited Vienna in 1838, he met Thalberg and recorded in his diary that he personally liked the man. "Early on Thursday, to Thalberg's," he noted, "who is very modest and rather well-mannered and respectable." He was still more impressed with Thalberg's playing. "Yesterday," he recounted, "the weather was fair and I visited Thalberg, who played much and beautifully; several things by F. Schubert, and then he sight-read my *Kreisleriana* with considerable perfection and grasp."[79]

Even before seeing Thalberg perform, Schumann claimed that moments in his fantasies and variation sets embodied transcendent qualities. In 1836, he described Thalberg's *Deux airs russes variés*, Op. 17, as "the most excellently successful of these compositions that has yet come before me." Schumann singled out the way Thalberg introduced the first of the folk songs: "An introduction takes shape, very imaginative and effective, and the child's song emerges charming and transfigured like an angel's head."[80] Schumann might have been referring to two moments in the introduction, shown in example 1.5. In the first, Thalberg reveals an embellished, minor-mode version of the theme. He prepares for this moment with an imitative treatment of the theme's head motive, and he reaches the dominant via a four-voice texture that traces chromatic progressions before trailing off into silence. In the second, the major-mode theme itself emerges from a densely voiced, chromatically inflected tremolo. It, too, fades to a murmur before the theme enters, briefly passing through an augmented triad. In both cases, Thalberg contrasts textural and harmonic obscurity with clear, singing lyricism. For Schumann, such lyricism was "transfigured" to suggest an ethereal being.

Schumann was not alone among German critics in claiming that Thalberg's virtuosity possessed transcendent qualities. Hanslick grouped Thalberg with a wave of virtuosos who brought a new element into Vienna's "sensually amusing, shallowly comfortable musical life" around 1836. This style of composing and playing, he wrote, "impressed sensuously without lacking spirit [*Geist*]." Hanslick heard a glimmer of transcendence in Thalberg's compositions: "delicate, elegant, brilliant, lacking in strength or depth, but not without a shimmer of spirit [*Geist*] and passion [*Schwärmerei*]."[81] Gustav Schilling was less equivocal in his encyclopedia entry on

A:

Example 1.5. Thalberg, *Deux airs russes variés*, Op. 17. Preparations for theme in Introduction.

Thalberg. Speaking mainly of Thalberg's prowess as a performer, he wrote, "His playing is neither correct nor merely precise, not elegant and not brilliant; all that says too little, even if we added a thousand more adjectives: his playing is truly colossal. Whoever hears him, blindfolded, would never believe that the piano on which he played was a mere piano. . . . So powerful is the spirit [*Geist*] he breathes into his playing."[82]

Schumann, then, mediated between two ways of seeing Thalberg. On one hand, he described Thalberg as a composer primarily concerned with designing accessible, sensuous pleasures. On the other, he commended Thalberg as a virtuoso who redeemed this pleasure, particularly in music that subverted the transparent

B:

Example 1.5. (*continued*)

clarity conventional in postclassical piano music. Rather than snugly placing the pianist-composer or individual works in one or the other category, these writings reveal the flexibility of Schumann's views about superficiality, pleasure, and transcendence. In the next two chapters, we will see that Schumann's concept of "poetic" interiority did not reject the figurational and structural idioms of popular pianism, nor did it abnegate the sensual pleasures of virtuosity. In fact, Schumann developed this ideal partly through his critical and compositional engagement with the cutting edge of postclassical pianism.

2 Florestan's Wine, Clara Wieck's Spirit: Postclassical Virtuosity and Poetic Interiority

As we saw in chapter 1, Schumann often described the "poetic" as an antidote to the sensuous pleasures of popular postclassical showpieces. He hinted at this alternative while critiquing "ingratiating" or "flattering" delights, satirizing vapid countesses and attachés, and describing shallow luxury items. By becoming poetic, he suggested, music could transcend superficiality and sensuousness and, crucially, aim for a different kind of cultural prestige.

In this chapter, I trace how Schumann's critical writings identified instances of poetic virtuosity during the early 1830s. Such virtuosity, for him, embodied qualities of interiority. Schumann described transcendent interiority in various guises: introspective, ethereal experiences for the listener, glimpses of a performer's or composer's inner self, or some animating spirit or concealed depth within the composition. Three clusters of sources reveal the flexibility of this concept, showing how Schumann applied it to different situations and agendas. All emerged during a formative period of his career when he was beginning to enter public debates about virtuosity. His 1831 "Ein Opus II" essay on Chopin's "Là ci darem la mano" Variations, Op. 2, was his first published piece of writing. (It also began his strained relationship with Gottfried Wilhelm Fink, editor of the *Allgemeine musikalische Zeitung*.) This essay finds poetic interiority in a single showpiece, revealed to individual musicians and listeners in a specific context. However, Schumann's responses to Clara Wieck during the early 1830s show that, for him, the poetic was not exclusively a property of compositions and could emerge from a performer's style and persona. Finally, Schumann's 1835 review of Ferdinand Hiller's Etudes Op. 15 attempted to validate his ideal of poetic interiority by incorporating it into a critical and analytical methodology.

Despite the Philistines-versus-*Davidsbündler* rhetoric that pervades Schumann's writings, the poetic did not inhabit one side of an easily demarcated dichotomy. Schumann's writings on Thalberg, as we saw at the end of chapter 1, reveal the overlap between the sensuous pleasures of piano virtuosity and the inner, even ethereal qualities Schumann believed he was detecting and valorizing. The poetic interiority Schumann heard in Chopin, Clara Wieck, and Hiller occurred along this hazy border.

My discussion here emphasizes this porousness. These writings discuss repertoire (or performances of repertoire) within the postclassical tradition. They thereby illuminate a side of the virtuosity discourse that scholars have largely overlooked. One of the broadest currents of this debate—and the one scholars most frequently cite—urged performers and composers to ally themselves with the Austro-German canon. In many cases, such virtuosos strove to embody ideals of reverent interpretation. Clara Wieck Schumann earned plaudits as a Beethoven and Bach interpreter beginning in the mid-1830s, Liszt played Bach, Beethoven, and Scarlatti to convince critics of his credentials, and Joseph Joachim founded his reputation on the perceived insight with which he rendered canonized masterworks. Original showpieces could also reflect a canon-centric view of serious virtuosity. These included Brahms's 1859 Piano Concerto No. 1, Op. 15—whose first movement positions Brahms within a symphonic tradition through its intertextual allusions, classicizing strategies, and sheer scale—and Mendelssohn's historicizing 1841 *Variation sérieuses*, Op. 54, which includes chorale and fugal variations and alludes to Beethoven's String Quartet Op. 95.[1]

From almost the beginning of his career, Schumann did turn to the canon to elevate virtuosity, as subsequent chapters will show; however, his writings also reveal a concept of transcendent virtuosity that emerged from cutting-edge developments in popular pianism. The music of Chopin and Moscheles was just as important to Schumann's aesthetic as that of Schubert and Beethoven. Poetic showpieces and performances, here, did not reject postclassical idioms, even though they often subverted the formal and textural transparency that we saw in Hummel's Concerto No. 2 or Thalberg's "Norma" Fantasy.

Moreover, poetic interiority did not abnegate virtuosity's sensuous or pleasurable aspects. Several strands of the virtuosity discourse did attempt to distance serious virtuosity from its physical or crowd-pleasing facets. As we will see in chapter 6, Eduard Hanslick described select virtuosos as "priests," a metaphor that connoted self-denial and distance from worldly concerns. Eduard Krüger's writings for the *Neue Zeitschrift*, cited in the Introduction, draw a boundary between physical display and inner content. With his descriptions of "martyrdom" and the "smoke of a sacrifice," Krüger implied that the ideal performer entered a radically ethereal realm. By contrast, Schumann acknowledged that poetic interiority was just another variety of pleasure, one that (he believed) stimulated the imagination or spirit as well as the senses. The writings I present in this chapter constantly emphasize that the sensuous aspects of this music were important to its effect—its visceral engagement with the instrument, the delight it offered listeners, or the desire it stimulated. In poetic virtuosity, for Schumann, the body and senses resonated sympathetically with a transcendent interior.

The Schumannian Poetic

Scholars have long recognized Schumann's concept of the poetic as a cornerstone of his music and writings, and they occasionally use the term as a general descriptor for his aesthetic. John Daverio's Schumann biography dubbed the composer "Herald of a 'New Poetic Age,'" Hubert Moßburger's essay on Schumann's harmonic language terms it "poetische Harmonik," and Holly Watkins has recently explicated what she calls Schumann's "poetic depth."[2] Studies of the Schumannian poetic stress its roots in Romantic literature and literary theory. They also shy away from virtuosity, instead stressing the cycles of piano character pieces. Watkins, for example, uses Schumann's *Nachtstücke*, Op. 23, as a case study. This focus, in part, represents a response to ways in which Schumann's 1830s piano cycles resist conventional analytical approaches and defy easy generic classification. Indeed, many nineteenth-century writers critiqued his works as bewildering or incoherent. Daverio developed literary frameworks for considering this music precisely in order to find new, historically grounded ways to understand its logic.[3] By contrast, Schumann's 1830s showpieces fall into more familiar genres—variation sets and a concerto, for example—even if they approach them in strikingly unconventional ways.

Schumann never presented a systematized, explicit definition of what he meant by "poetic." His writings discuss the poetic more through imagery and association than through rigorous argumentation, often using the term within clusters of synonyms and antitheses. In his 1835 New Year's address for the *Neue Zeitschrift*, for example, he described his journal's goal:

> Our intention was . . . to struggle against the recent past as an unartistic one for which only the great increase of the mechanical offers any compensation and to prepare for and help to precipitate a young poetic future."[4]

Even in this proclamation, Schumann avoided firm dichotomies. The meaning of "mechanical" is vague, though his 1854 *Gesammelte Schriften* suggests that it encompassed the efflorescence of public interest in virtuosity. The anthology changed the wording so that the *Zeitschrift* struggled for a "new poetic age" against a recent past "that only led to the increase of external [*äußerlicher*] virtuosity."[5] Schumann's address also hints that even the "intensification of the mechanical" represented some (if by itself inadequate) contribution.

In numerous writings, though, Schumann suggested that music became poetic by opening up a transcendent interiority within itself or the listener. As we saw in chapter 1, he described Chopin "unveiling profound poetic states," an inner depth that Thalberg's etudes supposedly missed. The different versions of the New Year's editorial suggest that "poetic" music transcended both the "mechanical" (to become organic, animated by inner life) and the "external" (to harbor an internal essence). In some cases, Schumann specifically imagined that "poetic" music reached not just the senses but the spirit. In an 1838 review of Moscheles's Etudes Op. 95, he described the ones titled "Kindermärchen" and "Traum" as "the most delicate and poetic of the collection." Schumann wrote, "Here, where it plays across the spirit-realm, beyond the sensuous [*Uebersinnliche*], music exercises its full power."[6] Schumann took a different rhetorical tack in his review of Julius Benedict's *Variations sur un thème favori de "La straniera,"* Op. 16. In this case, he used the term to describe a characteristic built into the composition itself, demanding "poetic unity"—a quality of inner connection accompanied by non-corporeal "thoughts" and "fantasy"—instead of Benedict's outlay of pleasing melodic turns and physical virtuosic gestures: "The days are past when a sugary figure, a yearning appoggiatura, an E-flat-major run over the keyboard, raised astonishment: now, one wants thoughts, inward connection, poetic unity, the whole bathed in fresh fantasy."[7] Schumann appealed to both interpretations of poetic interiority in a review of Moscheles's Piano Trio Op. 84: he praised the composer for allowing "the idea to reign," using "poetic raw materials [*poetischen Grundstoff*]," and conveying "noble states of the soul."[8] Watkins has traced Schumann's concept of musical interiority in general to Jean Paul's definition of metaphor, presented in his 1801 *Vorschule der Aesthetik*. (Schumann kept the *Vorschule* in his library and annotated it during the early 1830s.) Jean Paul defined metaphor as a device that gave spirit to matter, and vice versa. In Watkins's formulation, "music's body—its physical reality as (external) sound—demands to be read as a sign of (internal) spirit."[9]

The poetic did carry other implications for Schumann, and my discussion in this chapter does not exhaust its constellation of meanings. As the New Year's editorial illustrates, he also believed that poetic music stood in a youthful vanguard rebelling against an older order. His review of Moscheles's trio praised the composer for joining "the younger ranks" against "mere formalism [*Formwesen*], the reigning fashion [*Modeherrschaft*], and Philistinism."[10] The Schumannian poetic could imply a fusion of art forms. Many scholars have shown that, when the composer sought to convey interiority in his own music, he used narrative strategies that Romantic literary theorists believed stimulated the reader's imagination and required inner reflection.[11] (I return to this aspect of the poetic in chapter 3.) Finally, at the extreme of generality, Moßburger notes that "poetic" could be synonymous with "original," "fantastic," "new," "unknown," and "dream-like."[12]

By idealizing art forms, individual works, and historical periods as "poetic," Schumann was employing a trope common in German Romantic literature and aesthetics. Such statements surface in writers he mined for his *Mottosammlung*, a collection of quotations on music.[13] One passage from Novalis in the *Mottosammlung* comes close to the composer's ideal that poeticizing meant giving matter a soul or spirit: "Nowhere is it more striking than in music that it is only the spirit [*Geist*] that poeticizes objects and the changes of matter."[14] More broadly, many late eighteenth- and early nineteenth-century German writers and philosophers lamented their own time as a "prosaic" one, a drab period of cultural decline, and presented a "poetic" age as an antidote. Novalis's unfinished 1799 encyclopedia, *Das Allgemeine Brouillon* mused in an entry on "Cosmology," "The prosaic nature of the current heaven and the current earth. The world period of usefulness. The direction of the world—the beginning of a new, cultivated [*gebildeten*], poetic period."[15] Goethe, in his 1817 essay "Stages of Man's Mind," saw a "poetic" age not as a future hope but as a primordial golden age "elevated by the power of the imagination." The "prosaic" present, he lamented, had declined into "sensuality" and the "dissolution into the ordinary."[16] This is not to argue that Schumann's use of the term "poetic" maps cleanly onto Novalis's or Goethe's; he did not use the terms "poetic" and "prosaic" as antitheses, for example. Rather, Schumann customized this ideal to fit his own purposes and aesthetic.

The interiority that Schumann idealized reflected not only the rarefied realm of Romantic philosophy but also more widespread cultural attitudes. Schumann was immersed in a middle-class culture preoccupied with the inner life. Historian Peter Gay has traced this obsession throughout Western European and American bourgeois society: in ideas about music as well as the ubiquitous confessional diaries and soul-baring letters, the thriving market for autobiographies, and the cult of the egocentric Romantic hero.[17] Schumann encountered intense, even frightening descriptions of music's power to catalyze inner experience in the literature he read—fiction by E. T. A. Hoffmann, for example. (He confided to his diary in 1831 that "one scarcely dares to breathe" while reading Hoffmann. Two of his piano works, *Fantasiestücke*, Op. 12, and *Kreisleriana*, Op. 16, draw their titles from Hoffmann.)[18] Stories such as "Rat Krespel," "Don Juan," and "Ombra Adorata" depict transformative musical ecstasies that momentarily release listeners from the realities of the everyday, physical world. Others satirize characters who regarded music mainly as a form of light entertainment or external ornament, as in the title character's exasperated rant from "*Kapellmeister* Kreisler's Musical Sufferings."

The ideal of transcendent interiority informed Schumann's writings on topics other than virtuoso piano music, including many reviews that do not mention the word "poetic." One thinks, for example, of his essay on Mendelssohn's *Lieder ohne Worte*, Op. 30, in which he imagined the composer creating melodies in moonlit moments of solitary, inspired improvisation. Or when he described the introduction to Schubert's Symphony No. 9 as "veiled in secrecy" and a horn solo in the second movement as a "heavenly guest passing through the orchestra."[19]

This belief in interiority was one facet of the ideology of serious music: one way in which Schumann and his contemporaries elevated music's cultural prestige. Several of the writings I explored in chapter 1 raise this issue explicitly. By becoming poetic, Schumann suggested, music rose above the status of superficial luxury items and frivolous entertainments. The sources I consider here make the point more implicitly: Schumann did not locate this virtuosity in the world of fashion and the senses but within an inner, ethereal one. Through interiority, music transcended (without suppressing) merely physical labor, pleasure, or recreation. Instead, it spoke to the inner self that middle-class audiences were self-consciously cultivating.

In fact, however, Schumann's "poetic" music was closer than he acknowledged to the pleasures that Fink touted in Czerny's showpieces or that the *Journal des Luxus und der Mode* described in many kinds of cultural consumption (see chapter 1). The poetic emerged from the same broad current as these pleasures: the desire to enliven the mind with cultural products available to the middle class, the drive to free the listener from everyday routine, and the search for artistic novelty. The difference lay in the writers' specific stances. Schumann and his literary influences suggested that the pleasures of interiority transcended not just stress and tedium but the sensuous world altogether. They described the search for originality as a redemptive revolution or an encounter with the otherworldly rather than a parade of stimulating novelties. And, crucially, they disavowed or at least deemphasized the real-world role of supposedly poetic music—its undeniable status as luxury item and recreational pursuit. For all Schumann's attempts to locate Chopin, Clara Wieck, and Hiller in ethereal realms, playing and listening to their music was a form of entertainment, relaxation, and enjoyment, one that required leisure time and disposable income. Gay himself points to the recreational value of introspection when he describes it as a "favorite, and wholly serious, indoor sport."[20]

Schumann evocatively described this inner experience in the realm of virtuosity when he reviewed Chopin's Etude Op. 25, no. 1 ("Aeolian Harp"). Both this and the next etude of the set, he wrote, were "poetic creations." He described hearing Chopin himself play the piece during an 1835 visit to Leipzig:

> One would err to think that he makes all of the little notes clearly audible; it was more a wave of A-flat-major chords, here and there lifted to a new height with the pedal. But throughout, one could wondrously hear through the harmonies a melody in large notes, and only in the middle section a tenor voice, near to the melody, emerged clearly from out of the chords. After the etude, it was like after seeing a blissful image in a dream that one, already half awake, wanted to catch again. Speech can say little about this, and praise nothing at all.[21]

Schumann called the piece "more a poem than an etude," but he did not deny that it displayed physical dexterity. "Imagine that an Aeolian harp had all of the scales," he wrote, "and that the artist's hand cast these together in all manner of fantastic embellishments." Chopin's etude consists of rapid arpeggios divided by short changes of direction. The notation itself prescribes the finely shaded performance Schumann remembered: figuration appears in small notes, melodies in large. The result takes to an extreme the textural obfuscation that characterizes junctures of Thalberg's *Deux airs russes variés* (see chapter 1). Amid the undulations of harmony, Chopin's melodies tread the border between clarity and obscurity. Schumann imagines the main theme emanating through the rushing blur of figuration. The pianist sporadically shadows it with inner voices, only to let them vanish into the wash of sound.[22] At the very end, melody itself collapses into texture, reaching the tonic on the weak fourth beat before blending into the closing arpeggios.

Chopin's etude, for Schumann, stimulated pleasure, an image the listener longed to repossess. However, the imagined listener experiences and manifests this pleasure in introspective dreams rather than in the external world. Instead of applauding or exclaiming with delight, he or she longs to turn inward again. Schumann described the dream-image using the adjective *selig*, which connotes "blissful" in the "blessed" sense, and he wrote that the effect bordered on the ineffable. Schumann even came close to describing the performance itself as ethereal rather than corporeal: though he recognized the agency of the performer's body, he described an instrument played by the wind, an invisible source of virtuosity. According to his review, Chopin's etude stimulated an inner, transcendental experience through the composer's own performance and the textural obscurity he scripted into his composition. Virtuosity, here, became poetic.

"Ein Opus II": Encountering Transcendent Interiority

Schumann's first published essay—his review of Chopin's *Variations sur "Là ci darem la mano,"* Op. 2—charted such an intersection between virtuosity and interiority. Around the time he was abandoning his dream of virtuoso stardom, Schumann made his debut as a music critic with an article on the Variations that appeared in the *Allgemeine musikalische Zeitung* on December 7, 1831.[23] This essay, "Ein Opus II," is one of the most often-anthologized nineteenth-century writings on music, and scholars have used it to explore the literary style of Schumann's criticism.[24] It also marked the beginning of Schumann's public, printed engagement with the virtuosity discourse and made a complex argument about the kind of experience that Chopin's showpiece offered.

As well-known as "Ein Opus II" has become, several of its features have concealed important aspects of this argument. The review as nineteenth-century and present-day publications have it is fraught with textual omissions. The largest and perhaps most surprising is the absence of Schumann's planned conclusion. Originally, Schumann wrote a second part of the review that picks up where all the published versions end. When "Ein Opus II" appeared in the *Zeitung*, Gottfried Wilhelm Fink lopped off this conclusion, stopping the review midstream. Schumann attempted to have the full essay published in Ignaz Castelli's Viennese *Allgemeiner musikalischer Anzeiger*, but to no avail.[25] He did not rectify the omission in his own 1854 *Gesammelte Schriften*, and Leon Plantinga described the conclusion as lost.[26] However, a draft of the conclusion exists at the Robert Schumann Haus archive in Zwickau. Contextual evidence suggests that it reflects, if not the exact wording, at least the substance of what Schumann submitted to the *Zeitung*.[27] Aside from this large omission, when Schumann republished the essay in 1854, he changed many details of the text.

The style of the essay presents its own challenges: "Ein Opus II" contains virtually no technical discussion of Chopin's Variations. The review is a short story involving Florestan, Eusebius, and Raro, plus a narrator named Julius. (Schumann had not yet coined the term *Davidsbund* but would do so soon.) The young men extol the originality of Chopin's showpiece and behold otherworldly visions from Mozart's *Don Giovanni*, the source of the theme. Florestan himself spins an elaborate comparison between Variations and opera. His narrative emphasizes the scenario for "Là ci darem la mano"—Don Giovanni's encounter with Zerlina—but incorporates other characters (Leporello and Masetto) and other scenes (the opera's finale, for example). Aside from describing the contrasting characters of the variations, he does not explicitly discuss Chopin's harmonies, forms, and textures. Sanna Pederson's reading of "Ein Opus II" stresses that Schumann was modeling a particular way of discussing and subjectively experiencing music for his readers and that he was not necessarily arguing for a specific appraisal or interpretation of Chopin's composition.[28]

Chopin's Variations themselves also seem an unlikely candidate for this kind of review. As Jim Samson and John Rink have noted, the piece reveals Chopin's immersion in postclassical piano music.[29] It inhabits the same genre as Herz's "Violette" Variations and other popular variation sets: it includes an extended, quasi-improvisatory introduction, a complete statement of its borrowed theme, several variations (five in this case) that retain the structure of the theme and usually keep its melodic contours audible, a penultimate slow variation, and a dance-meter rondo finale. The fast variations feature keyboard idioms and transparent textures conventional in this repertoire, and, as in many Herz variation sets (including "Violette"), the slow variation segues directly into the finale. Chopin's very choice of theme reflected not reverence for a classic but an awareness of popular trends: potpourris and variation sets on Mozart themes flooded the sheet-music market, and Mark Everist has counted 160 works based on *Don Giovanni* published in Paris alone. Plantinga writes of "Ein Opus II," "It is astonishing that [Schumann] should be able to make this judgment on the basis of the "Là ci darem" Variations alone."[30]

Untangling the interplay of postclassical virtuosity, sensuous pleasure, and transcendent interiority in Schumann's story-review requires us to consider "Ein Opus II" in its most extensive form (including the lost conclusion) and alongside other contemporary responses to Chopin's Variations. Schumann was indeed modeling an attitude toward listening. However, this wider context also shows that he regarded Chopin's Variations as the catalyst for this experience. He echoed other critics who believed that this showpiece transcended merely physical display, and he recognized that Chopin was subverting the structural and textural conventions of postclassical variation sets.

Schumann first encountered the Variations while studying with Friedrich Wieck and watching Clara Wieck's early career take flight. Friedrich assigned Schumann to practice the Variations during the summer of 1831, and the hopeful virtuoso's diary reveals that he alternately "reveled in Chopin" and ran up against frustrating technical roadblocks. Meanwhile, Clara, who had just made her public debut in 1828, programmed the Variations as one of her signature showpieces between 1831 and 1838.

Friedrich identified the work as an ambitious project for Clara that would set her apart from other virtuosos. In part, the piece's sheer difficulty attracted him. In 1831, for example, he was preparing to take Clara to Eisenach but received a letter warning him that a local pianist would already be performing a work on Clara's program, Pixis's Concerto Op. 100. Friedrich canceled the visit but retorted, "She also plays the great *Phantasie-Bravourstück* by Chopin . . . a work that, until now, has been considered impossible to play in the spirit of the composer. My Clara, then, could have certainly counted on the same recognition in Eisenach that was given her, in the form of a true triumph, in Dresden, Leipzig, Altenburg, Weimar, and other places."[31] Friedrich himself wrote in Clara's diary,

"Chopin's Variations, Opus 2 . . . is the most difficult piece of music I have yet seen and played. This original, inspired composition is still so little known that almost all pianists and teachers regard it as incomprehensible and unplayable."[32] (Ever the possessive, ambitious manager, Friedrich frequently wrote portions of his daughter's diary, recording viewpoints that he believed would do her credit.) Schumann's early *Zeitschrift* collaborator Julius Knorr performed the Variations in Leipzig in 1831, and the *Allgemeine musikalische Zeitung* described the piece as "enormously difficult."[33]

Friedrich also believed that the "Là ci darem" Variations possessed culturally and aesthetically elevated qualities that set it apart from other popular showpieces. He made this claim in an 1832 review of the Variations for the journal *Caecilia*. His essay was designed in part as a self-interested effort to bolster Clara's credibility as a virtuoso. In 1831, he sent a draft to his brother-in-law in Paris, urging him to get it published in the *Revue musicale* in advance of his and Clara's tour there. He also sought to have it published in Leipzig, where he felt that audiences and critics did not sufficiently admire his daughter.[34] Friedrich acknowledged that the Variations drew upon recent styles of popular virtuosity, but he dismissed Chopin's influences as merely superficial. The Variations, he wrote, "bespeaks a very ample acquaintance with the lightweight, graceful, but purely mechanical Viennese style of playing" and "knowledge of the newest, savory, perhaps frivolous, but elegant and very tasteful French school" of Herz, Moscheles, and Kalkbrenner. Wieck claimed that Chopin maintained his originality, and he praised the work's "surprising and entirely new" passages. For him, these touches were not merely astonishing but transcendent. Chopin's Variations, he proclaimed, was worth "the attention of virtuosos who seek to represent something higher than mere technical proficiency." As Schumann did in his review, he developed a narrative interpretation of Chopin's piece involving Don Giovanni, Zerlina, Leporello, and Masetto.[35] In Wieck's discussion, changes of style and figuration take on quasi-literary meaning, and he used the comparison to underline the piece's originality: "Chopin chose the duet from *Don Juan* as its theme, not merely to write variations on it, but . . . to depict the entire daring, wild, foolhardy, love-indulging life and deeds of a Don Juan. He has done this, in my opinion, in the most ingenious and bold features [of the Variations]." In a brazen claim for prestige, Wieck wrote that the Variations would be "understandable and graspable and, from the standpoint of harmony, significant and most interesting for the cultivated [*Gebildeten*]."

Other listeners similarly immersed in postclassical piano music believed that, for better or worse, the Variations was a distinctive, unconventional showpiece. The Viennese *Allgemeiner musikalischer Anzeiger* reviewed the score in 1830 and made claims that anticipated Friedrich's. The anonymous reviewer remarked that Chopin, "without neglecting the brilliant exterior of the piece," also gave it "the stamp of intensive, real individuality" and "at least in the eyes of the connoisseur [*Kenner*], secured a lasting value for this work."[36] (Like Wieck, the *Anzeiger* was no neutral source: its publisher, Haslinger, also published the "Là ci darem la mano" Variations.) Friedrich Wieck recorded that, when Clara played the work for the composer Ludwig Spohr, he criticized some aspects of her playing but at least found the work "extraordinarily imaginative and original."[37] Other critics were not so complimentary. When the *Allgemeine musikalische Zeitung* published Schumann's truncated "Ein Opus II," it also ran a negative review of Chopin's Variations. The reviewer (possibly Fink himself) cringed at several of Chopin's dissonances and criticized what he called "over-full" textures.[38] Ludwig Rellstab's journal, *Iris im Gebiete der Tonkunst*, complained that Chopin had added an upbeat to Mozart's melody, which amounted to "vandalism" and "revealed an exceptionally deficient feeling for melodic construction and for beauty in rhythm." The reviewer sneered that Chopin's "rough, Slavic nature" might be to blame.[39] Perhaps because of its harmonic and textural unconventionality, Clara at first performed the Variations in the middle of her concerts (sometimes to end the first half) and instead used variation sets by Herz as closers.[40]

More than these writers, Friedrich Wieck detailed specific features of Chopin's Variations that, for him, embodied qualities of imagination and originality. His programmatic reading highlights moments when Chopin leads virtuosic figuration through surprising, digressive formal and harmonic pathways or when he pushes the boundaries of postclassical textural transparency. In studies of Schumann's review, John Daverio and Stephen Downes have noted one of these cases, the minor-mode slow variation.[41] Friedrich described it as "full of original and poetic features—greater than many longer Adagios."[42] The first half of the variation adheres to Mozart's phrase and harmonic structure. As shown in example 2.1, though, the second half modulates to the flat submediant, a key unanticipated in the B-flat-major theme. The modulation yields a new melody in octaves, a lyrical outpouring that initially articulates a four-measure phrase but becomes an open-ended string of runs by measure 13. The flat-key efflorescence, then, temporarily dissolves the classical phraseology of Mozart's theme and suspends the inexorable, predictable progress of the variations. Chopin's figuration itself juxtaposes extremes of profusion and stasis—between the dense passagework of measure 10 and the rolled harmonies of measure 11, or between the sustained chord in measure 12 and the blindingly fast runs that follow.

Wieck also singled out the finale's harmonic language. "How rich in harmonic twists, how new!" he exclaimed of the rondo form's second episode.[43] As shown in example 2.2, the passagework ranges widely amid distant tonal centers and abounds in striking harmonic gestures. Chromatic mediant relationships separate the ending of one sequence from the beginning of another. In its final stages, the piano's passagework orbits B minor and C-sharp minor (enharmonically spelled flat-II and flat-iii, respectively), and the solo ends on a diminished-seventh chord. Only four measures of tutti reveal a last-minute path back to tonic.

The densely textured style of bravura writing in the slow variation and finale informs some of the other variations. Shown in example 2.3, Chopin's Variation 1 only barely adheres to the thematic and textural transparency standard to postclassical variations sets. The sixteenth-note triplets weave above and below Mozart's theme. The first measure spotlights the contour of the melody and leaves

Example 2.1. Frédéric Chopin, "Là ci darem la mano" Variations, Op. 2. Variation 5 (excerpt).

the triplet sixteenths in the mellow middle voice—in the second, by contrast, figuration climbs over the melody and into a brighter register. Chopin refracts the phrases through kaleidoscopic shifts of color. In the first two measures, the accompaniment alternately thickens the texture by shadowing the theme and lightens it with a striding accompaniment. Other patterns double the right hand's triplet sixteenths or involve hand-crossings. Syncopated accents allow

Example 2.1. (*continued*)

high notes to ring out and accentuate the brilliance of the runs. Wieck described it as "very difficult and bold, splendidly worked out, a true Don Juan variation." By contrast, Rellstab's *Iris* complained that Chopin "almost overcrowds the theme with runs" throughout the piece.[44]

Schumann couched some of his claims about the Variations in terms that echoed his teacher's. Eusebius introduces the piece with his often-quoted proclamation,

Example 2.2. Chopin, "Là ci darem la mano" Variations. Finale, second episode. Chromatic-mediant joints between phrases shown in boxes.

"Hats off, gentlemen, a genius." Schumann made an even stronger statement about cultural prestige when Florestan mused that the work "could have been something by Beethoven or Schubert, had they been piano virtuosos." (Florestan's compliment contains an inaccuracy: Beethoven had made a career as a virtuoso pianist.)[45]

More than Friedrich Wieck and the *Anzeiger*, Schumann made interiority the focus of his essay. "Ein Opus II" traces a narrative arc in which the young men begin in the everyday world of casual, recreational music-making and gradually

Example 2.2. (*continued*)

(B minor)

(C-sharp minor)

Last-minute path back to B-flat

Example 2.2. (*continued*)

Example 2.3. Chopin, "Là ci darem la mano" Variations. Variation 1.

become absorbed in an inner world, one contained within Chopin's score and unlocked in their own minds. When Eusebius walks in, score in hand, Florestan and Julius are sitting at the piano, apparently playing through four-hand music. As Julius pages through the music, he beholds fantastic beings hidden within Chopin's flourishes and modulations. In imagery that evokes Chopin's elaborate figuration and wide-ranging harmonic vocabulary, Julius imagines "strange eyes—flowers' eyes, basilisks' eyes, peacocks' eyes, maidens' eyes" peering out of the score while Mozart's theme "wound through a hundred chords." Each "eye" adds to a disorienting chain of associations. Whereas the "maidens' eyes" perhaps invite Julius to peer closer, those of the "basilisk" (a mythical creature whose gaze can prove lethal) would have been more unsettling than alluring. Peacock feathers only have eyes in the metaphorical sense and add a hint of exotic mystery and opulence, evoking the strangeness and the seeming excessiveness of Chopin's figuration. In one uncanny moment, the score begins to move and come to take on inner life: "Leporello seemed as if he were winking right at me, and Don Juan flew past me in his white cape."

Throughout his tale of poetic absorption, Schumann also recognized the postclassical framework of Chopin's Variations, and he praised it for stimulating sensuous pleasure alongside inner experience. While paging through the score, Julius noted that "in many places, it became brighter [*lichter*]," suggesting the brilliant, transparent passagework in several variations. As Downes has noted, detailing Don Giovanni's pursuit of Zerlina gives the story an erotic frisson.[46] Hearing the Variations intoxicates the young men: they rush to Raro, "heated with wine and Chopin." He laughs off their find and shows little interest. The 1854 version has him say only, "I know you and your newfangled enthusiasm." In 1831, though, Raro said more: "I know you and your newfangled enthusiasm for Herz and Hünten—but bring me the Chopin sometime anyway."[47] The detail reveals that the young men followed and enjoyed the latest postclassical showpieces (as Schumann himself did) and situates Chopin within that tradition.[48] Schumann's "Ein Opus II" presents the view of virtuosity that later informed his Thalberg reviews, one in which popular pianism offered both pleasure and transcendent interiority.

And, for all Clara and Friedrich Wieck's caution about the Variations, they succeeded as a crowd-pleaser. Chopin himself wrote to his family that when he played the piece at his Vienna debut, audiences applauded so much after each variation that he could barely hear the orchestral ritornelli.[49] Clara ultimately did use the Variations as a concert-closer. Her programs from a concert in Magdeburg on November 25, 1834, and in Hannover on February 7, 1835, even designate it "auf Verlangen," performed "by request" of her supporters.[50]

The poetic transcendence Schumann heard in Chopin's Variations reflected his own experience as a pianist who immersed himself in the latest postclassical repertory. Erika Reiman has revealed that Schumann's piano cycles, often recognized for their radically unconventional structures, are in fact modeled on popular genres: dance medleys such as Schubert's waltzes and Weber's *Aufforderung zum Tanze*.[51] In "Ein Opus II," the young composer-critic also articulated his own aesthetic within the realm of popular piano music, here in a genre designed for virtuoso concerts rather than the domestic drawing room.

Engagement with popular genres and mixtures of the familiar with the otherworldly also characterized the literature Schumann read. Several of Jean Paul's novels use plot formulas from so-called trivial literature as points of departure. Reiman has argued that Schumann imitated his favorite novelist when he invoked and transformed the dance-medley genre in his piano cycles.[52] More generally, the plots of novels and stories by Jean Paul and Hoffmann often feature scenes in which everyday life takes on fantastic, even magical qualities—sometimes, music itself serves as an agent of reenchantment. Another of Novalis's fragments evocatively describes such transformations: "The world must be romanticized. . . . By giving the common a higher meaning, the everyday a mysterious character, the known the dignity of the unknown, the finite the appearance of the infinite, I romanticize it."[53] Like these literary sources, Schumann's "Ein Opus II" crosses a border from the everyday to the mysterious, from a casual gathering to fantastic depths within the music. It also hints that Chopin's piece "romanticizes" postclassical virtuosity with poetic interiority. (Schumann had not necessarily decoded Chopin's own aesthetic—rather, he idiosyncratically interpreted the Variations from his own perspective, influenced by German Romanticism. Chopin never responded to "Ein Opus II," but he did see a copy of Wieck's review and wrote in an 1831 letter, "I could die laughing at this German's imagination." The programmatic conceit he called "really very stupid."[54])

The inward arc of "Ein Opus II" peaks when Florestan arrives later at Julius's residence. Lying in a dreamlike state on the sofa, he probes his own memory of the music and his imaginative response (emerging from his trance only to ask for more wine). "'Chopin's variations,' he began as if asleep, 'have been running through my head.'" Though immersed in his inner world, Florestan does not forget the Variations' display of physical skill. In the *Zeitung* (but not in the *Gesammelte Schriften*) version of the essay, Florestan muses, "In Eusebius's playing I missed Paganinian performance and a Fieldian touch."[55] Florestan imagines diverse scenes from *Don Giovanni*—now vivid and detailed rather than veiled and obscure—and matches them with the music. Here, Schumann's *Don Giovanni* narrative resembles Friedrich Wieck's, albeit compressed and spoken by the half-dreaming Florestan. Though Florestan demurs from discussing passages of music in detail, Schumann lavishes the most narrative substance on sections that Friedrich Wieck had identified as particularly unconventional—as if the digressive formal and harmonic schemes called forth a richer array of dream-images. In the Adagio variation, for example, Florestan hears a seduction narrative. The stentorian opening suggests a "moral warning" and the appearance of "B-flat major" "the first kiss of love." (Schumann might have made a typographical error and meant the striking G-flat modulation. If not, he might been referring to the very last measure of the variation, in which a solitary G natural forecasts the major tonic.) Florestan calls the polonaise-finale the best part of the work. He packs in a flurry of imagery that evokes the combination of dance meter, disorienting harmonic progressions, and cascading passagework. The finale, he says, is "the whole of Mozart's finale: popping champagne corks, clinking glasses—Leporello's voice in the midst of this, the grasping, snatching spirits, the fleeing Don Juan."

In the end, Florestan passes entirely beyond Julius's sofa and the details of Chopin's music. He compares the feeling of hearing the showpiece to his memory of beholding the Italian Alps. His description completes the inward journey, moving to a memory unique to Florestan himself. The realistic and the fantastic mingle at the boundary between outer and inner worlds:

> When, particularly on a beautiful day, the evening sun climbs red and pink up glaciated peaks, then flattens and disappears, and over all the mountains and valleys there lies a quiet air, but the glacier stands still, cold and strong, like a titan awakening from its dreams.[56]

Florestan enjoins his friend—and the reader—to follow him: "Wake to new dreams, Julius, and sleep!"

Raro Speaks on "Opus II"

In the "Ein Opus II" that appeared in the *Allgemeine musikalische Zeitung* and Schumann's *Gesammelte Schriften*, the story ends with Florestan's Alpine vision. However, Schumann originally included an epilogue in which the younger *Davidsbündler* bring Chopin's "Là ci darem" Variations to Raro. The sole extant source for this epilogue does not necessarily provide a definitive version of what Schumann sent Fink. The Robert Schumann Haus archive identifies it as an "Entwurf" (a draft) dating from 1831. The two-page autograph manuscript is an incomplete copy of the "Ein Opus II" essay—the first page begins in the middle of Florestan's dream, and the second contains the epilogue. It is not a fair copy and contains several scratchings-out and revisions. The manuscript itself is barely legible in some places, and deciphering it requires inferences from an expert in the composer's handwriting.[57]

Nevertheless, contextual evidence suggests that the draft epilogue reflects the substance (and perhaps the details) of what Schumann submitted. First, the opening page of the manuscript contains the text that appeared in the *Zeitung* with only some minor changes of wording. Second, the draft epilogue fits smoothly into the "Ein Opus II" narrative. A Roman numeral "II" appears at the head, announcing it as the second part of the review—a follow-up letter by Julius, we learn. It seamlessly continues the story and ties up its loose ends. Schumann describes the promised visit to Raro and addresses one of the first part's philosophical cliffhangers. Julius had ended the first half of the review on an ambiguous note, chiding Florestan that his interpretation of Variations was entirely "subjective." Through Raro, Schumann maintained that his judgment rested on a concrete appraisal of the piece. Third, Schumann's manuscript of a later, unpublished essay titled "Odeon" offers another supporting clue. (He intended "Odeon" as a preface to the complete "Ein Opus II" review. Parts of it later surfaced in Schumann's *Davidsbündler* essays for *Der Komet*.) Here, Schumann carped that Fink had omitted the "actual critical part" of "Ein Opus II."[58] In the epilogue draft, he presented Raro as a "critic" given to sober analysis.

Because this epilogue has never been published, I translate its complete text here:[59]

II

My last letter, which must have still been warm when you obtained it, is almost like a parable![60] For the Italian sky therein, by which I seem to be surrounded this moment, you have Chopin and Florestan to thank.

We were very eager for Meister Raro's judgment over Chopin, because he is often all-too Sebastian-Bachish toward youths (and fully so toward composing men) and is a born enemy of everything partial, weak, and sickly ethereal. He also understands how to cool his feeling, molding from that blaze a holy, clear fire of ether.

Finally he lectured us. "Your joy over the new work," he began, "does not displease me. You know how little I can suffer picturesque music in general. But, for one thing, Chopin can't help it, because he was only channeling the hand of his genius (and that hand, then, is to be commended), and, for another, because it is entirely different merits that distinguish his work."

Florestan paced restlessly back and forth, because all critics' analysis and anatomical measuring is hateful to him, because, as he says, it is the death of both poetry and the genius's life.

"The prolonged exaltation, which seems to me an apotheosis of Mozart, allowed him to avoid all the misleading paths that often dazzle the poet. [Raro uses the word *blenden*, which connotes a deceptive or blinding dazzle.] Except for one single passage (the octave passages on the penultimate page), where the character of the window-concert is not sufficient to completely represent the energy of the thoughts—except for this fantasy-passage there is not a dull, weak minute. This grace, which permeates the whole, this giving and taking, this overflow and restraint, distinguishes every bar."

Small wonder that Schumann later tried to republish the review with the epilogue.[61] By lopping off Raro's lecture, Fink made it seem as if Schumann was depicting impulsive reactions unsubstantiated by consideration of Chopin's music. (It is possible that Fink did not deliberately misrepresent Schumann's argument and simply truncated the review to save space. In any case, Schumann had little justification for his complaint: when he wrote to Fink, he gave him permission to strike out sentences as he saw fit.[62]) The negative review of Chopin's Variations that Fink ran alongside "Ein Opus II" contributed to this impression: Fink introduced its author as a careful analyst who had spent weeks studying the score before writing.

In the "Sebastian-Bachish" Raro, though, Schumann had already advanced his own learned critic. Of course, Raro does not offer extensive commentary on the Variations in this epilogue, and he does not present a systematic or concrete explanation of just how Chopin's piece conveyed or embodied interiority. Nevertheless, Raro's willingness to single out a short passage at the end of the finale portrays his response as the result of a detailed study of the composition. (It seems likely that Raro meant measures 93–96. Here, Chopin's texture simplifies as the hands move in parallel octaves, and the finale's flow of bold harmonic progressions pauses as the figuration cycles repetitively through the flat submediant.) More than Eusebius, Florestan, and Julius, the epilogue notes, Raro can distance himself from his own subjective response to music, "cooling" his enthusiasm and "anatomically measuring" the composition. Schumann anticipated the multiple perspectives of his later reviews by allowing Florestan to remain skeptical of this "critical" approach.

Raro validated the younger men's enthusiasm about Chopin's Variations and, like them, described transcendent interiority as one of its most striking, commendable characteristics. This interiority, Schumann stresses through Raro, was not a subjective response that could have applied to any music, but a quality somehow intrinsic to Chopin's piece. After examining every measure of the score, Raro credits the Variations to Chopin's genius—an inner spirit rather than a desire to please or flatter his listeners. The offending octaves, he claims, mark the only place where the virtuosic passagework fails to mirror inner content, the "energy of [Chopin's] thoughts." In a striking metaphor, Raro says that the result is an "apotheosis of Mozart." He thereby praises the resplendence of Chopin's virtuosity, noting that it glorifies Mozart's theme and stimulates engagement and euphoria. His language resembles some of the reviews I presented in chapter 1, which describe variation sets "delighting in" popular themes and generating perpetual pleasure. However, Raro hints that the ecstasy of Chopin's virtuosity also possesses an element of ethereal transcendence: an apotheosis occurs when a mere mortal is elevated to divine status.

Raro's speech culminates the overall argument of Schumann's essay—that physical virtuosity, compositional style, pleasurable listening, and transcendent interiority could fuse. This apotheosis occurs not within a symphony, sonata, or other genre at the heart of the canonic tradition, but within a postclassically structured set of opera variations, one that stretches convention with digressive harmonic schemes and complex textures. At this intersection of virtuosity with interiority, Eusebius perceives genius, Julius glimpses a living world hidden in the score, and Florestan traverses inner realms of fantasy and reflection. If the draft epilogue reflects the final but unpublished version, Raro himself finds a transcendent essence within the showpiece.

Poetic Performance: Schumann's Aspiration and Clara Wieck's Trademark

"Ein Opus II" described the poetic qualities of Chopin's "Là ci darem" Variations as coming primarily from the composition, albeit within a context of convivial and spontaneous playing, contemplation, and discussion. However, Schumann also imagined that performances themselves could convey transcendent interiority. "Ein Opus II" hints at this possibility. When Eusebius played the Variations for Julius and Florestan, he "played as if inspired and brought out countless vivid, living shapes. It was as if the fresh spirit of the moment elevated the fingers above their mechanism."[63] (The *Gesammelte Schriften* changed the wording to specify that inspiration helped Eusebius's fingers to surpass their usual technical capabilities.) In this vision of Chopin's virtuosity, the performance and the composition form a feedback loop of inspiration: guided by his delight in Chopin's piece, Eusebius's performance gives inner life to the variations, and the effect seems to transform Eusebius's body itself.

While he was practicing the Variations, Schumann aspired to achieve this kind of transcendent performance himself. During the summer of 1831, the hopeful pianist kept a practice diary, devising technical exercises and recording his short-lived successes and more frequent frustrations.[64] In a diary entry from July 18, 1831, he described his ideal:

> I think there are three periods for artists who already stand at a certain level: in the first period of study the spirit and the recent fascination of the object keep one fresh and vigorous and lift the fingers beyond themselves; in the second, the imagination's flowering gradually falls off, the notes are written there, they must be reckoned with, the keys are depressed, sounds fail to come out. What should I say about the third, where spirit and form, mechanism and imagination flow into each other, that a person is corporeal music? Let me see these paradises of yours![65]

In this narrative, the performer journeys through stages of imperfection: initial enthusiasm, then struggles with inescapable technical demands. The synthesis he describes anticipates the way his later writings on the poetic mingle pleasure and transcendence, the sensuous and the ethereal. Schumann aspired to invest his physical music-making—"mechanism"—with inner qualities—"spirit" and "imagination." The combination of "spirit and form" hints at ensouling inanimate matter, so that the pianist at once transcends mere physicality while also giving the spirit of the music a corporeal body. Schumann's mention of not one but multiple paradises combines ecstatic pleasure and transcendent rapture.

Here, it is mainly the pianist who experiences transcendent interiority. The diary hints that Schumann believed he had reached the third stage of this progression in his own performances of Hummel's Concerto No. 2 and Moscheles's "Alexander" Variations. Given the right performance, then, even postclassical standards that little resembled Chopin's chromatic, densely textured passagework could manifest an inner spirit. In the end, however, Schumann never publicly performed the "Là ci darem la mano" Variations. Despite some days when he reported making good progress, his practicing ended in frustration, especially as his hand injury became increasingly prohibitive. In this sense, the diary entry gives a wistful glimpse of Schumann's largely unrealized ambitions.

Schumann's published writings, however, portrayed Clara Wieck as the epitome of poetic performance. Wieck was a multifaceted artist from the beginning of her career. She engaged with various facets of contemporary concert life and stimulated multiple strands of reception. She programmed the latest postclassical best sellers by Herz, distinguished herself as a Beethoven interpreter (first programming the "Appassionata" Sonata in 1835), played opera fantasies by Liszt and Thalberg, improvised, and introduced audiences to music by Chopin, Henselt, Robert Schumann, and herself. Critics viewed her through several lenses. Janina Klassen has noted two particularly prominent tropes in Wieck's reception. First, critics emphasized that she conveyed an impression of technical and interpretive mastery—surprising vocabulary to see in reviews (written by men) of a teenage, female pianist during the nineteenth century. One likened her to "The Maid of Orleans [Joan of Arc] at the piano." Second, critics linked her with the "art religion" of the time and used religious imagery to describe her. From early in her career, Wieck was compared to a "priestess," a "prophet," an "angel," and Saint Cecelia.[66]

During the 1830s, Schumann emphasized that what truly distinguished Clara Wieck's virtuosity was a quality of interiority. He and many other contemporary writers made inwardness another important facet of her public image. For them, this quality came partly from the tone Wieck produced at the piano, from the sonic results of her physical engagement with the keyboard. Schumann explained his impression in an 1832 review for *Der Komet* that covered her July 9 and July 31 Leipzig concerts. He later recycled several sentences from this review as aphorisms in his *Gesammelte Schriften*, but the original review (which has gone unexplored in the scholarly literature) contains more extended, concrete descriptions. Schumann compared Clara Wieck with French-German pianist Anna Caroline de Belleville. He acknowledged that de Belleville, a former Czerny student, possessed the more polished technique. However, he suggested that Wieck's tone and the way she voiced textures allowed her playing to transcend the merely sensuous or pleasing:

> On the other hand, [de Belleville] perhaps lacks the magical middle-shadings of the secondary voices. Because just as the bass should be the fundamental roots translucently overhung but not covered by the other voices—so with Clara they branch out through the whole. Belleville's tone flatters the ear without demanding more; Clara's sinks into the heart and speaks to the soul [*Gemüt*]. The former is poetized about—the latter is poetry.[67]

Though he commended both virtuosos, Schumann drew a distinction between the ingratiating qualities of one and the inner qualities of the other. For him, the textures Wieck created—her nuanced balance between different lines—became organic and alive, bound by inner connections like roots and leaves. Her playing, he claimed, did not stop with the ear but reached the listener's interior and became poetic.

The details of Wieck's performances evade reconstruction for present-day scholars. What evidence survives suggests that tone production was an important part of her training and approach. Claudia de Vries has shown that Wieck's playing, as specifically as we can reconstruct it from contemporary sources, reflected a concept of piano sound that gained ground during the first decades of the nineteenth century.[68] Wieck seems to have produced a continuously warm legato tone, not the crisply articulated gestures of earlier generations, the extravagant gestures that Liszt developed, or the barely audible nuances for which Chopin was known. Her physical bearing seems to have been composed but nonetheless flexible—again, unlike Liszt, whose extravagant gestures provoked strong positive and negative reactions.

In any case, Clara Wieck's contemporaries usually described her sound evocatively rather than analytically. Whereas Schumann portrayed her tone as penetrating the listener's heart, Gustav Schilling's 1838 encyclopedia had it move the other way to reveal her own "soul":

> [Wieck's tone] is not merely round and tender, like perhaps that of a Hummel was, not merely elegant like that of a Moscheles, not merely brilliant and grand, like that of a Kalkbrenner; it is also not merely sentimental like that of a Liszt, or distinguished through many bizarre features like that of a Chopin, but rather it is all of these things together, enlivened by an enchanting geniality, that makes of the most triumphant dexterity only a flexible, docile servant.
>
> Like these young masters [Mendelssohn and Henselt] she has become one with her art so much that her entire being seems to come up from within it. Every tone that she attacks is a sound from her own soul. Her playing is the innermost life in all its shadows and light, down to the finest nuance.[69]

A *Neue Zeitschrift* review of Wieck's 1835 Hannover concert took yet another view of her interiorized virtuosity. The critic credited her hands with drawing new qualities from the piano itself: "Meanwhile, Clara Wieck's masterful hand [*Meisterhand*] elicited from the instrument new, unknown tones for us, and the fullness, sweetness, elegance, energy, and surety of her playing let her achievements appear inimitable even to connoisseurs."[70]

Schumann also hinted in his *Komet* review that Wieck guided her playing with extraordinary insight that allowed her to move past superficial surfaces. For him, she uncovered things hidden from—and even hazardous to—other musicians. "Early, Clara drew the veil of Isis aside," he wrote. "The child looks calmly into the sea of beams—an older person would have been blinded in the radiance." Schumann's metaphor amalgamates the act of "unveiling" with spiritual revelation and initiation into secret knowledge: Wieck beholds an Egyptian goddess known for her power as a magician and often depicted with a solar disc on her head. He wove a complementary metaphor of depth and risk when he wrote, "Only to win the pearl does one seek the dangerous depths of the sea." When he later turned the passage into an aphorism, he had Florestan clarify, "Clara is a diver."[71]

A few years after Schumann wrote his *Komet* review, one of Clara Wieck's other listeners specifically claimed that her interpretations of Beethoven reached spirit-filled depths that eluded her colleagues. The Austrian poet Franz Grillparzer wrote his 1838 poem, "Clara Wieck und Beethoven," in response to her performance of the "Appassionata" that year in Vienna. Here, the virtuoso unlocks the "diamond-hard" shrine of Beethoven's artistry not through learned investigation or strenuous struggle but through inborn insight: "Daydreaming in young girl fashion / She sinks her white fingers into the water. / They seize and lift and grasp—it is the key!" Grillparzer's Clara Wieck uses her physical performance at the piano to liberate and command noncorporeal beings. "The spirits / Ascend, then drop and bow / To the lovely, innocent mistress / Whose white fingers lightly guide them as she plays," he writes.[72]

Schumann's accounts from the early 1830s, though, stress the way that Wieck played rather than what repertoire she performed. In 1832, she was not yet programming Beethoven and Bach, nor was she championing Schumann and Mendelssohn and playing Chopin's etudes, nocturnes, and mazurkas. Wieck did perform the "Là ci darem" Variations on her July 9 concert, but she also offered more accessible postclassical fare: Herz's "Violette" Variations, Op. 48, and *Variations de bravoure sur la romance de "Joseph,"* Op. 20, as well as François Pixis's Concerto Op. 100.[73] Schumann even implied that on this occasion she was more successful with Herz's "superficial" variations than with John Field's Piano Concerto No. 2.[74] For Schumann, everything Clara Wieck touched took on interiority.

Aspects of Wieck's persona other than her tone and interpretations shaped these views. Among these, her gender produced the most complex range of responses. On one hand, it is hardly surprising that nineteenth-century critics should praise a female pianist for displaying her soul and penetrating the heart. However, Schumann and his contemporaries did not regard transcendent interiority as quintessentially feminine. Schilling's writer, after all, also commended

Mendelssohn and Henselt for envoicing their inner selves. Schumann's "Ein Opus II" pursues Zerlina through Chopin's Variations, but the context is masculine and homosocial: a male composer creates poetic interiority, a man plays the piece, and male friends experience it together. Numerous other Schumann essays similarly depict male musicians through the rhetoric of interiority. Wieck's listeners did undeniably filter her performances and compositions through her gender. Schilling's writer, for example, suggested, "She never transgresses the boundaries of womanly grace, and what appears to be elegant lightness with Mendelssohn sounds from her like powerful momentum [*Schwung*]."[75] Other critics distanced her from stereotypes of femininity. Schilling's writer and the 1835 Hannover critic cut against notions of feminine submissiveness: Wieck has a "master's hand," and her genius turns virtuosity into a "servant." A review of her 1856 Vienna concerts praised her for "unit[ing] feminine delicateness and tenderness with a rare strength one is used to hearing only in male virtuosos."[76] (For more about gendered responses to Clara Wieck Schumann's works and performances, see chapters 5 and 6.)

Critics also drew attention to her nationality. For example, an unsigned 1838 *Neue Zeitschrift* editorial compared Clara Wieck, Liszt, Thalberg, and Henselt by placing them in different categories and ranking them according to different criteria. Thalberg represented a "flattering Italian" school, Liszt a "French Romantic," and Wieck and Henselt a "German sentimental," a classification that hinted at stereotypes of German depth and inwardness.[77]

Finally, Wieck's status as a wunderkind shaped her reception. She was not yet thirteen at the time of the Leipzig concerts Schumann reviewed. His sentence about her ability to withstand the Isis's radiance drew upon a Romantic idealization of childhood, the belief that children had special insight that adulthood would only cloud. He commended Friedrich Wieck for not squelching Clara's vision: "In every child there lies a wondrous depth; do not dull or flatten it."[78] Even though Clara Wieck was eighteen when Grillparzer wrote his poem, he nonetheless portrayed her as an insightful child.

As the 1830s unfolded, Schumann increasingly commended Clara Wieck's programming. In the two years after her Leipzig concerts, she began performing Beethoven sonatas and Bach fugues; Chopin etudes, nocturnes, and other solos; and music by Schumann and herself. She often combined them into what Valerie Woodring Goertzen has called "mosaics" of solo pieces, in which her improvised transitions connected the canonized with the current.[79] On March 20, 1835, for example, she gave her own concert in Hamburg and opened the second half of the program with such a mosaic: the second and third movements of the "Appassionata," Bach's Fugue in C-sharp major from the *Well-Tempered Clavier* (book 1), Chopin's Nocturne, Op. 15, no. 2, and her own "Caprice à la Boleros" from her *Quatre pièces caractéristiques*, Op. 5.[80] As the decade went on, she added music by Mendelssohn and Henselt. Her programs often advertised the newness of her repertoire. When she performed a Chopin nocturne and two etudes from his Opus 10 in Plauen on February 14, 1834, for example, they were listed as "compositions of the new Romantic school."[81]

Prompted by her programming, Schumann and other writers used images of depth and interiority to rank Wieck at the head of a historic vanguard that was elevating German musical life. Schumann wrote in a review of her *Soirées musicales*, Op. 6:

> One must surely know how, as a virtuoso, she already stands on the highest peak of her time, from which nothing remains hidden to her. Where Sebastian Bach delves so deeply that even a miner's lamp threatens to get lost, where Beethoven reaches into the clouds with his Titan's fist, what the most recent time, which seeks to mediate height and depth, has brought—all these things the artist knows and tells us of in lovely, maidenly cleverness.[82]

Carl Herlossohn's *Damen Conversations Lexikon*—a Leipzig publication for whose early volumes Schumann contributed several articles about musical terms—explicitly described her as a virtuoso who transcended the sensual present and the convention-bound past. The unsigned article on "Deutschland" appeared in 1835, by which time Wieck was programming her solo mosaics. The article tells a tale of decline into fashion and mechanism: "The concert music of the virtuosos had reached its highest peak, but it degenerated into an attempt only to overcome whatever mechanical difficulties were imaginable. . . . Piano playing had become empty strumming, and one drifted around in clichéd, meaningless phrases." The writer presented Wieck as part of a new, redemptive moment: "But a modern school demanded at once deep content and—instead of the hollow, spiritless mechanism dressed up in fashionable glitter that said nothing—poetry and romantic verve. The first important virtuoso who followed this new path was Clara Wieck."[83]

There was more to Clara Wieck Schumann, of course, than her status as Robert's quintessential poetic virtuoso. Her practices and artistic identity transformed over the course of her career, as did Robert's role in her performances. During Robert's formative years as a critic and composer, though, he regarded her as a pianist whose very keystrokes transcended the superficial and (merely) sensuous and whose concerts brought interiority to the stage.

Systematizing the Poetic: Schumann's Manifesto and Hiller's Etudes

Schumann positioned his ideal of transcendent interiority within a more systematic framework in one of the foundational articles he wrote for the *Neue Zeitschrift*, his 1835 review of Ferdinand Hiller's Twenty-four Etudes, Op. 15. The essay served as a timely demonstration of critical rigor. Schumann had increased his responsibility for the journal, having assumed sole editorship and ownership that year. The new name of the journal—*Neue Zeitschrift für Musik* rather than *Neue Leipziger Zeitschrift für Musik*—suggested heightened ambition, a reach for significance beyond Leipzig itself. Moreover, Schumann's 1835 New Year's editorial noted that the journal needed defending: some (unspecified) readers, he regretted, had disagreed with him and his colleagues or complained that their lack of compositional achievements undermined the journal's credibility.[84] In the Hiller review, Schumann attempted to defend his music-critical aesthetic and demonstrate his acumen as an analyst. He explained, for example, his quasi-literary style of criticism: "We regard as the best criticism that which through itself leaves behind an impression similar to what the original work that stimulates it brings forth." He also heralded a rebellion in which "an entire youthful generation" was "unchaining a whole century, still hanging . . . on to an antiquated kingdom."[85]

Alongside these broader defenses, Schumann subjected the etudes to a concrete, multifaceted evaluation. Like the *Davidsbündler* Raro, he attempted to demonstrate that his judgments and interpretations rested on concrete musical analyses. The review proceeds in three sections, one dedicated to aesthetic ("the poetry of the work, bloom, spirit"), one to theoretical (i.e., harmonic and formal), and one to "mechanical" (i.e., pianistic) questions. Schumann emphasized the interdependence of these issues, which he described as "the bloom, the root, and the fruit" of a composition. The essay weighs Hiller's enharmonic spellings, assesses pianistic demands, and includes a formal diagram of the first etude. In a striking claim for a twenty-five-year-old newcomer to music criticism with no teaching career, Schumann introduced himself as a "pedagogue."[86]

Ultimately, Schumann used this critical and analytical apparatus as a divining rod for interiority within the etudes. For all his claims of rigor and objectivity, his discussion leaped easily from discussing style and structure to finding more intangible qualities: transcendent depth and inner experience. Here, poetic interiority was the standard—not, for example, a command of classical forms or demonstration of musical learnedness. Even though Schumann suggested that these qualities lay within the compositions themselves, he only obliquely explained the mechanisms by which he believed Hiller created them. He described interiority as a hallmark of Hiller's overall style, which displayed "imagination [*Phantasie*] and passion (though not enthusiasm or inspiration as in Chopin) cloaked in a Romantic *chiaroscuro*." Chiaroscuro itself is a painting technique that uses strong contrasts of light and shadow to create the illusion of depth. In a claim that echoes Florestan's comparison of Chopin with Beethoven and Schubert, Schumann wrote that "[Hiller's] second, seventeenth, twenty-second, and twenty-third etudes are . . . among the best things that have been written since the F-minor sonata of Beethoven and other things by Franz Schubert, which seem to have first opened up this kingdom of marvels."[87]

For Schumann, however, Hiller's music was not exclusively ethereal. He claimed that the composer's physical engagement with the piano and immersion in the Parisian virtuoso scene had formed his style. Born in Frankfurt in 1811, Ferdinand Hiller studied with Hummel in Weimar. He spent the years between 1828 and 1835 in Paris, where he befriended and performed music by Chopin, Liszt, and Berlioz. (Upon returning to Germany, Hiller built a career that extended beyond the piano. He succeeded Mendelssohn as the Gewandhaus conductor, composed in various media, wrote several books, and hosted a salon.) "For young composers who are also virtuosos," Schumann wrote, "nothing is more inviting than to write etudes, if possible the most tremendous. A new figure, a difficult rhythm, are so easily invented and harmonically developed."[88] He specifically suggested that Hiller had produced his etudes under the influence of Chopin, "who knows his instrument as does no other," and designed them for his own or his students' practicing.

Schumann displayed his authority as critic by claiming that several of Hiller's etudes failed to capture the interiority he commended in others. He reserved his harshest words for Etudes Nos. 7 and 18:

> I have already said that these two etudes were the weakest of all and promised to say why. Well, here it is: because Chopin has already written two etudes, one in F minor, the other in C minor, that Hiller must have known before he wrote [Nos. 7 and 18]. Now, he does not want it to be noticed that there's something similar and becomes tender all at once, which one is not at all used to from him—but no souls speak like this.[89]

As shown in example 2.4, Hiller's etudes use accompaniment patterns more familiar in Chopin's Opus 10 etudes. In both cases, Hiller keeps the harmonic vocabulary straightforward and the texture transparent, and he subsumes virtuosic figuration under melodies inflected by appoggiaturas and grace notes. The "tender" result bears little resemblance to the *agitato* of Chopin's Op. 10, no. 9 or the surging march of no. 12. Such ingratiating and (supposedly) derivative music, Schumann complained, lacked a soul.

The second of Hiller's etudes, by contrast, illustrates the chiaroscuro Schumann praised. His description intertwines dreamlike introspection with fantastic imagery and terrestrial depth: "A dream. Subterranean pursuits. The spirits of the earth sing and hammer; fairies lean on diamond flowers. Everything is jolly. The dreamer awakes: 'What was that?'"[90] Hiller's etude sows textural and tonal obscurity beneath its arpeggios and trills. As shown in example 2.4, the first three measures alternate between hollow, perfect consonances and dissonant major seconds. The transition to the second theme places closely voiced diminished and half-diminished sevenths in the bass. Subtle rhythmic ambiguity exacerbates the textural obscurity: most harmonic changes occur a sixteenth note before the beat.

On a larger level, the etude withholds tonal and formal clarity. Earlier in the essay, Schumann urged composers to complicate and obscure classical paradigms:

> Now, the analyst of the above etude does not at all belong to those who like to begin in C major, bring in the second theme in G major, and then, after a stopover in (at most) B-flat, D minor, but then A minor, repeat the first theme in C major, add the second in the same tonality, and conclude at once; instead, he loves a certain order in disorder [*Ordnung in der Unordnung*].[91]

Etude No. 2 blurs the boundaries of its sonata form. The secondary key, B-flat, initially emerges in minor. The exposition does not present a B-flat-major triad until its last chord (and even then softens the sense of arrival by placing this

Hiller, No. 7:

Chopin: Etude, Op. 10, no. 9:

Hiller, No. 18:

Example 2.4. Ferdinand Hiller, Etudes Op. 15.

chord in first inversion). It segues directly into the diminished harmonies that fill the development. Instead of spotlighting brilliant passagework, Hiller generates harmonic ambiguity and textural murkiness from which the defining outlines of a sonata form emerge only blurrily, like Schumann's subterranean dream images.

A Poetic Virtuoso Takes the Stage: Schumann's Unfinished Piano Concerto

Several of Schumann's own virtuosic compositions from the 1830s, like those of Chopin and Hiller, subvert postclassical transparency and clarity and employ musical metaphors for poetic interiority. Schumann's unfinished Piano Concerto in F Major offers one example. Designed as a vehicle for his own use, the concerto represented Schumann's first major compositional project. He began working on it in 1829 while in Heidelberg, brought a draft of the exposition to Leipzig in 1830, and believed that he had completed the solo part of the first

Chopin: Etude, Op. 10, no. 12:

Hiller, No. 2:

Example 2.4. (*continued*)

movement in August 1831. Perhaps because of his hand injury, he abandoned the project and completed neither the orchestration nor the other two movements. Schumann's sketchbook from this period contains drafts and revisions of the first-movement solo part. Using instructions the composer himself wrote down in the sketchbook, Claudia Macdonald has reassembled these drafts into an edition.[92]

Though Schumann never attempted to publish the work or perform it with orchestra, he did play the first movement as a solo at private gatherings. His diary records his thoughts about one such occasion, a soiree hosted by Friedrich Wieck on August 14, 1831. He disagreed with Friedrich Wieck and Heinrich Dorn (Schumann's composition teacher at the time), who heard in the piece a "[John] Field-like character that is thoroughly foreign to me." Instead, Schumann wrote, Florestan believed that the movement contained "more shapes and speaking characters." This was, he wrote, "my first piece that inclined toward the Romantic."[93]

The movement reveals Schumann's immersion in postclassical virtuosity and knowledge of performance practicalities. Solo-orchestra intertwining, for example, is as limited as it is in Chopin's and Herz's piano concertos: the scoring reflects the reality that a pianist could find him- or herself playing a concerto with unrehearsed orchestras, string quartets, or as a soloist. Macdonald has revealed that Schumann charted the formal proportions of Herz's Concerto No. 1 and used them as a model for his own. She also notes that many of his themes, harmonic gestures, and figurational patterns derive from Moscheles, Hummel, and Herz.[94]

Within this postclassical framework, the Concerto in F Major developed an idiosyncratic sound for the hopeful star. The culminating displays in particular confronted audiences with a style of virtuosity that differed strikingly from Herz's or Moscheles's. Like those of Schumann's postclassical models, they unfold cadentially directed modules of figuration over vamp-like accompaniments. However, Schumann also breaks from these patterns to lead the soloist through disorienting chromatic digressions and complex, layered textures. Example 2.5 shows one such juncture, drawn from the recapitulation's culminating display. At measure 294, the figuration shifts from the tonic F major to F-sharp minor, disrupting the flow of glistening arpeggios and pinging upper notes with a sudden harmonic jolt and tumbling into a string of descending scales. A series of sequences at measure 297 highlights not the brilliant upper range of the instrument but the darker lower register: the sixteenth-note figuration appears as an inner voice within a four-part contrapuntal texture, wreathed with chromatically inching voices. Even the reapproach to the striding accompaniment pattern traces a circuitous route through a chromatic bass line and a sustained augmented sixth articulated by pulsating, syncopated bass notes. In a section where listeners expect a flow of brilliant figuration, Schumann asks them to follow the passagework through dense contrapuntal textures and tortuous harmonic pathways.[95]

Other passages of the concerto complement this style. The lavishly ornamented second theme, for example, dissolves its melody into a digressive tonal trajectory. After evading a cadence, the phrase extends to wander through a chromatically oscillating bass line. A surprise dip into flat harmonies produces an augmented sixth—suddenly embellished with shimmering tremolos—that itself evades traditional resolution. Macdonald has also noted that, throughout the concerto,

Example 2.5. Schumann, Piano Concerto in F Major (1831). Culminating display in recapitulation. Adapted from Claudia Macdonald, "Robert Schumann's F-Major Piano Concerto of 1831," 491–492.

Example 2.5. (*continued*)

Schumann subverts climactic arrivals. The final culminating display, for example, ends the movement with a sudden fadeaway, the pianist's scales slowing to a halt and blending into a horn call. She also observes that Schumann's figurational patterns, unlike Herz's or Field's, often impart smooth melodic profiles.[96]

Read alongside Schumann's diary entry and later essays, such passagework begs to be interpreted not merely as a leap for novelty and idiosyncrasy, but as an attempt to imbue his virtuosity with poetic qualities of depth, spirit, and interiority. Indeed, the harmonic turns and complex textures resembled features Schumann and his teacher admired in Chopin's "Là ci darem la mano" Variations. According to their essays, such features redeemed Chopin's bravura display and, for Schumann himself, stimulated poetic transcendence. And, perhaps, they invited the richly shaded voicing Schumann commended as a mark of interiority in Clara Wieck's playing. Through Florestan, Schumann himself hinted that the unfinished concerto contained an inner essence that spoke and took human form.

In chapter 3, we will explore one significant performing context in which Schumann's poetic virtuosity took shape. This music and the cultural currents it entered offer insight into questions that Schumann's Hiller and Chopin essays beg but do not address: for what audiences did Schumann design his poetic showpieces?

3 Poetic Showpieces in the Cultivated Salon

As we saw in chapter 2, Schumann first articulated his concept of the poetic in writings about postclassical pianism: Chopin's "Là ci darem la mano" Variations, for example, and Clara Wieck's performances. For Schumann, such virtuosity embodied interiority, depth, and spirit. During the early 1830s, Schumann himself composed several variation sets in which he sought to combine postclassical virtuosity with poetic interiority.

This chapter shows how this music took shape and found supporters in the Leipzig, Heidelberg, and Zwickau salons Schumann frequented. Here, he developed a concept of transcendent virtuosity that emphasized not public concerts and professional virtuosos but salons of amateur players and musical connoisseurs. Scholars have already noted Schumann's extensive engagement with contemporary salon life. As David Ferris has shown, Schumann and other writers for the *Neue Zeitschrift* idealized private performances as forums in which virtuosos encountered less pressure to please a large, heterogeneous public and could instead connect with a more rarefied, connoisseur audience. Ferris and Anthony Newcomb have both observed that though Clara Wieck rarely programmed Robert's music on her public concerts, she did perform it for small gatherings of connoisseurs.[1]

My discussion considers some heretofore unexplored ways in which Schumann's early salon music poeticized virtuosity. To some extent, speaking of "salon music" as a category is misleading: music for domestic concerts and convivial gatherings could range from solo miniatures to large chamber pieces, even the cantatas Felix and Fanny Mendelssohn composed for their family's *Sonntagsmusiken*. The only limit was a household's resources and tastes. The two Schumann variation sets that I explore here, however, specifically grew out of salon music-making. Schumann started composing his 1831 "Abegg" Variations, Op. 1, while thriving as a salon pianist in Heidelberg, and he published it as a lightweight piece accessible to accomplished amateurs. Another variation set, the 1835 *Fantaisies et finale*, is an early, unpublished version of the *Études symphoniques* that Schumann briefly considered complete and ready for the press. Its style and genesis, too, bear traces of the domestic music and amateur pianists Schumann encountered. Throughout the Variations and *Fantaisies*, Schumann invoked early Romantic signifiers for poetic interiority and intellectual cultivation, some of which derive from literary aesthetics as well as from contemporary concepts of erudite conversation.

A cluster of sources related to Schumann's relationship with Leipzig salon hostess Henriette Voigt shows that he did encounter connoisseur amateurs who embraced his abstruse brand of pianism. Schumann's ideal salon was not only a vision that he discussed in his writings but a reality that he believed he encountered at Voigt's. These sources do not provide a panoramic view of contemporary salon life or domestic music-making. Rather, they constitute the richest extant record of Schumann's engagement with a single salon and its patron, and they offer a new glimpse of one specific context that shaped the composer-critic's engagement with virtuosity during the 1830s.[2]

This aspect of Schumann's work reveals an often-overlooked part of the virtuosity discourse. In present-day scholarship and in many contemporary writings, the archetypal serious virtuoso wears a somber, austere expression. Such virtuosos allied themselves above all with music professionals, often against dilettantes, whom contemporary writers considered insufficiently serious. Their most well-documented activities occurred in public forums. For example, Dana Gooley has characterized important parts of the German antivirtuosity polemic as a "professional defense" carried out by "a small but inspired and enthusiastic class of musical professionals" bent on influencing the public.[3] Eduard Krüger (whose essay "Ueber Virtuosenunfug" was cited in the Introduction) wholeheartedly contributed to this discourse. Unlike Krüger's fictional Dilettante, his Music Director knows how to appreciate musical "content."[4] One of the best-researched patterns in nineteenth-century virtuosity has been the consolidation and prestige of the canon in public concerts.

In Schumann's variations and at Voigt's musical gatherings, by contrast, transcendent virtuosity bore the knowing smiles, casual poses, and delight in game-playing and witty conversation that characterized the salon and its guests. They illuminate a complementary story about the virtuosity discourse, one that took place in private settings and involved connoisseur dilettantes as well as professionals. In many cases, these sources foreground musically accomplished women who played important roles in Schumann's career. Though salon music-making by no means excluded men, it gave women more opportunities to participate in and even lead musical life than public concerts did. More generally, nineteenth-century piano music for domestic performance aimed primarily at a female market. Private music-making, of course, was not insulated from the public sphere. Amateur musicians formed their musical tastes under the influence of professionals, and well-connected salons hosted professional performers. These showpieces and writings on salon virtuosity also entered a wider, public arena, such as when accounts of salon performances appeared in music periodicals. Even so, Henriette Voigt's statements about virtuosity originated in private writings. And, in the "Abegg" Variations and Fantaisies, poetic virtuosity did not necessarily come from professional musicians performing in temple-like concert halls. Rather, it issued from the fingers of pianists who played lightweight, popularly-styled music in domestic settings, possibly for convivial gatherings of musically cultivated insiders.

The Power of the "Cultivated" Salons, and the Case of Henselt

Salon music possessed a double image in the nineteenth-century imagination. On one hand, critics disassociated serious music and salon performance more often than they linked them. Carl Dahlhaus did draw a distinction between salon music written for socially elite connoisseurs (that of Chopin, for example) and what he dismissed as trivial salon music marketed to a wider, less exclusive public.[5] Nevertheless, nineteenth-century critics often painted with a broader brush and relegated piano music designed for domestic performance to a generally lower rung of an aesthetic hierarchy. Gender played a significant role in this discourse, in which critics (most of whom were men) devalued music written primarily for women to play. They heard in such music stereotypically effeminate sentimentality and concern for fine detail at the expense of large structure. Jeffrey Kallberg, for example, has shown that the ambivalent critical reception of Chopin's nocturnes hinged on their association with "tea table" performance.[6]

Several of Schumann's own writings contributed to this stereotype. In a scathing 1841 review of Robert Müller's *Poésies musicales*, Op. 5, for example, he wrote, "Musicians know what to expect from these compositions: a mixture of sentimentality and piano passagework, as is especially prized in salons." The quasi-narrative review of Thalberg's and Kalkbrenner's opera-based showpieces we encountered in chapter 1 places vapid, effeminate aristocrats and superficial virtuosity in a high-society salon. In a review of showpieces by Thalberg and Döhler, Schumann speculated that aging virtuosos might regret their misspent youths and long for "the true home of art, which is never to be found in the salons of the great and rich."[7]

On the other hand, Schumann also recognized a different side of salon music. Some of his writings anticipate Dahlhaus's judgment about different levels of salon pieces. As we saw in chapter 1, for example, he described Thalberg's "Moïse" Fantasy as representative of a "better style of salon music."[8] More important, Schumann knew that the salon venue could provide a haven and crucible for poetic virtuosity. Salon life in and beyond Germany displayed considerable musical diversity. Audiences ranged from devotees of the latest Herz variation sets to string-quartet enthusiasts, and gatherings ranged from those where music was the main attraction to those where it played in the background. Music-making in private circles nourished many musicians Schumann championed. Felix Mendelssohn been groomed for a musical career at his family's *Sonntagsmusiken*, and, when he arrived in Leipzig to lead the Gewandhaus Orchestra, he became a favorite guest in local salons.[9] Ferris observes that, when Clara Wieck was concertizing in a new city, she arranged semiprivate performances for individuals important in local music life. Such events helped secure the successes of her public performances.[10]

Schumann imagined an ideal salon in his 1836 review of the *Grand duo concertant sur des thèmes de "Robert le Diable"* by Chopin and cellist August Franchomme. The duo, for Schumann, embodied qualities of interiority. "Whatever Chopin touches assumes shape and spirit," he wrote, even this "smaller salon style." Chopin developed his themes "so fantastically, here veiling, there unveiling, that they continue to resound in the ear and heart."[11] As the imagery suggests, the showpiece intersperses Meyerbeer's themes with transitions in which Chopin's ornate, chromatically inflected figuration weaves around Franchomme's more lyrical, harmonically straightforward writing.

Schumann's imagined audience for the Grand Duo contrasts strikingly with the frivolous salon he depicted in his Thalberg and Kalkbrenner review. This was, he wrote, "a piece for a salon where now and then the head of a famous artist disappears behind a count's shoulders—therefore not for tea parties, where conversation is struck up, but rather for the most cultivated [gebildetste] circles, which give the artist the attention his station deserves."[12] Schumann did not necessarily exile aristocrats from this salon; however, the elitism of this circle lies in its artistic and cultural awareness—its "cultivation"—rather than in wealth or ostentation. In such a salon, virtuosos could meet listeners attuned to the subtlety and spirit of poetic music.

The Neue Zeitschrift's promotion of Adolph Henselt put this ideal into practice. More than most nineteenth-century pianists, Henselt relied on private performances to establish his career. He was active in Germany from his 1832 debut until only 1838. After that, he traveled to St. Petersburg, gained a series of appointments as a piano pedagogue and administrator, and remained in Russia for the rest of his life. Even while active as a performer in Germany, Henselt gave few public concerts, and most of his performances were for private audiences. (Contemporary accounts suggest that he suffered from intense performance anxiety.) His compositions first reached a wide public when Clara Wieck programmed them starting in the late 1830s and when reviews of his work appeared in the Zeitschrift and other periodicals.

Especially when heard in private and performed by the composer himself, Schumann and his reviewers claimed, Henselt's music synthesized virtuosity with inner depth and personal authenticity. In an 1838 review of Henselt's Etudes Op. 2, Schumann imagined an intimate performance with listeners gathered around the piano: "One should hear all of this from Henselt himself . . . when he is truly used to his instrument and becomes one with it, forgetful of time and place, unconcerned whether artists or princes stand next to him. . . . One must call him a God-inspired singer." His description of the lyrical etudes uses images of concealment to contrast their virtuosity with transparent postclassical brilliance. "But Henselt's charming melodies," he wrote, "only become that way through the mysterious figuration with which he conceals his melodies, so that they resemble rich fruit issuing from green leaves and branches."[13] As Ferris has noted, an 1838 Zeitschrift review even suggested that public performance did not quite capture Henselt's artistry:

> The larger public still knows only one side of him, however. Those who have been lucky enough to hear him in an intimate circle will never forget how his whole essence was revealed in music, and the inner richness, pressing out, set all external

means into motion, and made itself known in song, gentle at one moment, elevated the next, which floated over his playing like a secret music.[14]

One of the *Zeitschrift*'s most elaborate essays about Henselt came from an amateur musician, Sophie Kaskel, who embodied the "cultivation" Schumann imagined in his Chopin–Franchomme review. Kaskel was born in 1818 into a Dresden banking family that avidly engaged in music patronage. The Kaskels socialized with the Wiecks and Mendelssohns and hosted a performance by Chopin. Sophie herself studied piano, composed and published piano pieces and lieder, and later wrote children's books.[15] Her review described a Henselt performance she had heard eight days earlier. Though it is unclear whether she meant a salon or public concert, her essay establishes an intimate tone. She styled the review as a letter from her alter ego "Sara" to a "dear [female] friend."[16] Her identification of female characters itself evokes a private, domestic sphere, whether for Henselt's own performance or Sara's discussion.

Kaskel made the supposed difference between superficiality and interiority the crux of her evaluation. Thalberg, she wrote, only knew how to make "something out of nothing." In a departure from Schumann's views, she attributed Chopin's popularity to the "mechanical interest" and novelty of his music. For Kaskel, Henselt's variations and etudes possessed an inner, authentic essence that redeemed their virtuosity. "Henselt writes only music—he is all melody," she wrote. His virtuosity therefore could "penetrate to the heart" with its "simplicity and truth." One scarcely notices the pianistic effects in his music, she claimed, because he used them "only as a means, never as an end."[17]

For Kaskel and Schumann, the prevailing lyricism of Henselt's showpieces was what transcended the "mechanical." Like several other performer-composers Schumann promoted during this time, Henselt worked mainly within postclassical genres: during his German years, he wrote opera-based variation sets and lightweight etudes. These works often blend lyrical effusions with brilliant passagework. Many of Henselt's Etudes Op. 2, for example, relegate virtuosic figuration to an accompaniment that supports simple melodies with only the lightest ornamentation. The title of his Andante and Allegro Op. 3 seems to promise a contrast similar to what we find in Mendelssohn's Introduction and Rondo Capriccioso, Op. 14—a lyrical opening and a glittering conclusion. Henselt's Allegro, by contrast, places the virtuosic figuration in a sweeping accompaniment that supports a simple melody bereft of ornamentation. At the end, an extension of the last phrase seamlessly blends into a cascade of arpeggios, placing figuration in the spotlight for the first time.

When she promoted Henselt, Kaskel was also modeling an ideal listener for *Neue Zeitschrift* readers. She asked the reader to imagine herself as the "dear friend"—or, for a male reader, as an eavesdropper on the exchange. To buttress her claims, she invoked qualities that enhanced her authority: her refined connoisseurship and knowledge of the latest piano music, her elite social status (she received invitations to the kinds of events Henselt played), and her letter's mix of friendly intimacy and discerning evaluation. Listeners as cultivated as she, Kaskel implied, shunned virtuosic music that (for one reason or another) could be construed as "mechanical" and embraced inward virtuosity such as Henselt's.

In the case of Henselt, then, salon performance nurtured what Schumann promoted as a transcendent approach to virtuosity, one that reached a broader public through the *Neue Zeitschrift*, Clara Wieck's concerts, and the publication of his showpieces.

Schumann in the Salons

Schumann developed his own virtuosity through domestic and salon performance, and Claudia Macdonald has described him as a "gentleman amateur" prior to 1831.[18] Amateur musicians in Leipzig and Zwickau, particularly several members of the Carus family, played formative roles in his musical education. In his 1843 obituary for the Zwickau merchant, arts patron, and amateur violinist and bassoonist Karl Erdmann Carus, Schumann recounted that he had discovered the chamber music of Haydn, Mozart, and Beethoven at Carus's house.[19] Schumann frequented the home of Agnes and Ernst August Carus—the latter was a physician, Leipzig University professor, and nephew of the merchant-bassoonist. There, Schumann met important figures in Leipzig musical life, including Friedrich and Clara Wieck and the opera composer Heinrich Marschner. Friedrich Wieck himself also hosted musical soirees. At the Wiecks' and Caruses', Schumann played and listened to a wide variety of music: chamber works by Schubert, operatic numbers, light dance music and lieder, variations by Chopin and Herz, Bach keyboard fugues, and concerto movements by John Field. He also performed his own early compositions (to mixed reception), including his unpublished *VIII Polonaises*, WoO 20, the unfinished Piano Concerto in F, and *Papillons*, Op. 2.[20] During the year he studied law in Heidelberg, Schumann boasted in a letter to his brother that he was the "darling of the Heidelberg public," and that he performed several times a week in the homes of socially prominent citizens.[21] Schumann gave relatively few public performances during his brief career as a pianist. By contrast, his private performances were far more frequent, if sparsely documented.

Salon music-making set the tone for Schumann's compositional production even after he abandoned his performing career. Many of his 1830s piano works inhabit genres more associated with domestic performance than with the public concert. Erika Reiman has shown that piano cycles such as *Papillons* and *Carnaval*, Op. 9, draw upon dance medleys such as Weber's *Aufforderung zum Tanze* and Schubert's waltz sets.[22] The same is true of the "Abegg" Variations and the *Fantaisies*, both of which use idioms conventional in popular variation sets, cater to the abilities of accomplished amateurs, and incorporate light dance music of the kind that filled piano-owning households.

Schumann developed his style of virtuosity partly through the improvisations he played in intimate settings. Like many contemporary pianists, Schumann used improvisation both as a mode of performance and as a way to hone his technique and develop compositions.[23] Admittedly, evidence regarding what Schumann's improvisations actually sounded like is frustratingly vague. No transcription of one exists, and he never wrote about his improvisations in concrete detail. When witnesses did describe his style, they often compared the results to lyrical character pieces rather than bravura tours de force. Oswald Lorenz recalled that when conversation stagnated at the Leipzig *Kaffeebaum*, Schumann liked to extemporize music that resembled the "Eusebius" movements of *Davidsbündlertänze*, Op. 6.[24] These accounts often come from the mid- to late 1830s, by which point Schumann had injured his hand, changed his career path, and possibly modified his style of improvisation.

However, when sources do attempt to capture Schumann's piano playing—both in improvisations and set pieces—they consistently describe nontransparent textures as one of his idiosyncratic, defining features. Gustav Jensen's 1883 Schumann biography quotes several firsthand accounts. Jensen himself recalled walking in on Schumann improvising at home. Schumann, he remembered, retained the clarity of the melody but set it against a murky background in which harmonies and motives blended and interpenetrated. "The playing struck me as idiosyncratic," he remembered. "It always sounded as though the pedal was half pushed down, the figures were swimming into one another so. But the melody always stood out softly, truly as if in the light of dawn or dusk." (Jensen heard an echo of that improvisation in Schumann's *Nachtstücke*.) When Schumann played his own music, Jensen noted, he made heavy use of both pedals and gave downbeats only the slightest accentuation. Julius Knorr, a founding member of the *Neue Zeitschrift*, described in Schumann's improvisations a "soft, blurry style of playing, which died away in the ear in a way that won one's heart." Alfred Dörffel, who occasionally played for Schumann as a student (and later wrote a significant review of the Piano Concerto Op. 54), seconded their descriptions: "He always left the damper pedal somewhat open so that, to an extent, the middle voices melted into one another."[25] If these later performances resembled those Schumann gave during his stint as a locally famous virtuoso, textural obfuscation represented part of his identity as a pianist, a personal trademark that supplemented (and possibly contrasted with) his playing of postclassical standards by Moscheles and Hummel. Such nontransparent pianism found a more legible place in his compositions.

A Party Game about Poetic Virtuosity: Schumann's "Abegg" Variations

In his first published composition, *Thème sur le nom "Abegg" varié*, Op. 1, Schumann used a nontransparent style of virtuosity to create musical metaphors for interiority and cultivation. In addition to the piano textures, Schumann's strategies of nontransparency include several instances of structural blurring and subversion. He published the work in November 1831, only a month before he made his critical debut with the "Ein Opus II" essay we explored in chapter 2.

The "Abegg" Variations grew out of Schumann's salon performances. He sketched and possibly test-ran the work while enjoying his reputation in Heidelberg. In a letter to his Heidelberg classmate J. August Lemke, Schumann reported that the work would soon appear in print and, as if thanking his local supporters, extravagantly promised, "All Heidelberg will receive free copies."[26] Though Schumann dedicated the work to the most likely fictional "Countess Pauline d'Abegg," he might have met a real-life inspiration at his Heidelberg house performances: Meta Abegg, the daughter of a local city councilor. Schumann initially designed the Variations as an all-purpose vehicle for solo or concerted performance, similar to Chopin's "Là ci darem la mano" Variations. In his drafts, the piece was scored for piano and orchestra and featured a slow orchestral introduction.[27] By the time it went to press, however, Schumann was beginning to abandon his dreams of virtuoso stardom, and the "Abegg" Variations had become a concise solo piece marketed to fleet-fingered domestic pianists. Partly in reference to the elegant waltz theme, John Daverio observed that the piece "exudes the rarefied air of the salon."[28]

The Variations employ a postclassical framework. Ludwig Rellstab reviewed the piece in 1832 for *Iris im Gebiete der Tonkunst* and placed it squarely within this repertory: "They are the work of a gifted pianist, are as grateful and brilliant as many similar pieces by Czerny and Herz, and consequently merit equal recognition."[29] In one of the only positive reviews he ever gave Schumann's music, Gottfried Wilhelm Fink of the *Allgemeine musikalische Zeitung* described the Variations as appealing and accessible. The theme, he wrote, was "well-invented and attractive" and the variations themselves "not too difficult for good players."[30] Schumann's third variation displays glittering, "brilliant" figuration typical of postclassical showpieces. The obligatory slow variation transitions to the finale, a plan with precedent in Chopin's "Là ci darem la mano" and Herz's "Violette" Variations. Hans Joachim Köhler and Matthias Hansen point out specific passages that Schumann might have modeled on Chopin's "Là ci darem" and Moscheles's "Alexander" Variations.[31] With the dedication to "Countess d'Abegg," Schumann located his piece—albeit tongue-in-cheek—within the glamorous world of high-society salons that popular showpieces evoked (see chapter 1). Perhaps because of its postclassical layout, the Variations have not figured in recent scholarly attempts to interpret the abstruse style of Schumann's 1830s piano music, such as Daverio's or Reiman's.

Schumann's early showpiece wears its radical features lightly, and its poetic virtuosity arises from a musical game. The composition's most obvious idiosyncratic feature sets this process in motion: as the full title advises, the theme is based on the notes A-B-flat-E-G-G, evoking the dedicatee's name via musical cipher. Daverio noted that the theme creates a hint of quasi-literary substance within the music by inviting listeners to "read" a message.[32] I would add that Schumann's cipher also situates the Variations within the practice of salon gameplaying by presenting a musical pun and challenging listeners to discern the connection between title and theme. Numerous documents of salon life record that guests enjoyed games of wit and wordplay. Besides providing recreation, such activities allowed players to show off their erudition. Schumann's own review of Kalkbrenner and Thalberg depicts a game of charades in progress as the Countess's guests listen to music and display their literary knowledge. When Schumann attended soirees at Henriette Voigt's, he and other guests (including prominent musicians such as Mendelssohn and William Sterndale Bennett) played musical, verbal, and artistic games. On one occasion, the hostess wrote a poetic couplet on each guest's place card. On others, guests drew caricatures and ad-libbed humorous canons.[33]

Music often formed an integral part of salon games. Mary Ann Smart has described an operatic parody popular in 1840s Parisian salons called *L'Incendio de Babilonia* that required guests to appreciate references to well-known operas and operatic conventions. She also unearths allusions to characters from Bellini's *I puritani* hidden in solo songs meant for domestic performance, allusions that knowing listeners would have caught and enjoyed.[34] Within Germany, Ronyak has connected settings of *Die schöne Müllerin* to convivial role-play in Friedrich August and Elisabeth von Stägemann's Berlin salon.[35]

Rellstab poked fun at the "Abegg" Variations in his review but recognized the musical code as a playful display of cleverness. Once he understood the "musical joke," he "read therein the name of the most likely beautiful and talented countess at least as often as Roland read the name of Angelica in the tree-bark." His simile at once recognizes the ubiquity of the "Abegg" motive and suggests that Rellstab himself might have groaned at the cipher: in Ariosto's *Orlando Furioso*, Roland goes mad after reading Angelica's name alongside evidence of her love for another knight. Perhaps with tongue in cheek, Rellstab suggested that Schumann should have included other learned treatments of the "Abegg" motive—fugues or canons, for example—which would have made the Variations more "attractive for the musical intellect." After all, he wrote, "this is the work's entire purpose." Rellstab went on to propose other words that could be musically encoded, laying out a musical "luncheon": "Caffé" (coffee), for example, and "Fisch" (fish). By making a literary allusion, adopting a satirical tone, and generating his own ciphers, Rellstab accepted Schumann's invitation to a round of witticisms.[36]

Schumann's variations change the nature of the puzzle and lead performers and listeners through an elaborate process of thematic concealment. Though scholars have yet to recognize this aspect of the showpiece, it was the most radical way in which the "Abegg" Variations subverted postclassical convention. As we saw in chapter 1, postclassical showpieces produced "brilliant" sounds through glistening, transparently textured figuration. In variation sets, individual variations kept the theme itself clearly audible by retaining its melodic contours or adhering closely to its harmonic scheme. Czerny's treatises stressed that letting listeners hear well-loved melodies was one important way of generating pleasure. In the "Abegg" Variations, by contrast, Schumann used complex textures that obscured the theme's melody, harmonies, and in some cases phrase structure. Example 3.1 excerpts the first three variations. Variation 1 presents a particularly striking case. A string of figurational patterns frustrates any expectation of pristine textures. The first four measures switch abruptly between chromatic chords and cascading arpeggios, rapid chromatic scales, and a combination of arpeggios and repeated notes. In measure 13, brilliant runs converge with an accompaniment

Example 3.1. Schumann, "Abegg" Variations, Op. 1. Strategies of thematic concealment.

Variation 2:

Example 3.1. (*continued*)

that bleeds into diminished-seventh chords one note at a time. The second half of the variation overlays running arpeggios, harmonic "blurs," and syncopated figures that obscure the regular meter.

The variation also subverts thematic transparency. It mirrors the formal and harmonic outline of the "Abegg" theme, neither adding nor subtracting measures.[37] However, the rapidly changing figuration makes the boundaries of phrases difficult to discern, doubly so when accents fall in the middle of measures. The first four measures cloud the theme's dominant and tonic harmonies with embellishing diminished-seventh chords. One must also listen carefully to hear the "Abegg" theme itself. The variation begins only with the notes A and B-flat before veering away into a series of ascending sequences. The melodic contour of the theme does not appear explicitly until measure 8, where it remains buried beneath the arpeggios and, after only four measures, fades into a diminished harmony.

Schumann's reviewers, even as they recognized the showpiece's postclassical framework, cautioned readers that the variations were not what they would expect. Fink described the variations as "not of the usual mold" and "very curious."[38] Rellstab was more specific, noting, "In the variations, the theme as good as disappears and is almost never to be discovered, except here and there in basso marcato, but even then only the first bar and not the rest of the melody."[39] His description might seem overstated for present-day listeners used to freer variation techniques in, for example, Elgar's *Enigma Variations* or Copland's *Piano Variations*. However, it recognizes that the theme was not as easily audible as it would have been in a comparable work by Czerny, Kalkbrenner, or Herz.

Each of the "Abegg" Variations differently conceals the waltz theme. Variation 2 renders the theme's harmonic structure practically indiscernible. Most harmonies

Variation 3:

Example 3.1. (*continued*)

from the theme remain present, but Schumann displaces and intersperses them with chromatically sliding chords. The only sign of the "Abegg" melody itself is in the right hand, which opens with A and B-flat but then spins the half-step into a winding, chromatic line. The equally chromatic left hand adds another layer of concealment, weaving around the right hand and pushing against the meter with its constant syncopation. Variation 3 presents a brilliant texture but only reveals the opening of the "Abegg" theme at the written-out repeat. Schumann highlights this statement by momentarily confusing the roles of accompaniment and main voice, gradually turning the striding eighth notes into held quarter notes and then into the *marcato e legato* melody itself. As if to further disorient the listener, Schumann veers away from the melody with a chain of parallel first-inversion chords.

Whereas conventional, brilliant variation sets charmed listeners with embellishments of a readily audible theme, tracking the relationships between theme and variations in the "Abegg" Variations requires one to peer through dense tangles of figuration and obfuscating harmonic progressions and to notice fleeting, unexpected glimpses of the head-motive. The result not only continues the cipher-theme's playful riddling; it also engages a perceptual faculty called *Witz* that figured prominently in early Romantic literary aesthetics. Musical wit is a topic scholars have explored far beyond Schumann, often in compositions that cleverly subvert formal conventions. For Schumann, *Witz* specifically meant the art of making and grasping farfetched comparisons. According to Jean Paul's *Vorschule der Aesthetik*, which Schumann kept in his library and annotated during the 1830s, *Witz* allowed one to discover "partial equality *hidden* in greater inequality."[40] Scholars of Schumannian *Witz*, notably Daverio, Reiman, Ferris, and Watkins, have stressed its literary roots.[41] Schumann himself wrote in his diary in 1828, "No one can seek deep, ingenious [*geistreich*] *Witz* like Jean Paul."[42] Jean Paul's novels, which Schumann read voraciously beginning in his late teens, display *Witz* with sentences that create surprising, colorful comparisons, and large-scale digressions that challenge us to discern the main thread of a narrative. In addition, Friedrich Schlegel's writings (which Schumann mined for his *Mottosammlung*) often discuss *Witz*.

Beginning with Daverio's pathbreaking use of literary frameworks for understanding Schumann's style, *Witz* has provided scholars with a versatile tool for approaching the composer's 1830s music, especially the piano cycles. Here, *Witz* serves as a unifying strategy, a means of suggesting and discerning elusive, recondite connections between fragmentary, incongruous movements. *Witz*, Daverio summarized, can convert "a seemingly random juxtaposition of antithetical terms into a meaningful configuration."[43] His examples include what he called the "subcutaneous" linking motives in *Carnaval* (based, like the "Abegg" theme, on musical ciphers), distinctive accompaniment patterns that connect movements of *Papillons*, and harmonic and figurational topoi that migrate between the *Novelletten*. Reiman has found *Witz* in the cycles' digressive formal schemes.[44]

The "Abegg" Variations offers a different but complementary view of Schumannian *Witz*. Granted, Schumann's Opus 1 is not as radical as the piano cycles he composed over the next few years. It would be hard to construe the individual variations as fragmentary and, unlike the dance medley or character-piece set, the variation genre presupposes that its components form a coherent whole. Instead, the "Abegg" Variations displays musical *Witz* in its abstruse connections between theme and variations. Schumann's variations, as Rellstab noted, were so nontransparent that the theme seemed to "disappear." They challenge listeners to divine their thematic and formal parallels and to situate them within Daverio's "meaningful whole." Some of Schumann's strategies of obfuscation anticipate features of his piano cycles. He uses the "Abegg" melody as a subcutaneous motivic trace—a snatch of melody glimmering beneath the figuration or hinted at in wandering chromatic lines. Unconventionally complex textural and harmonic detail clouds the harmonic and phraseological bedrock that the variations share. The variations also navigate disorienting contrasts comparable to the piano cycles' connection-obscuring changes of style: between the simple, repetitive waltz theme and the kaleidoscopic Variation 1, or between the chromatically opaque Variation 2 and the brilliant Variation 3. In contrast to the piano cycles, however, Schumann's "Abegg" Variations does not invoke musical *Witz* as an exercise in creating compositional unity. Rather, *Witz* arises here from concealment and obfuscation. To use Jean Paul's words, Schumann replaced the variation genre's conventional transparency with "greater inequality," leaving behind only a "hidden" unity for listeners to discern.

Like the cipher-theme itself, these *Witz*-provoking connections link the "Abegg" Variations to salon culture. Scholars have amply demonstrated the literary roots of *Witz*, but the concept also informed nineteenth-century conceptions of cultivated conversation, the kind one encountered in intellectually elite salons. Carl Hill's history of German *Witztheorie* notes that *Witz* originated in eighteenth-century aristocratic salons, where it provided a model for erudite discourse.[45] During the nineteenth century, it endured in bourgeois literary salons. Peter Siebert, in fact, argues that the witticisms and bons mots one heard in such settings both influenced and grew from published *Witz*-driven aphorisms by Novalis, Schlegel, and the Berlin poet and salon hostess Rahel Levin. In this context, *Witz* served as a stimulant to clever conversation, a way for an interlocutor to turn the separate details of a conversation into what Siebert calls a "veiled totality."[46] It embraced surprising connections that did not unfold as straightforward arguments or narratives but took the meandering paths of unpredictable conversations. As Thomas Kabisch has noted, the witticism needed to appear spontaneous in order to impress.[47]

Some of the aestheticians Schumann read alluded to this convivial context. Friedrich Schlegel, in one of his fragments, defined *Witz* as "logical sociability."[48] His formulation evokes the exchange of ideas among human speakers and, perhaps, imagines anthropomorphic thoughts themselves joining into friendly combinations. Jean Paul's *Vorschule* described *Witz* as a "social power" (his language could refer to conversations or the publication of literary works).[49]

Schumann himself seems to have recognized *Witz*'s connection to erudite conversation. While many sources reveal his exposure to literary manifestations of *Witz*, his engagement with *ars conversationis* remains little-documented. His diary and other extant documents provide a partial record of when he visited the Voigts or the Caruses, what they discussed, what activities they enjoyed, and what music they played. They do not, however, tell us how Agnes Carus and her friends conversed. (They were certainly aware of Jean Paul's literary *Witz:* Henriette Voigt read Jean Paul's novels, and Agnes Carus once asked Schumann to compose a *Streckverse*, a style of prose poem Jean Paul favored.[50]) Nevertheless, Schumann's early essays in *Witz* call attention to its social component. His aphorisms often unfold as short exchanges in which Florestan, Eusebius, and Raro discuss music using inventive one-liners and far-fetched comparisons. In one, Eusebius muses, "A triad=the times. The third, as the present, mediates the past and the future." "A bold comparison!" Raro responds.[51] *Davidsbündlertänze* makes a similar impression through music. The piece includes inscriptions that assign each movement to Florestan or Eusebius, some of which describe moments in a conversation. "Eusebius added this superfluously," the text before the last movement reads, "but his eyes were glistening with joy." Schumann begs listeners to imagine the characters responding to each other's musical utterances, producing stark contrasts and subtle connections. It was not only in the introverted act of reading but in the art of conversation that Schumann's musical *Witz* took shape.

In both its literary and sociable manifestations, *Witz* was no mere display of cleverness but a metaphor for interiority, spirit, and transcendence. Another of Schlegel's fragments, for example, defined *Witz* as "an explosion of contained spirit" unleashed when the mind perceives unexpected similarities. Elsewhere, he depicted *Witz* as an outward manifestation of non-corporeal, even ethereal qualities: "*Witz* is the appearance, the exterior lightning bolt of imagination. Hence its divinity, the similarity of *Witz* to mysticism."[52] In the aforementioned diary entry, Schumann himself described Jean Paul's *Witz* as "deep" and "inspired." Jean Paul's novels, as Reiman notes, often use *Witz*-driven effusions of descriptive language when characters enter what the author called a "Zweite Welt" (a second world). Here, characters pass into idyllic realms beyond the everyday world, and they momentarily experience heightened powers of perception that give their surroundings a preternaturally vivid appearance.[53] *Witz* offered salon discussants what Siebert calls an "entryway into mystical thinking."[54]

Contemporary writers also described *Witz* as a mark of intellectual cultivation. "Witty ideas," Schlegel wrote, "are the proverbs of cultivated people."[55] Through *Witz*, Hill summarizes, middle-class writers and salon guests enjoyed the intellectual repartee associated with aristocratic circles while connecting it to their ideal of *Bildung*.[56]

Ronyak describes the Stägemann *Liederspiel* as "serious play," a game in which participants tried on different personas to foster their own subjective development.[57] The phrase aptly describes Schumann's Variations as well. The showpiece invites listeners to enjoy musical recreation even as they animate their spirits and imaginations, probe musical depths, and enter a cultivated social sphere. Schumann almost immediately afterward wrote about poetic virtuosity (not connected to *Witz*) in Chopin's "Là ci darem la mano" Variations. The "Abegg"

Variations was also part of his larger project to synthesize the pleasures of virtuosity, ideals of interiority, and aspirations for cultivation within lightweight, postclassically structured showpieces.

The Variations' "Finale alla Fantasia" brings this process into its most elaborate stage. The title itself seems to invert postclassical convention. Whereas such variation sets generally begin with quasi-improvisatory fantasias and end with up-tempo rondos, Schumann's finale concludes the piece with simulated musical free-association. Gooley, in fact, has noted that the opening of the finale resembles one approach to improvisation that nineteenth-century treatises recommended, in which a pianist repeats a simple chord progression and overlays it with figuration.[58]

Amid its evocations of improvisation, the finale retains the outlines of the rondo expected at this point in a postclassical variation set. Figure 3.1 shows the ABACA layout. The ruminative chord progression serves as a refrain and, as is typical of rondo finales, intervening episodes present less clearly thematic figuration. This structure has gone unnoticed, perhaps because Schumann obscures the rondo form, clouding it to enhance the illusion of spontaneous, exploratory playing. The harmonic structure, for example, softens the boundaries of the form. The repeated chord progression rests on a dominant pedal, opening each refrain in a state of harmonic stasis that hints obliquely at F major. In A and A″, tonic pedals emerge without emphatic preparation: the sequences that lead up to them touch but lightly on the dominant.

Schumann also disguises the form by inverting the thematic process typical of postclassical rondo finales. As we saw in chapter 1, refrains in such finales are usually based on a mostly complete statement of the theme, and episodes might draw upon the theme's motives. Schumann's refrain presents a particularly obscure reference to the "Abegg" theme: the repeated chord progression opens with the telltale A–B-flat motive and encapsulates the harmonic structure of the theme's first two phrases. Schumann thus continues the game of concealment at the very point where one would expect an undisguised appearance of the theme. Subsequent parts of the finale present more recognizable versions of the "Abegg" theme. The end of section A, for example, fills in its outline with broken octaves. The analogous point in A′ redistributes the notes A, B-flat, E, and G across the octave. Schumann reserves his most emphatic reference to the "Abegg" theme for the transition to the second episode. Here, he gives the leading motive a forceful sound through horn-like doublings and a triadic contour and sets it at the most harmonically distant point in the movement (a V^7/F-sharp). This surprising recall seems to unlock the finale's virtuosic climax, an expanse of thinly textured figuration. In the fantasia-like rondo, the "Abegg" theme functions neither as a motive for extensive development nor as a melody to be savored in its entirety but as a reminiscence to which different sections refer more or less obliquely.

Near the end of the finale, Schumann uses the "Abegg" motive to suggest a different musical metaphor for interiority. Section C halts on a cadential 6/4 that announces a cadenza. Instead of glistening figuration, Schumann calls for one of the most idiosyncratic sound effects in the piano literature. The pianist plays two

Section	A		B	A′	
Measures	1	22	31	40	47

F: V (pedal) ⟶ I   A:I   F:V (pedal) → I

Refrain, with harmonies from theme:

From A:

Cadenza:

Figure 3.1. Concealed rondo form of "Finale alla Fantasia," "Abegg" Variations.

(trans)	C		Cadenza	A″	Coda
54	63			75	89

Modulation ⟶		F: V (pedal)	I

From A′:

Transition:

Figure 3.1. (*continued*)

chords that embed the first two notes of the "Abegg" motive in an inner voice. After the second chord, s/he completes the motive by lifting the keys one by one. The motivic significance of the passage might be more readily apparent to the pianist than to the audience, and the effect risks becoming inaudible in any but the most intimate of venues.

The cadenza evokes a trope that fascinated Romantic writers and aestheticians: the distant or dying sound. Berthold Hoeckner has identified many representations of distance in Schumann's 1830s works and writings, including passages in the Fantasie Op. 17 and Sonata No. 1, Op. 11. One case closely resembles the "Abegg" cadenza. At the end of *Papillons*, the pianist similarly makes a chord vanish by lifting keys one by one. Schumann himself wrote that *Papillons* paralleled scenes from Jean Paul's *Flegeljahre* and that the ending corresponded to one in which the character Walt hears the sound of his brother Vult's flute fading into the distance.[59]

In the "Abegg" Variations, the dying sound does not hint at a specific literary image but replaces what would conventionally be a virtuosic flourish with an introspective turn. Schumann's favorite writers connected distant sound to interiority and the poetic. Jean Paul's *Vorschule* described how, as a decaying tone blends into silence, it seamlessly converts physical vibrations into inner memory or imagination: "It is more than an analogy to call [the Romantic] the undulating hum of a vibrating string or bell, whose sound waves fade away into ever greater distances and *finally are lost in ourselves and which, although outwardly silent, still sound within.*"[60] Novalis, Hoeckner notes, similarly mapped the contrast between distant, indistinct sound and clearly audible sound onto a dichotomy between the poetic and the prosaic.

In a pianistic analogue of Jean Paul's bell or string, Schumann's cadenza converts the "Abegg" motive into distant sound. The pianist articulates the first two notes (A and B-flat). The next three slip into the Romantic distance, their attacks lost in the second chord. Though listeners might perceive the E growing more prominent after the pianist releases the B-flat, the note makes its presence felt more by vanishing than in its onset. The G resounds as the last, already decaying remnant of the chord, and the pianist articulates its repetition only by releasing the bass C and depressing the pedal to add a faint shimmer of sympathetic vibration. Just as Jean Paul's sound waves imperceptibly cross from the physical world into the mind's ear, listeners might catch the last three pitches of the cadenza by missing or imagining them as much as by clearly perceiving them. After a party game that invited listeners to decode a cipher and exercise their musical *Witz*, Schumann's virtuoso draws them into the Romantic distance, where the memory of poetic virtuosity blends with introspective contemplation.

Henriette Voigt, Schumann's Ideal Salon Patron

Henriette Voigt was a salon patron who avidly supported Schumann's music and ideas throughout the 1830s. Indeed, Schumann's writings portray her as an ideal music lover. Sources related to her life and salon offer a largely unexplored glimpse of an important individual in Schumann's piano decade and, more broadly, one of the countless listeners and amateur musicians who contributed to the virtuosity discourse.

Schumann's friendship with Voigt spanned crucial years of his piano decade. They met on January 27, 1834, during the intermission of a concert given by their mutual friend, pianist Ludwig Schuncke. Schumann soon became a frequent guest at the Voigt home. Documents of their friendship include a rich body of correspondence, numerous diary entries, two musical dedications, and a substantial *Neue Zeitschrift* article titled "Erinnerungen an eine Freundin"—Schumann's eulogy for Voigt after her death from tuberculosis in 1839. Voigt's son-in-law, Julius Gensel, published both parties' extant letters to one another as well as a biographical article on Voigt herself.[61] Voigt's diary entries are available in Leipzig and London archives, transcriptions by Wolfgang Boetticher, and Schumann's eulogy, which quoted several of them.[62] Schumann biographies have stressed this friendship's personal significance. Voigt served as Schumann's confidante during his ill-fated engagement to Ernestine von Fricken, and she cared for Schuncke during his fatal illness in 1834. Schumann gave Voigt the *Davidsbund* nickname "Eleanora," hinting via Beethovenian reference that she had played the rescuer to his "Florestan."[63] Voigt, however, also held professional significance for Schumann. By 1834, the young composer-critic was in a formative stage of his career. The "Abegg" Variations had been in print for three years, and he had already published *Papillons*, his Paganini Etudes Op. 3, the Intermezzi Op. 4, and the Impromptus Op. 5. The first issue of the *Neue Zeitschrift* would appear later that year. Over the next several years, he published his most significant 1830s piano music, including several piano cycles, the Fantasie Op. 17, three piano sonatas, and the *Études symphoniques*. During this time, he found at Voigt's a receptive venue for his compositions and journal.

Voigt's background prepared her to be a well-connected, musically accomplished salon patron. She was born Henriette Kunze in 1808 in Leipzig.[64] After her father died in 1817, funds from her godfather enabled her to pursue an education in Berlin, initially with the goal of becoming a governess. There, she studied piano with Ludwig Berger and counted Wilhelm Taubert and Felix Mendelssohn as fellow students and occasional duet partners. Pleased with her progress, Berger encouraged her to perform in public, but Voigt declined and, throughout her life, played only in private settings. Upon her return to Leipzig, she married the not-yet-established textile merchant Karl Voigt. While her husband built his business, Henriette brought in extra income teaching piano lessons and, after the business became successful, gave free lessons to girls who could not afford them.

Even amid Leipzig's lively salon scene, Voigt's musical gatherings emerged as particularly vibrant. Her home had a large hall appropriate for dancing or musical performances, and the family hosted prominent local and visiting artists.[65] These included Carl Loewe, Moscheles, Mendelssohn, Taubert, Bennett, Chopin, Henselt, Theodore Döhler, the soprano Clara Novello, and others. Voigt herself performed alongside her guests. She played duet arrangements of chamber and orchestral works with Mendelssohn and Schubert's *Divertissement à la hongroise* with the pianist Camille Stamaty. She accompanied violinists Karol Lipiński and Ferdinand David in Beethoven sonatas, including demanding works such as the "Kreutzer."[66] Schumann's diary often mentions spending time at Voigt's, where he conversed with many of the musicians he was promoting in the *Neue Zeitschrift*.[67] "The musician, it seemed, was the master of the house, and music its highest goddess," he wrote in Voigt's eulogy.[68] An obituary for Voigt that appeared in the *Zeitschrift* described her as "the premiere dilettante of our city" (using "dilettante" in its positive sense to denote a devoted amateur).[69]

Beyond the walls of her home, Voigt immersed herself in Leipzig's musical life. She sang in the Gewandhaus chorus, and her diary records her enthusiasm for Mendelssohn's oratorio *Paulus*. She attended orchestral concerts and wrote after hearing Mendelssohn perform Beethoven's Piano Concerto No. 4, "I had a pleasure as I had seldom had before in my life and I sat there, without breathing, without moving a limb, for fear of disturbing it." She read the *Neue Zeitschrift*, and one diary entry expressed her agreement with Moscheles's positive review of Schumann's Sonata No. 1.[70]

Schumann's remarks on Voigt's musical views seem almost too good to be true—too in sympathy with the ideology he was promulgating in the *Zeitschrift* to be wholly uncontrived. Indeed, when Schumann published his "Erinnerungen," he was not merely tendering a personal tribute but making a statement about an idealized listener and patron in a public forum that extended far beyond Leipzig. Like Kaskel's Henselt review, the eulogy modeled particular attitudes and behaviors and attributed them to a musically cultivated woman. However, Schumann made his most striking statements about Voigt by quoting at length from her diary, and Boetticher confirms that he did not distort these entries. Her letters and activities, too, corroborate the image Schumann presented. However much Schumann idealized her, Voigt was not a wishful fiction but a real music lover.

Voigt admired and advocated for many of the same composers Schumann was promoting, and she kept abreast of their latest work. Schumann's "Erinnerungen" reports that, after her studies in Berlin, Voigt mostly played Berger and Beethoven. After she met Schuncke and began taking piano lessons from him, she became more aware of "newer directions" in music and developed a love for Schubert, Chopin, and Mendelssohn. Before long, Friedrich Rochlitz, founding editor of the *Allgemeine musikalische Zeitung*, was seeking her out to hear her discuss and play "young artists."[71] Mendelssohn himself wrote to Voigt asking for repertoire suggestions on January 10, 1835: "Oh, by the way, can you tell me of any really beautiful, new pieces for piano, with or without accompaniment? There, [in Leipzig] you are right at the source."[72]

Some of Voigt's diary entries echo statements that Schumann made in the *Zeitschrift*, and she may have formed her views partly through their interactions. Her entry from August 31, 1836, for example, resembles Schumann's 1835 New Year's address, in which he had portrayed the current age as an artistically vacuous one awaiting redemption. "I can't help myself," Voigt wrote, "I see present musical activities and creations only as a period of transition (though I allow exceptions), from which still better and clearer things must develop—it is a struggle and a fight, but victory surely is not far off."[73] Voigt also shared some of Schumann's literary tastes. Her diary records that she read E. T. A. Hoffmann's *Kreisleriana* and Jean Paul's *Siebenkaes*, and Julius Gensel reported that a shared love of Jean Paul had first sparked conversations and courtship between Henriette Kunze and Karl Voigt. Schumann himself sent Voigt a letter in which he encouraged her to compare *Papillons* to the close of Jean Paul's *Flegeljahre*.[74]

Voigt often articulated her musical tastes through statements about virtuosity. In her letters and diary, Voigt often emphasized negative views of virtuosity and did not discuss individual compositions in concrete detail. Nevertheless, reading her writings offers broader insight into why she considered virtuosity a significant, fraught issue, one that raised important questions about how she experienced music and regarded herself as a music-lover. Rather than revealing herself as an anti-virtuosity listener, Voigt sketches the frameworks within which she scorned certain music and hints at the ideals she attached to music she prized. In one diary entry, for example, she likened virtuosos to circus entertainers:

> I have always felt an aversion to rope dancers' and equestrians' feats and the like, and the same feeling seems to have glided unconsciously into my artistic views. For, if I allow myself to be astonished for a moment, my inborn revulsion soon returns. Please, no rope dancing in music: how this sanctuary is profaned through it.[75]

As I mentioned in the Introduction, such comparisons proliferated in nineteenth-century writings about virtuosity, and they reflected musicians' anxiety about their cultural prestige. Certain approaches to virtuosity, they suggested, threatened to turn music into a display of physical dexterity rather than a vehicle for serious thought, lowbrow entertainment rather than a cultivated pursuit. Voigt's entry uses similar rhetoric but says more about her self-image as a listener than about professional anxiety. Her aversion to "rope dancing in music" suggests that she saw herself as immune to the charms of plebian spectacle and that, for her, virtuosity risked falling into this category. By defending the "sanctuary," she demanded that music resonate with the spirit rather than with the senses or the body. Or, to state it more neutrally, she surrounded music she preferred with spiritualizing rhetoric and thereby affirmed its cultural and aesthetic prestige. Another diary entry drew a similar distinction between physical execution and inner cultivation: "What a sad feeling hearing a family of virtuosos always gives me! When the whole life of a person is directed only at mechanism, the very essence of the spirit [*Geist*] is already sorely wasted."[76]

Voigt's entry from September 22, 1838, does not directly reference music but offers further insight into her self-image. Here, she records her disgust for ostentatious luxury:

> Today I was in a shop where the newest goods of the fair were to be seen in great quantities, and only objects of finery! All of the people who were buying, all of the throng who were selling, a running and pressing to the point of madness! All were running in confusion and many almost lost their minds over what they wanted to set down!—Against my will, a tear sprang to my eye, and I felt the weight of heaven and earth on my heart—I thought: all of this striving, for what? Why?—Not to live? No, but to decorate life![77]

As we saw in chapter 1, Schumann's critique of pleasurable virtuosity frequently invoked images of aristocratic frivolity and shallow luxury. By quoting Voigt in his eulogy, Schumann complemented this strand of his criticism and upheld her as a music lover impervious to the allure of fashion. Voigt's involuntary tears paint her as a woman of interiority: repelled by superficiality, she turned inward. A caveat I offered in chapter 1, though, bears reiterating. Voigt's antiluxury stance was just that—a rhetorical stance. After all, her salon treated guests to numerous luxuries: Voigt had refined her own musical tastes through extensive recreational piano playing and study with a widely known teacher, and her gatherings boasted an elite roster of prominent musicians. Had she tried to reconcile this contradiction, Voigt herself (like other nineteenth-century writers) likely would have insisted that these accoutrements reflected inner cultivation rather than outer wealth and that the pleasures they offered transcended superficiality or sensuousness.

When Voigt's diary turned to specific composers of virtuosic music, she often critiqued postclassical bestsellers such as Czerny and Herz. In an entry from 1837, she described Henselt as an antidote to Herz's brilliant virtuosity: "Henselt is an extraordinary player, an original through and through, and also in his compositions—he astonishes without dazzling, because his achievements are not merely of the Herzian kind."[78] In an entry from January 12, 1835, she remarked, "Rochlitz brought me Czerny's latest work, original clutter of notes and shallowness."[79]

Voigt demonstrated support for Schumann's favored approaches to virtuosity more through her actions than through her recorded words. Her salon became a venue for Schumann's own work. He sent her a copy of his Toccata in an 1834 letter and, on September 16, 1836, played through his *Concert sans orchestre* at her home. In an effort to lift Voigt's spirits during Schuncke's illness, Schumann presented her with a copy of the "Abegg" Variations.[80] He also improvised at the piano for Voigt and her guests: one of his diary entries from October 1836 records that he "improvised on Chopin's C-sharp-minor etude and nocturne in the dark and with much inwardness."[81] (Schumann probably meant the Etude Op. 10, no. 4, and Nocturne Op. 27, no. 1.) Voigt's home also provided a stage for composers Schumann was promoting, including Mendelssohn and Henselt. She also hosted a visit from Chopin during his 1836 visit to Leipzig, heard him play his recent music (including selections from his Etudes Op. 25), and recorded her delighted response in her diary.[82]

Voigt did not merely listen to Schumann's music—she actively promoted it. Most of the surviving documents concern her responses to Schumann's character pieces and piano cycles rather than the variation sets. Even so, these works feature the same strategies of formal and textural obfuscation and *Witz*-provoking connections that characterize the "Abegg" Variations and (as we will see) the *Fantaisies et finale*. In response to Mendelssohn's plea for new repertoire, Voigt sent him *Carnaval*.[83] In a letter from March 20, 1838, she reported to Schumann that Rochlitz admired his *Fantasiestücke*, Op. 12, and *Davidsbündlertänze*, which suggests that she had been discussing these works with the former critic and perhaps even playing them for him.[84] In 1838, the year before her death, she traveled to Berlin and championed Schumann at the soirees she attended. She wrote to him, "Think of a soul who thinks of you much and seeks to express your thoughts, speaks of you with solid conviction, and happily draws the sword for open feuding when it is called for in order to defend your ideas against the firmly immobile ones of the Philistines."[85] Aware that Berliners were reading the *Neue Zeitschrift* but not generally aware of Schumann's compositions, Voigt played his music: "Yesterday I was at a large social gathering . . . and when I played your *Fantasiestücke* after the table was clear, that is, by evening light, people were very satisfied and charmed, and I was endlessly happy. I played with special enthusiasm, to which the bubbling champagne and much interesting conversation might have contributed somewhat."[86]

Schumann planned on dedicating to Voigt a variation set that exemplifies his poetic pianism. He composed his *Variationen über den "Sehnsuchtwalzer" von Franz Schubert: Scènes musicales sur un theme connu* between 1833 and 1834.[87] (Its genesis, then, began a year before he met Voigt.) The work remained unfinished, and Schumann later gave Voigt the dedication of his Sonata No. 2, Op. 22. He recycled the introduction to the "Sehnsuchtwalzer" Variations in the "Préambule" of *Carnaval*. Scott Messing has observed that the Schubert variations "evoked an aura of feminine domesticity," both because the waltz itself was designed for at-home performance and because Schumann regarded Schubert as a quintessentially feminine composer.[88]

The "Sehnsuchtwalzer" Variations eschew transparent, postclassical procedures. More pianistically understated than the "Abegg" Variations, the piece features none of the earlier work's light-fingered runs and generally remains within the piano's middle register. As in the "Abegg" Variations, though, each variation masks the theme with obfuscating rhythmic, harmonic, and textural configurations. Variation 5, excerpted in example 3.2, banishes all trace of Schubert's melody. Somewhat like the second "Abegg" variation, it hides the harmonies in chromatically oscillating voices, and it foments metric ambiguity by placing the left hand's arrivals a sixteenth note before the beat. Variation 1 fractures the theme by alternating single-line melodic gestures with densely voiced chromatic progressions. Schumann marks the variation "parlando" to suggest a rhythmically flexible performance.

Such *Witz*-provoking variations seem calculated to match the interiority Schumann heard in Schubert's waltz. In 1834, Ludwig Schuncke composed his own *Variations concertantes*, Op. 14, on the "Sehnsuchtwalzer" and also dedicated the piece to Voigt. Schumann discussed Schuncke's variations in a later review and remembered telling his friend that he found it "inappropriate to use such a deeply felt [*herzinnig*] theme in such a heroic piece."[89] It remains unclear how much Schumann had already composed of his own Schubert variations when he met Schuncke in 1833, and how much he added or altered while they worked and lived side by side. Depending on the precise chronology, Schumann may have designed his piece as a response to Schuncke's, answering his friend's "heroic" bravura with introverted, abstruse pianism. Schumann's "Sehnsuchtwalzer" Variations also seems tailor-made for Voigt herself, who appreciated Schubert, expressed scorn for the brilliant sounds of Czerny and Herz, played exclusively in private settings, and supported Schumann's 1830s piano music in all its stylistic abstruseness. With its dedication to Voigt and its link to Schuncke, the "Sehnsuchtwalzer" Variations crystallized a relationship between three music-loving friends who discussed virtuosity and shared music in convivial settings.

Voigt's salon, in short, featured the idealistic aesthetics, literary sensibility, barely veiled elitism, and love of games that characterized Schumann's own salon showpieces (and 1830s piano works more generally). Schumann was already

Theme:

Variation 1:
L'istesso tempo
parlando e molto teneramente
p

Variation 5:
(p)

Example 3.2. Schumann, *Variationen über den "Sehnsuchtwalzer" von Franz Schubert.* Theme, Variations 1 and 5. Text from Andreas Boyde, ed., *Robert Schumann, Variationen über ein Thema von Schubert* (Leipzig: Hofmeister, 2000). © Friedrich Hofmeister Musikverlag, Leipzig.

developing his approach when he met Voigt, and she became his receptive listener and eager promoter. His poetic music found a niche not only in the half-fictionalized world of Florestan, Eusebius, and Raro and within the professional sphere of the *Neue Zeitschrift*, but also in the real-life salon of a middle-class woman. Though Voigt was atypical in her status and connections, she gives us a selective glimpse of the diverse public of amateurs who responded to and helped drive the virtuosity discourse, and her writings and activities sketch a portrait of the one amateur musician closest to Schumann during the 1830s.

A Poetic Network at the Limits of the Salon: Schumann's Unpublished *Fantaisies et finale*

While he was associated with Voigt's salon, Schumann composed an expansive variation set in which musical *Witz* connects a wide range of musical styles. Like the "Abegg" Variations, the *Fantaisies et finale* inflects variation form and virtuosic display with musical metaphors for poetic interiority. Schumann began work on the *Fantaisies* late in 1834 and provisionally completed it in 1835. However, he scrapped this version and continued revising the work. Scholars know the *Fantaisies* today as a preliminary version of the 1837 *Études symphoniques*. At this writing, one can access the *Fantaisies* through Schumann's working manuscript housed at the Bibliothèque du Musée Royale de Mariemont in Belgium, a copyist's manuscript at the Gesellschaft der Musikfreunde in Vienna, and an edition presented in Damien Ehrhardt's unpublished dissertation.[90] Studies of the *Études* mention the *Fantaisies* as one step in its genesis, but no scholarship has explored the context and intricacies of this work on their own terms.[91]

Though Schumann ultimately chose not to publish the *Fantaisies*, he briefly considered it finished and ready for the press. He had a copyist's manuscript prepared and may have intended to send it to either the Härtel or Haslinger firms— he was corresponding with both about the work in 1835 and 1836. Schumann designated the *Fantaisies* Opus 9 (the number that ultimately went to the roughly contemporaneous *Carnaval*) and dedicated it to "Madame le Baronne de Fricken" (mother of his then-fiancée, Ernestine von Fricken).

Charted in figure 3.2, the *Fantaisies et finale* differs substantially from the *Études symphoniques*. It includes six variations that Schumann excluded from the later, published work. Five of these were published posthumously in 1873, and Schumann left a sixth incomplete.[92] The *Fantaisies* does not include six variations Schumann later composed for the *Études* and arranges published and posthumous variations in an order that little resembles the later work. The *Fantaisies* also differs from the *Études* in several smaller details: its theme, for example, takes several harmonic turns that Schumann changed for the *Études*, and the first variation, marked "Un poco più vivo" in the *Études*, is marked "Grave" in the *Fantaisies*.

Schumann's contact with amateur musicians in Voigt's and other salons left traces on the *Fantaisies*' genesis and panoply of styles. The theme itself was Schumann's revision of a melody for flute by Ernestine's father, Baron Ignaz Freiherr von Fricken. Schumann's full title acknowledges his source: *Fantaisies et finale sur un thême de Mr. le Baron de Fricken*. An amateur composer, the Baron had written his own (now lost) set of variations on the theme and exchanged letters about the project with his prospective son-in-law. The dedication to Ernestine's mother further situated the piece within a refined, domestic setting.

Ernestine von Fricken herself was part of this circle, not just as Schumann's love interest but as a musician in her own right. Ernst Herttrich suggests that Schumann might have designed the piece specifically for her to play, which would have united the composer's fiancée and intended in-laws in a single composition.[93] Ernestine has played a thankless role in Schumann biography: today, she is known primarily for having been briefly engaged to and then jilted by the composer. Somewhat as they have done with Henriette Voigt, biographers have underplayed her musical capabilities and significance for Schumann's art. (Her connection to *Carnaval* is well-known but does little to credit her actual musicianship—one of the work's musical ciphers derives from the name of her hometown, Asch.) In fact, Ernestine was an accomplished pianist who probably

Fantaisies et finale

Figure 3.2. Schumann, *Fantaisies et finale* and *Études symphoniques*, Op. 13. Sequence of variations. Position of fantasies in *Études* or "Posthumous Variations" (abbreviated PV) shown in parentheses.

Études symphoniques

Figure 3.2. (*continued*)

6 (PV 3)

7 (Etude X)

"Trio" (PV 5)

Fantasy 7 da capo

8 (Unfinished)

9 (Etude IV)

10 (PV 4)

Finale (Etude XII)

Figure 3.2. (*continued*)

Études symphoniques continued

Figure 3.2. (*continued*)

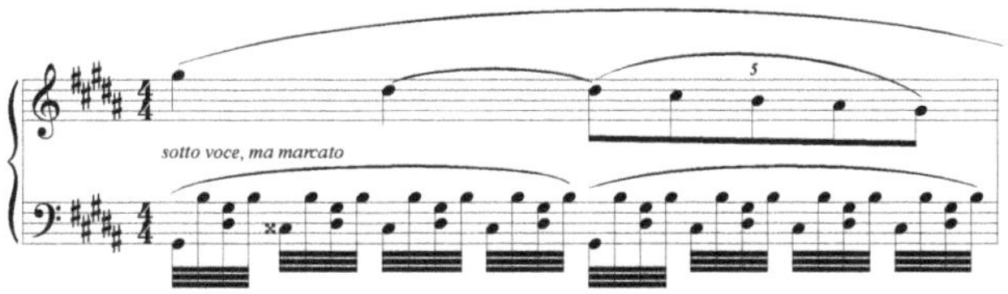

could have handled the pianistically demanding *Fantaisies*. She had auditioned for and secured a place in Friedrich Wieck's studio. As a locally well-known pianist, she received an entry in Gustav Schilling's music encyclopedia. The author noted that Ernestine had mastered repertoire by Hummel, Moscheles, and Kalkbrenner even before studying with Wieck. "Barely 18 years old in 1835," the author wrote, "she must already be counted among our premier virtuosos."[94] He specifically praised her excellent technique and ability to master difficult compositions rapidly. Because of her close relationships with Voigt, Schumann, and Schuncke, the entry affiliates her with what it called the "new Romantic school." After the death of the man she eventually married, Ernestine gave benefit concerts in Asch, Adorf, and Plauen until the year before her own death in 1844. She often programmed repertoire by Beethoven and Chopin (but not, understandably, by her ex-fiancé). Much like Henriette Voigt, Ernestine von Fricken was an accomplished pianist who at least for a time, seems to have been receptive to the music Schumann was writing and promoting.

The *Fantaisies*' play of musical styles captures the heterogeneous music-making typical of salons like Voigt's or the Caruses', where a single gathering could mingle Schubert waltzes, piano transcriptions of orchestral works, Beethoven, flashy variations by Döhler and Chopin, Schumann's own improvisations, lieder, and operatic selections. The *Fantaisies* shifts unpredictably between domestic dance styles, bravura variations, and piano textures redolent of symphonic music. Fantasies 4 and 10 are lightly ornamented waltzes. With a syncopated melodic line that simulates rubato, Fantasy 10 specifically calls to mind the music of Chopin. (Schumann was around this time writing a Chopin pastiche for *Carnaval*.) Other variations, including Fantasies 5, 7, and 9, feature the chordal, richly doubled textures that gave the *Études* their "symphonic" descriptor (see chapter 4). No reviewer could compare the *Fantaisies* to works by Herz and Czerny, as Rellstab did with the "Abegg" Variations. The virtuosic variations feature little of the transparent, brilliant textures standard to postclassical showpieces. The theme itself resembles a cross between a funeral march and a chorale, a far cry from the dance-style or operatic themes standard in popular variation sets. Nevertheless, postclassical convention structures some aspects of the work. The finale is a rondo based on an operatic theme from Heinrich Marschner's 1829 German Romantic opera *Der Templer und die Jüdin*. The fugal Fantasy 1 calls to mind two showpieces the *Neue Zeitschrift* reviewed in 1834 and 1835: Thalberg's "I Capuleti" and "Norma" fantasies, both of which demonstrate contrapuntal dexterity in their first variations.

Just as a writer or salon conversant could display *Witz* by finding recondite, surprising connections between disparate ideas, Schumann used fleeting, unexpected links between contrasting variations to tie together this crazy quilt of styles and genres. Although every variation derives from the von Fricken–Schumann theme, adjacent or proximate variations also refer to one another. Here, witty connections resemble the intermovement links one finds in Schumann's piano cycles more than they do the thematic cat-and-mouse game of the "Abegg" Variations. Outbursts of virtuosic figuration find mirrors in intimate, lyrical variations, and apparitions of the theme interrupt ornamented waltzes. Like the "Finale alla fantasia" in the "Abegg" Variations, the title of the *Fantaisies* evokes improvisation. It asks the listener to imagine cross references and changes of style emerging from exploratory, spontaneous juxtapositions and transformations. According to the logic of Romantic *Witztheorie*, this network not only unified the work—it also embodied qualities of spirit and imagination and situated the *Fantaisies* within a cultivated sphere.

Two pairs of adjacent variations illustrate Schumann's cross-references: Fantasy 7 and what we might call its "Trio," and Fantasies 2 and 3. Fantasy 7 brings the piece to its virtuosic peak with detached chords and a running bass line. The "Trio" retains virtually all of its melodic gestures. The excerpt shown in figure 3.2 mirrors Fantasy 7's opening descending contour and the neighbor-note motion that follows. The second repeated section of the "Trio," like that of Fantasy 7, begins with two measures of sequences and continues with scales placed in the inner voices. At the same time, the lyrical doppelgänger changes its predecessor's C-sharp minor to D-flat major, turns its chords into widely spaced melodic lines, and defuses its rhythmic drive by placing some of these gestures within a syncopated inner voice. Fantasy 3, like Fantasy 2, uses a bass line that resembles the theme's opening arpeggio, but it strips away Fantasy 2's textural complexity in favor of a two-part texture and replaces Fantasy 2's arching countermelody with a series of sequentially repeated units.

In the waltz-like Fantasy 4, Schumann brings together several intervariation quotations while disguising the theme's harmonic and phrase structure. The variation begins off-tonic by reinterpreting the opening harmony as a $V^{4/2}/iv$ that resolves to the major subdominant. When C-sharp minor does materialize, the waltz topic evaporates, and spectral tremolos outline the theme's arpeggio motive. Although these opening measures follow the theme's harmonic outline, the sudden change of texture creates the illusion that the theme is being quoted out of context, as do the ruminative repetitions that follow. The remainder of Fantasy 4 departs more radically from the theme's structure. Two measures (9 and 10) approximate the harmonic and motivic content of four of the theme's measures. The moment analogous to the theme's fourth phrase—where we might expect a return of the opening waltz—yields another quotation, this one from Fantasy 2. Schumann extends the ending of the variation to accommodate yet another surprise citation of the theme's opening arpeggio. What began as a tonally ambiguous waltz, then, digresses into a string of memories. Later, the waltz-variation itself becomes a musical reminiscence when the opening of Fantasy 6 nods to its dotted head-motive.

The overall trajectory of the *Fantaisies* also yields an unexpected transformation. The most familiar pattern in variation sets—whether by Herz or Beethoven—is to culminate with the most elaborate, pyrotechnic variations, possibly pausing for a slow penultimate variation. The *Fantaisies* unfolds a different process that peaks with Fantasy 7 and gradually sheds texture and momentum over the next several variations. By Fantasy 9, rests separate the chords, emphasizing the decrease in energy. Fantasy 10 takes rhythmic and textural dissipation to the extreme, its lagging melodic line gently out of phase with the spare accompaniment: the virtuosic juggernaut of Fantasy 7 becomes a languid waltz almost bereft of ornamentation.

Although Schumann briefly considered the *Fantaisies et finale* complete, he continued working on it for two more years and ultimately arrived at the *Études symphoniques*. On the copyist's manuscript for the *Fantaisies*, he already outlined a new sequence of variations: theme, I, II, V, PV4, IV, PV3, X, PV5 (and presumably X da capo), PV2, finale. This planned revision navigates a different path through intervariation contrasts and connections. Here, the series of variations ends with the second "Posthumous Variation," emptying into a web of memories from across the set before the finale breaks forth.

The Salon Beholds the *Siegeszug*: Schumann's Marschner-Based Rondo

The rondo finale of the *Fantaisies* alludes to a source beyond the theme and its variations: the Romanze "Wer ist der Ritter Hochgeehrt" from *Der Templer und die Jüdin*. Example 3.3 presents Schumann's refrain alongside the Romanze, a song for the character Ivanhoe and a chorus of Saxon knights and ladies. Present-day studies widely acknowledge the quotation. However, no documents from Schumann's lifetime mention it, and scholars only began discussing it in the later nineteenth century.[95] For this reason, the Marschner reference presents a problem similar to the supposed quotation of Beethoven's "An die ferne Geliebte" in Schumann's Fantasie Op. 17. Though many scholars accept the quotation as part of Schumann's design, others suspect that, because it lacks contemporaneous acknowledgment, it is the creation of a later critical tradition.[96] For the *Fantaisies et finale*, such critical silence is hardly surprising, since few substantial reviews of the *Études* and no reviews of the *Fantaisies* appeared during Schumann's lifetime (see chapter 4).

Contextual and musical evidence, however, make a strong case that Schumann purposefully cited "Wer ist der Ritter" within the *Fantaisies'* allusive network and that listeners like the Voigts, von Frickens, Wiecks, and Caruses would have appreciated it.[97] Schumann was familiar with Marschner's works, including *Der Templer*. Marschner and his music circulated in the Leipzig salon circles Schumann frequented during the early 1830s. Schumann's diary records that he personally met Marschner several times at the Carus and Wieck homes, where he and other guests sang Marschner's lieder and selections from his operas. In 1834, Clara Wieck began composing variations (now lost) on a theme from Marschner's *Hans Heiling*, which her father planned to show the composer.[98] Schumann would have been in Leipzig for the 1830–1831 run of *Der Templer* itself. Later, in 1847, he wrote in his "Theaterbüchlein" that *Templer* was "after Weber, the most significant German opera of recent times."[99] Schumann's critical writings promoted Marschner as a German alternative to French and Italian opera and opera-based showpieces. An 1835 aphorism on Rossini for the *Zeitschrift* has Florestan exclaim:

Marschner:

Example 3.3. Heinrich Marschner, "Wer ist der Ritter Hochgeehrt," from *Der Templer und die Jüdin*. Schumann, *Fantaisies et finale*. Rondo refrain. Signature motive shown in boxes.

Schumann:

Example 3.3. (*continued*)

Doesn't the stenographer Herz, who only has his heart in his fingers—doesn't Herz, I say, receive four hundred *Thaler* for a volume of variations and Marschner scarcely more for all of *Hans Heiling?* Once more I say—it makes the tips of my fingers twitch.[100]

Schumann's interest in Marschner continued after the 1830s and, in 1842, the *Neue Zeitschrift* printed Carl Koβmaly's multi-issue essay on the composer.[101]

For fans of German Romantic opera, the connection between Schumann's refrain and Marschner's Romanze would have been difficult to miss. Schumann exaggerated when he described Marschner as sadly neglected. *Der Templer* became one of the most widely known German operas of its time, and "Wer ist der Ritter" was one of its most popular numbers. *Der Templer* received over two hundred performances in Germany, England, Denmark, the Netherlands, and Russia during Marschner's lifetime. As late as the 1880s, Eduard Hanslick called it a "favorite opera of the Germans."[102] "Wer ist der Ritter" appeared in several sheet-music editions for solo voice or men's chorus, and Hanslick described its popularity as comparable to that of a folk song. A. Dean Palmer even reports that audiences sang along with the choral interjections.[103]

Musical evidence corroborates the contextual. Schumann cites Marschner's Romanze at the very point in a rondo finale where a composer would conventionally present a popular operatic theme.[104] Unlike typical opera-based rondos, Schumann's refrain does not use a complete statement of the melody. Instead, it opens with Marschner's leading motive but departs from it to create a new rounded binary form. Though the citation is partial, Schumann uses the romance's most recognizable motive—shown boxed in the example—and mirrors the dotted rhythm that completes the phrase. In "Wer ist der Ritter," the motive begins the phrases in Ivanhoe's verse, rebounds several times in his refrain, and returns in the choral responses. In Schumann's refrain, it also marks significant junctures, appearing at the beginnings of phrases and winding through the inner voices before the rounding of the form. Schumann's quotation, while consonant with postclassical convention, also conforms to his own borrowing practices, which took a less transparent approach to citation. The "Abegg" finale also begins with a partial (and even more veiled) statement of the theme. If the Beethoven quotation in the Fantasie Op. 17 was intentional, it follows a similar pattern, beginning with the head of the borrowed melody and then developing related but original material.

The Marschner citation crowns the witty discourse that runs throughout the *Fantaisies.* Studies of the *Études symphoniques* usually interpret the allusion as Schumann's tribute to William Sterndale Bennett, the showpiece's dedicatee.[105] In this reading, the text "proud England, rejoice!" playfully nodded to Bennett's nationality. However, this interpretation appears doubtful in the case of the earlier work. Schumann may have later recognized the connection between the Romanze and his English colleague, but he had drafted the *Fantaisies* before Bennett visited Leipzig in 1836. Rather, the allusion opened the rondo with an act of witty name-dropping. Instead of exposing an entire theme, it required knowing listeners to recognize a pithy reference to a composer Schumann and his friends knew musically and socially.

The specific source of this allusion contributed to the *Fantaisies'* aura of cultivation and interiority. Schumann's 1833 aphorism implies that, whereas Herz's heart lay in his fingers, Marschner's music possessed qualities that transcended physical display and easy popularity. Koβmaly's 1842 essay made a similar claim and gave it an air of nationalist chauvinism. Invoking a cliché common in nineteenth-century German music criticism, he contrasted Marschner's "depth" with the supposed "shallowness" and "triviality" of French and Italian opera.[106]

Schumann's choice of theme also suggested a nationalist stance, albeit allusively and without the starkness of Koβmaly's essay. The finale employs a formal strategy most commonly used as a vehicle for savoring current Franco-Italian operatic hits to trumpet one by a composer of German Romantic opera who was at home in Leipzig's middle-class salons.[107] In fact, early reviews of *Der Templer* noted the *volkstümlich* style of "Wer ist der Ritter"—it was one of the opera's most conspicuously "German" numbers.[108] The text for the Romanze paints an aggressive picture of knightly valor in which Ivanhoe, his beloved Rowena, and the chorus extol Richard the Lionhearted's bravery, honor, and record of putting his Muslim adversaries to flight during the Crusades. "Wer ist der Ritter," like the opera as a whole, revels in Walter Scott's idealized Middle Ages and its fairy-tale qualities of nobility, virtue, and—at the hands of Marschner and his librettist—Germanness. (*Templer* even gives the heroic "Sachsen" Germanized names while retaining French names for the antagonist Normans and Templars.) The titanic chords of Schumann's finale re-create the full-throated choral singing of Marschner's chivalric Romanze and eschew the glittering textures of postclassical variation sets. Schumann ended his salon showpiece and its display of *Witz* and cultivation by nodding to an idealized, medievalist vision of Germanness—a cultural preoccupation as current for him and his listeners as Schubert waltzes and Beethoven symphonies.[109]

Like the masterstroke of a witty conversationalist, Schumann's allusion seems to materialize spontaneously but creates a new, surprising relationship between two disparate ideas. In an 1834 letter to Baron von Fricken, Schumann wrote, "I would like to build the funeral march gradually into a really proud *Siegeszug* [victory procession] and moreover bring in some dramatic interest."[110] (By "funeral march," he could have meant the theme itself, the "Grave" first variation, or both.) In this context, "Wer ist der Ritter" becomes a victory banner, an antidote to the Baron's theme. The finale unequivocally turns minor into major and answers a descending triadic theme with an ascending one. By moving from the somber theme to the triumphant rondo, Schumann created a third referent: the breakthrough finales of Beethovenian and post-Beethovenian symphonies. Indeed, Schumann's description of "funeral marches" and "victory processions" hints at the quintessentially Beethovenian narrative of struggle and victory or tragedy and triumph, one particularly associated with the "Eroica" Symphony. (On the "Eroica" and the *Études symphoniques*, see chapter 4.) One of the finale's climactic moments encapsulates this narrative. A retransition layers dotted figuration from one of the rondo episodes over the head-motive of the Baron's theme, now in D-flat major and resounding in various registers. In a multifaceted display of musical *Witz*, Schumann knit together two borrowed, seemingly unconnected sources, answering the implied sorrow of one with the victory celebrated in the other and drawing upon a narrative that Voigt knew and venerated as a music lover steeped in Beethoven.

Schumann's *Fantaisies* suggests that this victory belonged to a circle of cultivated music-lovers such as he was meeting in Leipzig salons. If the heterogeneous piece seems to follow the something-for-everyone aesthetic Schumann and his *Zeitschrift* writers derided in Thalberg's opera fantasies, the "everyone" here embraces aficionados of German Romantic opera, salon hostesses who demanded spirit and interiority in their music, amateur composers of solemn themes, devotees of Beethoven, Chopin, and Schubert, and virtuosos attuned to the formal intricacies of Schumann's 1830s piano music. Schumann's *Fantaisies* concluded its assortment of styles with a triumphant climax. It was perhaps not coincidental that Schumann was also composing *Carnaval* around this time. This other cornucopia of diverse styles also ends with a densely chordal victory march (albeit one in 3/4 time), this one explicitly for the *Davidsbündler* to launch against the Philistines. Such triumphant endings reflected the mixture of idealism, elitism, and intimacy that characterized Schumann's social circles. Henriette Voigt, after all, later wrote in her diary about a struggle to transcend the prosaic present, one she believed would end in victory. Schumann had reason to be triumphalist about Voigt's salon, in which he found support for his music and ideas and broadened his professional horizons.

4 Virtuosity and the Rhetoric of the Sublime

During the 1830s and early 1840s, Schumann engaged with an approach to virtuosity that differed from the poetic interiority we encountered in chapters 2 and 3. These compositions and performances channeled virtuosity to overwhelm the listener with sheer intensity, power, difficulty, or even borderline-unpleasant discord. One such moment occurs in the coda of the Toccata, a passage I excerpted in example 0.1 in the Introduction. In an effect Charles Rosen described as calculated for "shock value," Schumann combined driving figuration with a sudden metric shift—it gives the double-notes a quality of breakneck acceleration, as if the cascade of figuration has momentarily overrun the piece's metrical organization.[1] An even more idiosyncratic flourish caps the final movement of the *Concert sans orchestre*, Op. 14. After over six hundred measures of perpetual-motion figuration performed *prestissimo possibile*, the finale launches into the cadenza shown in example 4.1. Rather than playing pearly, transparent flourishes, the pianist embellishes a closely voiced diminished seventh with rapid-fire alternation between chords. The *Concert* finale peaks with clangor rather than glitter.

Critics recognized this intensity. Austrian composer, critic, and pedagogue Ignaz von Seyfried compared the *Concert* finale to fearsome, unstoppable forces of nature. He wrote in the Viennese *Allgemeiner musikalischer Anzeiger*, "The finale . . . is like a violent, booming cataract whose flood of waves stops for nothing, that storms forth raging over rocks and crags and, in wild swoops, sweeps everything before it that ventures to restrain its clangorous course."[2] As I noted in the Introduction, Ernst Ortlepp's review of the Toccata compared Schumann to Beethoven. Ortlepp thereby hinted not only at Beethoven's image as the quintessential great composer but also at the powerful, massive effects that characterize many of his works.

These discussions evoked a variety of aesthetic experience that philosophers and aestheticians referred to as the sublime. The sublime emerged from a long discursive history. *On the Sublime*, by the Greek critic Longinus, dates from the first century. The concept particularly preoccupied eighteenth- and nineteenth-century writers, including Edmund Burke, Immanuel Kant, Friedrich Schiller, Johann Gottfried von Herder, and Jean Paul. They shared the belief that one experienced the sublime by observing phenomena of unsettling power and

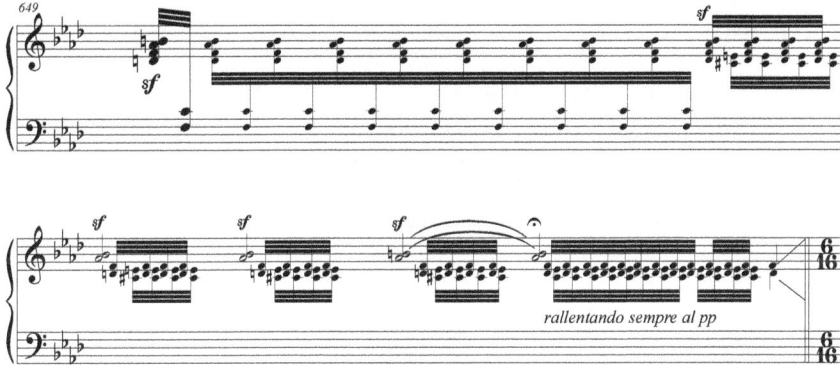

Example 4.1. Schumann, *Concert sans orchestre*, Op. 14, movement 3. Cadenza.

grandeur. Such experiences overwhelmed the beholder's sensory and cognitive faculties, inspired a mixture of fear, attraction, and admiration, and could catalyze ecstatic, elevating experiences. Writers illustrated the sublime using a constellation of images, ranging from the vastness and might of nature to the traits of admirable, formidable individuals. Nineteenth-century listeners and present-day scholars often locate musical manifestations of the sublime in symphonies and large works for chorus and orchestra, particularly Beethoven's. Among virtuosos, Liszt embodied the sublime for many of his listeners. Documents of his reception read like a compendium of sublime imagery: reviewers compared him to Greek god-heroes (Atlas, for example) and powerful nature (Niagara Falls, for example), described him engaged in violent, all-consuming struggle, and reported feelings of trembling and awe.[3]

As we will see in this chapter, Schumann and his contemporaries made the sublime part of their project to define certain instances of virtuosity as serious or transcendent. For them, such showpieces and performances could give listeners the mixture of thrill, sensory overload, and discomfort that the sublime entailed. In other cases, they imagined virtuosity conveying the heroic, superhuman striving that represented one manifestation of the sublime. The rhetoric of the sublime echoes through three episodes during and shortly after Schumann's "piano decade." First, Schumann himself extended the mantle of sublimity to Franz Liszt in his reviews of the virtuoso's 1840 Leipzig and Dresden concerts, thereby drawing upon and contributing to this facet of Liszt's image. Second, reviewers suggested that the finale of Schumann's own *Concert sans orchestre* conveyed sublime violence and intensity through its style and structure. Third, reviewers hinted at allusions to Beethoven symphonies in Schumann's Toccata and *Études symphoniques*, Op. 13, that have gone unacknowledged in the scholarly literature. They point to ways in which the two showpieces draw upon music that epitomized sublimity for the nineteenth-century imagination.

Virtuosity and the Rhetoric of the Sublime 125

These pieces and performances represent one facet of Schumann's engagement with postclassical virtuosity. Some incorporate or adapt postclassical conventions and idioms, from the Weber *Konzertstück* Liszt performed to the rondo finale of Schumann's *Études*. More important, many of the critics we will encounter pointedly contrasted this music with brilliant piano virtuosity. Whereas Ludwig Rellstab heard in the "Abegg" Variations an idiosyncratic mix of postclassical convention and bewildering variation technique (see chapter 3), these writers made a much starker claim: that the music at hand rejected the pleasure and accessibility they expected in popular showpieces.

Though these writings often seem to draw sharp binaries, they fit into a more complex discourse. As we have seen in the past three chapters, Schumann himself took a nuanced view of the postclassical repertoire, and his critical and compositional approaches to virtuosity engaged with a wide range of strategies and ideals, including many rooted in postclassical pianism. The rhetoric in his and his critics' reviews did not signal a wholesale rejection of postclassical virtuosity or the aesthetic of pleasure; instead, they attempted to describe the sound and the cultural status of specific showpieces and performances (partly by contrasting them with more accessible virtuosity). Moreover, contemporary aestheticians recognized that the sublime did not truly negate pleasure but was itself a form of pleasure—one that inhered in sheer intensity and perceived exclusivity.

Despite the wealth of sources on the sublime and its application to music, my purpose here is not to argue whether Schumann's or any other composer's works evince what one might call a sublime style.[4] Just as I have been interpreting the category of serious virtuosity as an ideal that could be reinterpreted and negotiated, I view the sublime itself as a rhetorical strategy and an aspiration. In this case, my approach specifically takes into account an argument made by the late Wye J. Allanbrook—that, because the sublime was usually defined as a subjective experience, there is no sublime musical topic, no stable lexicon of stylistic elements we can identify as sublime independently of context.[5] Instead, I ask what aspects of this music critics recognized when they evoked the sublime and what claims they were staking in doing so.

This chapter not only explores a variety of musical transcendence that differs from poetic interiority: it also draws us into a different side of Schumann's piano-decade activities, specifically his relationships with some professional virtuosos. Liszt's Leipzig and Dresden concerts gave Schumann a long-awaited chance to hear the international star. Schumann dedicated the Toccata to his friend and fellow *Neue Zeitschrift* founder Ludwig Schuncke, the *Concert* to Ignaz Moscheles, and the *Études* to William Sterndale Bennett. Considering details of the first two works alongside contemporary critical discourse suggests that Schumann dedicated them not simply out of admiration, but because they resonated with aspects of their dedicatees' personae and public images.

To some extent, then, this chapter moves away from the domestic, amateur-friendly salon I explored in chapter 3 (one in which many significant participants were women) and edges toward a more professional, male-centric one. I do not mean to present this shift as straightforward. Public and private musical life and amateur and professional performance interpenetrated, and salon performance was open to both men and women (as was professional concertizing, to a lesser extent). Virtuoso showpieces themselves were often all-terrain musical vehicles. Performers could render concertos as solos, Liszt performed his opera fantasies in public concerts as well as Parisian salons, and Chopin's "Là ci darem la mano" Variations and Henselt's music inhabited public and private venues. Nor am I suggesting that the sublime was Schumann's default response to professional virtuosos—many of his writings on such figures describe other qualities and consider other issues. Even so, the rhetoric of the sublime figured prominently in Schumann's engagement with the star virtuosos I discuss here.

More broadly, these sources reveal a new side of the nineteenth-century preoccupation with the sublime. Musicological scholarship on this topic has focused on symphonic or large choral works.[6] Two of the most often-cited contemporary texts on the musical sublime are E. T. A. Hoffmann's 1813 essay on Beethoven's Fifth Symphony and Christian Friedrich Michaelis's 1805 essay that applies Kantian categories to symphonies by Haydn, Mozart, and Beethoven.[7] Outside of Liszt, the virtuoso sublime in the nineteenth century has received little attention. Scholars summarizing historical viewpoints, in fact, often emphasize sources that drew a boundary between virtuosity and the sublime. Mark Evan Bonds writes that, for eighteenth-century theorists, the concerto "could project a sound as forceful as that of the symphony" but "was never able to free itself entirely from the specter of empty virtuosity. Self-serving display was simply not consistent with the idea of the sublime."[8] Katharine Ellis has noted that Berlioz's writings often contrast the sublimity of Gluck and Cherubini with embellishment-laden salon music. When Berlioz turned to heavily embellished music by Paganini, Liszt, and Beethoven, he displayed what Ellis calls "critical unease." In some cases, he attempted to justify embellishment and in others regarded it as a weakness of otherwise admired artists.[9] Scholars have also generally stressed that writers used the rhetoric of the sublime to capture an affect—the sheer intensity of a Liszt concert, for example, or the "infinite longing" Hoffmann heard in Beethoven's Fifth Symphony.

In fact, Schumann and other writers invoked overpowering, unsettling sensations, heroic virtuosos, and Beethoven not merely to describe but to valorize. They used the rhetoric of the sublime to claim elevated cultural prestige for certain works or performances and to compliment listeners drawn to them. In some cases, these critics were attempting to counter the resistance they believed this music was inspiring or would inspire. The sublime, they claimed, turned virtuosity away from ease and pleasure and toward what they considered more serious, inaccessible categories.

The Rhetoric of the Sublime

The sublime differed from Schumann's concept of "poetic," an ideal that scholars frequently cite as a key to his music (see chapter 2). Whereas Schumann believed that poetic music embodied qualities of interiority, the sublime entailed overwhelming intensity.

Contemporary thinking about the sublime, however, was also part of Schumann's intellectual framework. Several authors he drew upon during the 1830s attempted to define and explicate the sublime: Jean Paul (in his *Vorschule der Aesthetik*), Friedrich Schlegel, Herder, and Hoffmann.[10] These sources emphasized the visceral intensity of sublime experience. Kant's influential works take a metaphysical approach to the sublime, arguing that the subject only experiences the sublime by cognitively mastering and transcending overwhelming experiences after the fact. By contrast, the writings closer to Schumann located sublimity within moments of intensity and overload themselves—in Hoffmann and Herder, within specifically musical moments. Herder illustrated the "auditory" sublime by describing musical passages of extraordinary disruptiveness or intensity. Hoffmann found the sublime not only in the ineffability of instrumental music but in the "monstrous," terrifying forces Beethoven unleashed. Jean Paul also took an auditory (not specifically musical) approach and described threatening or startling sounds as ideal catalysts of sublime experience. These views resonate with Robert R. Clewis's argument that the sublime is an affect: an experience so intense that it temporarily defies our ability to rationalize it.[11]

In his own critical writings, Schumann similarly stressed the immediate intensity of the sublime. He invoked the sublime most frequently in his essays on Beethoven symphonies. Florestan's 1835 Shrovetide speech, for example, compares a performance of the Ninth Symphony to shattering natural forces. The *Davidsbündler* describes speaking to his "trembling" neighbor about the finale's *Schreckensfanfare*. "Cantor, beware of storms," Florestan whispers. "Lightning sends no liveried servants before it strikes—at the most a storm in advance and then a thunderbolt." (To Florestan's irritation, the neighbor—apparently an old-fashioned church musician—makes pedantic objections rather than marveling: "But such dissonances must be prepared!"[12]) In 1841, Schumann described a Gewandhaus performance of Beethoven's Fifth: "[This symphony] wields its power unchanged over every age, just like many great phenomena of nature that, no matter how often they recur, fill us with fear and admiration."[13] Schumann's 1836 essay, "A Monument for Beethoven," described the transition between the third and fourth movements of the Fifth as a vertiginous glimpse of the immeasurable. "Not a breath," he wrote. "A thousand hearts hang by a hair over an unfathomable depth."[14] Schumann also drew upon the sublime's association with formidable, mighty individuals, as when Florestan compares the Ninth's first movement to "the entire, slowly striding majesty of a god."[15] At times, Schumann mingled the rhetoric of the sublime with images more associated with the poetic; in one passage of the Shrovetide speech, Eusebius ponders depths within Beethoven's very name.[16]

Alongside definitions of an affect, philosophies of the sublime provided frameworks for interpreting its cultural significance. Philip Shaw has noted that, as far back as Longinus, writers used discussions of the sublime to imagine that an artist could both overpower and inspire his audience, or to explain why listeners would embrace artworks that confronted them with violence and discomfort.[17] As writers explored such issues, the sublime, even if ostensibly an abstract philosophical concept, accrued an array of political agendas. Studies of the philosophical tradition have noted that Kant sympathetically identified the French Revolution as sublime. Both Nicholas Mathew and Sara Hibberd have recently explored instances of "sublime" music (by Beethoven and Cherubini, respectively) being used for political ends during the Congress of Vienna and after the French Revolution.[18]

More important for my argument is the politics of cultural status. During the nineteenth century, the sublime became one part of the vocabulary that elevated music's prestige among the arts and within society—or at least the prestige of certain works and performances. In this sense, it served a purpose similar to Schumann's concept of poetic interiority, even if its implications differed. For many writers, identifying a work, performance, or musician as sublime made a claim for seriousness and prestige. The sublime, in music or otherwise, supposedly appealed only to certain individuals. Kant, for example, insisted that only the educated man receptive to abstract ideas could contemplate the sublime.[19] Michaelis maintained that "frivolous, feeble, limited temperaments" could not appreciate sublime music, which spoke only to people of "spirit [Geist] and sensitivity, people of the noblest intellect."[20] Gustav Schilling's article, "Erhaben und Erhabenheit" (The Sublime and Sublimity), for his 1835 music encyclopedia similarly cautioned that listeners needed "powerful awareness" to appreciate the sublime.[21]

Even though writers claimed that the sublime denied the subject pleasing experiences in favor of fearsome, overwhelming, or even painful ones, they also acknowledged (in different ways) that the sublime offered its own form of pleasure. According to some of its acolytes, the sublime brought intellectual and spiritual ecstasy, a feeling that Kant called "enthusiasm" and that Schlegel and Hoffmann described as a longing for the infinite. Burke wrote that, when observed from a safe distance, dangerous and threatening phenomena can be "delightful."[22] (For Burke, "delight" differed from "pleasure"—the latter was consistently positive and pleasing, whereas the former embraced a more complex set of sensations.) Schumann's own essays on Beethoven describe a panoply of musical thrills and depict the Davidsbündler responding to them with admiration and ecstasy. The prestige that writers constructed for the sublime represented its own kind of pleasure—that of elitism, of perceived membership in a rarefied audience that claimed special intellectual and aesthetic sensibilities.

In the eighteenth- and nineteenth-century imagination, such delights turned the beholder toward lofty ideals and experiences. Joshua Rayman's study of Kant and morality summarizes, "The sublime affords us an egress from the sensuous world in which the beautiful would gladly hold us forever captive."[23] Although some writers pursued metaphysical considerations about transcending the physical world altogether, others discussed more concrete implications and described disregard for comfort and luxury as hallmarks of sublime affects and individuals. To cite one vivid example, Schiller allegorized the sublime using Odysseus's dalliance with the nymph Calypso: Calypso symbolized beauty and sensuality that ensnared the hero until the sublime, embodied in Mentor (Athena in disguise), inspired him to turn toward home, battle, and higher ideals.[24] Schiller's use of a goddess (appearing as a man) notwithstanding, writers usually considered the sublime a quintessentially masculine category and relegated women to the merely beautiful.[25] The rhetoric of the sublime, then, could freight music with qualities that included ennoblement, transcendence, intellectual sophistication and fortitude, and masculinity.

Schumann's readings on music exposed him to many instances in which critics invoked the sublime for this purpose. Some (such as Schilling and Michaelis) mentioned the sublime by name and cited philosophical writings. More often, writers described sensations and images that evoked the sublime but did not explicitly name the concept. This is particularly true of reviews that addressed specific compositions and performances: Hoffmann's and Schumann's Beethoven essays, for example, and the numerous reviews that ascribed sublime intensity to Liszt's virtuosity. Hoffmann's essay exemplifies the polemic work to which writers could put the rhetoric of the sublime. Hoffmann sought to convince doubting connoisseurs that Beethoven's symphonies were not disorganized bombast but, through their very intensity, ecstatic glimpses of the infinite. Such masterworks, he claimed, realized the full potential of instrumental music and won admiration only from sufficiently perceptive listeners. Hoffmann also set Beethoven's works above light, popular instrumental pieces. Alongside more philosophical sources, such reviews represented an important way in which Schumann encountered the rhetoric of the sublime.

Several of Schumann's own Beethoven essays used the rhetoric of the sublime for a complementary purpose. Schumann did not suggest that Beethoven needed defending, but he did claim that true appreciation of his music belonged to the few—specifically, the half-fictionalized *Davidsbündler*. Schumann repeatedly acknowledged that even Philistines could experience Beethoven's sublimity. Florestan's Cantor trembled, the Fifth's power extended "over every age," and the "Monument" essay suspended a "thousand hearts." However, he also asserted that most concertgoers could have only a limited understanding of Beethoven's sublime symphonies, one that stopped at superficial admiration or misguided attempts at interpretation. Florestan mocked uncomprehending listeners such as the Cantor. He also complained that audience members with (he alleged) a limited understanding of music were presumptuously claiming to understand Beethoven's precise meaning and to pass judgment on the symphony. "Do they really believe, when they smile and applaud, that they understand him who strove so, who struggled so in countless battles?" Florestan seethed. "They, who could not give me an explanation of the simplest musical rule, want to presume to judge a master overall?"[26] The "Monument for Beethoven" essay similarly contrasted the titanic greatness of Beethoven's music and persona with the shallow applause of the multitude. In both essays, Schumann avoids claiming that he himself holds the key to Beethoven's music, emphasizing only that the Beethovenian sublime was palpable for multitudes but held depths and heights beyond Philistine reach.

In Schumann's writings and reception, the rhetoric of the sublime also offered a powerful way for critics to portray unconventionally intense virtuosity as serious, elevated, and admirable. And, it offered a way to compliment audiences who embraced this music by describing them as an exclusive group attuned to ideals higher than pleasure and ease.

Schumann Promotes Liszt in Germany

Schumann used the rhetoric of the sublime for this purpose when he supported Franz Liszt during the virtuoso's March 1840 concerts in Leipzig and Dresden. As Gooley, Leppert, and Ellis have noted, Liszt's performances and compositions helped inspire his sublime image. Critics and caricaturists drew attention to his extravagant performing gestures. In Liszt's compositions themselves, simultaneous, frequently shifting layers of figuration seem to divide the pianist's body and persona between distinct gestures and affects. Climaxes often result when dense sonorities push the piano toward its maximum capacity for sound. In Gooley's evocative analysis, "The sheer quantity of information [Liszt] put forth was far beyond what audiences were accustomed to hearing and seeing at a virtuoso concert and exceeded what their minds could reasonably process. Listening to him was the aural equivalent of experiencing the sublime."[27]

Schumann generally located sublimity in Liszt's performances, or at least in the effects his showpieces produced onstage. His first published essay on Liszt, an 1839 review of the 1837 *Grandes études*, invokes this performative sublimity amid an ambivalent statement about Liszt's music. As Wolfgang Seibold and Leon Plantinga have noted, Schumann was critical of the *Études* as compositions.[28] He interpreted them as evidence that Liszt's development as a virtuoso had taken precedence over and hindered his development as a composer. Schumann even suggested that Liszt had become a prolific transcriber to compensate for his compositional deficiencies. (See chapter 5 for additional discussion of this essay and its presentation of Liszt as a composer.)

Near the end of his review, Schumann's perspective and implied value judgment changed, moving away from a critique of compositional technique to imagine the *Études* in performance: "To conduct a critique of them in the usual manner—picking out and correcting some parallel fifths and cross relations—would be a useless bother. One must hear such compositions—they were wrung from the instrument with the hands, and they must resound for us through the hands on the instrument."[29] Schumann described the etudes as sites of superhuman struggle and intensity, works that challenged players to harness and deliver titanic forces. His image of hands "wringing" the music from the instrument already suggests this quality. He continued, "These are etudes of storm and dread, etudes for at most ten or twelve [pianists] in the world; weaker players will only raise a laugh with them."[30] Schumann imagined Liszt himself struggling with and mastering forces almost beyond his control. Sound and visual spectacle, he maintained, were both important: "And, one must see the composer; for just as the appearance of every virtuosity elevates and strengthens, how much more so when we see the composer himself struggling with his instrument, subduing it, making it respond to his every tone."[31] Schumann, at this point, had never personally witnessed Liszt's playing, and the performances he describes are hypothetical. (He could have learned about Liszt's style from journalistic accounts or from Clara Wieck, who had encountered Liszt during her recent Vienna tour.) At the end of his review, Schumann reiterated his skepticism about the *Grandes études* but left open the possibility that Liszt's performance might make up for what he considered their compositional weaknesses. He eagerly awaited the day when Liszt would perform in Leipzig: "He himself will then give the best review of these works at the piano."[32]

Schumann's reviews of Liszt's Leipzig and Dresden concerts continued to depict the virtuoso using sublime imagery. Unlike the *Grandes études* review, Schumann's tone here was consistently positive, even effusive.[33] Schumann foregrounded Liszt's effect as a performer, both of his own works (including opera fantasies and Beethoven and Schubert transcriptions) and of music by other composers. Aware of the hype and controversy Liszt was generating, Schumann took one of his few trips on assignment for the *Neue Zeitschrift* and covered Liszt's March 16, 1840, Dresden performance and accompanied the virtuoso to Leipzig. In his Dresden report, Schumann wrote that a Liszt concert was an overpowering experience. The virtuoso possessed a "power to subjugate an audience to himself, to elevate it, carry it, and let it fall " (rather than charming or delighting it) unequaled by any artist save Paganini.[34] Schumann's review of Liszt's first Leipzig performance invoked the sublime's associations with human heroism: Liszt's playing was the "expression of an altogether daring character, to whom fate has given, in order to dominate and conquer, not dangerous tools [of war], but the peaceful ones of art."[35]

As the climax of the visit, Schumann singled out Liszt's performance of Carl Maria von Weber's *Konzertstück*, Op. 79, at his second concert. On this occasion, the audience probably heard Liszt's own version of the concerted showpiece. Liszt published an edition of the *Konzertstück* in 1883, replete with *ossia* parts and added solos. Reviews from the 1840s, as Gooley has shown, suggest that the later edition reflects the way Liszt customized the work during his touring years. Liszt turned Weber's postclassical figuration into dense, chordal passagework—single-line scales become double octaves, for example. The Weber itself had a widely recognized chivalric program in which a knight returns from the Crusades to his lady; in this context, Liszt's alterations accentuated the program's themes of peril, combat, and euphoric triumph. Liszt also added a cadenza to the opening and had the solo join the orchestra for its march-style climax—both touches, Gooley argues, encouraged audiences to identify Liszt with the story's knight.[36]

When he described the Leipzig *Konzertstück* performance, Schumann portrayed Liszt himself as a heroic, even superhuman virtuoso. Rather than evoking medieval scenes, he followed a common practice of comparing Liszt to Napoleon, in this case a Napoleon wreathed in the violent ecstasy of battle:

Just as Liszt grasped the piece straightaway with a strength and grandeur of expression, as if it was an attack on the battlefield, so he led it on, increasing from minute to minute up to that passage where he seemed to place himself at the head of the orchestra and exultantly led it himself. At this point, he indeed seemed to resemble the commander to whom we also compare him in outward appearance, and the applause for the performance was not unlike a *Vive l'Empereur* in its strength.[37]

The next day, Schumann wrote to Clara Wieck that Liszt had "played like a god" and inspired an "indescribable furor" of applause.[38] For Schumann, being conquered by Liszt was an occasion for ecstasy, trepidation, admiration, and awe.

Describing Liszt as a purveyor of sublime experience did not merely convey the style or intensity of his performances: it also made a polemical statement on his behalf. Liszt's efforts to build an audience in Germany initially met with resistance. Naysaying critics regarded him more as a bombastic entertainer than as a serious artist. Liszt suffered a disappointing initial reception in Leipzig. Audiences took offense at the exorbitant ticket prices he or his agents charged at the first concert, and he even annoyed Schumann by complaining about the dearth of local aristocracy.[39] Liszt's strategies for winning his audience over included performing canonic repertoire (notably Bach's Concerto in D Minor for three keyboards, BWV 1063), featuring works by local composers (including Schumann's *Carnaval*), and giving benefit concerts.[40]

To these strategies of image construction, I would add that Schumann used the rhetoric of the sublime to defend Liszt. Schumann and Liszt were often critical of one another's personalities and music. In his public statements about the Leipzig concerts, though, Schumann attempted to recuperate Liszt's image. Since the articles appeared several weeks after the Leipzig concerts, they did not attempt to rescue the performances immediately at hand as much as they addressed readers across Germany, where Liszt was continuing his conquests. What less sympathetic critics depicted as overhyped bombast, Schumann presented as sublime and worthy of admiration. In fact, he alleged that Liszt's detractors were simply not musically initiated enough to appreciate his virtuosity: Schumann acknowledged the controversy Liszt stimulated, but he maintained that "most voices, and especially all great artists" sided with the pianist.[41] The prestige Schumann extended to Liszt, then, redounded to his own journal and readers. For the listener willing to embrace Liszt's style of virtuosity, Schumann promised, the reward was the exhilarating feeling of being conquered by a heroic pianist who earned the admiration of an elite stratum of listeners.

The gendered rhetoric in these reviews clarifies Schumann's claim. Schumann's Liszt "struggled," "subjugated," and resembled a military hero. By contrast, as I showed in chapter 1, Schumann often used effeminizing imagery to denigrate the accessible pleasures that more typically brilliant showpieces offered: works by Kalkbrenner, Döhler, and early Thalberg, for example. His reviews included jabs at "countess pianists" who played "ingratiating" music that "more masculine players" would scorn, and he depicted Thalberg and Kalkbrenner as refined but sycophantic guests at a frivolous, aristocratic salon. As we saw, Schumann believed that poetic interiority redeemed (without negating) the sensuous pleasure of virtuosity.

Schumann presented sublime virtuosity as a different antidote—a hypermasculinized, bracing one. In addition to his imagery of domination and heroism, Schumann also portrayed Liszt as masculine by contrasting him with Thalberg. (The review thus sounded an echo of the Liszt–Thalberg rivalry that had played out in Paris three years before.) The Leipzig review quoted an unnamed Viennese artist's observation that, whereas Thalberg "resembled a handsome countess with a man's nose," Liszt "could sit for any painter as a model for a Greek god." Schumann added, "There is a similar difference between [Liszt's and Thalberg's] art."[42] Earlier in the review, Schumann had specifically likened Liszt to Jupiter, the most quintessentially sublime of the Olympians.[43] Such comparisons remained silent about aspects of Liszt's persona and practices that overlapped with Thalberg's, including his extensive aristocratic connections.[44] When read alongside his critique of postclassical pleasure, though, Schumann's reviews of Liszt urged readers to reject a style of virtuosity based on pleasure and accessibility and to embrace the difficult rewards of the sublime—qualities that Schumann categorized according to class and gender, using contemporary stereotypes to stigmatize one and valorize the other. He invited readers to brave Liszt's storms and conquests along with throngs of listeners and "great artists" rather than emulating vapid, pleasure-seeking countesses and attachés.

Virtuosic Peaks as Theme-Destabilizing Catastrophes: Schumann's *Concert sans Orchestre*

When contemporary critics used the rhetoric of the sublime to discuss Schumann's own showpieces, they made similar claims. They read these qualities not into a combination of stage presence and musical style. as Schumann did in his Liszt reviews, but into the formal and stylistic contexts in which these compositions presented virtuosic display. When writers on the *Concert* turned to the pyrotechnic finale, they often described sublime imagery and sensations, such as Seyfried's "booming cataract." (My discussion here concerns the 1836 published version of the *Concert*. In 1853, Schumann revised and republished the work as his Sonata No. 3.)

Some of the finale's relentless ferocity comes from its metrically dissonant virtuosic idiom. Schumann's opening, shown in example 4.2, is rife with what Harald Krebs has termed displacement dissonances.[45] Its salient motive shifts metric stress to the second sixteenth note of each measure so that clashes between the pianist's right and left hands pervade the opening. Ends of phrases push the accent deeper into the measure, and the subsequent transition settles into a metrically dissonant groove. The *presto possibile* marking adds to the sense of barely controlled momentum by asking the pianist to play—or to give the impression of playing—at the limit of human capability. The *Concert* finale itself frequently returns to such figuration throughout more than six hundred measures of perpetual motion.

Writers also suggested that the finale's idiosyncratic formal structure contributed to the impression of overwhelming force. After likening the movement to a raging waterfall, Seyfried continued, "It is one, single phrase characterizing the

Example 4.2. *Concert sans orchestre*, movement 3. Opening. ("X" in figure 4.1.)

phenomenon of this powerful breaking wave, which, although occurring in shadowy gradations, nonetheless never stops."[46] Wilhelm Joseph von Wasielewski's 1858 biography of Schumann also evoked violent nature when discussing the finale. His account called attention to the listener's subjective experience. The third movement takes up the "heaven storming" character of the first, he writes, only this time, "a second, calming element scarcely becomes noticeable. Rather, everything drives to the close in an incessant storm, as if in desperation. In such form, it offers no resting point. The enjoyer is torn away without being able to come to his senses—in the end, the sensation is thrust on him of being thrown into a sea of tones whose waves break repeatedly over his head."[47]

Both writers did exaggerate for poetic effect: Schumann introduces several contrasting, "calming" subjects, and the finale does not literally consist of a single, unbroken phrase. However, their descriptions capture some of the most striking structural features of the movement. Figure 4.1 charts this form—the theme from example 4.2 is labeled X. Linda Roesner has described the finale as one of what she calls Schumann's "parallel forms."[48] That is, it rotates twice through the same sequence of themes, the second time transposing themes other than X up a fifth. Seyfried and Wasielewski, though, draw our attention not to the movement's larger parallelism but to the details of how Schumann moves between themes and sections. As both writers suggest, Schumann continually offers but denies the listener relief from the opening. The finale introduces two lyrical themes, marked Y and Z in the figure. Each time, material based on the turbulent opening and transition interrupts and replaces them.

Schumann presents virtuosity as the agent of this ongoing disruption—metrically dissonant passagework intrudes upon, destabilizes, and submerges the lyrical themes. Whereas Czerny had described the alternation of lyricism and virtuosity as a means of guaranteeing the listener's pleasure, Schumann turns such an alternation into a process Seyfried and Wasielewski likened to mighty waves breaking through all resistance or submerging the listener. The disruption is both affective and tonal: each lyrical theme begins in a secondary key preceded by dominant preparation, but each digresses from its local tonic and back into the roiling virtuosity without having reached a firm cadence. We are left with a series of thwarted themes and modulations, musical collapses that the second half of the finale only reiterates and in some cases intensifies.[49]

The theme marked Y introduces this strategy, as shown in example 4.3. It opens with several evenly proportioned, metrically consonant phrases in the Neapolitan. However, this stability begins to collapse when the theme moves toward C minor and when figuration based on the transition interrupts the phrase and drags the finale briefly back to F minor. Theme Z, a series of descending, sequentially structured phrases, features a somewhat less abrupt disruption. In its second appearance (marked Z2), the final phrase completes only its first two measures and moves into a transition based on its own motive. After only eight measures, the transition gives way to a different, metrically dissonant transition based on theme X.

First thematic rotation

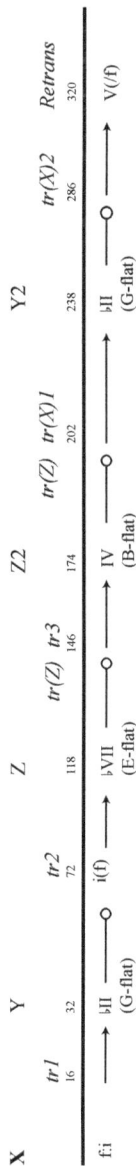

X	Y		Z		Z2			Y2		Retrans
	tr1	tr2		tr(Z) tr3		tr(Z) tr(X)1			tr(X)2	
	16	72	118	146	174	202		238	286	320

f:i ——○——→ i(f) ——○——→ ♭VII ——○——→ IV ——○——→ ♭II ——○——→ V(/f)
      (G-flat)   (E-flat)   (B-flat)   (G-flat)

Second, parallel thematic rotation

X	Y		Z		Z2			Y2		Retrans, Cadenza
	tr1	tr2		tr(Z) tr3		tr(Z) tr(X)1			tr(X)2	
	348	403	449	477	533	569		620	286	641

f:i ——○——→ i(f) ——○——→ IV ——○——→ I ——○——→ VI ——○——→ V(/f)
      (D-flat)   (B-flat)   (F)   (D-flat)

Coda

X	Coda
650	662

f:i ——○—— F:I

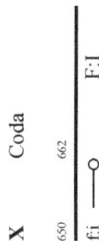

tr = transition (based on material introduced in m. 16)
tr(X) = transition based on X
tr(Z) = transition based on Z
Retrans = retransition
——— = disrupted theme or transition
——○ = disrupted theme or transition

Figure 4.1. *Concert sans orchestre*, movement 3. Formal outline.

Example 4.3. *Concert sans orchestre*, movement 3. Theme Y.

The most intense virtuosic catastrophes occur at the hinges of the parallel form. As shown in example 4.4, Schumann reintroduces theme Y and extends it for an additional twenty measures. Yet another transitional variant of X interrupts, here intruding upon the last measure of its final phrase. This transition leads to a dominant pedal at measure 312: after several hundred measures of thwarted themes and suggested-but-not-confirmed secondary keys, the movement finally

Example 4.3. (continued)

hurtles toward a recapitulation and a strong arrival on tonic. The tempo increases to Vivacissimo and then to Più presto, creating the impression that the performer has somehow pushed beyond maximum velocity. As a series of chords cascades toward the recapitulation, Schumann suddenly deploys the most radical metric dissonance of the *Concert* when the meter changes from 6/16 to 5/16. In this context, compressing the measure into an asymmetrical shape scripts a headlong acceleration more than it creates a perceptible friction against the established

Example 4.4. *Concert sans orchestre*, movement 3. Retransition.

Example 4.4. (continued)

meter. Dominant preparation itself seems to unravel when, instead of resolving a vii°⁶ᐟ⁵/V to V in measure 328, Schumann hammers the diminished harmony against the lone C, engulfing the dominant with dissonance. Theme X returns, only to initiate a parallel sequence of interrupted themes. The analogous moment immediately before the coda—the aforementioned clangorous cadenza— intensifies the dissonance. In the final stages of the finale, Schumann uses metrically dissonant virtuosity to overwhelm theme X itself. In the last return of the theme, the antecedent phrase of its second period hangs unresolved and gives way to the coda. During the coda, the main motive of X intrudes in the bass but is swallowed by arpeggios that establish F *major*, a redirection that Seyfried likened to "a meteoric appearance."[50]

Reviewers claimed that the *Concert sans orchestre* was not merely shocking but transcended the pleasurable brilliance that more accessible showpieces offered. Seyfried, for example, described Schumann as a "priest of art," a "spirit directed only toward the important and dignified."[51] Ignaz Moscheles and Franz Liszt made similar claims that centered on the work's ambiguous generic identity. The oxymoronic title of the *Concert* is misleading: it resembles a three-movement sonata with few if any concerto-like features. Schumann initially sought to publish the work as a sonata with four or five movements but, early in 1836, decided to include only three movements and title it a concerto.[52]

Both composer and publisher might have appealed to the concerto genre instead of the old-fashioned sonata to give the work an air of modernity. Haslinger suggested this motivation in a June 13, 1836, letter to Schumann. "I regard your idea for the *Concert* as very appropriate for the times (with which one must always move)," he wrote.[53] Seyfried interpreted the title as a marketing ploy: "The designation was most likely chosen for the sufficient reason that the very title 'Sonata' today belongs to the category of scorned items with which even a hungry smuggler would barely want to occupy himself."[54]

Liszt and Moscheles, though, took the title as an invitation to contrast Schumann's *Concert* with more conventionally brilliant concertos. Both recognized that the work closely resembled a large sonata. However, they focused more attention on affect than on genre. Schumann's showpiece, they wrote, denied listeners accessible, brilliant pleasures. For them, the *Concert* only appealed to knowledgeable, serious listeners ready to grapple with its complexity and abrasiveness. They made this argument by drawing attention to the finale's inaccessible, unsettling, even shocking features.

Schumann had probably been hoping for such a review from Moscheles. Dedicating the *Concert* to Moscheles marked a high point in Schumann's long-standing admiration for the older pianist-composer. As we have seen, he performed Moscheles's "Alexander" Variations during his years as an aspiring pianist and briefly planned on studying with him in Vienna. Schumann finally met one of his piano idols when Moscheles gave a concert in Leipzig on October 9, 1835. After Moscheles returned to London, Schumann corresponded with him. He wrote in March 1836 asking permission to dedicate the *Concert* and followed with several requests for Moscheles's latest scores. Schumann gave generally positive reviews to Moscheles's piano, chamber, and orchestral works.

Around the time when Schumann was writing the *Concert*, he was specifically touting Moscheles as a virtuoso-composer who had recently rejected an aesthetic of pleasure. In 1835 and 1836, he reviewed Moscheles's Leipzig concert as well as his three latest piano concertos: Nos. 5, 6 ("Fantastique"), and 7 ("Pathétique"). Schumann recounted that, during the 1810s, Moscheles's music (such as the "Alexander" Variations) reflected a time when "the word 'brilliant' gained momentum and legions of girls fell in love with Czerny." However, he claimed that the 1830s were seeing a new Moscheles who wrote music in a more "Romantic" vein suffused with a "magical, murky light."[55] As Claudia Macdonald has noted, Schumann singled out the somber orchestration and unusual key of Concerto No. 5's slow movement (E minor in a C-major concerto) and the close interaction of piano and orchestra throughout the latter two works. He probably also noticed other striking features of the concertos. The "Fantastique" incorporates wide-ranging tonal contrasts, for example, and the culminating displays of the "Pathétique" move through expansive phrase structures.[56]

For Schumann, these works showed that Moscheles had renounced his former desire to please a broad public. In his review of Moscheles's Leipzig concert, he wrote of his latest works, "Now he enters darker, more mysterious paths, unconcerned with whether this will please a large audience as he did before."[57] Schumann reiterated his point when he reviewed the "Pathétique" concerto in 1839. "This time Moscheles renounces popularity right from the start. The concerto is titled 'Pathétique,' and so it is—what do 99 out of 100 virtuosos care about that!"[58] Schumann's 1835 and 1836 Moscheles reviews preceded and overlapped with the genesis of his *Concert*. He never described Moscheles's virtuosity as awe-inducing or heroic, as he did with Liszt's, or as shocking or overpowering, as other critics did with the *Concert*. Schumann's reviews, however, do suggest that he dedicated the *Concert* not simply out of admiration, but because he believed that his showpiece would resonate with Moscheles or bear comparison with his recent concertos.

Moscheles returned the compliment. He discussed the *Concert* in a December 20, 1836 letter to Schumann, and Schumann printed a substantial excerpt in the *Neue Zeitschrift* on February 24, 1837. Moscheles favorably contrasted the work with conventional concertos and their accessible, transparent sounds. He described the *Concert*'s effect as a nearly unpleasant feeling of being shattered or shocked:

> In concertos, one is (unfortunately) used to seeing, alongside unity in style,
> consideration taken for glittering bravura or coquettish elegance, which could find
> no place in this work. The seriousness and passion that pervade it stand very much
> in opposition to what a concert audience of today expects. For one thing, it doesn't
> want to be deeply shaken [*tief erschüttert*].

Moscheles reserved the piece for listeners steeped in inaccessible, complex music. The typical concert audience, he claimed, "lacks the aptitude and musical dedication to understand and grasp such harmonies and ingenious interlacings, which is only possible for ears and dispositions experienced in the higher speech of the heroes of art."[59] Moscheles's gendered rhetoric is not as heavy-handed as that in Schumann's Liszt reviews, but it made a similar point about pleasure, seriousness, prestige, masculinity, and "deeply shaking" musical experiences. Schumann's *Concert*, for Moscheles, rejected a style he feminized as "coquetry" and instead shared an exalted plane with artistic "heroes."

Liszt's made similar claims about the *Concert* without Schumann's prodding. Liszt discussed the *Concert* in an 1837 essay on Schumann's piano music for the *Revue et Gazette musicale*. (He also commented on the Impromptus Op. 5 and Sonata No. 1, Op. 11.) Liszt even suggested that the title of the *Concert* was misleading, not because of its form but because it forwent brilliant textures and an accessible style: "It is an error, we think, for him to give it a title that seems to appeal to a large number of listeners and promises a brightness for which one will search in vain."[60] He described the finale as a "sort of toccata" with "harmonic combinations whose strangeness, even without the excessively rapid tempo, could nevertheless shock the ear a bit."[61] Liszt placed the *Concert* and Schumann's other works within a category of music "that the shadow envelops for a long time, whose veiled beauties only reveal themselves to the attentive eye of one who searches with love and perseverance but in front of which the crowd passes *unaware* and distracted."[62]

These remarks might seem ambivalent, but Liszt presented them as compliments. He wrote that, by categorizing Schumann's works as he did, he was differentiating them from music that achieves fast popularity but remains ephemeral, forgotten by posterity. (Liszt acknowledged a third category that achieved universal recognition and critical acclaim, but he demurred that critical discussion of such music is superfluous.) Liszt maintained that, though Schumann's music hardly seemed destined for popular success, "there is not an elevated intellect who would not perceive, at first glance, its superior value and rare beauties."[63] Liszt seems to contradict himself by first describing a persistent analyst and then one who perceives value immediately. What his statements share is the claim that Schumann's admirable qualities were apparent to listeners whose understanding surpassed the "crowd's." He also encouraged younger pianists to profit by Schumann's example as a representative of a musical style that "encounters much opposition among us" but "today is the only one that contains the seeds of longevity."[64] Liszt's review delighted Schumann. After reading it, he wrote to Clara Wieck, "By the way, Liszt has written a large, very just article about me in the French journal. . . . He has greatly pleased and surprised me with the essay." Two years later, he wrote to Ernst A. Becker that Liszt's essay was one of "the best things written about me, as far as I can judge."[65]

Like Schumann's reviews of Liszt's Leipzig concerts, both Liszt's and Moscheles's writings on the *Concert* reveal acts of self-positioning—in the case of Moscheles's remarks, from Schumann himself. Schumann opted not to print portions of the letter that offered a more ambivalent evaluation of the *Concert*. Moscheles believed that the finale's relentlessness went too far. "I wished for somewhat more contrast to the billowing rhythm, in which different elements merge into one," he wrote. "Take these critical remarks only to mean that, alongside the many beauties of this movement, I do not welcome the things that stand out too stridently or that would be just as inspired [*geistreich*] with somewhat more polished harmony."[66] Schumann did not quote these admonitions. Though Schumann did not generally review his own compositions, the *Zeitschrift* occasionally published reviews of his music by other critics. His decision to publish and tailor Moscheles's letter was one case in which he influenced the journal's evaluation of his music: it might even suggest the way he himself wished the *Concert* to be heard.[67] When Moscheles's remarks appeared in print, they seemed to describe the entire *Concert*, and they presented its propensity to "deeply shake" the listener as unequivocally positive—a turn away from frivolity rather than a hazardous experiment with discordant virtuosity. Schumann appended to Moscheles's remarks his own exhortation, striking a modest tone yet framing the letter as high praise: "Florestan and Eusebius, make yourselves worthy of such a favorable judgment."[68] Schumann's editing illustrates that, in the realm of music criticism, the distinction between strident bombast and thrilling sublimity depended on the beholder's value judgment.

Liszt's appraisal of Schumann also reflected back on him. The review followed on the heels of Liszt's contest with Thalberg. During the rivalry, Liszt had published music-critical essays with an eye toward bolstering his own legitimacy, including one that savaged Thalberg.[69] As Liszt explained to Wasielewski, he later decided to change his tone and publish a positive review of some new piano music.[70] Despite its generally admiring tone, his Schumann essay fulfilled the same purpose as his earlier writings by presenting Liszt as an authoritative standard-bearer of serious taste. Liszt implicitly included himself among the "elevated intellects" able to appreciate Schumann and suggested that he, too, embraced an embattled musical style that promised longevity. In Liszt's and other responses to the *Concert*, the rhetoric of the sublime and the denial of pleasurable brilliance served multiple interrelated purposes: describing and valorizing a style of music, defining a rarefied audience for it, and positioning the critic himself as one such listener.

Virtuosic Peaks within Beethovenian Narratives

Schumann's Toccata and *Études symphoniques* invoked the sublime in a more allusive way. Critics compared both pieces to Beethoven, claiming that they absorbed some of Beethoven's loftiness and thereby distanced themselves from popular virtuosity. In different ways, both showpieces evoke Beethoven's "heroic," middle-period symphonies, specifically the "Eroica." They thereby referred to music whose extremes of musical tension (even violence), apotheosis culminations, and (especially in the "Eroica") implied narratives of masculine heroism embodied the sublime for its enthusiasts.[71] Schumann was hardly alone in using Beethoven to present virtuosity as serious or elevated. Liszt, for example, published transcriptions of all nine Beethoven symphonies. As Jonathan Kregor has shown, they attempt to capture every detail of Beethoven's orchestration and "require a skill of execution tantamount to the exaggerated stature of the composer Beethoven."[72] As we saw in chapter 2, Clara Wieck established herself as a Beethoven interpreter beginning in the mid-1830s. In Schumann's showpieces, Beethoven's music does not offer material for performance or transcription but models for largely original virtuosic showpieces.

Ernst Ortlepp explicitly presented the Toccata as evidence that the young composer embraced ideals higher than popularity and accessibility: "He will certainly reach, as he goes, a very different goal than that of fashionable composition, which contains no higher thought than to make every morsel bite-sized for the people."[73] Not that the Toccata rejects postclassical keyboard styles. The piece is based on perpetual-motion double notes, a standard postclassical figuration. Numerous nineteenth-century etudes (such as Johann Baptiste Cramer's) showcase such passagework, as do various piano works by Hummel and several sonata-form showpieces titled "Toccata." Schumann had studied one of the latter, Czerny's Toccata Op. 92, under Friedrich Wieck. His own Toccata went through at least one preliminary version, and one title he considered, *Etude fantastique en double sons*, links it to this subcategory of piano piece.[74]

For Ortlepp and other critics, the sheer difficulty of the Toccata contributed to its lofty inaccessibility. Some mentioned performances by Ludwig Schuncke, the showpiece's dedicatee, when describing this aspect of the showpiece. Unlike Moscheles and Liszt, Schuncke was an up-and-coming virtuoso rather than an international icon. Hailing from a Stuttgart family of musicians, he had concertized throughout Germany and resided in Paris between 1827 and 1830. He and Schumann met in Leipzig in late 1833, became close friends, and shared an apartment between March 1834 and Schuncke's death from tuberculosis in December of that year.[75] Schuncke wrote reviews of virtuosic piano pieces for the *Neue Zeitschrift* that complemented Schumann's. (These include a derisive review of Kalkbrenner's *Variations sur une mazourka de Chopin*, Op. 120.[76])

Schumann and other critics presented Schuncke as a virtuoso who boasted a powerful, athletic stage presence and could master Herculean pianistic challenges. Ortlepp wrote that, in Leipzig, the only pianists who could handle the Toccata were Schuncke and Clara Wieck. In 1835, the *Musikalischer Anzeiger* described the Toccata's difficulty in terms of masculine daring and prowess (the fourteen-year-old Wieck's performance notwithstanding). The Toccata presented a "gigantic task" to which Schuncke, a "matador of the piano" had been equal. Other pianists were encouraged to try but should be prepared to fall short:

> But, whoever does not feel equal athletic strength within himself and is not ensnared by arrogant vanity should in no way consider beneath his dignity to attempt it—*quid valent humeri, aut quid ferre recusant* [(Consider well) what weight your shoulders can and cannot bear]. Such a person never again dares to and instead continues down his own street quietly and with due reverence, thinking, *non omnia possumus omnes* [None of us is capable of everything] to console himself.[77]

After Schuncke's death, Schumann published several essays on his friend's music. They eulogize the young virtuoso with a hint of sublime imagery—one passage describes him "flying over the keys like an eagle and with Jupiter's lightning bolts." In his 1840 Liszt reviews, Schumann likened Liszt's playing and appearance to Schuncke's.[78]

Ortlepp also hinted at sublimity written into the Toccata's very style. John Daverio pointed out that, by comparing Schumann to Bach, Paganini, and Beethoven, the critic was pointing out salient features of the Toccata—its motoric virtuosity, for example, and its intricate counterpoint. Daverio suggested that the Beethoven mention commends the full-fledged sonata form.[79] I would argue that Ortlepp's comparison also recognized some finer details of the Toccata: the critic knew his Beethoven well and wrote a quasi-fictional book on the composer in 1836.[80] At crucial junctures, Schumann's Toccata blends virtuosic figuration with some signature elements of the first movement of Beethoven's "Eroica" and Beethoven's middle-period, "heroic" style more generally.[81]

This connection, heretofore unrecognized, fits into a larger pattern of Beethoven citation in Schumann's 1830s works. Between 1832 and 1835, Schumann wrote a set of unpublished etudes based on the second movement of Beethoven's Seventh Symphony, his *Etüden in Form freier Variationen über ein Beethovensches Thema*. (Nicholas Marston notes that the final variation also quotes the first movement of the Seventh Symphony and alludes to the first movement of the Ninth.[82]) The Fantasie Op. 17 contains what many scholars hear as a quotation of "An die ferne Geliebte." In several cases, Schumann turned specifically to the "Eroica" Symphony and the related "Eroica" Variations, Op. 35.[83] His Impromptus are modeled on the latter work. In Schumann's own review of his Opus 10 Paganini transcriptions, he imagined a combination of the Beethovenian and the Paganinian when he wrote that, while working on the fourth etude (based on Paganini's Caprice No. 4), "I had a notion of the funeral march from the heroic symphony by Beethoven. Perhaps one will find it himself."[84] Paganini's and Beethoven's opening phrases indeed follow a similar contour. Though the melodic echo in the violin caprice itself was probably coincidental, Schumann's transcription adds open fifths in the bass that lend the piece an air of funereal gravity and strengthen the proposed allusion. Finally, the first movement of Schumann's unpublished Symphony in G Minor—which he worked on concurrently with the Toccata—contains passages Marston has shown to be influenced by the "Eroica" first movement itself.[85]

The Toccata also documents the young Schumann's Beethoven obsession. Its most pointed reference to the "Eroica" occurs at the retransition from development to recapitulation, shown in example 4.5. Octave passagework from the first half of the development turns into a double fugato on a syncopated subject. Stretto entries accumulate, and textural complexity reaches a maximum in measure 142, where the syncopated rhythm persists in the dovetailing contrapuntal lines. Immediately before the recapitulation, this rhythm takes over when the retransition suddenly breaks into syncopated chords. Though the harmonies are simply dominant sevenths, Schumann accentuates their inherent dissonance by giving the right hand double tritones and placing the chord in second inversion. This retransition mirrors one of the most often-remarked upon passages of the "Eroica." A fugato—whose subject uses a syncopated rhythm similar to Schumann's—begins

Example 4.5. Schumann, Toccata Op. 7. Retransition.

Example 4.6. Toccata. Opening (excerpts).

in Beethoven's development, but, as in the Toccata, metrically and harmonically dissonant chords grow out of the subject itself and engulf the texture. Schumann did give his fugato a different function within the Toccata's sonata form. Nineteenth-century programmatic readings of the "Eroica" often described this moment as a catastrophic collapse from which the development gradually recovers.[86] Schumann's fugato devolves into hammered-out chords that prepare for a climactic moment of tonal resolution and thematic reprise. However, both works use counterpoint overwhelmed by metric and harmonic dissonance to mark a turning point in their development sections.

Other passages of the Toccata employ structural aspects of the "Eroica" first movement and heroic Beethoven. Schumann's opening gesture, shown in example 4.6, evokes an orchestral tutti more than it does a pianistic flourish. Its brusqueness has a similar effect to the two orchestral hammer blows that open Beethoven's symphony. As Joel Lester has noted, the motto's syncopated rhythm and built-in half-step and neighbor-note figures anticipate the syncopated bass and salient motives of the first theme group—much, I would add, as Beethoven's chords contain the seeds of the "Eroica" first theme.[87] The bravura double notes become part of a Beethovenian argument in which the exposition's thematic material grows from a concise motive, one which itself begs interpretation as a heroic gesture.[88] Schumann's figuration echoes the call to action with densely chordal fanfares in measure 22.

The Toccata adopts Beethovenian formal proportions in some respects. The work is an "Eroica" among double-note showpieces: weighing in at 378 measures (counting repeats), it is more than twice as long as Czerny's Toccata. The expansive coda consumes approximately a fifth of these measures, a share of the sonata form comparable to the "Eroica" coda. Though nineteenth-century commentators regarded the "Eroica's" climactic coda as one of its most important features (and often situated it within the implied heroic narrative), summarizing codas are common in Beethoven's works and, indeed, in post-Beethovenian instrumental music.[89] The Toccata's coda does resemble the first stage of the "Eroica's." It presents a climactic apotheosis of the first theme group's defining motive, reworking it to consume one measure, stringing together iterations of this shortened version, and making them reverberate across the keyboard. Regardless of whether Schumann had such a specific model in mind for this section, his coda presents the Toccata's crowning pyrotechnics as a bracing peroration that channels the sublime climaxes of heroic symphonies rather than the transparent brilliance Czerny and Fink described as generators of pleasure and refreshment. At the start of the coda, the texture at once thickens and simplifies, the contrapuntal lines snapping together as bounding chords and relentlessly driving double stops. The first theme group's motive unequivocally confirms the tonic even as Schumann increases its metrically dissonant momentum. At the climax of the coda, the pianist's hands alternate dense, four-voiced chords, bounding toward one another from opposite ends of the keyboard.

It would be misleading to map the entire "Eroica" narrative onto the Toccata. Unlike the symphony, the showpiece features few moments that suggest the danger of musically expressed defeat. The Toccata presents no analogues for other striking features of the "Eroica" that drew the attention of contemporary commentators: the premature horn call before the recapitulation, for example, or the ostensibly new theme in the development.[90] Schumann's coda fades to a *piano* at the last minute, the climactic double stops reduced to murmuring, gently syncopated accompaniment. In the end, the Toccata demurs from Beethovenian climax and turns inward.

Nevertheless, Schumann's Toccata does create a Beethovenian process in moments evocative of heroic entrances, the overwhelming massing of metric and harmonic tension, and prolonged, triumphant apotheoses. Jean Paul's *Vorschule*, arguing for a flexible definition of the sublime, proposed that Jupiter's mere eyebrows could hint at the god's thunderbolt and hence convey his full sublimity.[91] Similarly, these signature moments, even if presented within a seven-minute concert etude, lent Schumann's showpiece an aura of sublimity, grandeur, and heroism. By incorporating them into his Toccata, Schumann presented virtuosity both as heroically difficult and as part of a Beethovenian trajectory of striving and apotheosis. In the Toccata, the deeds of a seemingly superhuman virtuoso (such as Schuncke) found their reflection in the showpiece's design.

For Schuncke, the Toccata complemented his compositional as well as his performing persona: he shared Schumann's penchant for modeling keyboard works on Beethoven. In a review of Schuncke's 1833 Allegro Passionato Op. 6, for example, Gottfried Wilhelm Fink described him "stepping into Beethoven's realm and following this hero's example in form."[92] Fink specifically referred to the

Allegro's motivic unity. He might also have recognized that Schuncke recalls motives from the slow introduction during the main body of the movement, a gambit with several Beethovenian precedents, notably the first movement of the "Pathétique" Sonata. In one of his eulogizing reviews of Schuncke, Schumann recalled hearing his friend's Caprice No. 2, Op. 10, and suggesting that he subtitle it "Beethoven, scène dramatique." He qualified that the title was partly a joke and that the piece captured only "a small dark line on Beethoven's brow."[93] His jest, however, recognized that the Caprice featured a turbulent affect and suspenseful, rhetorical pauses reminiscent of Beethoven's minor-key sonatas.[94] Schuncke dedicated to Schumann his most ambitious work, his Sonata Op. 3. Leon Plantinga, Joachim Draheim, and Ruskin King Cooper hear echoes of Beethoven in the work's expansive, tightly organized form and the scherzo's resemblance to that of the Ninth Symphony.[95] The fugato-coda of Schuncke's first movement might draw upon Beethoven's late sonatas, such as the "Hammerklavier." Schumann apparently dedicated his Beethoven-citing Toccata to Schuncke to return the honor.[96]

For Schumann himself, the Beethoven-ized Toccata made an ambitious statement about his own professional identity. During the early 1830s, Schumann was shaking off his local reputation as an aspiring virtuoso and attempting to define himself primarily as a composer. Shortly after resigning himself to his hand injury, for example, he had the first movement of his unfinished, partly Beethoven-based G-minor symphony premiered in 1832. The only preliminary version of the Toccata to survive in its entirety is titled *Exercice* and preserved in an autograph fair copy. Gooley has argued that the *Exercice* shows signs of having developed from Schumann's improvisations and that the Toccata's sharply chiseled sonata form distanced the composer from spontaneous creation at the keyboard and asserted his skill at designing large, traditional forms.[97] The Beethovenian elements of the Toccata—which do not appear in the *Exercice*—also supported Schumann's self-redefinition. In addition to making the Toccata echo with the voice of the archetypal "great" composer, they aligned Schumann with the Beethovenian sublime and its aura of transcendence, power, and cultural prestige. The Toccata evoked a composer whose music, Schumann would claim in his reviews, enjoyed near-universal admiration but remained beyond Philistine comprehension. To paraphrase Schiller's Homeric allegory, Beethoven (rather than Mentor) drew the ex-virtuoso and his showpiece away from "mere" pleasure and toward loftier values.

Schumann's *Études symphoniques* does not cite signature Beethoven passages as the Toccata does. Nevertheless, one of the most substantial contemporary reviews of the *Études* invoked Beethoven to explain the work's mixture of genres: etude, variation set, and a "symphonic" element. In his 1837 essay for the *Neue Zeitschrift*, Carl Ferdinand Becker imagined a dialogue between six fictional speakers, five of whom struggle to understand the piece. The first expresses confusion that a set of variations should be titled "etudes." Two others pedantically criticize Schumann's use of a D-flat-major finale for a C-sharp-minor piece and his supposed failure to follow Marpurg's rules of counterpoint. A speaker to whom

Becker attributes an "intelligent expression" strikes a more sympathetic tone and attempts to elucidate the work by comparing it to a symphony, specifically the "Eroica" finale. "I regard the whole piece as nothing other than the last movement of a symphony for piano and hope that I have hit the nail on the head," he says. "Haven't you noticed that everything grows bit by bit until the actual finale breaks through and moves forward in a flood? If these are etudes or variations, then the finale of Beethoven's 'Eroica' is also nothing more."[98]

Becker points out the variation set's continuous buildup of intensity and breakthrough finale. When Schumann transformed the unpublished *Fantaisies et finale* (discussed in chapter 3) into the *Études*, he reordered the variations, omitted six, and composed six new ones. Gone are the fleeting intervariation links and sharp contrasts of style that characterized the *Fantaisies*—the new showpiece moves forward with inexorable, constant momentum. Variations fill in the theme's opening arpeggio with increasing density, and tempos gradually become more driving. Especially after Etude IV, the variations employ textures that nineteenth-century and present-day commentators often describe as orchestral.[99] Bereft of the ornamented, transparent passagework that gave the postclassical style its brilliant sound, they present richly doubled figuration and showcase muscular, full-fisted playing. The finale—whose rondo form is one of the set's few postclassical features—crowns the work with leaping chords and octaves. Transitions between some variations abet the buildup, and a network of secondary keys adds a tonal arc that resolves only with the finale. (Etude III ends on the mediant, Etude VII is entirely in the mediant, and Etude XI is in the minor dominant.) Compared to the *Fantaisies*, the *Études* presents a more goal-directed, linear version of the path from "funeral march" to "victory procession" that Schumann hoped to create.

The *Études* also wears a more professional, public face. Whereas the full title of the *Fantaisies* acknowledged that Baron Ignaz von Fricken had composed the theme, the *Études* relegates this information to a footnote and does not even name him: the theme, it reads, was "composed by an amateur." And, whereas Schumann had dedicated the *Fantaisies* to the Baroness von Fricken, the *Études* went to William Sterndale Bennett (who admired the work but never seems to have performed it publicly).[100] Music-lovers could of course enjoy "symphonic" music at home through piano transcriptions. Schumann, however, discarded the aspects of the *Fantaisies* that most clearly evoked domestic music: its ornamented, waltz-like variations. The new title instead evoked the genre that was becoming the flagship of public orchestral concerts and the ultimate test of a composer's craft and ambition. Indeed, the change of titles removes any reference to improvisation. It asks the listener not to imagine spontaneous, intimate piano performance but architecture crafted by a symphonic composer.

Becker compared this new work not to brilliant, postclassical showpieces but to the "Eroica's" variation-based finale. He does not necessarily make an argument about compositional intent: rather than explicitly proposing that the *Études* is based on the "Eroica" finale, he offers a more general claim that that they similarly transcend the status of conventional variations or etudes. No documentary evidence acknowledges that Schumann turned to the symphony when composing the *Études*. Structural commonalities between the works, however, do leave open the possibility that the "Eroica" finale—easily one of the best known set of symphonic variations in 1837—provided a model for some aspects of Schumann's own "symphonic" showpiece. Beethoven's finale mingles traditional variations with freer approaches to the theme (including extensive development sections) and presents variations in several nontonic keys. In Michael Broyles's account, it combines the incremental intensification characteristic of the variation genre with a more sonata-like process of tonal resolution.[101] The same could be said of the *Études*, though they do not use free development sections and feature a smaller palette of tonalities. (Two variations, Etudes VII and IX, do depart significantly from the phraseological structure of the theme.) As I noted in chapter 3, Schumann's statement about funeral marches and victory celebrations is suggestive, since contemporary critics often read such images into the second and fourth movements of the "Eroica." In any case, more important for my argument is Becker's larger claim: that Schumann's piece belonged in a more prestigious category than that of etudes or variations, that it fit into a genre routinely touted as a catalyst for the sublime, and that it merited comparison to one of Beethoven's sublime signature works. If the rhetoric of the sublime in this case resists recovery as a compositional strategy more than it does in the *Concert* or Toccata, it retains its agenda of elevating virtuosity and identifying the initiated listener.

Epilogue: The Shocking Amalgamated with the Venerable

Later nineteenth-century critics continued to valorize showpieces and performances using the rhetoric of the sublime. Eduard Hanslick's writings on Brahms's 1859 Piano Concerto No. 1, Op. 15, offer one example. Scholars have generally emphasized that the concerto was a milestone in Brahms's development as a symphonist. James Hepokoski has revealed it as a "monumental manifesto" in which Brahms positioned himself within the German symphonic tradition and produced a concerto "more symphonic than virtuosic."[102] It would be misleading to describe Brahms's piece as antivirtuosic. Rather, it stages piano virtuosity in ways that differ from conventional concertos. The first movement's sheer scale and formal complexity, for example, were unprecedented in the concerto literature. Here, the pianist's muscular octaves and densely textured passagework are most elaborate during the extensive, tension-ridden development and tragic coda. The movement follows not a trajectory toward transparent brilliance but what Hepokoski reads as a narrative of struggle and defeat. The premiere was coolly received, and Brahms could not find a publisher for the full score until 1874.

When Hanslick reviewed English pianist Leonard Borwick's 1891 performance of the concerto, he employed rhetorical strategies similar to those I have highlighted in Schumann's writings and reception. Brahms's concerto, he wrote, demanded a virtuoso of "spiritual [*geistig*] and physical strength." Its expansive layout and allusions to Beethoven's Ninth Symphony, for Hanslick, allowed Brahms to reject the pleasurable and brilliant for the fearsome elitism of the sublime: "Never before had a piano concerto appeared with such serious and severe speech, so thoroughly symphonic, and staving off all merely brilliant effects." The result was a concerto "more repulsive than attractive" filled with "thunderous, searing passion" and "echoes of Beethoven's Ninth."[103]

The compositions and performances we have been exploring in this chapter also engaged with another thread of the virtuosity discourse. According to this ideal, performers and composers established themselves as serious and transcendent by engaging with a canon of eighteenth- and early nineteenth-century, usually Austro-German repertoire. Performers, for example, established themselves as inspired interpreters of musical works. As we have seen, Schumann's 1830s "sublime" showpieces engage the canonic tradition in their own ways: the Toccata and Études with their links to Beethoven, the Concert sans orchestre with its sonata layout. The same could be said of Liszt's Leipzig concerts—where he played Beethoven transcriptions and a Bach concerto—and Brahms's Piano Concerto No. 1.

The rhetoric of the sublime and engagement with the canon were not separate, much less contradictory, categories. After all, Schumann used Beethovenian elements to deliver overpowering virtuosic climaxes in his Toccata and Études, and in no way did Moscheles or Liszt hint that the Concert's appeal to the sonata tradition mitigated its shocking or inaccessible qualities. These strategies shared the stage with other visions of transcendent virtuosity. Clara Wieck, for example, performed Beethoven sonatas alongside Chopin's "Là ci darem la mano" Variations, and she established an aura of interiority both through her perceived interpretive insight and through her approach to voicing. (See chapter 2.) Liszt established himself as a sublime virtuoso while also performing canonic repertoire and practicing musical humanitarianism.

What these cases do illustrate is that multiple threads of the virtuosity discourse could interpenetrate in individual pieces and performances—threads that drew upon different ideological frameworks and rhetorical stances. The rhetoric of the sublime called attention to immediate, visceral effects, whereas canon veneration realized ideologies of historicism and the work concept. Critics invoked the sublime to valorize music that shocked audiences and provoked bewilderment or resistance. By contrast, engagement with the canon appealed to a body of classics whose greatness had become a foregone conclusion.

The next two chapters emphasize Schumann's engagement with the latter vision of virtuosity, particularly his exploration of the work concept (an ideal at the heart of canon formation) and his collaborations with performers who championed it. We will focus on Schumann's work during the 1840s and 1850s, when he gained recognition as a successor within the canonic lineage and entered into some particularly vibrant collaborations. As we will see, his work during these decades continued to display the multiplicity of perspectives and strategies that characterized his 1830s writings and compositions.

Part II

Schumann's Virtuosity and the Culture of the Work Concept

In his review of the 1836–1837 Leipzig Gewandhaus season, Schumann paused from discussing individual performances and imagined the concerts as a panoramic tableau:

> As my imagination strove to condense everything into one picture, all of a sudden a sort of blossoming mountain of the muses stood before me, upon which I saw under the eternal temple of the older masters new arcades, new paths, and among them, merry virtuosos and lovely singers like flowers and butterflies: all of this in such a rich fullness and bewildering alternation, that the common and insignificant overlooked themselves on their own.[1]

As Schumann's description suggests, the concerts blended venerated composers, canonized masterworks, and recent music that, for him, continued this legacy. The season had immersed audiences in Haydn (two unspecified symphonies), Mozart (including Symphonies Nos. 40 and 41), and Beethoven (including Symphonies Nos. 2, 4, 5, 8, and 9). Not that the concerts fixated exclusively on the past—Schumann described new wings and thoroughfares. For example, the orchestra performed overtures such as Mendelssohn's *Midsummer Night's Dream* and *Meeresstille und glückliche Fahrt* and William Sterndale Bennett's *Die Najaden*. The concerts also exemplified the heterogeneous programming typical of the first half of the century. Some virtuosos entered the temple performing concertos by Bach, Mozart, or Beethoven. Others offered popularly styled showpieces, such as when violinist Karol Lipiński played his variations on Rossini's *Il barbiere di Siviglia*, and vocalists performed operatic numbers by Donizetti, Mercadante, and Spontini.[2] In Schumann's description, this musical heterogeneity thrived in the shadow of the "eternal temple" and its new additions. If he seemed to portray virtuosos as decoration rather than superstructure, he nonetheless made it clear that they inhabited and enriched the mountaintop and its edifices.

Schumann painted a scene at once venerable and idyllic. Mount Parnassus, mythical home of Apollo and the nine muses, evokes timeless value and classical equanimity. The affective qualities Schumann described in this essay differed from those we have encountered so far in this book: not the otherworldly, mysterious effects the *Davidsbündler* heard in Chopin's "Là ci darem la mano" Variations, the convivial idealism of Voigt's salon, or the overwhelming power of Liszt's 1840 concerts, but Apollonian solidity and repose.

The Leipzig tableau captures the most often-cited way in which nineteenth-century virtuosos presented their work as having transcendent qualities: attempting to synthesize virtuosity and the work concept. The work concept is a complex, multifaceted ideal that is central to nineteenth-century musical aesthetics. At its heart was the belief that musical life should revolve first and foremost around the composition, performance, discussion—and, potentially, the veneration—of musical works. The work concept shaped musical life in ways ranging from abstract thinking about the ontology of music, to programming and performance practices, to publication endeavors (critical editions and study scores, for example), to compositions themselves.[3] By embracing it, musicians and listeners valorized the composer over the performer, the composition over its ephemeral performances.

No mere intellectual exercise, the work concept elevated music among the arts and within society. One of its most significant manifestations was a long process of canon formation. Beginning early in the 1800s but especially after midcentury, self-consciously serious concert programming centered on a body of eighteenth- and nineteenth-century, largely Austro-German repertoire, with Beethoven as its most iconic figurehead. Living composers, too, could position themselves and their music as a continuation of this lineage—sometimes with the effect of inspiring debate and controversy, as in the case of Liszt's symphonic poems. By solidifying and valorizing this canon, musicians, scholars, and critics made the case that music stood on par with literature, that it too boasted a body of classics and merited a place within the humanistic education prized by the nineteenth-century bourgeois.[4] This demographic was a driving force behind cultural nationalism, and, especially in Germany, canon formation and composer veneration also affirmed that certain music deserved to be prized as a centerpiece of national identity. More broadly, the work concept staved off the ephemerality of music, a property that vexed eighteenth-century philosophers (notably Kant). It reified music in a form that could be contemplated, curated, and interpreted that (in the nineteenth-century imagination) demanded precedence over individual performances.

For composers and performers of virtuosic music, the work concept addressed the anxiety I broached in the Introduction and have been exploring throughout this book: the cultural status of virtuosity. One particularly influential part of this work-centric aesthetic was the ideal of *Werktreue* performance. *Werktreue* demanded that the performer respect and realize the composer's intentions and demonstrate profound insight into a composition. (Nineteenth-century notions of what it actually meant to faithfully interpret a composition varied widely. In general, they were less literalistic than those of the present day: performance practice, for example, admitted improvised preludes and the modernization of expressive markings and piano textures.[5]) The philosophical roots of *Werktreue* date to the late eighteenth century, and the ideal became especially important around the mid-nineteenth. From Clara Wieck Schumann to Franz Liszt and Anton Rubinstein, virtuosos harnessed their performances to the prestige of the canon. *Werktreue* performance also offered one way to transcend the egotism and self-indulgent subjectivity commentators described as a pitfall of virtuosity. As Mary Hunter has argued, it modeled a concept of healthy subjectivity that many nineteenth-century intellectuals championed, notably Hegel. According to this ideal, the individual (here, the performer) merged his/her self with some greater, objective entity (here, the work) and transformed both in the process.[6]

The ideology of the musical work also shaped original showpieces. Composers of such music could present themselves not only as scriptwriters for astonishing performances but as architects who exerted compositional mastery over the virtuosic spectacle, created idealized musical works, and jockeyed for a place within the canonic tradition. A showpiece, in this view, matched virtuosity to a redemptive compositional foundation or essence. Scholars have recently traced this dynamic, for example, in Liszt's Weimar piano compositions. Jim Samson has shown how Liszt's engagement with the work concept transformed across the three published versions of the *Études d'exécution transcendante*: the 1826 *Étude en douze exercices*, the 1837 *Grandes études*, and the 1851 final work. All three sets are self-evidently musical works, notes on paper that do not leave space for improvisation. More than he did with the other sets, though, Liszt presented the *Études d'exécution transcendante* as a collection of ideal works. The etudes at once display a self-consciously "classical" approach to form and reflect contemporary aesthetics that defined the musical work as the organic development of a single idea. In some, Liszt clarified structural boundaries or made motivic unity more apparent. In others, he streamlined the *Grandes études'* sprawling forms to create what Samson calls "single, large-scale intensity curves" that build toward climactic moments of "tonal and thematic reprise."[7] David Trippett has made a complementary argument about Liszt's "Dante" Sonata. The sonata began in Liszt's improvisations and, when Liszt revised the work in Weimar, he accentuated the work's sense of large-scale organicism and structural integration—however, Trippett is careful to note that composition and improvisation interpenetrated in Liszt's creative process and cannot be readily disentangled.[8] Liszt's revisions to the sonata and the etudes supported his midlife career change. In 1847, he went from a touring pianist-composer to a *Kapellmeister* based in Weimar and devoted to writing large-scale works. (Liszt no longer toured extensively but did perform at his masterclasses and on highly anticipated public occasions.) His showpieces from these years helped to define him not only as a spectacular virtuoso but as a masterful composer who carefully designed his works—a composer who at once entered into dialogue with a venerated Classical tradition and realized a more recent aesthetic of organicism.

Chapters 5 and 6 will explore ways in which Schumann molded virtuosity to the work concept. His career unfolded during a period of bourgeoning canon formation and historicist consciousness among German composers, and the work concept was a career-long preoccupation. This issue became particularly important for him during the 1840s and 1850s, when he redefined his compositional approach and collaborated extensively with Clara Schumann and Joseph Joachim, two performers who brought the work concept and the culture of the canon to the concert stage.

5 Steps to Parnassus? Schumann's Equivocal Work Concept

This chapter will trace how Schumann sought to ally the spectacle of virtuosity with the aesthetics of the musical work, exploring several of his projects as transcriber, borrower, and critic. All were important to the way he publicly presented himself at significant junctures of his career. When contextualizing his argument about Liszt, Jim Samson summarizes that Schumann "sought to recover an eighteenth-century balance between virtuosity and work character."[1] Though Schumann regarded this balance as important, I would argue that his approach was equivocal. He flexibly and often ambivalently considered how his understanding of the musical work and the masterful composer existed in tandem or tension with the immediacy of live performance or the spontaneity of improvisation. (The latter could be enacted in actual improvisations or simulated in compositions and performances). Considering how Schumann navigated these questions reveals some of the work concept's blurry, negotiable boundaries. The ideal musical work was not a straightforward, monolithic category but a matter of presentation and reception—because of the high cultural stakes it brought into play, Schumann and his contemporaries debated or equivocated over its precise meaning in different situations.

Three episodes in Schumann's music and writings illustrate this balancing act. The "Parnassus" tableau's rhetoric of Apollonian solidity and equilibrium winds throughout them, but never uncontested or unqualified. First, Schumann described his Opus 10 transcriptions of six Paganini violin caprices as an attempt to reconcile Paganini's compositional and performing identities. He discussed this project in an 1836 essay, the only review he published of his own music. Second, during the 1840s, the *Neue Zeitschrift* published a string of elaborate, generalizing articles about virtuosity by critics other than Schumann. Two of the most prolific and important, Eduard Krüger and Herrmann Hirschbach, engaged in a short polemic skirmish and showed that they had fundamental disagreements about what the work concept meant for virtuosity. Finally, Schumann's Piano Concerto Op. 54 derived some of its tonal and structural features from Clara Wieck's 1835 Piano Concerto Op. 7, a case of intertextual interplay several scholars have noticed and that I unravel and contextualize for the first time. Robert, I show, at times emulated and at times mitigated the fantasy-like spontaneity he and other critics heard in Clara's concerto. His reinterpretation bolstered his midlife attempts to prove that his music embodied compositional self-possession, reflection, and mastery. Reviews of Robert's concerto, though, hinted that it also offered pleasures more sensuous and visceral than admiration for the composer's architecture.

Paganini, Liszt, and the Equilibrium of the Composer

From the time he abandoned his performing career and began to establish himself as a composer, Schumann wrote showpieces that conspicuously advertised his compositional mastery. As I showed in chapter 4, the Toccata alludes to Beethoven, the embodiment of the "great" composer, and the *Études symphoniques* effaces the quasi-improvisatory free association of the earlier *Fantaisies et finale* and suggest a link to the symphonic tradition. Schumann's 1835 *Études de concert d'après des caprices de Paganini*, Op. 10, richly document an attempt to mediate between his admiration for virtuosic performance and his attitudes about musical composition. Schumann's essay about the transcriptions anticipates arguments he later made in his 1839 review of Liszt's *Grandes études*. The 1830s Schumann is today best-known as a radical who developed musical analogues for literary narrative strategies and whose piano cycles and Fantasie Op. 17 bewildered listeners with their digressive, fragmentary structures. These essays and transcriptions reveal a different side of Schumann's piano decade, showing that he also turned to more traditional forms and ideologies when attempting to establish his authority as a composer-critic. At the same time, however, Schumann allowed his remembered or imagined encounters with live performances to coexist or compete with these compositional ideals. In his Liszt review, this dual perspective even made him uncertain about how one should evaluate virtuosic compositions to begin with.

Schumann's Opus 10 Paganini transcriptions have attracted little scholarly attention, and his essay about them has gone virtually unexplored.[2] Taken together, they complicate Schumann's well-known admiration for the violinist-composer. In most of his public and private writings about Paganini, Schumann stressed his effect as a performer. (Because Paganini performed his own compositions, these accounts also implicitly took account of the effects his music had onstage.) During his days as Friedrich Wieck's struggling piano student, Schumann traveled to Frankfurt with two Heidelberg classmates to hear a Paganini concert on April 11, 1830. Even before the trip, his diary recorded that he and his friends frequently discussed the violinist. The concert itself made a memorable impression on Schumann. In an 1834 review of violinist Henri Vieuxtemps, Schumann recalled Paganini's performance and described a hypnotic experience that gradually entranced the audience and brought them into an intimate communion with the virtuoso: "Then he began, and so thin, so small! Then, how he now cast his magnetic chains loosely and barely visibly into the masses, so that these swayed to and fro. Now the rings became more wonderful, more intertwined; the people pressed more tightly together, now he laced them ever more firmly until little by little they melted into one, to confront the master on an equal footing, to receive from him as one from another."[3]

Following the concert, Schumann's writings teem with admiring references to Paganini. Schumann's 1831 plans for *Die Wunderkinder*, a novel he envisioned but never wrote, included Paganini as a character. Paganini would have a "wondrous effect" on "Zilia," a novelized Clara Wieck. Schumann's sketches described "the ideal of technical perfection—the ideal of expression—the union of both in Paganini." Such qualities would stimulate "Clara's striving." By contrast, the sketch described Hummel only as "the technical ideal."[4] In one of his aphorisms, Schumann simply designated Paganini "the turning point of virtuosity."[5] At the time, Schumann was still struggling to begin a career as a pianist-composer. These writings hint that, just as Liszt reinvented his style of piano figuration in response to Paganini, the young Schumann found in Paganini an inspiration for developing his own approach to virtuosity.

Schumann recognized that Paganini could spur virtuosos to greater accomplishment on their instruments (and, perhaps, to anxious self-comparison). In one of his eulogizing reviews of Ludwig Schuncke, he remembered that "new Paganini ideals he detected within himself" had led the insecure youth to consider "shutting himself away for half a year and studying technique."[6] In 1832, Schumann himself published a set of six transcriptions of the caprices, his *Études d'après les caprices de Paganini*, Op. 3. Unlike Opus 10, which he described as a set of concert etudes, Schumann designed the earlier opus as a pedagogical work. It includes an introductory essay in which Schumann, injured but recently immersed in piano study, suggests exercises and practice strategies.

Schumann also developed the metric dissonance that pervades such showpieces as the Toccata and *Concert sans orchestre* partly through his attempts to capture Paganinian virtuosity. Harald Krebs has identified Paganini as an important influence on Schumann's use of metric dissonance.[7] The "Paganini" movement from *Carnaval*, after all, derives its furious momentum from perpetual-motion broken octaves in which the hands are displaced by a sixteenth note. In his transcriptions of the caprices, Schumann translated Paganini's violin figuration into metrically dissonant counterpoint that ranges from subtly syncopated grooves to shocking, sudden jolts. Krebs and John Daverio have shown that the transcriptions often seize upon and exaggerate metric dissonances already present in the caprices.[8] Daverio singled out the last etude of Schumann's Opus 3 set as particularly striking. In the coda, Schumann places Paganini's figuration in the bass and overlays chords that change on the second sixteenth note of the beat. Near the end, the pianist hammers at a metrically displaced dominant with an added minor ninth. In a diary entry from 1832, Schumann compared this specific passage to a caricature by Johann Peter Lyser titled "Paganini, der Hexenmeister." Lyser depicts the violinist in the heat of performance: the virtuoso stands on one leg, and his hair stands on end. Macabre spectres surround him. "Paganini in a magic circle—the murdered woman—dancing skeletons; and floating, magnetic hazes of spirits," Schumann wrote. "It often floated before me while I was working on the G-minor presto, and I thought that the close gladly recalls it."[9] Not that metric dissonance necessarily symbolized qualities listeners heard in Paganini's virtuosity—violence, the erotic, or the demonic, for example.[10] As we saw in chapter 4, reviewers suggested that the Toccata and *Concert* channeled Beethoven and violent nature, respectively.

Despite this larger pattern of admiration and emulation, Schumann presented his Opus 10 transcriptions as a critique of Paganini. Specifically transcribing the caprices already presented Paganinian virtuosity through a selective lens. Paganini's Twenty-Four Caprices Op. 1 did attract considerable public attention and became a landmark in the violin literature. However, no documentary evidence records that Paganini actually performed them in concert.[11] Instead, he programmed works that fit more smoothly into the postclassical tradition: his variation sets on popular themes and his brilliant concertos. Paganini's repertoire at the time of his 1830 Frankfurt concert included his Concerto No. 1, the "La Campanella" rondo from his Concerto No. 2, and his variations on *Il carnevale di Venezia* and Rossini's *Mosè in Egitto*.[12] Dana Gooley has shown that Paganini's variation sets wear their radical violin virtuosity lightly. They rapidly shift between contrasting techniques to imitate voices and suggest miniature comic dialogues.[13] It might have been such features that led Schumann, in a diary entry about the 1830 concert, to voice some reservations: "Doubts about his artistic ideals and his lack of the great, noble, priestly tranquility of art [*Kunstruhe*]."[14]

Schumann was more circumspect in his published essay on the Opus 10 transcriptions, muting criticism with admiration and humility. Regardless of whether or not we read his tone as sincere, it is hardly surprising that a then little-known composer transcribing works by an international musical celebrity—and then printing an essay about the project in a journal he himself edited—would adopt a cautious tone. He described the transcriptions not as radical reinterpretations, but as attempts to absorb and honor: "If it is praiseworthy to have lovingly absorbed the thoughts of one higher than oneself, to have reworked them, and brought them into the outside world again, I may perhaps possess a claim to praise."[15]

For all his laudatory rhetoric, Schumann made clear that he saw Paganini the composer as flawed and his caprices as subject to correction or at least enhancement. He hinted at a discrepancy between Paganini's performing prowess and compositional abilities:

> Paganini himself supposedly places his compositional talent higher than his eminent virtuoso genius. Even if one cannot completely agree with him, at least up to now, nevertheless his compositions, particularly in the violin caprices . . . show so much that is diamantine, that the richer settings required by the piano would solidify rather than evaporate them.[16]

Schumann did not describe the caprices as completely gemlike but praised them for containing many diamantine features (among, perhaps, less stellar ones). He depicted the transcriber not as an excavator chipping away at proverbial diamonds in the rough but as a setter firming up the originals.

Paganini:

Example 5.1. Paganini, Caprice, Op. 1, no. 12. Retransition and recapitulation. Schumann, *Études de concert d'après des caprices de Paganini*, Op. 10, no. 1. Retransition and recapitulation. Analogous V/V chords shown in boxes.

Schumann reworked the formal structures of some of the caprices. At the outset of his review, he qualified that his etudes were truly Paganini compositions "except for the bass lines, the denser, German middle voices, and the forms, which are made smoother."[17] In his first and third etudes, Schumann created "smoother" structures by converting Paganini's originals into more normative sonata forms. Whereas their source caprices stage fluid, ongoing transformations of figurational patterns, Schumann's transcriptions mitigate this seamlessness. They recast Paganini's virtuosity within more sharply demarcated structures in clearer dialogue with sonata-form conventions.

Etude No. 1, based on Paganini's Caprice No. 12, features the most extensive interventions. Paganini deemphasizes the boundaries of the sonata form to accommodate manipulations of the broken-octave figuration—he leads the soloist's virtuosity through wide-ranging, often surprising tonal and registral contrasts. Paganini approaches the recapitulation via a circuitous retransition. (See example 5.1.) After sustaining a $V^{6/5}/V$, he feints briefly at the minor dominant, descends into the violin's low register to present a snatch of the second theme in the distant key of A major, and only then takes a chromatic route to an unclouded dominant. The retransition itself forgoes the conventional double return of primary theme and tonic key and instead feeds directly into a tonic presentation of the second

Schumann:

Example 5.1. (*continued*)

theme group. A measure after the second theme begins, it veers into a series of modulating sequences that reapproach a dominant pedal, making it seem as though developmental processes are spilling into the recapitulation. The exposition similarly staves off structural linchpins with the tonally wandering second theme and with a transition as long as the first theme itself.

Schumann's transcription undercuts this strategy, stemming the caprice's boundary-overriding flow of figurational patterns at significant structural junctures. In place of Paganini's ambiguously delineated recapitulation, Schumann inserts a conventional double return—here, the recapitulation opens with the first theme, music with a memorable thematic profile whose parallel phrases unequivocally establish and confirm the tonic. Schumann precedes this arrival with a more directional retransition. He cuts six of Paganini's measures, replaces the $V^{6/5}/V$ with a V^7/V, and adds two that simply resolve the latter chord to the major dominant. Schumann also prunes the modulating passagework in Paganini's transition between the first and second theme groups, reducing six measures to four. Some of Schumann's textures plant formal signposts within the onrushing figuration. At the second theme group, for example, the accompaniment pattern momentarily changes, clarifying the start of a new section.

In Schumann's Etude No. 3, based on Paganini's Caprice No. 10, the formal alterations are less extensive, but their effect is similar. Paganini's caprice is already a sonata form with clearly articulated theme groups and a full recapitulation. Even here, Schumann's changes deemphasize Paganini's seamless figurational transformations and accentuate the caprice's classicizing structure. Paganini's primary and secondary themes grow out of a trill figure introduced in the second measure. As the violinist navigates the sonata form, he or she seems to spin constant variations on the trill, deriving the piece's thematic materials from a minute virtuosic gesture. Schumann's first theme group alternately foregrounds Paganini's figuration and buries it beneath a new melody. The changing texture emphatically demarcates the distinct phrases that make up the theme. The juncture between Paganini's exposition and development effects a seamless transformation across formal boundaries: his development starts with a treatment of the second theme and seems to pick up where the exposition leaves off. Schumann, by contrast, inserts an F-minor statement of the first theme at the start of the development. He thereby emphasizes that a distinct section is under way and invokes the eighteenth-century convention of beginning the development with a rotation of the opening theme.

Formal revisions were not the only changes Schumann made to Paganini's caprices. Even more than the Opus 3 transcriptions, the Opus 10 set wreathes Paganini's figuration in metric dissonance. As shown in example 5.1, Schumann clusters surprising accents around those already present in the Paganini, creating bursts of friction between polyphonic voices. Schumann's accompaniment to the first theme repeatedly stresses the second half of each beat, so that the broken octaves career through a field of syncopations. In some etudes, Schumann altered individual harmonies, creating bracing chromatic progressions in his Etude No. 4, for example.[18] As I noted in chapter 4, Schumann built an allusion to the "Eroica" funeral march into the fourth etude (or accentuated a resemblance he believed was already palpable), adding a canonic emblem to the showpiece.

The larger context of Schumann's essay presented these alterations as a way of giving the caprices smoothness and solidity and bringing Paganini's compositions into closer balance with his virtuoso "genius." At one point, Schumann suggested that the piano setting prompted him to rework harmonies and forms: a strange assertion, for why should a piano piece require more sharply chiseled, conventional sonata forms than a violin one? In a footnote to that comment, he offered a more pointed justification that critiqued Paganini's career path:

One must know the way these etudes [caprices] took shape and how quickly they were ordered for printing to excuse much in the originals. Herr [Karol] Lipiński relates that they were composed in diverse times and places and were given as gifts by Paganini to his friends in manuscript. When, later, the publisher, Herr Ricordi, requested an edition of the collection from Paganini, he hastily wrote them down from memory, etc.[19]

Paganini appears blameless in this account, the victim of dispersed manuscripts and the publisher's deadline. However, the footnote still alleged that Paganini's work as a touring virtuoso—constantly on the move, composing in the heat of his schedule, and more focused on managing concerts than on keeping track of and revising compositions—explained supposed flaws of the caprices.

In an outwardly modest act of self-promotion, Schumann presented himself as the one to identify and address these problems. He would, he implied, amend works by a peripatetic virtuoso whose compositional abilities did not yet match his performing powers. Now dedicated primarily to composition and criticism rather than performance, Schumann strove to distinguish himself from his longtime idol by claiming greater compositional mastery, equilibrium, and authority.

Schumann's 1839 essay on Liszt's *Grandes études* made a less rhetorically hesitant—but nonetheless still ambivalent—statement about a perceived mismatch between composition and virtuosic performance.[20] Whereas Schumann's perspective on Paganini fluctuated between the admiring and the critical throughout several public and private writings, his *Grandes études* review voiced such a tension in a single essay. The review was an important one for Schumann. Liszt was generating considerable press in Paris, and the *Zeitschrift* was reporting on his activities. In 1836, the journal ran a German translation of Joseph d'Ortigue's Liszt biography, giving it front-page billing in six consecutive issues, and Paris correspondent Joseph Mainzer opined that, unlike Thalberg, Liszt used virtuosity "purely as a means to develop his thoughts and ideas."[21] Schumann's *Études* review, though, marked the first time the *Zeitschrift* tackled Liszt's compositions and the first time the editor himself weighed in on the virtuoso. While preparing the essay, Schumann studied other Liszt scores, including the *Apparitions*. He also compared the *Grandes études* to their earlier version, the *Étude en douze exercices*. The *Exercices*, as Samson shows, employ figurational idioms standard in postclassical piano music, and they usually feature concise, simple forms. The *Grandes études*, by contrast, unfurl Liszt's signature piano writing: the rumbling bass flourishes of No. 8, for example, or the alternating hands in No. 2.[22] Schumann commended the pathbreaking virtuosity. "The new ones, having gained in richness of means, seek to outdo the former in brilliance and fullness," he wrote, and he praised Liszt for "seeking the outermost extreme on his instrument."[23]

Nevertheless, Schumann believed that Liszt had thrived as a pianist at the expense of his compositional development. As in his more critical writings on Paganini, Schumann couched his criticism in claims that Liszt lacked qualities of stability or equilibrium. And, again, he blamed the constant traveling and touring, though he understood why Liszt would prefer the immediacy of piano playing to the labor of writing out scores. Disequilibrium, Schumann suggested, was apparent in Liszt's life and artistic persona:

> He seems to have found no rest for lasting studies in composition, perhaps also no master equal to him; all the more did he study as a virtuoso, for lively musical natures prefer tones that speak quickly to dry work on paper. Though he developed his piano playing to an astonishing height, the composer remained behind, and this always leads to an imbalance, which has noticeably avenged itself even into his most recent works.[24]

Schumann heard imbalance within the *Études* themselves. Comparing the earlier and later versions, he wrote, "The latter leave us vacillating about whether we should envy the boy more than we do the man, who seems to have not succeeded in finding peace." "To win the favor of his fatherland," which Schumann assumed to be Germany, "he would admittedly have to return to serenity and simplicity, which so agreeably express themselves in the older etudes. He would have to take the reverse process—that of simplification rather than complication."[25]

Schumann hinted that the problem was at least partly formal. When tracing Liszt's biography, he speculated that encountering Chopin "brought Liszt again to his senses. For Chopin has form: among the wondrous shapes of his music there always winds the rosy thread of a melody. But it was much too late for the extraordinary virtuoso to recover what he had neglected as a composer."[26] Here, Schumann links formal coherence not to sonata-like processes but to the consistent presence of a melodic profile. Of course, none of Liszt's etudes literally lacks melody. Schumann might have been recognizing that Liszt's etudes often transition between sections via extravagant cadenza-like passages. He might have also heard a lack of melody in Liszt's passagework, which embeds themes in shifting layers of figuration. In any case, Samson has shown that when Liszt streamlined forms, emphasized motivic unity, and thinned textures in the *Études d'exécution transcendante*, he followed (knowingly or not) the overall thrust of Schumann's review.

And yet, Schumann vacillated between criticizing the etudes as compositional structures and considering them from other perspectives: their potential effect in live performance, or their challenging, novel figuration. No sooner did he counsel Liszt to simplify his etudes than he added, "But, let us not forget that he wants to produce etudes, and that here the new, complicated difficulty of the composition excuses itself through this goal—the overcoming of the greatest."[27] Near the end of the essay, Schumann cast further doubt on his analyses. As we saw in chapter 4, he maintained that one needed to hear and see a performance (preferably Liszt's own) to truly appreciate and evaluate the *Grandes études*, and he began to imagine the overwhelming effect they might have. In the end, Schumann left two divergent images unreconciled—the shaky composition and the astonishing performance. If he expressed reservations about the etudes' structure and style, the review also shows a glimmer of the admiration he expressed for Liszt's 1840s concerts.

Divergent Work Concepts in the *Zeitschrift*:
The Krüger–Hirschbach Skirmish

Most of the Schumann reviews I have been considering in this book focus on specific pieces and performances. During the 1840s, his *Neue Zeitschrift* also published several essays in which other critics discussed virtuosity in sweeping, general terms. Rather than promulgating a single stance on virtuosity, these critics defended a range of viewpoints. In fact, two frequent contributors, Eduard Krüger and Herrmann Hirschbach, engaged in a brief but heated debate between 1840 and 1841. Both agreed that the work concept redeemed virtuosity but disagreed on how exactly this could happen.

Krüger emphasized reverence for musical works that, in his view, possessed what he called "content." As I noted in the Introduction (and as Gooley has explained), Krüger urged the virtuoso to subordinate his individual subjectivity to some larger entity, possibly the content-bearing musical work. Content, Krüger suggested, was a quality that transcended individual performances and was inherent to a composition. He propounded this view in his 1840 "Ueber Virtuosenunfug," a fictional dialogue between a Music Director and a Dilettante. Krüger did praise contemporary composers, including Mendelssohn, but he most often cited canonic repertoire as examples of works with content. At one point, the Director recalls hearing *Don Giovanni* played by a mediocre ensemble. But because the conductor was faithful to Mozart's tempo markings, he claims, "From the first notes of the introduction, my tears began to flow. . . . Everyone was uplifted and shaken to the depths."[28] The Director also maintains that, when audiences hear Mozart symphonies and piano works, they do not exclaim over "technique, fire, and flageolet" or the "peculiar" performer but about "poetic content."[29] In his most extreme statement about privileging the canonic work over the performance, Krüger's Director describes a five-year-old boy reading from the Bible: however halting and uncomprehending the delivery, "you feel warmed because . . . the godly content is indestructible."[30]

Hirschbach presented a different interpretation of the work concept in an article titled "Antiphilistroses" that appeared in the *Zeitschrift* on October 10, 1840. He later asked Schumann to advise readers that his essay was not a response to Krüger's, and indeed it does not mention Krüger by name.[31] Still, it would have been easy to read "Antiphilistroses" as a targeted rebuttal. It appeared only a month after Krüger's essay, and it compared critics who "were now lamenting about *Virtuositätsunfug*" to earlier reactionaries who had opposed Mozart and Beethoven. Such archconservatives, Hirschbach charged, were "bereft of every creative gift."[32] This language could have helped convince Krüger that Hirschbach was attacking him: Krüger was an organist, academic, and choral conductor, whereas Hirschbach was a composer well known for his chamber music. An anonymous *Zeitschrift* editorial on May 28, 1841, also interpreted Hirschbach's essay as a critique of Krüger's.[33]

Whereas Krüger emphasized the venerated past, Hirschbach looked to the future. He agreed with Krüger's pessimistic view of contemporary virtuosity but insisted that it would provide the basis for yet-to-be-written masterworks. "At most," he wrote, "one can reproach the virtuosos, but not the virtuosity of our time; in the future, more than one happily gifted composer will use it—for gigantic works." In fact, he criticized composers for neglecting to verse themselves in "the rich means of new virtuoso art." Like Krüger, Hirschbach viewed the virtuoso as subordinate to the composer—but to the living composer, to whose musical edifices even supposedly superficial virtuosos contributed: "Subordinate handymen are also necessary—to build pyramids." Hirschbach only condemned one kind of music outright: "Our art is a wonderland . . . but there is only one poison shrub: dance music and variations."[34] Hirschbach's argument reflected his situation as a professional composer, and he might have even felt threatened by Krüger's canon veneration.

Krüger's rejoinder on April 23, 1841, explicitly referenced and disputed Hirschbach's essay. He reiterated his point that virtuosos should transcend their egotism by interpreting the ideal musical work, and he kept to his implicit argument that one found such works in the canon. He ridiculed Hirschbach's remark about dance music and variations: "The poor man! He knows only tavern and salon waltzes and Gelineck's variations! Not Beethoven's, Mozart's, and Haydn's variations, or, from our own time, *Davidsbündlertänze*." He disputed Hirschbach's view of virtuosity as a compositional resource. "An artist has not yet been born from the instrument," he writes. "History shows that thus far it has been the other way around. Bach's cello solos began modern virtuosity for this instrument, Beethoven's symphonies the orchestral."[35] (Krüger neglected to note that numerous composers, including Schumann himself, did in fact learn to compose "on the instrument" through improvisation.) In Krüger's narrative, redeemed virtuosity did not require the composer to physically explore the instrument or join a process of historical evolution—it resided within the composer prior to his engagement with the instrument, and it already existed in the canon.

Hirschbach and Krüger never debated one another again, but they continued to publish essays for the *Zeitschrift* about their different interpretations of the work concept. Less than a month after responding to Hirschbach, Krüger published a more elaborate essay about his ideal, "Das Virtuosenkonzert: Gespräch." In this dialogue, a Virtuoso joins the Music Director and the Dilettante. The Director denies the Dilettante's claim that he believes "there is no music outside Mozart, Bach, and Beethoven."[36] Nevertheless, his arguments constantly return to the canonic tradition that he believes the Virtuoso is neglecting and to his belief that these masterworks transcended performance. "Whence these always recurring programs with variations by the concertizer, adagio by the same, *Concert brillant* by the same—while our eternal classicists lie hidden on the music stand or moldering as non-sellers!" The Director (again, inaccurately) describes Mozart's operas and Shakespeare's plays as works created on an ideal level, not tailored to their original performers.[37] Hirschbach reiterated his view in an 1843 essay, "Componist und Virtuos." He blamed audiences for insufficiently valuing the work of current composers, whose challenges and contributions he considered superior to those of touring virtuosos—more directed toward the "ideal."[38] Again, he predicted a future of redemptive masterworks.

The Krüger–Hirschbach skirmish was a brief episode in the virtuosity discourse, a flash in the pan compared to the Liszt–Thalberg or Schumann–Fink rivalries. It illustrates, though, that because the work concept admitted many interpretations, it could serve divergent attitudes and agendas related to performance, composition, and interpretations of music history. Presently available sources do not indicate whether Schumann himself took a side in their debate. That he printed both authors' essays suggests that he relished the discussion, and, ever the ambivalent critic, might have agreed with aspects of both arguments. Here, he used the *Zeitschrift* to provide a forum in which critics debated how the ideal musical work could yield transcendent virtuosity.

Schumann Adjusts His Style and Aesthetic

During the 1840s, Schumann shifted his understanding of what composition entailed, how virtuosity functioned within a musical work, and what professional profile he wished to cultivate. These changes provide one important backdrop to his work on the Piano Concerto Op. 54. As is well-known, Schumann diversified his output after his 1840 marriage, partly to realize long-held compositional ambitions and partly because he was now the head of a family and needed to achieve greater public recognition. He did remain prolific as a composer of piano music but prompted greater fanfare with his symphonies, lieder, chamber music (notably the three string quartets, the Piano Quintet Op. 44, and the Piano Quartet Op. 47), and large theatrical works (especially *Das Paradies und die Peri*). The composer of abstruse salon music was entering Mozart's, Beethoven's, and Schubert's signature genres and jockeying for a place in their lineage.

Schumann's 1830s piano works, as is well known, had encountered a rocky reception. (This was particularly true of Schumann's cycles of short piano pieces, with their fragmentary movements, ambiguous tonal plans, recondite structural underpinnings, and diverse literary allusions.) Numerous writers alleged that the music was overly convoluted, even incoherent, and that it revealed a lack of compositional restraint. In 1832, Schumann sent his *Papillons*, Op. 2, to Hummel, who responded by advising him that the "rapidly succeeding changes of harmony" risked "preventing comprehensibility for the listener." Hummel cautioned that such "bizarreness" compromised the "beauty, clarity, and unity of a well-arranged composition." In 1834, Gottfried Weber of the journal *Caecilia* published a scathing review of the "Abegg" Variations, *Papillons,* the Intermezzi Op. 4, and the Impromptus Op. 5. In Weber's account, Schumann was making a "premature grasp for extraordinariness" and "prematurely emitted wild sparks." *Papillons*, he wrote, was not a well-planned work but consisted of "thought-splinters (*Gedankenspähnen*) dashed off before the public." Weber wondered whether Schumann would ever "find his way out of his present tangles . . . back to simplicity and naturalness and from there to the heights of art." A decade later, in 1844, Carl Koßmaly painted a similar picture in an *Allgemeine musikalische Zeitung* retrospective essay about Schumann's 1830s piano works. Though Koßmaly generally admired Schumann, he regretted that the composer might have gone too far in his "reaction against the commonplace and philistine." The resulting music "occasionally degenerates into the search for alienating, unheard-of phrases and completely unenjoyable bizarreness . . . a persistent detriment to pure, peaceful, artistic beauty." When listening, it was "as if one were lost in a thick, overgrown forest, the path barred from moment to moment by mighty tree trunks or knotty roots, powerful vines and sharp thorns, and could escape only with difficulty."[39]

Contemporary reviewers heard a new Schumann—a more classicizing, Apollonian one—in his 1840s chamber and orchestral works. Not that the composer had rejected his earlier style: Julie Hedges Brown has shown that Schumann's 1840s chamber works use compositional strategies from his piano decade and bring them into dialogue with his new priorities.[40] Rather than an abrupt paradigm shift, his midcareer music shows a subtle rebalancing of techniques and goals. Critics wrote that the composer showed new self-possession and technical mastery, that he at once retained and tamed his penchant for expressive effusion. In 1843, for example, Robert and Clara Schumann gave a *Morgenunterhaltung* at the Leipzig Gewandhaus. The concert showcased Robert's new compositional portfolio (the Piano Quintet and the String Quintet Op. 41, no. 1), lieder by both spouses, and some canonic works in Clara's repertoire (Beethoven's Sonata Op. 101, and her piano rendition of Bach's organ Prelude and Fugue in A Minor, BWV 543). The concert was by invitation but made a public statement. The *Allgemeine musikalische Zeitung*, for example, reviewed the performance and reflected on Robert's new style in general: "Already, in his first symphony, Schumann has encouragingly demonstrated that he knows how to combine fresh blooming energy with artistic measure." An 1844 review of the Piano Quintet proclaimed, "The whole piece differs strongly from the works of Schumann's earlier period through its surety and self-possession in the use of all means, but also from many publications of the present time through its warmth of feeling and poetic abundance." August Kahlert, in an 1846 review of the Piano Quartet, opined that Schumann had surpassed Schubert. The latter, he wrote, had never learned to control his "overabundance" (possibly his wealth of melodic ideas) but "with Schumann, this overabundance is controlled." Essays about the Symphony No. 1 detected technical mastery, diligence, indebtedness to Haydn, Mozart, and Beethoven, and "natural, healthy sense."[41]

This pattern of Schumann reception took on a more polemical edge in the reviews Franz Brendel published after taking over the *Neue Zeitschrift* in 1844.[42] Brendel and his writers heard in Schumann's 1830s works a "subjective phase" and in the 1840s an antithetical "objective" one. It still remained for Schumann, they maintained, to synthesize these approaches: their demand reflected the Hegelian ideology that permeated writings on behalf of the New German School. *Zeitschrift* critics occasionally claimed that Schumann was on the cusp of a synthesis, but he never quite satisfied the journal's ideologues. Granted, these writings are of limited use for assessing Schumann's own aesthetic. In 1854, the composer himself wrote an irritated letter to *Zeitschrift* critic Richard Pohl and grumbled that "subjective" and "objective" categories were too simplistic. Though they imposed a framework that the composer did not endorse, the New German essays recognized and tried to map and interpret the shift between Schumann's 1830s style and his newer approach.

Schumann himself suggested that, in 1845, he changed not merely his style but his approach to composing. An often-cited diary entry from spring 1846 claimed that he was newly committed to intellectual reflection and planning:

> I wrote most, almost all, of my smallest pieces in moments of inspiration, many with unbelievable speed—so, my first symphony in B-flat in four days, a *Liederkreis* of twenty pieces in the same amount of time, and *Die Peri* likewise in a relatively short time.

> Beginning in the year 1845 on, when I began to invent and work out everything in my head, an entirely new style of composing began to develop.[43]

The composer and his critics identified different years as turning points. Nevertheless, both saw the 1840s Schumann moving away from effusive inspiration (possibly, the diary hints, experienced at the piano) and exerting more extensive and calculated control over the musical work.

Like critical claims about his 1840s style, Schumann's diary entry describes not a radical about-face but a shift of emphasis. The entry understated the planning that went into his 1830s compositions: manuscripts for the Toccata, *Études symphoniques*, and Sonata No. 2, Op. 22, for example, all reveal that Schumann made sketches and substantially revised his drafts, sometimes with the apparent goal of concision and clarity.[44] And, of course, it would be too simplistic to view intellectually considered composition and heat-of-the-moment inspiration as two sides of a dichotomy.

In any case, Schumann's diary entry reveals how he wished to regard and present his music at this point of his career. His music also reflects his self-proclaimed reorientation in concrete, if subtle, ways. In Daverio's analysis, Schumann's post-1845 music showed a new concern for *ars combinatoria*, spinning melodies by recombining pithy motivic ideas. It is surely no coincidence that Robert dated his shift to around the time when he and Clara were intensively studying Bach and writing their own canons and fugues; indeed, his mid-1840s compositions burst with contrapuntal textures. Daverio also notes that Schumann developed a more gradual approach to transition, tempering the stark contrasts that pervade his 1830s works.[45] Schumann's self-assessment resonated with advice that he gave to others: in personal letters and his *Hausregeln* for students, he urged intellectual reflection away from the piano rather than composing through improvisation.[46]

Schumann hinted that his "entirely new style of composing" also affected the way he approached virtuosic display. His description occurs within a four-paragraph diary entry that reflects on his overall development as a composer. In the first of these paragraphs, Schumann critiqued his early piano music. He regretted an imbalance between composition and performance similar to the one he had heard in Liszt and Paganini:

It detracted from the purely musical content of my earlier piano compositions that I believed that they also had to have a special musical interest for the piano player (through mechanically new difficulties for the piano).[47]

This paragraph does not lend itself to straightforward interpretation where specifics are concerned. Schumann did not explain precisely what he meant by the term "content" other than that it existed apart from the music's display of physical virtuosity. Contemporary discourse offers little helpful context: when critics expressed reservations about Schumann's 1830s piano works, none suggested that "mechanical" concerns were a problem. The diary entry does not presage an overall retreat from virtuosity, plentiful in Schumann's concerted works during the 1840s and early 1850s. What it does suggest is that, at least at mid-decade, Schumann believed that becoming the masterful, calculating composer he described in his diary meant somehow subordinating virtuosity within the musical work.

Schumann's 1851 revision of his *Études symphoniques* reflects this new attitude—possibly the diary entries and certainly his overall 1840s reorientation. Schumann republished several of his 1830s piano works during the late 1840s and early 1850s, among them the Impromptus, *Davidsbündlertänze*, Op. 6, and *Kreisleriana*, Op. 16. In many cases, he changed features that had mystified listeners, rounding off fragmentary endings and removing cryptic inscriptions.[48] He reworked the *Études symphoniques* and the *Concert sans orchestre* when the publisher Julius Schuberth acquired rights to them. The former reappeared as the *Études en forme des variations* in 1852, the latter as Grand Sonata No. 3 in 1853. In the *Concert*-turned-Sonata, the change represented a return to an earlier plan, reverting to the title and restoring one of the scherzo movements Schumann had initially intended for the work.

The *Études* underwent a more thorough rethinking. The new version omitted two variations, Etudes III and IX in the 1837 version. More than the others, these variations relate loosely to the theme. Etude III features wide-ranging arpeggios that recall Paganini's Caprice No. 1. It makes no obvious reference to the theme's opening arpeggio and, after a start on C-sharp minor, ends in E major. In Etude IX, detached sixths, thirds, and chords cascade down the piano *presto possibile*, outlining the arpeggio motive but stretching the theme's phrase structure beyond recognition. As Damien Ehrhardt has noted, the revised variation set is more unidirectional, forming two crescendos of increasingly dense figuration.[49] The result exemplifies the formal clarity Schumann's critics noticed starting in the 1840s. If the revisions reflected Schumann's diary entry about "mechanical interest," he may have decided that Etudes III and IX presented rewarding displays of virtuosity but compromised the "content." In that case, this content would have inhered in the newly clarified variation process and its long surges of energy.

This is not to suggest that Schumann had already viewed the *Études* with such a critical eye in 1837. As I argued in chapter 4, formal and tonal stretching represented one "symphonic" feature of the work that signaled Schumann's compositional ambition. The different versions of the *Études* document Schumann's journey between venues and viewpoints: from the quasi-improvisatory *Fantaisies* steeped in salon music-making, to the "symphonic" *Études*, to the variation-form *Études* reworked at the peak of Schumann's career. The 1852 revision bore traces of each earlier version (the theme, for example, and the rondo finale) even as its larger outlines reflect Schumann's midlife priorities.

Taming the Phoenix: The Piano Concerto Op. 54

The composition and premiere of Robert's Piano Concerto unfolded alongside his 1840s shifts of style and aesthetic. Robert began composing the work as a single-movement *Phantasie* in 1841, around the time critics began to credit him with greater compositional mastery and self-possession. The *Phantasie* never saw publication or public performance. Clara rehearsed the work with Mendelssohn and the Gewandhaus Orchestra, but the intricate piano–orchestra interaction produced rocky, discouraging results. Robert was unable to find a publisher. In 1845, around the point he himself identified as the beginning of a new compositional approach, he revised the *Phantasie*, designated it as the first movement of a piano concerto, and added the second and third movements. Soon after, Clara premiered the work in Dresden (December 1845) and Leipzig (January 1846).

The Piano Concerto has already prompted numerous studies, and its form and genesis are well-known. Claudia Macdonald has shown that many of its characteristics reflect criteria for concertos that Robert developed in his critical writings. She has also shown that Robert anticipated aspects of the first movement in an 1836 essay that proposed a compressed concerto form. Macdonald and Stephen Lindeman have situated Robert's concerto within the larger field of nineteenth-century innovations in concerto form; Juan Martin Koch has explored its tenuous relationship with the category of the "symphonic"; and Arnfried Edler and Thomas Synofzik have identified several quotations within the first movement.[50]

Without retracing this insightfully explored ground, I would like to propose some new ways in which the Piano Concerto balanced the spectacle of virtuosic performance with Schumann's 1840s self-presentation as a composer. Clara Wieck's 1835 Piano Concerto Op. 7 offers one window into this negotiation, a window we can polish by considering some unexplored aspects of both concertos' structures and receptions. Scholars often recognize Robert's concerto as a response to Clara's.[51] Hers was not the only work to which Robert was responding: he also drew upon his broad experience as a critic, listener, and performer of concertos. Contextual and musical evidence, though, reveal Clara's concerto as an important model for Robert's.

Robert emulated several distinctive features of Clara's composition, notably the way he formally and thematically unified his *Phantasie*-turned-first-movement. His expansive sonata form embraces contrasting sections that suggest a three-movements-in-one plan: after the exposition, Schumann inserts an "Andante espressivo" that serves as a brief interior slow movement, and the "Allegro molto" coda establishes a faster tempo and new meter. Transformations of two motives pervade the work, from the more conventional sections of the sonata form to the

Andante, cadenza, and coda. Such thorough structural integration was almost unprecedented in the concerto literature—almost, because Clara's concerto anticipated many of these strategies. Granted, Robert knew other cyclic concertos: Mendelssohn's Piano Concerto No. 1, Moscheles's Concerto No. 6, "Fantastique," and Wilhelm Taubert's Concerto No. 1. None, however, resembled his as closely as Clara's did. Mendelssohn, Taubert, and Moscheles only offer cyclic links in isolated moments of reminiscence. Mendelssohn and Taubert delay the final pyrotechnics with lyrical recalls of previous movements, and Moscheles's "Fantastique" invokes its first movement in the transition to its finale. Clara Wieck, by contrast, saturated her entire concerto with thematic links: the first theme, both sections of the slow movement, and the polonaise finale all transform a single motive presented at the solo's first entrance. Also like Robert, Clara created a continuous form that moves seamlessly between sections—in her case, between the different movements of her concerto. Clara uses an abbreviated sonata form for her first movement, which cuts off after its development and segues directly to the second. Transitions link all three of her movements. Again, several nineteenth-century piano concertos transition between movements or abbreviate sonata forms. No other concerto that Robert knew, however, combined an unbroken flow of contrasting movements or sections with pervasive motivic transformation to the extent that Clara's did. Her concerto offered the closest model for his first movement.[52]

Robert echoed other striking details of Clara's composition. Her A-minor concerto features a slow second movement in A-flat, an unusual tonal relationship that critics noted. Robert's concerto is also in A minor and modulates to A-flat for the "Andante espressivo." I will point out some additional tonal commonalities below.

Contextual evidence corroborates the musical links. Robert was intimately familiar with Clara's concerto and even played a part in its genesis. Clara began composing the concerto in 1833 after a disappointing tour of Paris: Friedrich wrote to his brother-in-law that, next time, Clara would make a bigger impression with an expanded portfolio of compositions. She was at work on a concerto, he wrote, that would "attract the attention of the connoisseurs [*Kenner*]." That same year, Robert wrote to Friedrich that Clara's concerto should be in C major or A minor, possibly because of his own delight in A-minor concertos by Hummel and Herz. At Clara's request, he orchestrated the finale. He reviewed the premiere of the full work on November 9, 1835, in Leipzig, and he discussed the concerto in an 1837 letter to Clara.[53]

Clara's and Robert's concertos formed part of a now-famous musical exchange that wound throughout their oeuvres. Some allusions and borrowings they openly acknowledged. The subtitles of Robert's Impromptus and the second movement of his *Concert sans orchestre* advertise that they use themes by Clara Wieck. Other references remained for listeners or scholars to discover: Robert's Sonata No. 1 Op. 11, for example, quotes a motive from the fourth of Clara's *Quatre pieces caractéristiques*, Op. 5. In some cases, it becomes difficult to tell where one partner's work ends and the other's begins. For example, an idea that resembles the Clara Wieck theme on which Robert based his Impromptus appears in one of his sketchbooks well before she composed it. After their marriage, Robert and Clara contributed selections to a joint song cycle, *Liebesfrühling*, Op. 37, studied Bach and Beethoven together, and presented one another with compositions as birthday and Christmas gifts. From early in their relationship, they also critiqued one another's work. Clara, for example, convinced Robert to rewrite the final movement of his Sonata Op. 22, reasoning that the original version was too inaccessible for concert audiences.

Robert's echoes of Clara's concerto are less overt than these better-known citations and exchanges. I would not argue that he expected contemporary listeners to hear his A-flat-major "Andante espressivo," for example, as an evocation of the earlier work (comparable to his quotation of *Papillons* in the "Florestan" movement of *Carnaval*). Rather, he drew upon and reinterpreted some of the most distinctive structural features of his wife's concerto. Robert's Piano Concerto became one of many instances in which he used allusion and modeling to position himself in relation to his contemporaries and predecessors. For example, Brown has shown that the finale of the Piano Quartet alludes to Beethoven's "Hammerklavier" Sonata and uses formal strategies associated with Robert's early sonatas and the music of Schubert. In her argument, the mix proclaims Robert's desire to reconcile his earlier, more radical music with the "classical" tradition he sought to enter and enrich. Mark Evan Bonds has shown that the transition between the third and fourth movements of Robert's Symphony No. 4—based on the analogous moment in Beethoven's Symphony No. 5—gives way to a light, even comic finale that deflects the expected Beethovenian climax and instead embraces the eighteenth-century symphonic tradition.[54]

Scholars who have noticed the link between Robert's concerto and Clara's have offered various interpretations. Macdonald describes Robert's concerto as a "tribute to Wieck . . . not just in its specifics, such as the related tonalities, but in the broader terms of its thematic unity as well." Daverio saw both homage and competition. He proposed that Robert, now completing his first large orchestral works, felt the need to assimilate his wife's influence while establishing his own independence. Daverio suggested, in fact, that Robert's Symphony No. 4, whose first version dates from 1841, also reveals Clara's influence with its compressed first movement and pervasive motivic connections. Christoph-Hellmut Mahling assumes less admiration on Robert's part. He portrays Robert writing his work as a form of criticism, an object lesson for Clara about how a concerto could transcend its status as a virtuoso vehicle. In all cases, accounts stop at specifying what features Robert drew from Clara's concerto and do not consider how he reinterpreted them.[55]

Considering this latter issue reveals a more complex mix of emulation, reinterpretation, and critique. Robert's response comes into focus when we consider the musical echoes within both concertos' larger structures and alongside their different receptions. Seen in this light, Robert engaged with the aspect of Clara's concerto that produced the strongest reactions among critics: its simulation of spontaneous, even quasi-improvisational performance. Of course, Clara's concerto is not literally an improvisation and only includes one short, written-out cadenza. Nevertheless, critics wrote that her concerto gave the impression of a virtuoso spontaneously exploring musical ideas or a composer making daring choices on a whim. At several important junctures of his concerto, Robert used strategies that, in Clara's work, evoked these qualities—he had, after all, titled the earlier version of the work a *Phantasie*. At the same time, he tempered these evocations. Especially in the published version of the concerto, Robert used these passages as pretexts for demonstrating his own compositional mastery and calculation.[56]

When critics heard spontaneity in Clara's concerto, their descriptions ranged from the explicit to the implicit and from the complimentary to the condescending. In 1837, for example, the Hamburg journal *Freischütz* neutrally commented that Clara's concerto was "more a *Phantasiestück* than a concerto . . . developed in a designedly rhapsodic way."[57] Janina Klassen's present-day study of Clara's compositions echoes the analysis, finding in the movements' continuity and wide-ranging tonal schemes "a quality of free fantasy."[58]

When Robert himself reviewed Clara's premiere, he reveled in descriptions of spontaneity:

> The first thing we heard flew like a young Phoenix before us and fluttered on high. White sighing roses and sparkling lily bells leaned up there, and down there nodded orange blossoms and myrtles between them, alders and weeping willows stretched out their melancholy shadows: in the midst of this all, though, a beaming maiden's face floated and sought flowers for a wreath.[59]

Robert depicted Clara gathering flowers, an activity in which one picks options as they come rather than planning in advance. In the review, he left unclear whether he was describing the concerto, Clara's performance, or the cumulative effect of both. (As we will see in chapter 6, Liszt described spontaneous, ever-changing inflections of melodies as a hallmark of Clara's 1830s playing.) In any case, his tone was largely positive. The title of the review, "Schwärmbriefe" (Enraptured Letters) hinted at his delight. Robert captured Clara's prolific performative or compositional invention with a stream of contrasting images: "Now a young Saracen hero, like an Oriflamme, appeared with lance and sword and jousted . . . and finally a French *elegant* gamboled, and hearts hung upon him." By likening Clara's concerto to a phoenix—a mythical bird who dies in flames, only to rise, reborn, from its own ashes—Robert aligned her with his *Davidsbündler* ethos of youthful rebellion. Clara's concerto, he suggested, had risen from the ashes of the present, reborn to poetic virtuosity.

Robert, however, also expressed reservations. In terms familiar from his Paganini and Liszt essays, he depicted a concerto whose abundance and momentum lacked a sense of stability:

> I often saw boats floating boldly over the waves, and only a more masterly grip on the tiller, a tightly pulled sail, was missing for them to cut through the waves as quickly and triumphantly as surely: here, I heard thoughts that often had not chosen the right interpreter to shine in their fullest beauty.[60]

In 1835, Robert suggested that Clara's intrepidness made up for it. "But, in the end," he wrote, "the fiery spirit that drove her and the longing that steered her flowed surely toward the destination." By 1837, his opinion soured. He voiced doubts about the concerto in a letter to Clara while she was touring in Vienna, and he even implied that the ever-controlling Friedrich Wieck might be pushing her to perform it. "Do you always play your concerto of your own accord?" he wrote. "There are stars of ideas in the first movement, but it never made a complete impression on me."[61] Here, he explicitly addressed the composition itself, and his language, while vague, implied that the first movement lacked wholeness or coherence.

Other critics were more direct when describing qualities of impulsiveness or incoherence. An 1838 review in the *Allgemeiner musikalischer Anzeiger* discussed Clara's music in patronizingly sexist terms. The reviewer explained away the slow movement's unexpected key as a female whim, writing, "Women have their moods, to which they are entitled and authorized, and even such innocent caprices often make them all the dearer."[62] The entry on Clara in Gustav Schilling's 1838 encyclopedia described her "youthful passion" in performance as both a strength and a foible. The author specifically criticized the structure of the concerto: "But with regard to the layout of the individual movements, the modulations, etc., from the standpoint of the strict critic, these expose many things that cannot be excused under the concept of genius and originality."[63] Such criticism might have been what convinced Clara to drop the concerto from her repertory after the late 1830s. After all, she had learned from her father to zealously seek the approval of musically cultivated connoisseurs, aware that they could propel or hinder her career.

Macdonald has shown that these critics, by cavalierly dismissing the work of a female composer, missed many important aspects of Clara's concerto. Her analysis reveals that the work evinces careful compositional planning. The striking A-flat of the slow movement, for example, is no caprice at all: Clara foreshadows it at the beginning of the first-movement development.[64]

Even so—and even if we disagree with these critics' value judgments and recoil at their language—the rhetoric of spontaneity recognized some of the most original features of Clara's showpiece. With its abbreviated first movement, cyclic unity, and wide-ranging tonal scheme, Clara's Opus 7 resembles a conventional style of improvisation that Czerny's *Systematic Introduction to Improvisation on the Pianoforte* termed "Improvisation on a Single Theme." In this format, the performer improvises several potentially continuous movements in contrasting forms and styles bound by a shared theme or set of themes. Clara's concerto shared these strategies with other compositions whose titles openly evoked the improvised fantasy: Schubert's "Wanderer" Fantasy, Hummel's "Oberons Zauberhorn" Fantasy, Op. 116, Robert's Symphony No. 4 (initially titled a "Symphonic Fantasy"), and, indeed, his unpublished *Phantasie* itself.

Accounts of Clara's performances during the 1830s describe her as an adept improviser of extended fantasies. Gottfried Weber reviewed a concert Clara gave when she was fourteen. Improvisation, Weber wrote, was what truly set her apart from other child prodigies:

> Aside from the applause that her truly extraordinary playing won, however, the little virtuoso Clara Wieck also won far greater and more solid applause from me

First movement, ritornello and first theme group:

Example 5.2. Clara Wieck, Concerto Op. 7. Intermovement and interthematic connections.

> when she performed extemporaneously—on a one-and-a-half-measure theme I
> gave arbitrarily—a somewhat long, free fantasia with a capability and wealth of
> ideas that would do honor to an experienced artist.[65]

A *Neue Zeitschrift* review of Clara's 1835 Hannover concert similarly noted that
in a salon performance, she had improvised on a theme given by an audience
member.[66] Despite Weber's astonishment, Clara did not gain a widespread reputation for this kind of freestanding improvisation after her early teens. More
often, she extemporized preludes and transitions to the short solo pieces on her
programs, improvisations that formed tonal bridges and occasionally anticipated motives of the next piece.[67]

Several details of Clara's concerto strengthen the illusion of spontaneous,
quasi-improvisatory performance, such as Robert heard at the premiere and other
reviewers specifically read in the composition. The introductions to movements
and the transitions between them, for example, contribute to the onrushing continuity and simulation of musical free association. As example 5.2 shows, each
metamorphoses a motive presented near the outset of the concerto into a new
theme, and each spotlights the piano solo: in performance, the virtuoso seems
to seize upon a short, previously heard musical idea and spin it into an array of

Transition, first movement to second:

Example 5.2. (continued)

melodies and affects. Clara begins this process at the concerto's first solo entrance. The piano takes the stage with *fortissimo* double octaves that alternate between ascending scales and descending arpeggios. At measure 33, the texture suddenly thins, and the piano glides over the dominant with a motive comprised of three ascending eighth notes. When the first theme arrives, its head-motive grows directly out of this figure. The transition between the first and second movements transforms the eighth-note motive into the Romanze theme. The orchestra uses the motive to reach the dominant of A-flat, and a short piano cadenza spreads the harmony across the keyboard. When the slow movement itself begins, the motive expands into a bel canto melody. Its unaccompanied beginning makes it seem—if only for a moment—an outgrowth of the cadenza, a transformation that occurs through solitary (faux) improvisation.[68] Finally, at the transition between the second and third movements, the pianist cycles through the motive, now chromatically rendered and in quarter notes. Evoking an exploratory probing of formal and tonal boundaries, the pianist makes the same ascent three times, each time juxtaposing A-flat (the key of the slow move-

Transition, second movement to third:

Example 5.2. (continued)

ment) with the dominant of A minor (the key of the finale). The third movement's polonaise theme emerges from this transition: in a sudden transformation, the tempo accelerates, the key changes, and chromaticism gives way to
diatonicism. (The result also echoes the first movement's primary theme, though
in a different meter.) The unity that pervades Clara's concerto, then, emerges in
these section- or movement-joining transformations. The overall structure

Schumann's Equivocal Work Concept 181

evokes not only the free fantasy but also the preludes Clara improvised, extemporized introductions that seemed to contain the tonal and thematic seeds of the subsequent set piece.

Other passages evoke bold, digressive performance through different means. In the first movement, the second theme and culminating display rocket across different key areas and blur formal boundaries (see example 5.3). Macdonald observes that Clara prepared the theme with only a one-measure, last-minute landing on V/III. I would add that the theme itself continues to vacillate between the two most likely secondary keys for a minor-mode sonata form, III (C major) and VI (F major). It opens in C and reaches a cadence, but a chromatic bass line almost immediately draws us away, and the theme ends in F at measure 75. The source of the theme strengthens the impression of spontaneity: it expands a motive from the middle of the first theme so that, again, the pianist seems to develop a small detail into a longer melody. The culminating display continues this unpredictable trajectory. As we saw in chapter 1, display areas in postclassical concertos generally confirm the key area at hand with series of short cadential gestures. Clara's, by contrast, makes the tonal ground constantly shift under the listener's feet. At first, the display cleaves to F major. However, the passagework soon prolongs C major, veers into a series of sequences, and then tonicizes G major. The final stage breaks from the rising-fifth pattern with a surprising turn to A-flat. The solo segues into the development without the conventional tutti—we might not even be aware that the development is under way until the modulating sequences have already begun.[69]

In Robert's Piano Concerto, the transition between the A-minor exposition and A-flat "Andante espressivo" at once emulates and mitigates these qualities of Clara's concerto. As studies of the work's genesis often note, Robert revised this passage when converting the 1841 *Phantasie* into the 1845 concerto. Unfortunately, the *Phantasie* itself is lost. The nearest extant source is a manuscript from July 1845 in which the copyist, Carl Mehner, wrote out a piano part for the first movement, after which Robert added the orchestration and made several revisions. It remains uncertain which autograph source Mehner was copying and how closely his piano part reflects the original *Phantasie*.[70] More important for my argument is that the manuscript records Robert's late stages of polishing the movement. He crossed out the eight measures that Mehner had placed between the end of the expositional culminating display and the start of the "Andante." He then inserted four pages that contain a new, two-measure ending for the display and twenty-two measures of tutti. The Mehner manuscript does leave some questions about the pre-revision transition unanswered. Schumann scratched out and added notes in the measure before his inserted pages, obscuring exactly how the culminating display would have connected to the transition. He also never wrote out the orchestral parts for the pre-revision transition. (Given the piano's I–V vamp, it could have used the same theme as the final version.)

Regardless of how Robert planned these details, I would argue that the pre-revision transition staged boundary-blurring continuity and soloistic sponta-

Example 5.3. Wieck, Concerto, movement 1. Culminating display from exposition.

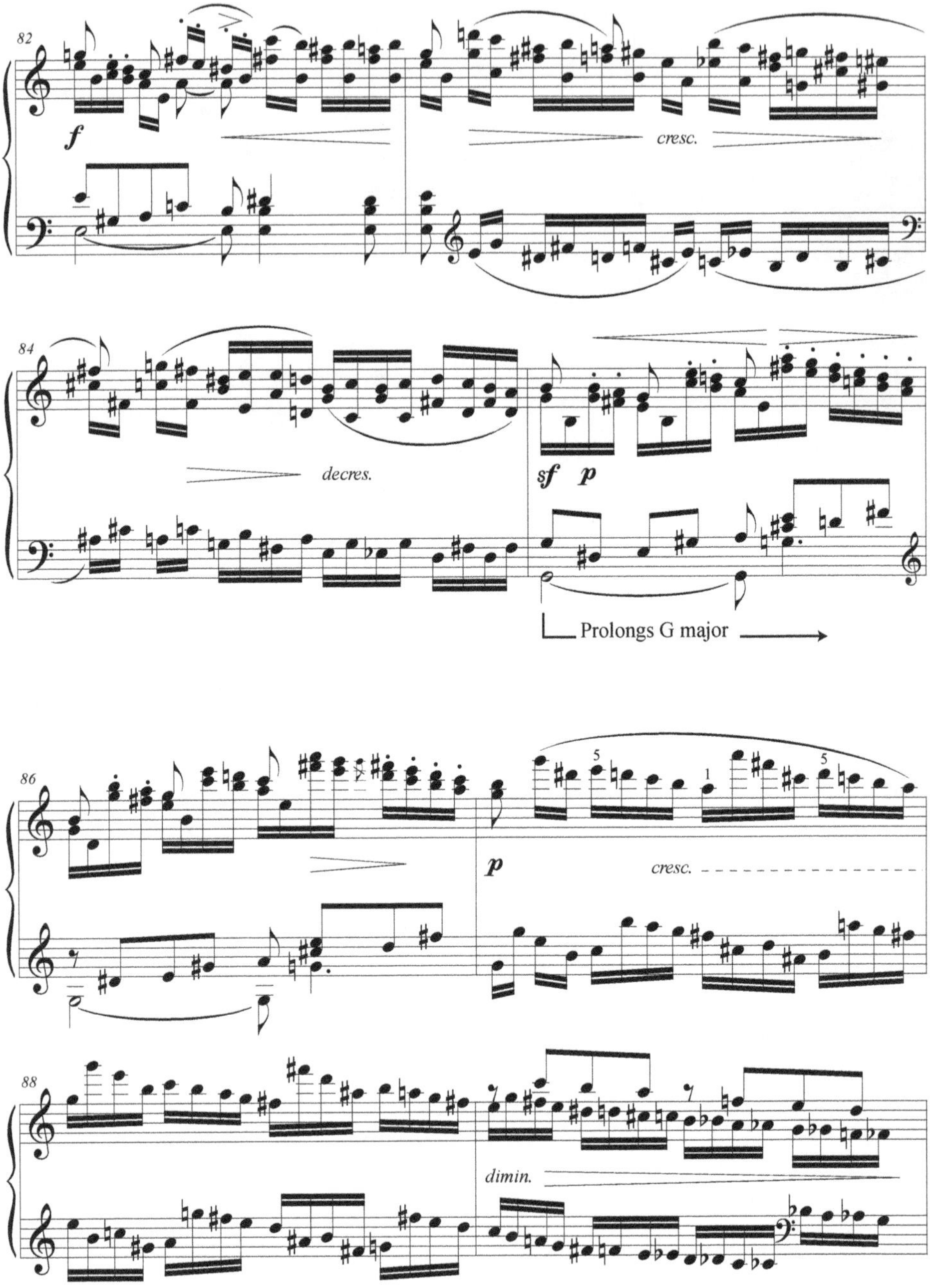

Example 5.3. (*continued*)

Example 5.3. (*continued*)

neity. As shown in example 5.4, this transition included an arpeggiated piano accompaniment that seamlessly grew into the "Andante espressivo." The constant triplets and the wide leap before the Andante would have required the soloist herself to lead the *ritardando*. The specific route to A-flat reinforces the illusion of soloist-driven transformation. Even more than Clara, Robert allows this flat-key efflorescence to take the listener by surprise. The piano figuration only foreshadows the modulation by turning C major into C minor three measures in advance, a slight harmonic shift that opens up the exposition's tonal boundaries. A-flat itself materializes when the soloist suddenly drops into the key, widens the arpeggios, and offers a lyrical version of the concerto's primary theme. The result would have resembled Clara's transitional strategies in her concerto and, perhaps, reflected Robert's original *Phantasie* title.

The Mehner manuscript also suggests that Robert initially planned to blend the culminating display into these transitional arpeggios. Most of the display relegates rapid figuration to a flowing triplet accompaniment in the piano's mellow middle range. The passagework briefly enters the spotlight sixteen measures before the transition begins, where the orchestra thins and the soloist's right hand takes the triplets. In the prerevision transition, these triplets simply descend into the piano's lower register and continue beneath the orchestra. The effect is not as disorienting as the end of Clara's first-movement exposition: Robert's culminating

Early version, as given in the Mehner manuscript:

Example 5.4. Schumann, Piano Concerto Op. 54, movement 1. Transition between exposition and "Andante espressivo."

display clearly ends in C major, and the orchestra delineates the form by entering for at least part of the transition. Nevertheless, Robert's transition creates a continuous fabric of piano arpeggios that stretches from the most brilliant moments of the exposition to the interior "slow movement."

The published revised version of the transition stems this flow of figuration. The change, on one level, reflects Robert's midcentury effort to distance himself from spontaneous or improvisation-driven composition. It might have also been a practical response to the difficulties Clara and Mendelssohn's Gewandhaus Orchestra had coordinating with one another. Edler notes that, by expanding the tutti, Robert clarified that the Andante represented a distinct section of the movement.[71] I would add that Robert also undid the earlier evocation of soloistic spontaneity. Here, the culminating display reaches a form-demarcating bravura conclusion: the triplets break into eighth notes and coalesce into a rising octave scale. The tutti transition that extends the energy of this climax elimi-

Published version:

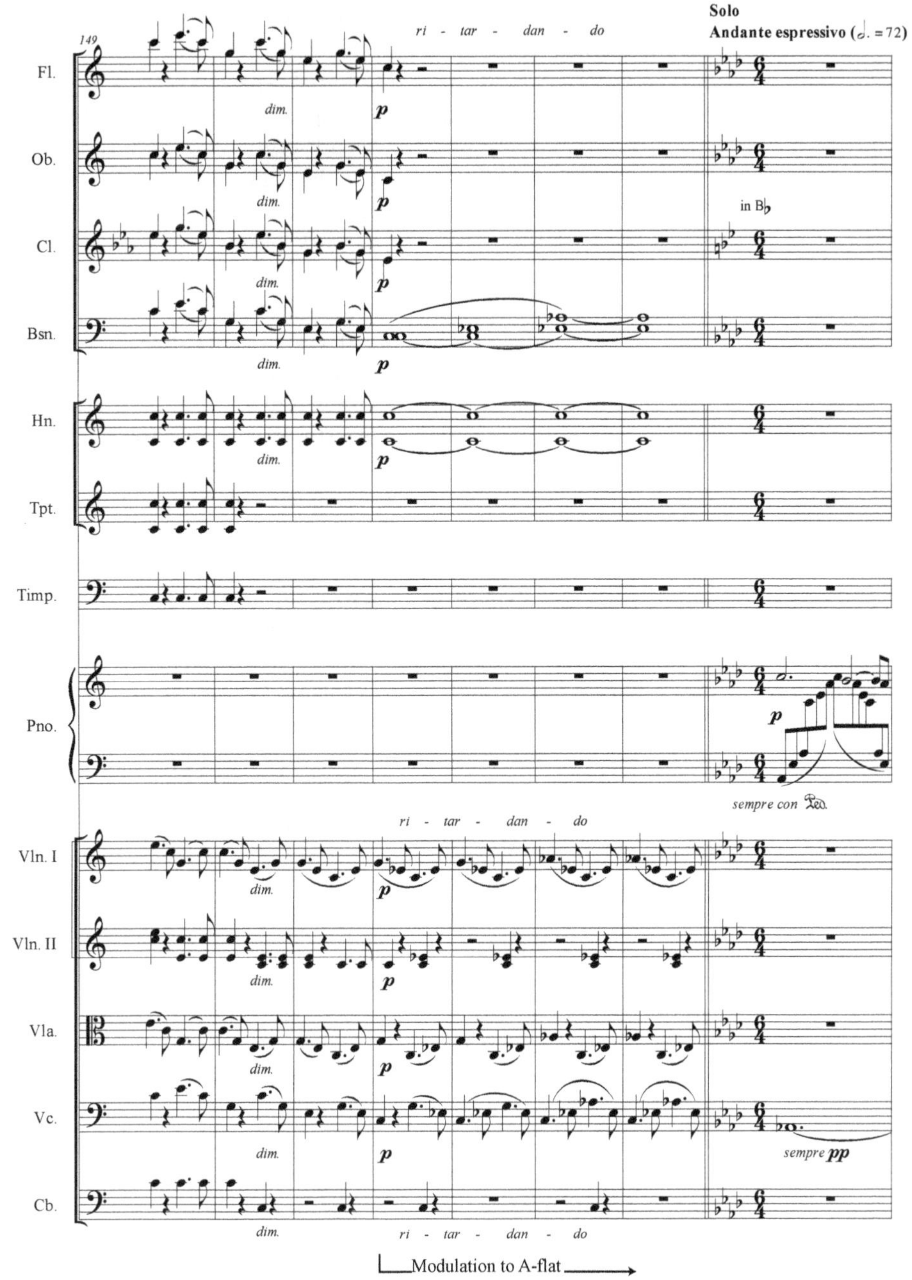

Example 5.4. (*continued*)

nates the piano entirely, and it softens the surprise value of the A-flat modulation by moving from C minor to A-flat two measures before the Andante begins. In the "Andante espressivo," then, the soloist enters a contrasting tonality and tempo that the orchestra has prepared in advance.

The "Andante espressivo" springs the most substantial departure Robert makes from Clara's concerto: his first movement uses a complete sonata form.[72] A first-time listener (especially one versed in mid-nineteenth-century developments in concerto form) might assume that the Andante is the beginning of a different movement and that what we have heard so far is a first movement with an abbreviated sonata form. In a single-movement work comparable to Weber's *Konzertstück*, the change could signal the next step in a several-movements-in-one plan. Schumann himself did not generally support abbreviated sonata forms. His largely positive 1836 review of Moscheles's Concerto "Fantastique," for example, expressed reservations: "Even if it does not appear impossible to create an agreeable whole with it, the aesthetic dangers appear too great in comparison with what can be achieved." He described the concerto as "fully effective despite its somewhat unsteady form."[73]

Robert used one of the concerto's most jarring moments to dispel any notion of an abbreviated sonata form. At measure 185, the movement suddenly reverts to Tempo I and launches into a sequential development shared between piano and orchestra. In an 1847 *Neue Zeitschrift* review of the score, Alfred Dörffel and Franz Brendel described this as one of the moments whose affective shift recalled Robert's more "subjective" 1830s music.[74] However, Robert used this disjuncture not to create a bewildering procession of fragmentary ideas but to reestablish the teleology of the sonata form. The clash of modulatory development against lyrical reverie sets his concerto apart not just from Clara's but from the broader field of piano concertos that included abbreviated sonata forms. The development turns to more lyrical figuration twenty measures later, but the mood swing has already made its statement. Heard alongside his 1836 essay (not to mention his essays on Liszt, Paganini, and Clara herself), it begs to be interpreted as an attempt to give the concerto qualities of repose, control, and solidity that Robert considered marks of the masterful composer.

The restarted development and full recapitulation assert Robert's identity as a composer who assimilated the associative, exploratory logic of the free fantasy but ultimately fit it to classicizing, sonata-form imperatives about large-scale tonal and formal balance. The "Andante espressivo" had incorporated the wide-ranging harmonic schemes and thematic transformation that characterized Clara's concerto and the fantasy tradition more generally. Eduard Hanslick, in a review of Clara's 1858 Vienna performance of Robert's concerto, evocatively described the section as an oasis-like break from the movement, "a small, mirror-clear lake between dark stones and trees."[75] Rather than using such contrasts to override sonata-form conventions, as Clara did, Robert only briefly suspends them. If one considers the Andante part of the development (as Macdonald does), Robert has clarified that the sonata form was never abandoned. A tonal gesture that one critic of Clara's concerto had described as a "caprice" here becomes a remote modulation rationalized by sonata-form conventions and grounded in the recapitulation. If one accepts Edler's equally plausible reading of the Andante as time out from the sonata form, an "arabesque" akin to the "Im Legendenton" section of the Fantasie Op. 17, the shift at measure 185 becomes even starker.[76] It forcefully relegates the Andante to peripheral (if captivating) status and restarts the sonata form.

Robert's transition between first and second theme groups also invokes but turns from a digressive pathway. Like Clara's, his exposition sustains a tension between III (C major) and VI (F major) as possible second key areas (ex. 5.5). The transition initially yields a melody in C that promises to start the second theme group (m. 36). The piano interrupts the cadence with bold octave figuration that reinterprets the final C-major chord as a V^7/VI. The brass and winds join in, converting the theme into an F-major orchestral fanfare in which the soloist has no part. Despite an emphatic cadence in F, the transition continues until arriving at a C-major variation of the primary theme. Also like Clara's, Robert's transition and second theme group take last-minute harmonic detours. At measure 56, for example, a cadence to F major seems to be under way, which would confirm the key of the fanfare. Only a vii^{o7}/V the measure before the second theme signals passage to C major. Even this tonal arrival is blunted when the second theme begins on a third-inversion triad.

For Robert, this digressiveness ultimately provided the pretext for a display of structural balancing and wit. Rather than crafting themes and display areas that venture fluidly between tonal areas, he assigned potential second key areas to distinct themes. He also resolved the tonal tension, clarifying that the F-major fanfare had been but a way station en route to the true second key: in the tutti after the exposition's culminating display, the fanfare returns in C major. Here, Robert reinterprets the formal significance of the theme, turning it from a catalyst of structural dissonance and momentary tonal uncertainty into a marker of tonal and formal clarification. The rising octave scales merge with the C-major fanfare, so that the culminating display's crowning flourish glorifies a moment that grounds an element from the tonally digressive transition. The recapitulation creates an even starker distinction between the fanfare's transitional and culminating roles. During the transition, the fanfare returns in a sudden burst of B minor, a key that, even more than the exposition's F major, introduces structural dissonance that propels the transition. The tutti that follows the recapitulation's culminating display at last brings the fanfare theme into A major. In the end, then, Robert used the transition to demonstrate his command of large formal processes—to show that he could work out its tensions across the entire first movement.

Though Robert's first movement draws the most from Clara's concerto, his second and third movements also reveal his attempt to demonstrate compositional self-possession. Robert, like Clara, included a transition between the second and third movements that effects a thematic transformation (not that he could only have derived this idea from her concerto). In Robert's case, the transition links the primary theme of the first movement to that of the finale. His transition does possess some of the ruminative quality of Clara's, repeating a motive in different harmonic contexts. However, whereas Clara's transition suddenly generates one

Example 5.5. Schumann, Piano Concerto, movement 1. Transition to second theme. Orchestral parts shown in piano reduction.

Example 5.5. (continued)

theme from another after a period of suspenseful repetition, Robert walks listeners through his transformation step by step. He first changes the motive from major to the original minor and back again. He then foreshortens the motive to emphasize its 3–2–1 descent. The descending third that opens the finale's first theme seems to emerge from these motivic and modal manipulations. Robert's transition resembles a painstakingly crafted gateway more than it does a sudden alchemic transformation—Macdonald even describes it as heavy-handed.[77] Robert also gives the motivic transformation to the orchestra rather than to the pianist, precluding the illusion of soloistic creation. The third movement concludes with a last display of classicizing logic. The development introduces a new theme in F major, and the coda "resolves" it in A major. The coda, then, ties up tonal loose ends amid the string of virtuosic flourishes. (Using codas to resolve structural dissonances is a hallmark of the Beethovenian symphonic tradition. To cite a non-Beethovenian example from the eighteenth-century concerto literature, the first movement of Mozart's Piano Concerto in A major, K. 488, introduces a new theme in the development and "resolves" it unexpectedly in the closing tutti.)

Critical responses to Robert's Piano Concerto differed almost diametrically from responses to Clara's. Reviews described his piece as an idealized work born of the composer's intellect rather than a script for a bold, exploratory performance.[78] These critics might have noticed features of the movement other than the Clara-emulating ones I have detailed: the way the orchestra gradually builds the fanfare theme from short motives, for example, or the cadenza's imitative, contrapuntal opening. An *Allgemeine musikalische Zeitung* review of the Dresden premiere claimed that Robert had entered a venerable tradition by mediating between inner inspiration, virtuosic display, and compositional mastery and learnedness: the concerto "provides new proof of the old claim that form and thoroughness of schooling lend themselves well to being united with an inspired [*geistreich*] conception, palpable invention, and all the brilliance of recent and latest technique." A review of the Leipzig premiere in the same journal paused from praising Clara's performance to note that the work was "beautifully felt, deeply thought through, and inspired" and that the solo–orchestra interaction shaped "a beautiful, rounded whole." In the *Dresdner Abendzeitung*, Julius Schladebach commended the composer's power to create a unified whole. He described "beautifully invented, interesting themes developed with inspiration; clear, very effective instrumentation; pleasing formal roundedness; artistic unity of idea and execution."[79] An 1850 article on Robert's life and compositions for the magazine *Die Grenzboten* claimed that the work continued a venerable canonic lineage. The reviewer wrote, "In its seriousness and dignity, the Piano Concerto worthily follows the works of Mozart, Beethoven, and Mendelssohn."[80]

The New Germans Dörffel and Brendel entered this strand of reception from their Hegelian perspective, claiming that the Piano Concerto brought Robert closer to a synthesis of his objective and subjective sides. "We feel this especially in the first and second movements," they wrote. "In them, the composer most fully preserves his profound inwardness, his particular nature, while striving for that objective expression."[81] They singled out the C-major statement of the fanfare at the end of the exposition as a climactic affirmation of self-mastery:

> The way the whole orchestra joins in, crowned by the trumpets as if with a cry of victory: is it not as if we were experiencing a moment of supreme joy in which the power of artistic genius bears us upward, far beyond this world? Does it not seem as if that power were celebrating the triumph of self-control?[82]

Despite the wide divergence of descriptions and value judgments, Robert's concerto did not suppress qualities of Clara's as much as it assimilated them. These critical responses, after all, also hinted at subjective freedom within the concerto—"sentiment" and "energy and passion." Though Robert's Piano Concerto kept some of the "young phoenix's" radical plumage, however, its flight reflected the agenda of a composer bent on demonstrating self-possession, planning, and formal order.

An Apotheosis of Postclassical Brilliance

And yet, despite their claims about intellectual depth and compositional mastery, critics also hinted that Robert's Piano Concerto possessed a double nature that emerged in its third movement. Some reviews took a dismissive tone when describing the finale. Following the Leipzig premiere, the *Allgemeine musikalische Zeitung* reported that the first movement's "lofty spirit" "understandably" took the prize.[83] Dörffel and Brendel alleged that the finale did not satisfy their hopes for Robert. It was "not as unified and self-contained as the previous movements: more fine, inspired detail work than a large, total impression." Their complaints evoked the shifting patterns of figuration and the stark contrast between the waltz-meter first theme and the second (where an extended hemiola creates a duple meter). The New Germans even heard the influence of Mendelssohn on the movement. For them, this was no compliment, since they regarded Mendelssohn as a regressive, convention-bound classicist.[84] Hanslick recognized the differences between the two movements without privileging either. He situated the finale within a conventional category of showpieces, and his piling up of adjectives exudes pleasure, even ecstasy, in the bravura display. "Full of life, brilliant, powerful, decorated over and over with newly charming passages, rushing forth in a single flow from beginning to end," he writes, "the final movement is a model of composition truly suited for the concert."[85]

The finale contains the most substantial expanse of postclassically textured, brilliant passagework in Robert's output. Macdonald writes that the finale "shuns virtuosity but at the same time gives the virtuoso . . . something to do. It stirs up excitement not through conventional bravura but through a dance of changing metric divisions that take a leisurely pace to a rousing climax and a splendid denouement."[86] Her analysis brings to light several subtleties of the finale, but I would contend that she exaggerates its suppression of conventional virtuosic figuration. In fact, the sonata-form third movement presents a brilliant inverse image of the first.[87] Whereas the first movement gives the piano solo a lyrical middle-register covering and complicates the sonata form, the third features a sharply chiseled structure that delivers transparently textured virtuosity in all of the expected transitional and culminating displays. Especially near the ends of these passagework areas, the solo executes single-line runs through the keyboard's upper octaves. The brilliance reaches a climax in the coda. A new figurational pattern emerges every eight to sixteen measures—scales, arpeggios, alternating octaves, broken sixths—and top notes ping higher and higher on the keyboard. Set to a light accompaniment, the perpetual eighth notes follow the flow of the first theme's waltz meter. After almost one hundred and fifty measures of such brilliance, the pianist returns to the pattern that began the coda, only to veer in a new direction that generates additional patterns.

In its finale, Robert's Piano Concerto ultimately offered a reward similar to the postclassical showpieces he knew, critiqued, and emulated: a trajectory leading to an ever-changing flow of transparent virtuosic figuration. As we saw in chapter 1, such figuration was designed partly to generate listening pleasure, and Hanslick revealed that the finale could elicit euphoria from even the most elitist critic. If the concerto's structural enterprise was what propped up Robert's professional image, it might have been the brilliant finish that sealed the work's popularity. In this sense, the Piano Concerto realized an important nuance of Robert's Leipzig Parnassus review: it aimed not only to impress listeners with compositional greatness and a contribution to the canonic tradition but to delight them—not only to cast masterworks in stone but to bedeck them with resplendent virtuosity.

6 Festivals of the Virtuoso Priesthood: Collaborating with Clara Schumann and Joseph Joachim

During the 1840s and 1850s, Robert Schumann collaborated extensively with two virtuosos who built their careers around *Werktreue*. One, Clara Wieck Schumann, we have already encountered in previous chapters. The other was violinist Joseph Joachim—the Schumanns first met him during the mid-1840s and began collaborating with him during the 1850s. As I noted in the introduction to Part II, *Werktreue* demanded a focus on canonic (usually Austro-German) repertoire, reverence for the composer's intentions (however these were defined), and profound insight into the musical composition. At its heart was an imperative that the performer should re-create the work in the spirit of the (possibly long-dead) composer. Writers variously described such interpretation as an abnegation of the performer's subjectivity or as a synthesis between the performer's subjectivity and the work or composer.

Critics idealized Clara and Joachim in quasi-religious terms. The most often-quoted instance comes from Eduard Hanslick's 1869 history of Viennese concert life, specifically in his description of an "Artistic Renaissance" after the 1848 revolutions. "In particular," he wrote, "four true priests of art have found consistent applause in Vienna through their long, frequent visits: Clara Schumann, Joseph Joachim, Johannes Brahms, and [baritone] Julius Stockhausen." These performers "personify for us the true mission of the virtuoso." The "priest" metaphor suggested reverence, even moral superiority. It claimed that these virtuosos enjoyed privileged access to the sanctum of serious music and upheld them as standard-bearers in the broader sacralization of art. In part, Hanslick's "true mission" entailed championing canonic repertoire: "By the middle of the 1850s (and especially after Clara's concerts), no pianist dared to offer a concert program on which Bach (occasionally Scarlatti or Handel), Beethoven, Chopin, and Schumann did not figure."[1]

Hanslick's honor roll harnessed this idealism to make a polemical point: his "priests" represented one faction in the debates over Liszt, Wagner, and the New German School. (Not that any group had a monopoly on *Werktreue*. Liszt, for example, also strove to demonstrate interpretive reverence.[2]) These debates hinged on the proper musical response to nineteenth-century historicism. Historicism was not one single ideology, and it did not simply mean venerating and imitating earlier styles of music.[3] Rather, it was a philosophical framework in which artists and intellectuals became hyperconscious of their historical position. Musicians and critics developed a variety of ways in which they interpreted music history and positioned themselves within it. Under the influence of Young Hegelian philosophy, proponents of the New German School claimed that supposed laws of history validated their music, which they believed continued a process of progress and synthesis. Around and after midcentury, Clara Schumann, Brahms, and Joachim openly opposed these claims. Particularly by championing Brahms's compositions, they promoted a different brand of historicism, one that sought to continue a supposedly timeless tradition of instrumental music.[4]

Robert Schumann joined and supported the latter circle. Most famously, his 1853 essay "Neue Bahnen" heralded Brahms as a composer "called to give utterance to the highest expression of our time in an ideal way."[5] Schumann appointed a circle of composers around Brahms, including Niels Gade, Theodor Kirchner, Stephen Heller, and Joachim himself. After a ten-year hiatus from music criticism, he essentially declared a new *Davidsbund*.

This chapter explores a different way in which Robert Schumann shaped the public personae of the virtuoso "priests." During the 1840s and early 1850s, I argue, his collaborations with Clara and Joachim helped them to establish themselves as performers who, in their own ways, embodied seriousness and historicism. These were transformative years for both virtuosos. Clara was changing her programming practices and intertwining her career with Robert's. Joachim was riding a wave of success as a Beethoven and Bach interpreter, and he was beginning to pull away from Liszt and toward the Brahms–Schumann circle.

Robert's role in these collaborations ranged from performance to composition. He participated in some of Clara's and Joachim's most significant concerts by showcasing his own works, conducting, and administrating. Several heretofore unexplored accounts of these concerts reveal their significance for the performers themselves and for the wider virtuosity discourse. Robert also composed concerted showpieces specifically for Clara and Joachim. For Clara, he wrote the Introduction and Allegro Appassionato Op. 92 (1849) and the Introduction and Concert Allegro Op. 134 (1853). For Joachim, he wrote the Phantasie Op. 131, and the Violin Concerto, both in 1853.

These works staged the aesthetic and cultural values that Clara and Joachim represented. Robert did publish Opuses 92, 131, and 134, making them widely available to performers, and he intended to publish the Violin Concerto. Nevertheless, the way they unfold virtuosic spectacle—their structures, styles of themes and figuration, and allusions to other compositions—specifically captures Clara's and Joachim's practices and public personae. Such affinities emerge not just through the composer's design but through the performers' agencies. Clara and Joachim chose to identify themselves with these showpieces, incorporating them into their existing practices. Evidence for my claim only comes through faintly in reviews of the scores, not least because Schumann's 1854 confinement in a psychiatric institution colored the reception of his late works. Instead, traces of the individual "priests" appear when we hear the music alongside other contextual sources, including programs, correspondence, and critical writings about the performers.

These writings and showpieces both document and complicate the virtuosos' austere images. On the surface, Hanslick's "priest" metaphor seems to separate Clara and Joachim from all things earthy and sensual, placing them in communion with quasi-divine forces. In this image, the concert appears as a reverently enacted ritual, presumably with the masterwork as sacred text. Numerous contemporary sources buttress this image. In fact, though, Clara's and Joachim's collaborations with Robert reveal the multifaceted aesthetic that, as we saw in chapter 5, informed Robert's Leipzig Parnassus essay and Piano Concerto. Here, the "temple of the masters" is at once honored and decorated, constructed from venerated pillars but also festooned with pleasurable virtuosity. Many of the concerts were convivial, festive occasions that turned historicist, self-consciously serious music into an object of mass celebration and consumption. The concertos incorporate postclassically styled passagework and other popular forms of virtuosity alongside evocations of the canonic tradition. Robert gave Clara and Joachim pedestals from which to assert their prestige and seriousness as well as platforms from which to elicit applause and reach for broad appeal.

Such virtuosity does not reveal a tension or contradiction but rather a blend of strategies fundamental to the culture of serious music. This musical scene was not a truly popular phenomenon in the way that political songs or fairground entertainment were. The educated middle class that sustained it was itself a demographic that avidly policed its own boundaries. As I noted in the Introduction, nineteenth-century critics distanced their preferred music from plebian, "uncultivated" activities and professions. At the same time, constructing music as a cultivated, serious pursuit not only depended on the metaphysics of Romantic aesthetics, the editing of critical editions, and awing audiences into respectful silence. It also thrived on choral festivals, oratorios that combined learned and accessible styles, and piano four-hands arrangements that turned Beethoven symphonies into equipment for social music-making. *Kunstreligion* needed recreation as well as rites, pleasure and delight as well as reverence and austerity.

The stories I trace here emphasize currents in virtuosity rather than the development of the composer's late style. Robert composed the Introduction and Allegro Appassionato in 1849, when he and his family lived in Dresden. The other performances and concerted works date from his last productive years, when he worked as municipal music director in Düsseldorf. After the composer's death, accounts of his life often described his time in Düsseldorf as a disappointing final decline. Recent scholarship, however, has revealed the 1850s as a highly productive, rich period for Robert. He undeniably clashed with his employers, suffered from ill health, and failed to inspire as a conductor. However, he was also enjoying widespread recognition for his compositions, working in diverse genres, and busy with literary pursuits. (He edited his *Gesammelte Schriften* and compiled *Dichtergarten*, an anthology of quotations about music.) The true disappointment is that his illness and institutionalization cut this period short.[6]

When scholars have explored the concertos, they have used them to define Schumann's late style and probe its troubled reception. Michael Struck has shown that responses to this music were initially positive. After Schumann's death, critics and scholars began to suggest that the same pieces revealed weakness, melancholy, and exhaustion—signs, they believed, of his mental illness.[7] The stigma of mental illness created a particularly tangled history for the Violin Concerto. Joachim and Clara suppressed the work after Robert's death, and it was not publicly performed until 1937. Yehudi Menuhin mounted a performance that December with the Saint Louis Symphony, but the Nazi propaganda ministry (unwilling to let a Jewish violinist have the world premiere) included it on a Berlin concert a month earlier.[8] Struck's and other recent studies of the late works have steered clear of clichés about composer pathology. Laura Tunbridge, for example, considers how the concertos evoke both public utterance and introverted subjectivity.[9] My discussion does not dispute their arguments—instead, I examine the concertos in a different context that emphasizes significant performers and performances.

The history of Schumann's late showpieces presents an irony. Though fine recordings of these works abound today, after his death they became some of his least performed instrumental compositions. And yet, in their original context, they supported what has been the most enduring strand of the virtuosity discourse: the ideal of *Werktreue*. The performances Schumann shared were ephemeral and the works he composed during this period later sidelined, but they nourished the careers of two virtuosos who epitomized what later generations usually meant by serious virtuosity.

The Priestess Virtuoso and the Genius Composer

During the 1840s and 1850s, Robert and Clara Schumann's collaboration became integral to their professional identities. Both were also transforming their individual styles and practices. I recounted Robert's midlife style change in chapter 5: his move to composing chamber, orchestral, and theatrical works and his attempts to demonstrate compositional mastery. It is also well-known that Clara changed the content and layout of her programs around midcentury. Examining this transformation reveals an important backdrop to her and Robert's collaboration and image.

Most strikingly, Clara dropped opera-based fantasies and variations from her repertoire. She also stopped performing Henselt's highly popular etudes and Thalberg's Caprice Op. 15. During the 1830s and early 1840s, Clara's concerts had inhabited the blurry or nonexistent boundary between cutting-edge popular virtuosity and concepts of transcendence and cultivation that I explored in chapters 1 through 3. She made Chopin's "Là ci darem la mano" Variations a signature showpiece beginning in 1831, championed Henselt beginning in 1837, and used Thalberg's fantasies as closers well into 1844. An audience got its final glimpse of Clara in Italianate opera melodies set in expansive variations and fantasies—and, for some critics, elaborated in ways that conveyed transcendent interiority. At an

1838 soiree in Dresden, for example, she used Henselt's *Variations sur "L'elisir d'amore"*, Op. 1, to close a concert whose second-half solo set featured Liszt's transcription of Schubert's "Lob der Tränen," a Henselt etude, and the second and third movements of Beethoven's "Appassionata." At an 1840 concert in Bremen, she entered the stage with the "Appassionata," performed shorter pieces by Scarlatti, Schubert, Chopin, and Mendelssohn, and exited with Thalberg's "Moïse" Fantasy.[10]

Clara began reformulating her concerts after she and Robert returned from her 1844 Russian tour.[11] Like Robert's stylistic transformation, Clara's change was more a nuanced rebalancing than a drastic shift. She retained many of her 1830s practices. For example, she continued to play Liszt's *Réminiscences de "Lucia di Lammermoor"* well into 1847. She also kept some of Henselt's shorter pieces in her repertoire, such as his *Wiegenlied*. The performances of canonic repertoire that led Hanslick to dub Clara a "priestess" continued practices she had begun early in her career, such as her Beethoven, Bach, and Chopin interpretations.

Phasing out opera fantasies and variations substantially changed the way Clara's concerts unfolded. The program for her December 10, 1846 concert at the Saal der Gesellschaft der Musikfreunde in Vienna illustrates her new practice. Clara's solo portions are shown in bold:[12]

Cherubini: Overture to *Faniska*
Beethoven: Piano Concerto No. 4
Haydn: Aria from *The Creation*
Robert Schumann: Canon [possibly from Opus 56 or 68]
Chopin: Barcarolle Op. 60
Stockhausen: *Schweizerlied*
Robert Schumann: Romanze [from Opus 28]
Mendelssohn: *Lied ohne Worte*, Op. 62, no. 6 ("Frühlingslied")
Scarlatti: Clavierstücke [An unspecified sonata]

Clara's midcentury concerts combined historicist repertoire and lied-style miniatures. Here and on other Clara Schumann concerts, the anchor was a large canonic work—or a recent composition pointedly in dialogue with the canonic lineage, such as Robert's chamber music. Without showpieces based on Italianate operatic hits, her concerts became more consistently Germanocentric. Performing of Chopin and Scarlatti did not compromise this focus. In his 1840 Berlin concerts, Liszt had grouped Scarlatti with Bach and Handel to convince critics of his historical awareness, and, during the later nineteenth century, publishers and critics increasingly presented Chopin as a branch of a largely Austro-German canon.[13] Clara's solo mosaics shifted from the middles to the ends of the concerts. Depending on the mix of repertoire, they could deliver pianistic acrobatics (Mendelssohn's *Spinnerlied*, for example) or withhold them (Robert's Romances). Now, when audiences got their last glimpse of Clara, they heard her entering the canonic tradition or summoning the intimacy and introversion of piano lieder.[14]

Clara found virtuosic variation sets that fit into her new practice. In 1848, she began programming Mendelssohn's *Variations sérieuses*, Op. 54.[15] The work gives virtuosity a historicist frame with its grim, chromatic theme in four-part counterpoint, fugal and chorale variations, and allusion to Beethoven's String Quartet Op. 95 ("Serioso").[16] She began programming Robert's *Études symphoniques* in the mid-1850s, and, in 1854, added Beethoven's chaconne-style C-Minor Variations, WoO 80, to her repertoire.

Unfortunately for present-day scholars, neither Clara nor Robert left behind writings that explicitly explain this change. In the end, we are left with several plausible, interrelated motivations. In an 1841 entry in her and Robert's marriage diary, Clara hinted that her own aesthetic was changing, that she was embracing a more canon-centric aesthetic and rejecting some of her 1830s repertoire as merely "mechanical." After playing Beethoven sonatas for two of Robert's colleagues, she wrote:

> Their cultivation is more directed at virtuosity than true music. A Bach fugue, for example, bores them. . . . I pity the musician who lacks a sense for this magnificent art. The less I play in public now, the more hateful mechanical virtuosity becomes for me! Concert pieces such as Henselt's Etudes, Fantasies by Thalberg, Liszt, etc. have become completely repugnant to me. . . . All of this can create no lasting pleasure! I will not play these things again unless I need them for a concert tour.[17]

In addition, Clara limited her international touring after her marriage. It seems reasonable to speculate that, working within a narrower geographical sphere and often playing for familiar audiences in Leipzig and Dresden, she opted to cultivate the prestige and Germanocentricity of the canon rather than popular showpieces that demonstrated her command of a cosmopolitan tradition. Clara's programming, too, was part of a broader midcentury shift in which heterogeneous musical variety shows that mixed popular hits with "serious" repertoire gave way to a firmer separation between canon-centric and more popularly styled concerts.

Clara's status as Frau Schumann also shaped her programming. She had sparingly programmed Robert's piano works during the 1830s, regretting that his music was too inaccessible for her audiences. After their marriage—and after Robert developed a more accessible, classicizing style—she made many of his works centerpieces of her repertoire. She premiered and extensively programmed his concerted works for piano and orchestra, especially the Piano Concerto Op. 54. When giving performances that did not involve an orchestra, Clara programmed chamber music and featured local string players—at smaller soirees, for example, or on the chamber-music concerts she organized while living in Dresden. Robert's chamber music with piano featured prominently in this corner of her repertoire. Clara most frequently performed his Piano Quintet Op. 44 but also programmed his piano trios, and, less often, the Piano Quartet Op. 47. Many of the Schumanns' concerts were what Claudia Macdonald calls "team programs" that included at least one of Robert's orchestral works and featured Clara in one or more concertos.[18] Even when she was not actually playing Robert's music, Clara's new programming practices reinforced her husband's image as a composer who was earning a place in the canon. On her and Robert's 1843 *Morgenunterhaltung*, for example, she surrounded her husband's chamber music with

Bach and late Beethoven. The program made clear which traditions Robert's latest work drew upon.

While Clara and Robert were navigating their mid-career metamorphoses, critics routinely presented them as an idealized partnership between a serious virtuoso and a genius composer. Their collaboration, then, went beyond simply sharing the stage—it also became the lens through which they and their contemporaries interpreted their different contributions, a framework in which they understood how their performances and compositions worked in tandem. Whereas we need to infer reasons for Clara's programming shift, this image of her and Robert pervades a wealth of primary sources. Though scholars unanimously acknowledge that Robert's music was central to Clara's repertoire, they have yet to map this thread of the Schumanns' reception. In accounts from the 1840s and 1850s, Robert created musical works through isolated, strenuous labor that demonstrated his compositional mastery, profundity, and place in the canon. Meanwhile, Clara brought his music to light with extraordinary insight and pianistic skill. Critics presented this partnership in explicitly gendered and hierarchical terms, stressing the subservience of the female virtuoso to the male composer: her receptivity, sensitivity, and devotion, and his intellectual prowess. At times, reviewers came close to describing Clara as a musical mother who gave birth to Robert's ideas or as a wife who served them to guests. Though such portrayals limited Clara to the role of interpreter, they presented the partnership as offering agency and prestige to both spouses. Through the bonds of marriage, *Werktreue* elevated both living composer and virtuoso.

A typical description occurs in a *Neue Musik Zeitung für Berlin* review of Clara's March 1, 1847, *Singakademie* concert. The reviewer praised Robert's Piano Quintet for its "thoroughly noble direction and happy mastery of form," features that grouped him "among the worthiest artists of the present day." He commended Clara for playing this and other works "clearly, with fine nuance, and with beautiful understanding." The reviewer suggested that Clara's wifely devotion gave Robert the pride of place Beethoven had occupied on her earlier concerts: "That her husband has perhaps stepped into Beethoven's place one can forgive the feminine artist, especially when she plays a Quintet of his composition as she did this time."[19] An 1844 review in *Die Grenzboten* depicted the Schumanns' collaboration with explicitly domestic language. "A matinée has the coziness one finds when invited into a family circle," it reported. "Clara was the housewife and entertained guests with her lieder, Beethoven, and the profound compositions of her husband." Beneath the convivial warmth was a core of *Werktreue*. The reviewer imagined that, as Clara played Beethoven, "The spirit of Beethoven stood behind her, smilingly beating time, and, when she stood up, he kissed her brow and then her beautiful, marble hands."[20] In both accounts, marital intimacy and devotion blended with the prestige of the canon.

Documents other than critical writings presented the Schumanns in this light. In an 1838 letter to Clara, Robert himself bemoaned the hand injury that had ended his performing career. He added, "Well, I have you as my right hand." The letter exuded admiration: Robert subsequently praised Clara's "mastery" and looked forward to the "happy hours you will give me through your art."[21] Intentionally or not, however, the metaphor also designated Robert the controlling, compositional mind and Clara the executor of his genius—Robert as inner thought, Clara as physical manifestation. An 1850 daguerreotype of the couple, their only photographic double portrait, suggests such a relationship in images. Clara sits at an upright piano, her hand on the keys. Robert stands opposite the piano, chin in hand. The pose emphasizes Clara's physical engagement with the instrument and Robert's inward, intellectual pondering. It subordinates her to him: a contemplative mastermind, Robert stands above and surveys his wife and the keyboard.

Franz Liszt's 1854 *Neue Zeitschrift* essay on Clara delivered the most substantial music-critical portrait of this idealized partnership.[22] By publishing this essay, Liszt was furthering a tangle of agendas. On the simplest level, he was promoting a tour Clara had begun after Robert's institutionalization: it was her first extended tour without Robert since she had performed in Denmark in 1842. Just that October, she had played Robert's Piano Concerto in Weimar, with Liszt conducting. Liszt might have also been attempting to mend personal fences with the Schumanns. He had offended the couple in 1848 when he arrived unfashionably late to a dinner party they were throwing in his honor. To make matters worse, he criticized Robert's Piano Quartet as "Leipzigerisch" (Leipzig-esque) and unfavorably compared the recently deceased Mendelssohn to Meyerbeer. ("Leipzigerisch" seemed to accuse Robert of provincialism and, via allusion to the Leipzig Conservatory, pedantry.) Finally, Liszt used this and other writings on the Schumanns to speak on behalf of his own work. In an 1855 *Zeitschrift* essay on Robert, Liszt presented him as an exemplar of the New German ideology—he wrote that Robert had followed the imperatives of historical progress by synthesizing literature and music.[23] The essay about Clara defended Liszt on a different front. Now settled into his *Kapellmeister* position, Liszt was working to establish himself as a composer of large-scale works. As James Deaville has shown, Liszt's detractors seized upon his virtuoso career to disparage his orchestral compositions. Even his supporters distanced their figurehead from his performing activities. New German polemicist Richard Pohl, for example, wrote that Liszt had become a great composer by transcending his earlier focus, not because of it.[24]

In his essay, Liszt used the Schumanns' example to defend virtuosity and, implicitly, his own career path. The couple, he wrote, symbolized the interdependence of performance and composition:

> Both practiced their art in different directions of equal significance. . . . Interpreters of the same poetic feeling, they beheld and heralded the same model of beauty, they were filled with the same revulsion at the trivial in art, the same reverence for the same characteristics. Going hand in hand, they bore the same candles and the same palms and received equal applause; because to honor one meant to honor both, who sang in different tongues but in splendid euphony.[25]

Liszt disputed the belief that composition was more significant than performance. "We declare ourselves opposed to the assumption that subordinates virtuosity—

here represented by a woman—to creative work," he wrote. Controversies about virtuosity would only be resolved "through the awareness that all members of the musical organism are as necessary as those of the human body to its free development."[26]

Despite his protestation, Liszt subordinated Clara to Robert as a woman and a virtuoso. He did not discuss Clara's performances of Robert's compositions and instead focused on the larger claim that her virtuosity became elevated precisely through her *Werktreue*. Liszt's argument reflected his own Weimar projects as well as his impression of Clara. In 1851, for example, he had published transcriptions of Bach organ fugues that scrupulously include every note of the originals and add no expression markings—they advertise Liszt's reverence for Bach's text. When Liszt performed his own large-scale compositions (such as the Sonata in B Minor), he now played from the score. As Kenneth Hamilton has observed, Liszt thereby "sought to demonstrate that his compositions were seriously thought out, and more than just offshoots of his concert improvisations."[27] Liszt attributed Clara's *Werktreue* to Robert's influence: "Because the relative equality of both artists does not preclude a definite superiority of the man over the woman, continual contact with so lofty and impressive an intellectual power [*Geisteskraft*] . . . as Robert Schumann's must have thrown the inextinguishable imprint of his profile on Clara's talent. And, in fact, Fräulein Wieck was still far from what Frau Schumann became."[28]

In Liszt's account, Clara Wieck had responded compellingly and spontaneously to musical details, accentuating rhythms more than they demanded and constantly changing the inflections of melodies. "Erratically and unthinkingly she followed her inclinations on nobly tangled paths, looked with delight on every flower, every star," he remembered. "Everything was spontaneous, sudden, enchanting, so that through her lack of deliberation and her naiveté, through her conspicuous lack of all fore- or after-thought, through a magical spell of her own charm . . . even the imperfections of her young being became almost more attractive than her more serious, solid characteristics."[29]

Liszt heard a radical difference in Clara's midcentury playing. Privately, he expressed some reservations when she played in Weimar. Liszt's student Marfa Sabinina remembered that his sole criticism of Clara's playing was that it was "too homespun [*hausbacken*]," an adjective that connotes a staid, unadventurous style.[30] In print, though, Liszt held up the midcentury Clara as a pinnacle of maturity and insight. He described her performances as painstakingly thought through. Before a concert, he wrote, Clara would test every note of the keyboard to calibrate her phrasing. In place of her earlier spontaneity, Liszt heard single-minded reverence and profound knowledge of the musical work. He described her in terms even more austere and religious than Hanslick would:

When she ascends the trivet of the temple, the woman no longer speaks to us. She neither entertains as a poet of earthy passion . . . nor does she attempt to gain our sympathy. An obeisant votary of the Delphic god [Apollo], full of faith and reverence, she serves his cult with shuddering, true conscience. . . . For her . . . all [in the score's "holy book"] is sacred and should be received free of doubt and with blissful veneration. And she is so ruled by devotion that the supple human element almost entirely retreats from this objective interpretation of art. And yet, no one will surpass her in the stirring truth with which she performs the sacred masters with complete understanding.[31]

If Liszt's essay contained the critical apotheosis of the Schumanns' partnership, the 1853 Lower Rhine Music Festival marked one of its performative high points. Along with Ferdinand Hiller and composer Julius Tausch, Robert organized the annual festival, corresponding with performers and conducting several concerts. Begun in 1818, the Rhine Festival was one of the oldest and largest such events in Germany. It featured three days of concerts in Düsseldorf, from May 15 through 17. The first two days emphasized choral and orchestral works. The first featured Robert's Symphony No. 4 and Handel's *Messiah*, the second Weber's *Euryanthe* Overture, selections from Mendelssohn's *Elijah*, act 1 of Gluck's *Alceste*, and Beethoven's Ninth Symphony. The third day was a "Künstlerkonzert" starring virtuoso soloists. Robert conducted Clara in his Piano Concerto and Joseph Joachim in Beethoven's Violin Concerto. Clara accompanied vocal soloists, Hiller gave a piano improvisation, and as an encore Joachim played the Chaconne from Bach's Violin Partita No. 2. Clara accompanied the Chaconne, possibly using the piano part Robert had composed the previous year.

The Rhine Festival centered on canonic composers and repertoire. Throughout the festival's history, Beethoven, Mozart, and Handel dominated the programs. The *Signale für die musikalische Welt* described Beethoven's Ninth as "the crown of the evening, indeed the entire festival." Because so many Rhine Festivals had featured the Ninth, the work was "in the flesh and blood of the participants."[32] James Garratt summarizes that the festivals "elevated the composer as a figurehead for the artistic and sociopolitical aspirations of its participants."[33]

This reach for cultural prestige mingled with festive socializing and recreation. The festival drew dedicated amateur musicians, particularly choral singers. By 1853, the size of the chorus had ballooned to 490. Philologist, archaeologist, and musicologist Otto Jahn attended the 1855 Rhine Festival (also held in Düsseldorf) and reported on a wide selection of delights. Participants and listeners enjoyed *Maitrank* (a punch made from Rhenish wine), attended large banquets, and refreshed themselves in parks and gardens. Local restaurants were packed, he wrote, and lodgings were scarce and expensive. Caecilia Hopkins Porter summarizes that the Rhine Festivals featured outdoor band music, dances, and fireworks.[34] Some of the repertoire itself set a popular tone or appealed to local Rhenish pride. Robert's *Fest-Overture über das Rheinweinlied*, Op. 123, for example, finished the third day of concerts in 1853.

The festival also affirmed the importance of canonic music to German cultural nationalism. Like other German cultural festivals—such as those dedicated to Luther, Goethe, and Beethoven—it stimulated middle-class participation in public life, the driving force of liberalism and nationalism. In the festival's early days, Andreas Eichhorn notes, it was considered important mainly for the Rhineland. By the 1850s, its profile had risen, and writers were praising it for displaying centerpieces of national musical identity and educating the *Volk*.[35] The festival created feelings of community and shared heritage through singing, socializing, listening, and venerating.

By performing Robert's Piano Concerto, Clara played a work that had come to emblematize their collaboration. As I noted in chapter 5, the concerto as a whole reflected Robert's own 1840s aesthetic of compositional control, and critics touted it as evidence of his compositional mastery and position within a venerable tradition. The concerto also became one of Clara's calling cards from the day of its premiere. Bernhard Appel has counted over one hundred of her performances, a list he notes is probably incomplete.[36] Clara herself described the concerto as a valuable addition to her repertoire, a much-needed vehicle for displaying her virtuosity within a concerted composition by her husband. When Robert added the second and third movements in 1845, she wrote in her diary, "I am delighted about it, because I have always lacked a large *Bravourstück* by him." Later, she exclaimed, "What a contrast between this and Henselt's Concerto [Op. 16]!"[37] Clara had also premiered the Henselt in 1845. Though critics praised her performance, they criticized the work: some claimed that it betrayed Henselt's discomfort with large forms. The initial reception of Robert's concerto, by contrast, lauded it as a composition perfectly matched with Clara's virtuosity. The *Allgemeine musikalische Zeitung* wrote of the Dresden premiere, "If, in the case of Henselt's recent concerto, we had to rate the performance far above the composition, here the two united as a perfectly beautiful, truly artistic whole."[38] The *Signale* praised the Leipzig premiere, writing that the concerto was "tenderly and softly felt, original in its combinations [of ideas], and entirely created for the noble playing of the pianist."[39] Robert surely designed specific features of the concerto to highlight Clara's pianistic trademarks. The lyrical first and second movements, for example, might have showcased her tone and voicing (see chapter 2). The concerto's classicizing touches—the fugal cadenza, or the finale's sharply chiseled sonata-form—complemented her historicist profile. More important for the Schumanns' overall image, though, were broader claims that the concerto represented an ideal meeting of composer and performer.

Critics hailed Clara's festival performance as a triumph for the couple's partnership. According to the *Süddeutsche Musik-Zeitung*, "[Clara Schumann] played the concerto by her spouse with a mastery that at once elevated the composition and enraptured the public to a storm of applause." The *Signale* reported that she "inspired everyone present with her performance of the A-minor concerto by her ingenious husband and, with the crowd's *Jubelzuruf*, was crowned with a laurel wreath." Ludwig Bischoff of the Cologne *Rheinische Musik-Zeitung* noted that he had initially disliked the concerto but that Clara's performance had changed his mind.[40] In these accounts, Clara was not the austere medium Liszt described. Rather, she provided a charismatic conduit from her husband's genius to the applause of a wide audience. At the festival, her performance was one of several pleasures and attractions that ranged from the self-consciously elevated to the plebian and from the musical to the social and culinary.

Robert and Clara took the stage at a crucial juncture in the evolution of the Lower Rhine Festival, and the press presented them as signs that the institution was moving in the right direction. The festival had halted during the 1848 revolutions and only resumed in 1851. The *Signale* described the Schumanns as agents of musical renewal. The festival, it proclaimed, showed that the Rhineland was still devoted to "the consecration of holy music." The reviewer went on, "How can this be lacking where men like Robert Schumann, at whose side stands an ingenious wife, and Ferdinand Hiller form the pinnacle of all art?"[41]

The 1850s also marked a tipping point in the professionalization of the festival. As Porter has shown, the third day of professional virtuoso performances became standard only during the 1850s. By this time, the overwhelming majority of vocal soloists and orchestral players were professionals, and the only amateurs who participated were choral singers. In Eichhorn's analysis, whereas the festival of the early nineteenth century had blurred the distinctions between professionals and amateurs, participants and audience, the festival after midcentury looked more like other formal, public concerts.[42] Even in the 1840s, some critics complained that professionalization was driving up ticket prices.[43] Ludwig Bischoff argued that the third day of concerts was appropriate and that Clara exemplified the kind of virtuoso the festival should welcome. He acknowledged that the purpose of the first two days was partly to create "powerful togetherness" through the massive choral and orchestral performances. However, he maintained that the festivals also edified musicians and the public, and that the third day of concerts served this end:

> Isn't it for [listeners who have no opportunities at home to see such performers] and for us all in general a festival to hear a Jenny Lind, a Clara Novello . . . a Clara Schumann, a Joachim? If one rails against the appearance of individual artists at music festivals, one must have no idea of the enormous influence a perfect individual artistic offering can have on the development of the musicians present and on the refinement of the listener's taste and judgment.[44]

At the Lower Rhine Music Festival, then, Robert and Clara Schumann emerged as two linked pillars: Robert, a composer who stood alongside Beethoven and Bach at a festival dedicated to composers and works at the center of German musical culture, and Clara, a virtuoso who brought masterworks to life and offered a model for musicians and listeners.

Staging the Partnership: The Introduction and Allegro Appassionato Op. 92

Like his Piano Concerto and chamber music with piano, Robert's Introduction and Allegro Appassionato is an extensive compositional document not merely of his own stylistic development but of his and Clara's collaboration. Composed in 1849, the work appeared on several of their team programs during the early 1850s.

The *Signale* review of the premiere succinctly invoked the Schumanns' idealized image: "One, with love, care, and the fullness of her charm and strength, brings into the world what the other builds in the isolated stillness of his rich mind [*Gemüth*] and in the depth of his inexhaustible creative genius."[45]

The Allegro Appassionato also staged the Schumann partnership through the way it presents virtuosity.[46] Considering this dual display clarifies a work that nineteenth-century critics and present-day scholars alike have regarded as problematic. The *Neue Zeitschrift* complained that, unlike the Piano Concerto, the Allegro Appassionato failed to steer a middle way between avoiding "old-fashioned odds and ends of passagework" and giving "effective and brilliant things" to the soloist.[47] Even admiring reviews presented it as prohibitively inaccessible. On one of the few occasions when Clara played the Allegro Appassionato after Robert's institutionalization, for example, the *Signale* commended her for making sense of the work: "Its beauties are not immediately apparent, and successfully tracing and illuminating them requires a musical understanding like Frau Schumann's."[48] Macdonald describes it as "hardly a concerto at all" but more like a symphony in which the orchestra overshadows the soloist.[49]

It would be more accurate, though, to describe the Introduction and Allegro Appassionato as a sonata-form concerto movement preceded by a slow introduction and overridden by an apotheosis coda. (The term "apotheosis" is Leonard Meyer's. Particularly characteristic of nineteenth-century orchestral works, such endings present climactic levels of intensity and generally offer an affirmative, majestic statement of a theme.[50]) Though the verb "overrides" risks anthropomorphizing the form, it captures the effect. As figure 6.1 shows, the coda warps the tonal conventions of the sonata form. Whereas the recapitulation would conventionally bring the second theme group to E major or minor, it instead lands in G major. Robert, then, tables the tonal tensions of the exposition proper to accommodate a climactic link to the Introduction.[51]

A horn-call motive shown in the figure binds the structure together. In the Introduction, the motive emerges as one phrase of a melody split between horn and clarinet. Fragments of the horn call return at pivotal moments in the form: they announce the second theme group and culminating displays and appear in the development. The horn call forms the substance of the apotheosis coda, which restores the motive to the full Introduction theme. In John Daverio's analysis, the work unwinds a dialogue between the "distance" of the Introduction and the "presence" of the Allegro's martial opening.[52]

Robert Schumann modeled this larger form and unifying strategy on the first movement of Schubert's Symphony No. 9. (Scholars and critics have yet to acknowledge this connection. The *Signale* might have hinted at it, remarking that Robert's music in general showed a "prevailing Beethovenian-Schubertian conception."[53]) The Introduction and Allegro Appassionato, then, represented one episode in the composer's lifelong engagement with Schubert. His early piano cycles and 1840s chamber music revel in Schubert's influence.[54] Schubert's Ninth Symphony itself played a catalyzing role in Robert's development as a symphonist, and Robert, in fact, helped to have the work premiered. During his 1839 trip to

Introduction

Sonata-form concerto movement

Exposition					Culminating display
P	Transition	S			
43	89	121	133		151
e		C (VI)			
G		R1	R2		R3

Recapitulation					Culminating display
P	Transition	S			
300	342	374	386		404
e		G (III, becomes I)!			
		R1	R2		R3

Development

188

R4   R5

Coda: apotheosis of Introduction

Tutti	Cadenza?	
441	451	457

R6

Figure 6.1. Schumann, Introduction and Allegro Appassionato Op. 92. Large-scale form and reminiscences of Introduction. R=Reminiscence of the Introduction's horn-call motive.

Introduction:

Second theme group, R1:

Second theme group, R2:

Figure 6.1. (*continued*)

Culminating display, R3:

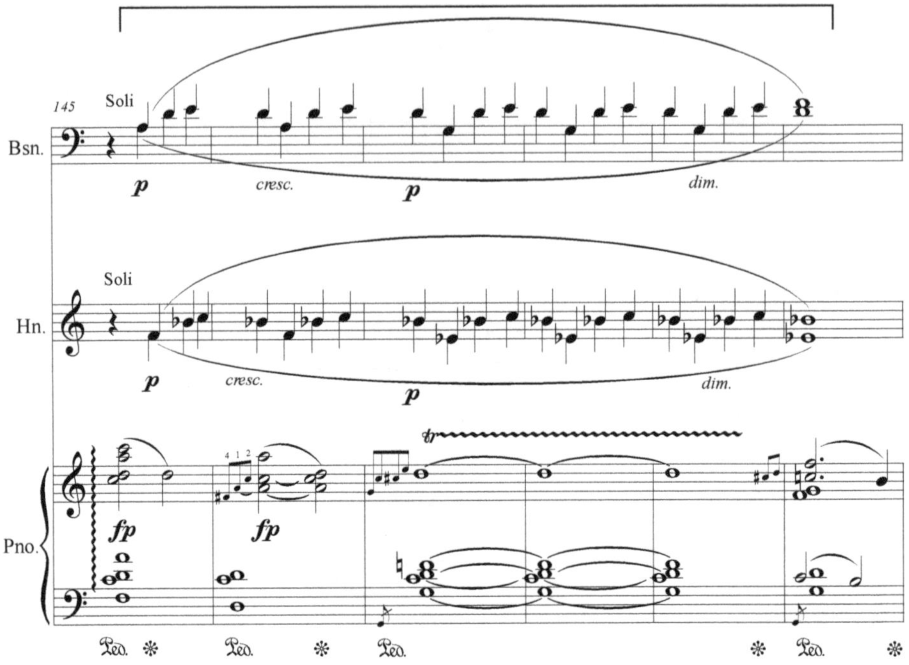

Figure 6.1. (*continued*)

Vienna, he learned about the as-yet-unpublished symphony from Schubert's brother, Ferdinand. Robert sent the Ninth to Mendelssohn, who conducted it at the Gewandhaus that year. Mark Evan Bonds has noted that Schubert's Ninth offered Robert a model for sidestepping Beethoven's potentially stifling influence in his own symphonies. During the early nineteenth century, the symphony was becoming the ultimate statement about a composer's ambition and style—critics demanded that a new symphony should position itself in relation to Beethoven's work and offer a self-consciously original contribution to the genre. In an 1840 essay for the *Zeitschrift*, Robert presented Schubert's Ninth as an exemplary post-Beethovenian symphony. He lamented that many current symphonies offered "pale reflections of Beethoven." Schubert's Ninth, though, revealed his "complete independence of the Beethoven symphonies" and original approach: "As if conscious of his own more modest powers, he avoids imitating the grotesque forms, the bold proportions we find in Beethoven's later works; instead, he gives us a creation of the most graceful form possible, yet full of novel intricacies."[55] Robert's own Symphony No. 1, composed in 1841, emulates many tonal, formal, and orchestration details of the Schubert.[56]

Like the Introduction and Allegro Appassionato, the first movement of Schubert's Ninth unifies a sonata form with a horn motive from the slow introduction—in Schubert's case, the unaccompanied horn solo that begins the symphony. Both works recall fragments of their horn calls at analogous formal junctures. Schubert's movement invokes its horn-call motive during the second theme group and the development. Schubert's apotheosis coda, like that of the Allegro Appassionato, restores the motive to its original thematic context, here in a triumphant orchestral tutti. (John Gingerich points out that, despite Schumann's claims about Schubert's independence, the symphony does reach a "heroic," Beethovenian ending.[57])

A concerted work that showcases a soloist's virtuosity, the Allegro Appassionato also reveals Robert's positioning himself within the symphonic tradition. The composer aligned himself with what he considered Schubert's pathbreaking model. Moreover, the way he adapted this model supported his midcareer project to demonstrate compositional control and clarity and to distance himself from the perceived tortuousness and abstruseness of his 1830s music (see chapter 5). The first movement of Schubert's Ninth features an expansive, three-key exposition. Here, the reminiscence of the horn call marks a surprising digression within the third key area, the dominant: as the trombones intone the motive, the exposition veers into the flat mediant inflected with minor harmonies and returns to the dominant when the recollection dissipates. In the Allegro Appassionato, by contrast, the horn-call reminiscences do not signal a departure from the conventional trajectory of the exposition but instead delineate traditionally significant junctures—the start of the second theme group and divisions between its themes and passagework areas. Both the Allegro Appassionato and Schubert's Ninth establish motivic connections between the horn motive and the expositional themes. Robert, though, makes his links more readily apparent: during the development, he juxtaposes the horn motive with a theme from the transition, clarifying how one can transform into the other.

In the Introduction and Allegro Appassionato, the Schubertian horn calls align with and seem to unlock the high points of pianistic virtuosity. The result is a showpiece in which flashy passagework emerges from moments that conspicuously bear the fingerprint of the unifying, integrating composer who speaks from within a lineage of symphonists. Figure 6.1 excerpts three such passages from the exposition. Each reminiscence summons increasingly extravagant virtuosity. Two reverberations of the horn call merge with a series of arpeggios that open the second theme group. Two more yield the showpiece's first extended passage of transparent figuration—continuous triplets that energize lyrical upper voices. We might suspect that the triplets form the culminating display: the passagework unfolds in repeated, cadentially directed modules, and it ends with a cadential trill. During the trill, though, four additional reverberations of the horn call unlock the true culmination.

It is tempting to hear in such moments the unequal balance of authority that critics commended in the Schumanns' partnership. After all, the horn calls remind us of Robert's integrative architecture before we get to enjoy the pianist's acrobatics. In the end, a coda derived from the symphonic tradition trumps the tonal logic of the sonata-form concerto movement.

A:

Example 6.1. Introduction and Allegro Appassionato. Virtuosic apotheosis during coda.

But Robert also allows the piano's virtuosity to match and compete with the orchestra's sonic power. The primary theme, for example, is split between an orchestral tutti and the piano's full-fisted chords. The culminating displays intersperse dense, rebounding chords with brass fanfares. These sections also stage sportive role reversal by giving the timpani the cadential trill while the pianist plays a string of dense chords.

More important, the pianist's—initially Clara's—virtuosity completes and culminates the apotheosis, excerpted in example 6.1. The coda grows out of piano arpeggios that promise a cadenza. During the tutti before these flourishes, the orchestra quoted the horn-call motive in G major. A first-time listener, then, might already be satisfied that the piece has completed a large-scale tonal and thematic

B:

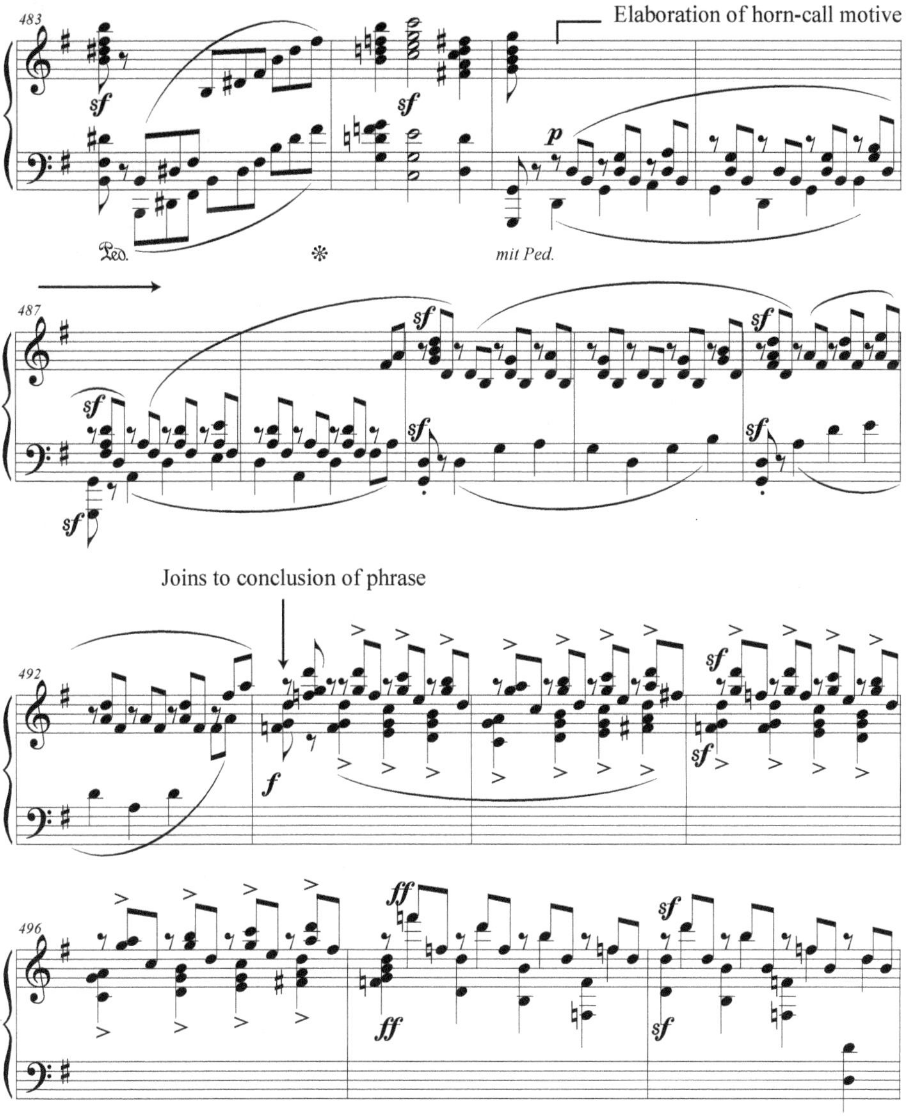

Example 6.1. (*continued*)

arc. He or she could assume that the arpeggios will lead to further passagework and a brief closing tutti. In the excerpt labeled A, however, the arpeggios become an accompaniment for the horn-call motive, now exchanged between horn and clarinet—the coda thus reunites the pair of wind soloists that opened the Introduction. As the arpeggios continue, the woodwind section plays the full Introduction theme, promising to restore the horn-call motive to its original thematic context. At the very moment where the horn call would lock into the theme, though, the piano interrupts with a dense G major chord. (The disruption clarifies that the woodwind choir did not represent the true culmination of the coda: the woodwinds play the Introduction theme in E-flat major, and the piano chord jerks the coda back to tonic.) The soloist at first bursts into transparent passagework, a flowing string of triplet figures. Ultimately, she changes her style to provide the promised horn-call motive and complete the Introduction theme. As shown in the excerpt labeled B, the pianist elaborates the motive across twelve measures, the longest presentation in the piece. Reverberations of the motive climb from the low register of the piano into the upper range, creating not transparent brilliance but a wave of virtuosic plenitude that consumes the keyboard. Just before this wave blossoms into a cascade of broken octaves, the piano links the horn call to the motive that completes the phrase. Whereas Schubert's Ninth peaked with a tutti fanfare, the apotheosis of the Introduction and Allegro Appassionato finds its structural and textural culmination in a moment of maximum virtuosic display.

Though critics generally agreed that the Introduction and Allegro Appassionato was too complex and densely orchestrated to appeal as the Piano Concerto did, it nonetheless encapsulates the Schumanns' midcentury image. The showpiece at once staked Robert's claim to the canonic lineage—presenting him as a composer who grasped and built upon Schubert's symphonic legacy—and framed Clara as a performer whose virtuosity glorified this tradition. Indeed, the Allegro Appassionato emphasized Clara's role as the charismatic champion who brought physical form to her husband's genius. Robert's integrative strategy in this showpiece is couched in a Romantic metaphor for distance: the horn call offers a conventional symbol for spacious landscapes and distant sounds. Robert himself wrote of his model, Schubert's Ninth, that its horn-featuring slow introduction was "veiled in mystery" and that a horn solo in the second movement seemed like "a heavenly guest passing through the orchestra." I would be loath to map a program onto the Allegro Appassionato, suggesting that the heralding horn calls literally represent the virtuoso's communion with the composer's ethereal genius. What is clear is the effect the piece has in performance—that it converts the distant marks of the composer's unifying strategies and canonic engagement into splashy passages that foreground the soloist's physical acrobatics, and that the coda gave Clara the virtuosically elaborated apotheosis that begs an ovation for Robert's Schubertian argument.

A Historicist Triumph in the Netherlands

Clara Schumann premiered the Introduction and Concert Allegro Op. 134 during her and Robert's 1853 tour of the Netherlands. It was the first extended tour on which their midcentury partnership—team programs, his orchestral works, and her new programming practices—won resounding critical and popular success. (By contrast, their 1846 Vienna tour had been a disappointment. Concerts were poorly attended, and the Piano Concerto received tepid applause.[58]) Between November 26 and December 20, Robert and Clara concertized in Amsterdam, Utrecht, The Hague, and Rotterdam. In Utrecht, the first stop of the tour, the concert began with Robert's Symphony No. 3, followed by an aria by Spohr and the Concert Allegro. On the second half, Clara played Beethoven's "Waldstein" Sonata and two Mendelssohn *Lieder ohne Worte* and accompanied vocal lieder. Clara's concerto repertoire for the tour also included Robert's Piano Concerto, Beethoven's Piano Concerto No. 5, Mendelssohn's Piano Concerto No. 1, and Weber's *Konzertstück*. Robert also featured his Symphony No. 2, *Der Rose Pilgerfahrt*, and his *Genoveva* Overture.[59]

Advance networking and promotion contributed to the tour's success.[60] Robert counted several professional allies in the Netherlands. He had befriended Dutch composer Johannes Verhulst, who studied with Mendelssohn in Leipzig between 1838 and 1843. When Verhulst returned to the Netherlands, he championed Robert's music and conducted the Symphony No. 1 in 1844. In 1837, Robert himself became a corresponding member of the Dutch Maatschappij tot Bevordering der Toonkunst (Society for the Cultivation of Music) and in 1843 was made an honorary member. The secretary of the Maatschappij's Rotterdam branch, Johannes Reinier Smalt, corresponded with Robert and Clara and helped to organize the concerts. Most of these took place under the auspices of local music societies, including the Maatschappij, the Felix Meritis society in Amsterdam, and the Gesellschaft Eruditio Musica in Rotterdam. Both spouses were impressed with the preparation of the orchestras. In a letter to her friend Marie Lindeman, Clara wrote that Robert "only had to stand and conduct."[61] (Surely a relief for both Schumanns, given Robert's struggles with the Düsseldorf orchestra.) The Schumanns' colleagues also arranged a warm, public welcome. After the December 1 concert in Rotterdam, Verhulst organized a torchlight procession to escort the Schumanns to their hotel. A chorus of over a hundred singers and a wind band serenaded them with music that included the "Waldchor" from *Der Rose Pilgerfahrt* and Mendelssohn's *Festlied an die Künstler*, Op. 68.[62]

Music journals and daily newspapers advertised the tour. *Caecilia*, the largest music journal in the Netherlands, trumpeted after the Utrecht concert:

> Netherlanders who honor art in its greatness and true beauty, and who wish nothing more passionately than to see it honored as such by true artists and to be performed, you are surpassingly fortunate! This desire you can now satisfy. Among you is a woman invited from abroad, Clara Schumann, a high priestess of art, a true representative of Bach, Mozart, Beethoven, Hummel, Chopin, and Schumann.[63]

A November 15 announcement even urged readers to approach the concerts with open minds: "It is hoped that there will be no wretched prejudging before the first concert."[64] The Schumanns' reception, then, was not a spontaneous reaction from the Dutch public. Rather, it reflected the labors of journalists, music societies, administrators, and orchestra leadership. It would also be an overstatement to describe the Schumann concerts as pan-Dutch popular phenomena: they succeeded with listeners who could afford tickets and were enticed by Schumanns' programming and image.

The tour did include some low points. Robert recorded in his diary on November 26 that Clara, pregnant with their son Felix, was feeling ill and that they had doubts about continuing the trip. He found a soiree at Prince Friedrich's in The Hague to be an annoying ordeal where guests chatted over the music. Both Robert and a reviewer complained that a December 9 performance in Rotterdam was poorly attended.[65]

Nevertheless, accounts consistently report that Dutch audiences responded to the Schumanns with enthusiasm, even furor. For example, a *Caecilia* review of the December 6 Hague concert reported that Clara's performance of a Beethoven sonata prompted such a "fortissimo" of applause that "no one would have thought that such a thing could happen in this proper capital city (half the capital is still hoarse)."[66] The reviewer playfully suggested that Clara was chastising the noisy crowd when she chose a *Lied ohne Worte* as her encore. Because *Caecilia* had promoted the concerts, its reports do not necessarily offer disinterested testimony. However, the Schumanns' private writings and the outcomes of the tour corroborate them. Clara's biographer, Berthold Litzmann, quoted her relating that she was "surprised to find the Dutch so enthusiastic and lively and, I would like to say, more cultivated than the Rheinish. We were very pleased with our musical beginning in Holland."[67] She wrote to Lindeman that she was called back for an encore at each concert.[68] In Robert's diary, the word "enthusiasm" becomes a refrain. Of the first Utrecht concert, he wrote, "Honors also came back to me, unexpectedly," and he described the "shouts of the audience" in Rotterdam.[69] Robert recorded more pragmatically that he and Clara were satisfied with the receipts. In fact, after prodding from Smalt, they extended the tour for one more concert in Rotterdam and one in Amsterdam.[70]

Reviewers and promoters proclaimed that these clamoring ovations were for music that embodied cultural and aesthetic prestige. Indeed, such prestige was itself one of the pleasures the concerts offered. Like the Rhine Festival, the tour turned the idealized Schumann partnership into an object of mass enjoyment and spectacle—here, not so much as icons of national and local pride but as a pair of admired guest celebrities. A *Caecilia* review of the November 30 Hague concert captured this convergence of sacralization and consumption: "The world of music was in good cheer. Old and young, the very musical, the half-musical, and also the not musical flowed en masse to the temple of music, to hear the newly arrived high priest and high priestess . . . to consider and judge them."[71] Appraisals of the Schumanns emphasized Robert's compositional genius and Clara's *Werktreue*. One review, when discussing Robert's Symphony No. 3, praised him as "the ingenious creator of so many beautiful, profound, original, and new things." The review of the December 2 Amsterdam concert gushed that it would be superfluous to speak of "the wonderful mastery with which Clara performed

Beethoven's E-flat ["Emperor"] Concerto; of the all-powerful genius with which she mastered, animated, and led the ingenious artwork."[72]

Mendelssohn's *Festlied* gave the torchlight procession itself a veneer of elitism and idealism. The chorus serenaded the musical celebrities with Schiller's, "An die Künstler," which begins, "The dignity of humanity is given to your hands." The text does present the artist as misunderstood and marginalized: "Rejected by her time, earnest truth in poetry flees / And finds refuge in the choir of Muses." If the Schumanns and their hosts paid attention to these lines, they heard a distant fantasy rather than a lament about real rejection—a proclamation that the music they were successfully promoting to a contemporary audience also transcended worldly tastes.

The Introduction and Concert Allegro stages the aspirations and strategies of the Netherlands tour. Though Robert dedicated the work to Brahms in 1855, he had composed it specifically for Clara and gave it to her as a birthday present on September 13, 1853. By this time, the Schumanns had been performing team programs for several years and were planning the Netherlands venture. The work met with success on tour. In 1854, the *Signale* reported that Clara had "created a sensation in Holland" with the Concert Allegro.[73] Like *Caecilia*'s reviews of the 1853 concerts, this account should not necessarily be taken at face value: Bartholf Senff's firm, which published the *Signale*, was considering acquiring the Concert Allegro. Again, though, other sources offer similar reports. *Caecilia* called the Concert Allegro "a new pearl of the composer's genius" and opined that Clara's November 30 performance of the work outshone the evening's vocal soloist. Robert described the audience's "enthusiasm" when Clara played it in Utrecht and Amsterdam.[74] The Schumanns included the Concert Allegro on three of their Netherlands concerts—since Clara had such a large concerto repertoire, they could have changed plans had the work met with indifferent reception.[75]

Like the tour itself, Robert's Concert Allegro intertwined popular appeal with the elevated profile he and Clara cultivated. Keyboard styles and compositional allusions transform into one another, fluidly moving between postclassical brilliance, nods to the venerated canon, and lied-style lyricism. Macdonald has shown that the Concert Allegro follows concerto convention more closely than any of Robert's other works in the genre; she suggests, in fact, that Robert designed it with criticism of the Allegro Appassionato in mind.[76] The culminating displays, for example, feature the modules of contrasting figuration standard to postclassical concertos. The overall lighter scoring gives the piano a clearer spotlight than the Allegro Appassionato did.

At the same time, I would add, the Introduction and Concert Allegro also captures Clara's "priestess" image: her historicist repertoire and flair for piano lieder. The piece, for example, bristles with neo-Baroque passagework. The first theme group concludes with a flurry of *fortspinnung*-style sixteenth notes. In conventional postclassical figuration, scale- and arpeggio-based roulades ascend to increasingly brilliant registers. Here, by contrast, the pianist moves through short, sequential patterns that fit within narrower, five-finger spans.[77] The opening of the slow Introduction reappears as a transition to the second theme, so that what had initially presaged neo-Baroque virtuosity now announces unornamented lyricism. The development also traces a journey from historicism to song. As Joachim Draheim has noted, it begins with strings of cadenza-like scales that resemble the opening of Bach's Chromatic Fantasy and Fugue (a work the Schumanns heard Mendelssohn perform during the 1840s and that Clara added to her repertoire in 1855).[78] The simulated improvisation breaks into motoric arpeggios propelled by a striding bass. As the bass settles into sustained notes, the arpeggios narrow and accompany a development of the second theme.[79]

Schumann also blurred the boundary between the second theme and the culminating display. Before the display begins, listeners pass through an intimate, lyrical portal in which sixteenth-note passagework flows without a striding, motoric bass. At the start of each measure, the pianist lingers over expressive gestures—a chromatic passing tone or suspension, or a bare octave decorated by a grace note. A two-measure passage of thirty-second notes forces an acceleration into the display itself and its sharply differentiated arpeggio patterns. Even in the culminating display, Robert mellows the brilliance of the virtuosity with lyrical inflections. Some passages present sixteenth notes beneath strings of accented appoggiaturas, and the portal figuration returns for two measures before the climactic scales and octaves.

Unlike the Allegro Appassionato, the Concert Allegro gives the soloist a substantial cadenza. As shown in example 6.2, the cadenza uses a process of diminution to give the second theme increasingly rapid, shimmering accompaniments. Initially, the pianist slips accompanying triplets between the hands, a texture typical of *Lieder ohne Worte* and comparable character pieces. In measure 246, the theme floats atop thirty-second-notes, and the bass vanishes to leave a brighter tessitura. The diminution peaks as a double trill that widens into overlapping tremolos. The pianist renders the first notes of the theme itself in trills, and a viola tremolo adds an extra layer of vibration beyond what the pianist's hands can accommodate.

This cadenza drew upon two repertoires that Clara cultivated. As we have seen, she often concluded performances with piano lieder—for a brief moment within a concerted work, the cadenza immersed audiences in the understated sound of Clara's signature concert closers. The diminution derives from an older source: the variation finales of Beethoven's Sonatas Opp. 109 and 111. In both, variations on slow themes accrue incrementally faster figuration and culminate in multilayered trills without actually speeding up the theme itself. Charles Rosen wrote that such moments "reach the extremes of rapidity and immobility."[80] The Concert Allegro cadenza creates a similar effect, retaining the theme and its tempo but dissolving the accompaniment into unmetered brilliance. The showpiece, then, elaborates a current style of piano music (one popular with amateur players) using a technique from one of the more esoteric corners of the repertoire.

Though Beethoven's late sonatas and quartets were not as widely performed then as his middle-period works and Ninth Symphony, the Schumanns and several musicians they knew drew upon late Beethoven in their performances and compositions. Clara played the late sonatas beginning in the early 1840s. She

Example 6.2. Schumann, Introduction and Concert Allegro Op. 134. Elaboration of second theme in cadenza.

performed the slow movement from the "Hammerklavier," Op. 106 and excerpts from Opus 101 at a private gathering in 1842, Opus 101 on the 1843 *Morgenunterhaltung*, and both Opus 101 and the complete "Hammerklavier" on her 1856 Vienna concerts.[81] Robert himself encountered Beethoven's late quartets at chamber-music parties during the 1830s, and Marie Sumner Lott has shown that his Quartet Op. 41, no. 1, entered a tradition of A-minor quartets that alluded to Beethoven's Quartet Op. 132. Mendelssohn modeled his Piano Sonata Op. 6 and Quartet in A Minor Op. 13 on late Beethoven works, and Brahms alluded to the "Hammerklavier" in his Piano Sonata No. 1, Op. 1.[82]

An apotheosis coda culminates the Concert Allegro's multifaceted display of historicism, seriousness, and wide appeal.[83] The coda of the Introduction and Allegro Op. 92 had grown out of what seemed like the beginnings of a cadenza, and it concluded the work with a complex process of thematic reassembly. The coda of the Concert Allegro employs simpler means and starker contrasts. Example 0.2 from the Introduction shows its beginning. Piano chords interrupt the cadenza mid-phrase, turning suddenly from the multilayered trills to a densely textured fanfare and changing the tone from intimacy to grandeur. The coda immediately subsumes the piano's sweeping passagework into a brass-driven chorale melody. Michael Struck has proposed that Schumann specifically derived the theme from the chorale "Du, meine Seele, singe"; however, he notes, the coda invokes a more general chorale topic even for listeners who do not recognize the specific source (or, for that matter, listeners who might not recognize the resemblance as a deliberate allusion).[84] Macdonald interprets the coda as a moment that spiritualizes the soloist's last virtuosic flourishes, an ending that leads us "to a glorious place where the soul sings."[85]

I would add that the apotheosis coda clothes the final burst of virtuosity with additional, interrelated qualities. By the middle of the nineteenth century, chorales had become a symbol of German rather than specifically Protestant identity. They could also serve as markers of historicist awareness; in Mendelssohn's *Paulus*, for example, Bach-style chorales align the work with the eighteenth-century oratorio tradition. Finally, the coda at once elevates the virtuoso and addresses a broad public. Apotheoses such as those in Bruckner or Beethoven symphonies or in Liszt symphonic poems created auras of monumental greatness and uplift. In Alexander Rehding's words, "triumphant fanfares, celestial harp arpeggios, and rousing, sonorous string tapestries . . . appeared to exude moral authority." This "imaginary equation between bigness and greatness," he goes on, supported the larger German project to give musical masterworks monumental significance.[86] Despite this ambitious ideology, apotheoses were not esoteric but straightforward, even obvious. Leonard Meyer therefore argued that apotheosis codas represented an egalitarian feature of nineteenth-century music, one that did not require musical learnedness or even consistent attentiveness to appreciate.[87] Granted, the coda of the Concert Allegro does not pack the sheer volume of a Lisztian or Beethovenian orchestral climax, and the orchestration remains thin to keep the piano audible. It does, however, deliver the textural plenitude, clarion major mode, sweeping melody, and euphoric, majestic (in this case, quasi-*religioso*) affirmation that defined the apotheosis.[88]

In this sense, the Concert Allegro's coda was another strategy that staged the Schumanns' lofty, "priestly" image even as it begged applause from a broad audience. Such a multifaceted and multivalent ending encapsulates the blend of prestige and appeal that the Schumanns successfully deployed in the Netherlands.

Staging Withdrawal and Elevation: The Showpieces for Joachim

During the brief time Joseph Joachim collaborated with Robert Schumann, the violinist was establishing himself as a paragon of *Werktreue*. Born in 1831 to a Jewish family in the German-speaking Hungarian town of Kitsee, Joachim received his early training in Budapest and Vienna. In 1843, his family sent him to Leipzig to study with Mendelssohn, where he and the Schumanns crossed paths socially and professionally. When Clara needed to cancel a concert in 1845, for example, Joachim filled in for her, playing the Mendelssohn Violin Concerto.[89] Joachim left Leipzig after Mendelssohn's death in 1847 and, between 1850 and 1852, joined Franz Liszt's circle in Weimar. The real collaboration between Joachim and the Schumanns began at the 1853 Lower Rhine Festival, where Robert conducted him in the Beethoven Violin Concerto and Clara accompanied him in the Bach Chaconne. By this time, Joachim had recently taken a job as a court composer and conductor in Hannover. He was also composing his first large-scale works, including his Violin Concerto No. 1, Op. 3, and his *Hamlet* Overture, Op. 4.

Joachim's career illustrates how central the Austro-German canon was becoming to midcentury concert life. In the 1830s, Clara Wieck's concerts mingled Thalberg's, Henselt's, and her own showpieces with works by Bach and Beethoven. Joachim, by contrast, founded his reputation on canonic repertoire almost from the beginning. His first major international success came in 1844, when he traveled to London with Mendelssohn and played the Beethoven to rave reviews. Throughout his career, the Beethoven concerto and Bach Chaconne remained among his signature pieces.

Joachim's performance at the Rhine Festival helped cement his image as an authoritative interpreter of canonic repertoire. A Hannover newspaper reported, "The colossal concerto by Beethoven became still more powerful under his magical bow-strokes."[90] The *Süddeutsche Musik-Zeitung* held, "Such a work executed with such mastery, entering so deeply into the spirit of the composition, is like an oasis in the desert. . . . There is classicism from the first to the last stroke—not a classicism that plays the coquette with the form, no, but 'one that is in spirit and truth.'"[91] The review quotes John 4:23, in which Jesus tells a Samaritan woman that, soon, "true worshippers will worship the Father in Spirit and truth." Like Liszt's description of Clara as a priestess of Apollo, the *Musik-Zeitung* valorized Joachim's *Werktreue* in religious (here, explicitly Christian) terms. The biblical allusion made a striking claim, that Joachim's insight into the concerto was comparable to a Christian disciple's knowledge of God.

In the months after the festival, Robert composed the Violin Concerto and the Phantasie Op. 131 specifically for Joachim. In fact, it was Joachim's encouragement that spurred Robert to write the concerto.[92] After the festival, he sent Robert his

Beethoven score as a gift and wrote, "May Beethoven's example inspire you to draw a work from your deep treasury into the light for the poor violinist, who, outside of chamber music, very much lacks something sublime for his instrument—you wondrous keeper of richest treasures!"[93] Robert replied that the score called up memories of Joachim's own performance: "It reminds me of the magician and sorcerer who, with an expert hand, led us through the heights and depths of this enchanting structure that most plumb in vain. When I read the concerto, I shall often think of that memorable day."[94] In October, Robert sent the manuscript of his own Violin Concerto to Joachim. He came close to saying that his memories of the violinist himself had shaped the composition. "I am enclosing something new here," he wrote, "which perhaps will give you an image of a certain seriousness, behind which a joyful tone often peeks out. Often you were present in my imagination when I wrote it." Either in error or jest, he also asked, "Cross out anything that doesn't look too hard to you."[95] Though Robert presented Clara with the Phantasie as a birthday gift, he wrote to Joachim, "I was thinking more of you when I wrote it."[96] Again, he asked him to identify impracticable passages. Joachim premiered the Phantasie in Düsseldorf in October 1853. He and Robert also planned to premiere the concerto that year, but disputes with the orchestra administration forced Robert to change the program.

After Robert's death, Joachim incorporated (or planned to incorporate) these showpieces into his relatively small repertoire of concerted works. He continued programming the Phantasie as late as 1887. Eventually, both Joachim and Clara did come to regard the concerto as a flawed composition that did not measure up to Robert's other works. In an 1898 letter to his biographer, Andreas Moser, Joachim wrote regretfully that the concerto revealed Robert's deteriorating mental health. "I cannot speak of it without being moved; it comes from the last half-year before the outbreak of the mental illness of the dear master and friend," he wrote. Joachim heard "sickly brooding" in the slow movement, and he suggested that the whole work betrayed "a certain fatigue that still tries to wring out some mental [geistig] energy."[97] After the composer's death, however, Joachim and Clara made tentative plans to premiere or publish the concerto. In 1857, Joachim arranged to rehearse the work with the Gewandhaus Orchestra. It was only afterward that he and Clara decided not to pursue publication. Their correspondence hints that the last movement presented the most significant problem—perhaps, for them, the only significant one. Before the rehearsal, Joachim wrote there were "wonderfully beautiful places in the first and second movements" but that the finale was "horrifyingly difficult." After the rehearsal, Clara wrote to Joachim that she shed bitter tears when she realized the concerto's flaws. She did not enumerate these weaknesses, but she suggested that Joachim might write a new finale to replace Robert's.[98] I cite these plans not to rescue the concerto from Joachim's 1898 criticism. (Ultimately, individual listeners and performers must decide for themselves whether they find the work compelling.) Rather, they demonstrate Joachim's considerable investment in the work's genesis and subsequent history, and they show that, at least for a time, he considered it a viable addition to his repertoire.

The concerto and the Phantasie stage aspects of Joachim's persona. In part, they do so through what we might oxymoronically call quiet apotheoses—codas that climactically present important themes but tone down the soloist's virtuosity, hold back the drive to the finish, and strike a placid, muted tone. At the end of the Violin Concerto's first movement, for example, virtuosic flourishes emerge only in the last eleven measures. For most of the coda, shown in example 6.3, the violin retreats from the center of attention. A *forte* pause on the dominant in the final tutti promises a cadenza, or at least a climactic burst of passagework.[99] Instead, the soloist settles into leisurely triplets that stay mostly within the violin's lower register. The orchestra itself dims the soloist's spotlight. The soloist's figuration accompanies the strings while they expand upon the second theme at a *piano* dynamic. As the theme rises through the violas and violins, its pitches overlap with and climb above the soloist's. The blending does not literally render the soloist inaudible, but it does intermittently obscure him, absorbing him into a soft-spoken, lyrical texture.

Several other moments in the concerto veer away from pyrotechnic display into lyrical quietude. In his letter to Moser, Joachim commented that the first-movement development was "almost too intimate for a concerto." Also shown in example 6.3, the development gradually slows and quiets the soloist. Scales and leaps from the first theme group settle into a treatment of the second theme. Even this lyrical oasis dissolves—a solo clarinet introduces a melody unanticipated in the movement, and the violin lets the second theme's main motive trail off. The violin trades the new theme with the clarinet and oboe, using the newly fragmented second theme as an accompaniment. By the end of the development, then, the soloist has abandoned virtuosic elaboration for intimate dialogue with the winds. The third movement presents an even more jarring retreat. Its development opens with a short theme that elsewhere introduces the transition and the coda, two sections driven by transparent virtuosic figuration. Here, the portal theme leads to a reminiscence of the second movement's syncopated accompaniment. As Laura Tunbridge notes, the violin blends into the texture and paradoxically becomes an accompaniment to the accompaniment.[100]

These passages emulate the way in which soloistic virtuosity unfolds in the first movement of Beethoven's Violin Concerto, the central work in Joachim's repertoire. Admittedly, no contemporary documents acknowledge links between the Beethoven and Schumann concertos. (This is hardly surprising because no nineteenth-century critics were able to review the score or a performance of the Schumann.) Even so, Joachim had played the Beethoven at the concert that sparked his collaboration with the Schumanns and specifically suggested the work as an inspiration for Robert. Reinhard Kapp has already pointed out one instance of Beethovenian modeling in Robert's concerto: the retransitions in both first movements employ similar harmonic gambits and establish similar affects.[101]

I would add that Beethoven's soloist, like Schumann's, retreats from pyrotechnics into quiet lyricism at unexpected junctures.[102] Beethoven also built his first-movement coda around a subdued statement of the second theme and withheld climactic passagework until the last minute. The soloist augments and repeats

Coda. Elaboration of theme in violas, second violins:

Example 6.3. Schumann, Violin Concerto, movement 1. Coda.

Development (orchestra shown in piano reduction):

Example 6.3. (*continued*)

the concluding subphrases, lingering over the theme and delaying closure. The orchestra joins the decrescendo with the expositional closing theme: an idea first introduced in a full tutti now vanishes beneath the soloist's sixteenth notes. The violin figuration descends into the lower register and only regains its clarion brilliance in the last measure. Beethoven also creates intimate, lyrical retreats by subverting two of the violin's cadential trills. First, as the second theme approaches, transitional passagework gradually slows and settles into a trill marked *dolce*. In both exposition and recapitulation, the trill becomes not a climactic gesture but a hushed background for the sparsely orchestrated second theme. The clarinet and bassoon present the first phrase of the theme beneath the trill and, rather than concluding the trill, the soloist ascends into the stratospheric upper register and adds the consequent phrase. Second, at the end of the culminating displays, the clarinet, bassoon, and strings prolong the trill as they trade the movement's primary motive *pianissimo*.

Robert was not only echoing the work Joachim had offered as a model—he was also evoking Joachim's own performance, an event he described as vivid in his memory and formative to the genesis of his Violin Concerto. The Schumann Violin Concerto, that is, stages textures, effects, and trajectories similar to those that Joachim navigated in the Beethoven.

Structural and thematic features of Robert's first movement flesh out this historicist framework. Alone among the composer's concerted works, it follows the eighteenth-century convention of presenting several main expositional themes in a long opening tutti. When rendered by the soloist, the D-minor primary theme resounds in dense triple stops. The texture, melodic contour, rhythms, and even specific harmonies and voicings echo Joachim's other signature piece, the (D-minor) Bach Chaconne.

Robert might also have designed the concerto's moments of soloistic withdrawal to emphasize Joachim's famously still, absorbed style of performing. Though my argument about this aspect of the concerto is necessarily speculative, contextual evidence lends it strong support. Robert's own correspondence emphasized his live encounters with Joachim's playing, and he even suggested that he wrote the Violin Concerto accompanied by memories of Joachim's festival performance. Numerous critics described Joachim's onstage demeanor as one of his most striking characteristics. As Karen Leistra-Jones has recently shown, Joachim did not make large, theatrical gestures while playing, nor did he even seem aware of his audience. Rather, he appeared to be totally engrossed and projected disciplined restraint. Joachim's contemporaries, Leistra-Jones reveals, read his performing style as a sign of personal authenticity. For example, Moser's biography of the violinist—a publication Joachim essentially coauthored—portrayed him as the antithesis of Liszt, in whose theatrical performing style the authors read a lack of authentic feeling.[103] In the broader context of Joachim's career, this discourse bolstered his image as an authoritative interpreter.

Although Leistra-Jones's sources date from the 1860s and after, Joachim was already cultivating this performing style during the 1850s, when he began to collaborate with the Schumanns. Whether critics described Joachim as awkward or simply placid and restrained, they agreed that he seemed to be in a world by himself, admirably (even transcendently) withdrawn from his surroundings. Ludwig Rellstab wrote of Joachim's 1853 Berlin debut:

> His external appearance, the clumsy, unfree demeanor, the half-shy, half-morose physiognomy, is nothing less than winning—he demonstrates in his entire being that the outward world barely touches him, that it is his art alone that engrosses him entirely. Even his success . . . seems to leave him indifferent![104]

Dwight's Journal described his Rhine Festival performance:

> The effect of his genius is heightened by the calm and simplicity of his manner. The applause hardly touched him more than if it had been addressed to his neighbor. All this quiet self-possession, and yet the greatest power and passion held in with bit and bridle.[105]

The review also expressed astonishment that Joachim maintained his calm during the most demanding passagework: "He seems to ride over the most tremendous difficulties as if to him they were mere child's play." An 1852 London review marveled at the facility with which Joachim took a breakneck tempo through the finale of the Mendelssohn concerto.[106]

Robert's Violin Concerto captures these qualities. The work gives the soloist a script in which he pointedly withdraws from virtuosic spectacle to linger over quiet, intimate effects, moments that seem to pause the teleology of the concerto and arrest its drive toward increasingly florid virtuosity. Concert reviews imply that Joachim's demeanor was consistent, that he appeared absorbed whether he was shaping a lyrical theme or executing a run. Nevertheless, structurally significant moments of Robert's concerto project the serenity, withdrawal, and restraint that critics heard and saw in Joachim's performances—his apparent disinterest in coaxing his audiences' applause or making extravagant gestures. Beethoven's concerto also provided such a script, albeit one composed well before Joachim's lifetime.[107]

The concerto's larger form, however, has the virtuoso withdraw from virtuosic spectacle only intermittently. In a letter thanking Joachim for hosting him and Clara in Hannover, Robert remembered his friend's playing not only as elevated but as pleasurable and athletic. "And I have dreamed of you, dear Joachim," he wrote. "We were together for three days—you had heron feathers in your hands, from which flowed champagne."[108] The first movement coda ultimately releases a flow of virtuosity, turning the triplets into triplet sixteenths at the last moment. Like the third movement of the Piano Concerto Op. 54, the polonaise finale delivers transparent passagework in its transitions, culminating displays, and coda. In a letter to Robert in Endenich, Joachim remembered rehearsing the concerto with Clara at the piano. His description of the finale mixed Polishness, militaristic masculinity, and danceable pomp: "Do you remember how you smiled and were happy when we said that the last movement sounded as if [Polish national hero Tadeusz] Kościuszko published a polonaise with [King John III] Sobieski: so stately [it was]?"[109] The coda of the polonaise generates increasingly brilliant textures. Scales in sixteenth notes become arpeggios that climb progressively higher, scales peppered with repeated notes, and finally arpeggios in thirty-second notes. Such passagework might have used Joachim's stillness to a different purpose, requiring him to toss off brilliant runs with apparent effortlessness.

The Phantasie stages its own narrative of elevation and absorption. The showpiece encompasses an array of popular styles, and contemporary critics noted its lightweight tone. The *Signale* reported of Joachim's 1854 Leipzig performance, for example, "We regard the Phantasie for violin as Schumann's best concert piece. It is written in a good tone for the public."[110] Like the Allegro Appassionato and the Concert Allegro, the Phantasie is a sonata-form concerto movement with a slow introduction. The first theme of the sonata form announces an appealing, accessible style. Its repeated anapest rhythms and persistent stress on the second and fourth beats impart a jaunty dance character more typical of a light rondo finale than a first movement.[111] The culminating displays deploy the modular structure and transparent textures conventional in postclassical concertos. Claudia Macdonald hears lighthearted humor in the sudden shifts between lyricism and acrobatics.[112]

The Phantasie also incorporates a popular form of virtuosity through the *style hongrois*, or "Hungarian-Gypsy Style."[113] John Daverio has already noted that the slow introduction evokes the *style hongrois*, and considering this instance of musical exoticism in greater detail illuminates the way in which the showpiece stages and self-consciously elevates virtuosity.[114] *Style hongrois* concert works reference *verbunkos* music, a tradition originally cultivated in Hungarian villages, influenced by Central European and Turkish traditions, and performed by "Gypsy" bands composed largely of Romani musicians. Beginning in the late eighteenth century, a Westernized version of *verbunkos* enjoyed great popularity. Composers invoked the style in *Hausmusik* and concert works. Some wrote entire pieces in the *style hongrois*, whereas others included *style hongrois* sections or movements in otherwise nonexotic compositions. Vienna led the way in cultivating and disseminating *verbunkos* and the *style hongrois*: Viennese audiences thrilled to "Gypsy" bands, publishers printed reams of such music, and composers including Haydn and Schubert contributed to this repertory.

Robert Schumann encountered and composed music that simulated "Gypsy" music-making throughout his career. During the 1830s, he recorded in his diary and letters to Henriette Voigt that he enjoyed Schubert's *Divertissement à la hongroise*, a veritable catalogue of "Hungarian-Gypsy" musical idioms. Though he never mentioned it in his diary or letters, he would have likely encountered *verbunkos* music during his 1838 and 1846 visits to Vienna. Schumann composed several short piano pieces in the "Gypsy" style for amateurs and beginners: his 1851 *Ballscenen*, Op. 109, for piano four hands includes an "Ungarisch," the third of his *Clavier Sonaten für die Jugend*, Op. 118, contains a "Zigeunertanz," and his 1849 *Lieder für die Jugend* contains two "Zigeunerliedchen" on Spanish texts translated by Emanuel Geibel. Robert's song "Zigeunerleben," Op. 29, no. 3, for small chorus, piano, and optional triangle or tambourine uses an original text by Geibel that evokes scenes of "Gypsy" wandering. As Julie Hedges Brown has noted, Robert also

Example 6.4. Schumann, Phantasie Op. 131. *Hallgató* in slow introduction. Orchestral parts shown in piano reduction.

invoked the *style hongrois* in some of his large chamber works. The finale of the Piano Quintet Op. 44, for example, begins in the style of a fast *style hongrois* rondo.[115]

The introduction's quasi-improvisatory runs and embellishments simulate the *hallgató* style, in which the leader of a band (usually a violinist) improvises on a slow melody, overloads it with ornamentation, and at times renders the original tune all but unrecognizable.[116] In published arrangements and collections of "Hungarian-Gypsy" music, *hallgató* sections often appear as fantasia-like introductions to faster, dance-style pieces. Robert's Introduction serves a similar purpose, though the dance-like music that follows does not bear any obvious exotic markers. As shown in example 6.4, the violinist alternates between plaintive me-

Example 6.4. (*continued*)

lodic gestures and rapid, rhythmically asymmetrical scales. In measure 16, for example, the faux improvisation transforms an appoggiatura-inflected melody into an ornamental turn. At measure 20, the soloist cycles through and varies the first eight measures, adding new melodic and harmonic turns: the Phantasie, then, does not begin with an open-ended cadenza but by heavily embellishing two parallel phrases. Although the introduction does not use any "Gypsy modes" or their characteristic augmented seconds, the runs suggest exotic modality with sharp-fourth scale degrees and dissonant leaps. The minor dominant in measure 16 also hints at modal harmony. Throughout the introduction, the violinist executes standard *hallgató* gestures, leaping rapidly between contrasting registers and adding ornaments to each successive note of a melodic figure. The orchestra, as is conventional in *hallgató* music, accompanies with sustained chords. The end of the introduction simulates the spontaneous solo–band exchanges that characterized *hallgató*: we quickly move back and forth between the violin's embellished, quasi-improvisatory outbursts and the orchestra's punctuating chords.

The *style hongrois* delivered quotidian entertainment and, at the same time, evoked what nineteenth-century listeners heard as idealized—if uncultivated—expressive and performative prowess. This seeming paradox emerged from the position of the Roma within Central European culture. As internal Others, the Roma were marginalized and regarded as mysterious, exotic, and threatening but were also readily visible in daily life and cultural products. *Verbunkos* and *style hongrois* music functioned as light entertainment, thanks to the ubiquity of "Gypsy" bands and bestselling "Hungarian"-style sheet music. At the same time, the style also symbolized heightened musical expressivity. As Jonathan Bellman has shown, the centuries-long oppression of the European Roma (which ranged from economic exploitation to homicidal persecution) and stereotypes about melancholic, hyperemotional, freedom-loving "Gypsies" shaped the style's perceived affective qualities. The *style hongrois*, he writes, could signify "both metahuman despair and a savage joy." [117] Shay Loya similarly observes that it stood for "soulfulness and precivilized freedom that stand in some contrast to the perceived tamer mainstream music of Europe."[118] The *hallgató* style in particular was designed to simulate an unmediated, extravagant display of passion and virtuosity. ("Simulate" is an important qualifier. Whether rendered by "Gypsy" bands or conservatory-trained violinists, such music enacted a cultural stereotype for an expectant audience.) All these connotations relied on a backhanded idealization of "Gypsy" musicians as gifted but uncultivated, even primitive. The stereotypical "Gypsy" played instinctively and impulsively, forgoing refinement, restraint, intellectual reflection, or literacy.[119] Many of these stereotypes—melancholy, homelessness, and abandoned music-making—surface in Geibel's text to "Zigeunerleben."

Within its mélange of popular styles, Robert's Phantasie makes a point about virtuosity and cultivation. At several junctures, Robert converted *style hongrois* violin playing into virtuosity that evoked the German culture of serious music and Joachim's own transcendent withdrawal. The development, for example, returns to the introduction's *hallgató*. Leaps of a seventh cascade into increasingly rapid flourishes, suggesting an ornate improvisation on the exposition's second theme. As if called forth by the rhapsodic emoting, the A-minor introduction theme reappears in the orchestra. The reverie suddenly disperses when the violin breaks into motoric arpeggios. At the retransition, the figuration expands into broad arpeggios that enliven a dominant pedal—the texture alludes to a distinctive and formally analogous point in the first movement in Mendelssohn's Violin Concerto.[120] The reference carries both personal and ideological significance. Mendelssohn himself had been Joachim's mentor. More broadly, he epitomized nineteenth-century German ideals of musical cultivation. Born into a highly literate, educated family, steeped in Bach and Beethoven, trained in counterpoint from the beginning of his education, and a founder of the Leipzig Conservatory, he embodied a model of musicianship antithetical to the "Gypsy" stereotype.

The Phantasie culminates by forgoing, even erasing, exotic and popular virtuosity. The cadenza itself does not include any *hallgató* playing, even though it might seem a logical place for it. After showing off his multiple-stop technique, the violinist twice repeats a lyrical phrase over a tremolo accompaniment, the second time embellishing it with an appoggiatura. Scripted though the cadenza may be, it seems to catch the soloist in the act of spontaneously creating and refining a melody bereft of exotic markers. The coda recapitulates the A-minor introduction in C major but eliminates any trace of exotic virtuosity. Like the first movement of the Violin Concerto, it presents a quiet apotheosis. The chords that open the coda seem to promise a triumphal return. However, the dynamic dips to *piano*, and the strings and winds weave around the soloist's figuration. Reminiscences of the introduction surface in the soft-spoken counterpoint. As shown in example 6.5, the coda

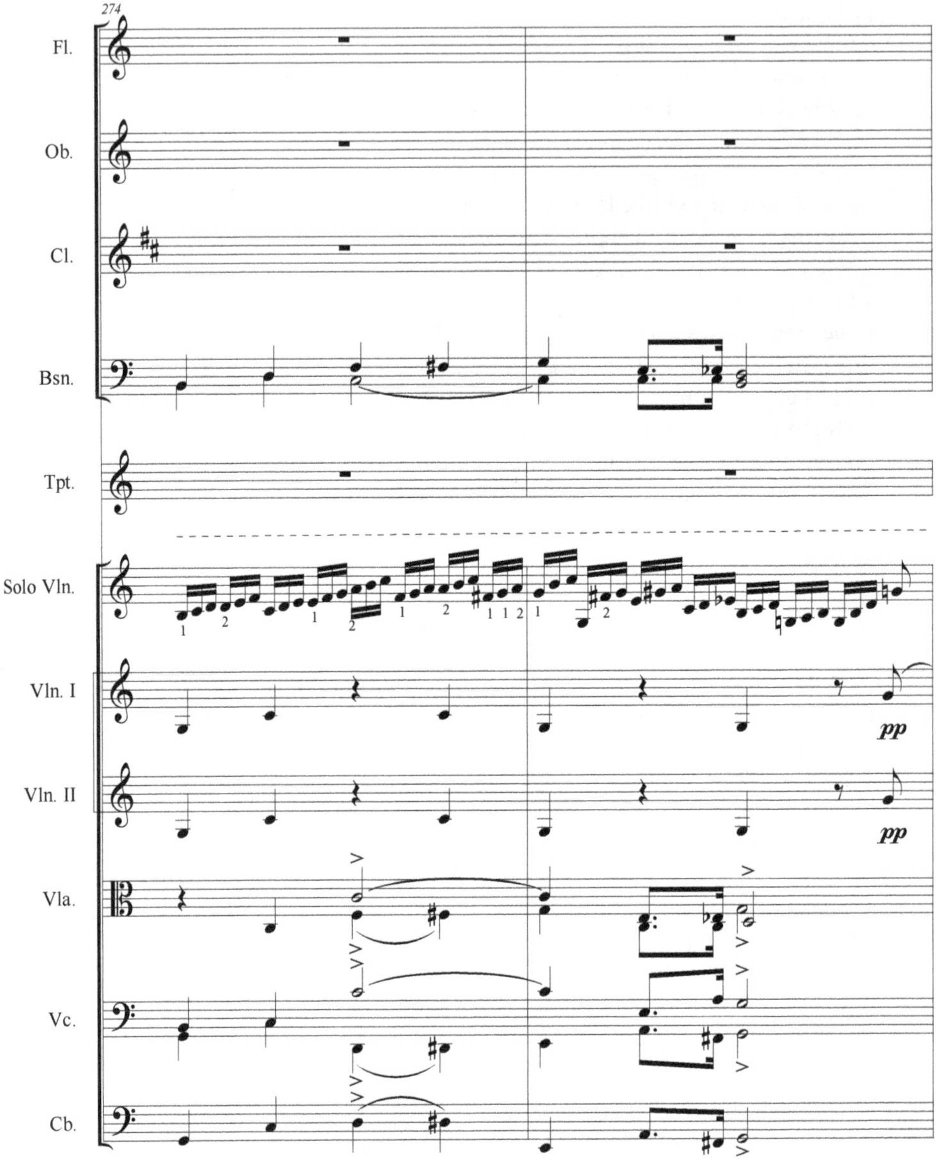

Example 6.5. Schumann, Phantasie Op. 131. Coda.

Example 6.5. (*continued*)

Example 6.5. (*continued*)

again seems ready to burst into brilliant runs at measure 270, where the violin accelerates into rapid scales and the orchestration thins. Instead of supporting a grand climax, the winds and strings enter *pianissimo* and divide the introduction's theme between them. The violin's scales broaden into broken octaves that double the orchestra, forming a connective tissue between the sections. Both introduction and coda gently undermine our sense of a motoric pulse— as the theme repeats the main motive, it places metric and dynamic stress on different notes. (Compare, for example, measures 276 and 277.) The coda, then, presents a last display of technical agility, but it eschews the transparently textured, metrically regular momentum of the culminating displays, the unpredictable flourishes of *style hongrois* virtuosity, and the light dance style of the first theme. What had been a canvas for *hallgató* emoting now reminds listeners of Robert's compositional craftsmanship—his ability to tie up thematic and tonal loose ends—and stages a nonexotic, restrained virtuoso.

Robert's Phantasie thereby entered a tradition of compositions that mediated between *style hongrois* music and signifiers of learnedness and cultivation. For example, the finales of Brahms's Piano Quartet No. 2, Op. 26, and Robert's own Piano Quintet intellectualize their *style hongrois* components. Brahms motivically deconstructs his *style hongrois* sonata-rondo theme during an extensive development section charged with syncopated rhythms. Robert's quintet includes a fugato based on the *style hongrois* main theme and, in the coda, contrapuntally combines it with a motive from the first movement. Daverio has argued that the Brahms's Double Concerto Op. 102 pursues such an amalgamation. The *style hongrois* pervades the first and third movements and shapes Brahms's harmonic vocabulary and motivic processes; in Daverio's analysis, the work reflects Brahms's larger project to synthesize expressive passion with structural rationality.[121] Like these works, the Phantasie Op. 131 offers the pleasures of exoticism as well as those of cultural prestige. It presents the *style hongrois* as a musical delight to be consumed, a pretext for expressively charged virtuosity. At the same time, it also allows composer and performer to assert their affinity for a self-consciously cultivated tradition.

Joachim's practices as a performer-composer wrote large the combination of exoticism, popular style, and self-conscious seriousness that characterizes individual works such as Robert's Phantasie. Though Joachim was most admired for championing Beethoven, Bach, and Mendelssohn, he also composed and performed *style hongrois* showpieces. His best-known composition was his Violin Concerto No. 2 in D Minor, Op. 11, "Auf Hungarischer Weise." His Variations on an Original Theme, Op. 10, for viola and piano, ends with two *style hongrois* variations, one *hallgató* and one in a faster, dance style. Composers other than Robert Schumann wrote *style hongrois* pieces for Joachim. He received the dedication of Liszt's Hungarian Rhapsody No. 15 and arranged it for violin and piano. In an 1854 letter to Liszt, Joachim suggested that they might perform "the Hungarian Rhapsody that I proudly call my own" together when he visited Weimar. The letter also showed that Joachim understood the appeal of "Gypsy"-style music. Describing Hans von Bülow's performance of Liszt's *Fantasie über ungarische Volksmelodien*, he wrote that the work won over even the stodgiest listeners: "The formal freedoms...have something so gripping about them that even the most confirmed classicists 'Gypsied' along [*mitzigeunerten*] with true love."[122] Brahms dedicated the Double Concerto to Joachim as a token of reconciliation after several years of estrangement, and Daverio proposed that the work alludes to their friendship by showcasing a popular, exotic style that both men enjoyed.[123]

In an 1861 letter to Brahms, Joachim hinted that he regarded the *style hongrois* as an integral part of his profile, a musical idiom that he believed he could use with fluency and even ownership. He discussed Brahms's Piano Quartet No. 1, Op. 25, the manuscript of which the composer had sent him. When he came to the "Rondo alla Zingarese," Joachim wrote, "In the last movement you have really given me a thrashing *on my own territory*."[124]

Joachim's predilection for the *style hongrois*, though, never compromised his status as the quintessential cultivated violinist of his time or his assimilation into German musical culture as a Hungarian Jew. Joachim grew up speaking German, not Hungarian. The letter to Brahms suggests that, as much as he viewed the *style hongrois* as his own territory, he also identified with German culture to the point of chauvinism. He wrote, "I wish that, in the near future, my countrymen (who behave somewhat arrogantly) would be so compellingly convinced by the Germans of the latter's intellectual [*geistigen*] preeminence. They would then amiably accept the inevitable and rejoice that one recognized their mother tongue."[125] (Joachim seems to be referring to political tensions within the Austrian empire between Hungary and the Vienna government.) Scholars have debated the nuances of Joachim's assimilation. Beatrix Borchard portrays him as man caught between cultural, national, and family tensions. She argues that *Zerrissenheit* (inner conflict) was central to his relationships and self-image. Robert Eshbach has countered that, although Joachim certainly encountered anti-Semitism from his colleagues, these insults stung especially because he unequivocally saw himself as a German musical insider from the beginning of his career. After all, he had consorted with Beethoven's friends during his early adolescence, played in the Gewandhaus Orchestra during some of his formative years, and studied at the University of Göttingen.[126]

In either case, Robert's Violin Concerto and Phantasie represented one step in Joachim's ascendency to this position. It might be assuming too much to interpret the Phantasie as an assimilation narrative that restrains and Germanizes Joachim's "Hungarian" virtuosity. (Robert did not discuss Joachim's Jewishness or Hungarianness in any surviving documents. Joachim might even have concealed his Jewish identity from the Schumanns, at least initially. According to Moser's biography of Joachim, King George V of Hannover himself was initially unaware that he had hired a Jewish music director. When he learned, he compelled Joachim to be baptized.) Rather, the designs of the showpieces more generally foregrounded Joachim's historicism, Germanness, and seriousness. His ownership over these works gave him a privileged relationship with Robert and even made him a curator of the composer's legacy. More broadly, the performances Joachim shared with the Schumanns won him recognition and began to tie his career to Robert's and Clara's.

While he was collaborating with Joachim, Robert Schumann himself was more immediately preoccupied with a different issue relevant to his own professional life: midcentury musical factionalism. During the early 1850s, Joachim sought both Robert and Liszt as mentors. His Violin Concerto No. 1, published in 1855, shows what he learned in Weimar—melodies linked through thematic transformation, for example, and an expansive, single-movement structure. Joachim sent his *Hamlet* Overture to Robert and asked for suggestions. Joachim did not definitively break with the New Germans until after Robert's death. In 1857, he wrote to Liszt that he could no longer support his music and in 1860 signed a public declaration against the New Germans along with Brahms. Even at this early date, though, Robert regarded Joachim as an important member of the Brahms-centered circle that he proclaimed in "Neue Bahnen." In the letter that contained the Violin Concerto score, he wrote, "I believe that Johannes is the true apostle" and described Liszt as "the Judas Iscariot on the Ilm." Such remarks, he wrote, were "only for the apostle Joseph." A month later, Robert saluted Joachim as "Dear *Kriegscamarad!*" He continued the military metaphor when discussing the "Neue Bahnen" essay: "Since I sent a few twenty-pound shells into the enemy's camp a few days ago, peace has been more or less preserved."[127]

Robert, then, pulled Joachim toward the Brahms–Schumann circle and away from the New Germans. (Not that he was solely responsible for Joachim's shift of affiliation. Joachim came to regard his style of performing as incompatible with Liszt's, and he bristled at anti-Semitism within the Weimar circle.[128]) The very showpieces Robert composed for his young ally presented his virtuosity within a classicizing frame that differed from Joachim's Lisztian Concerto No. 1. The New German controversy added yet another meaning to the Mendelssohn allusion in the Phantasie: the showpiece conspicuously evoked a composer whom Franz Brendel and other New German critics dismissed as a regressive classicist. After Robert's death, Joachim decisively joined the Brahms–Schumann circle and supported their version of musical historicism.

Epilogue: Schumann in the Canon

Ultimately, the late concertos that Schumann composed for Clara and Joachim gained only a precarious foothold in the canon. The stigma of mental illness haunted their reception. Critics also looked askance at their crowd-pleasing features and conventional concerto structures. Works designed for two of the quintessential serious virtuosos of the nineteenth-century later disappointed critics as "mere" showpieces. An 1875 review of the Concert Allegro damned it with faint praise. The work "gripped [us] more as a competent virtuoso piece than through the poetry of tones," the reviewer wrote. "The tutti were for the most part worked out entirely according to the traditional concerto pattern."[129] When an 1856 memorial concert for Robert featured the Phantasie, Richard Pohl wrote that the piece was a poor choice: "It is a *Gelegenheitstück*, and not even a successful one."[130] In a sense, Pohl was right. Robert's Phantasie, like his other concerted showpieces, was designed to script spectacular, crowd-pleasing performances and written for a specific performer. For Pohl, the work inadequately represented a composer fast becoming a monument within the canon.

Other Schumann compositions did enter the canon and became works with which pianists demonstrated their affinity for that tradition. Sculptor Friedrich Christoph Hausmann inscribed his 1896 bust of Clara Schumann with the primary theme of Robert's Piano Concerto.[131] He thereby monumentalized Clara's partnership with her husband long after the latter's death. Robert Schumann's 1830s piano cycles became a mainstay of the recital repertoire. Ironically, because these pieces drew upon domestic genres as much as they did the canonic tradition and because Robert only gained widespread critical acclaim after changing his style during the 1840s. Clara first publicly performed *Carnaval* in 1856.[132] As she added this and other cycles to her repertoire, other pianists followed suit.

Clara's work as an editor of her husband's music additionally furthered its canonization and maintained her own status as its privileged interpreter. With Brahms's assistance, she produced a collected edition of Robert's works that was published between 1881 and 1893. Robert thereby became one of the select composers considered significant enough to warrant comprehensive critical editions. (*Robert Schumanns Werke* was not truly comprehensive: it omitted several unpublished works, such as the Violin Concerto and third violin sonata.) Clara consulted other musicians about the *Werke*, but she assumed control of the final product, and the edition bore her name. On her own, Clara published a practical instructive edition of Robert's piano music in 1887, a contribution to the growing literature of piano "classics" edited by noted performers. As Nancy Reich has shown, these editions revealed Clara's attitudes about *Werktreue* and her ownership of her husband's legacy. Clara produced the instructive edition partly in response to Hans von Bülow's editions of Bach, Beethoven, Chopin, and other composers— indeed, she hoped to edit Robert's music before von Bülow did. Claudia de Vries notes that, in contrast to von Bülow's extensively annotated editions, Clara's contains few markings not found in the first editions and manuscripts.[133]

Though some of the pieces Robert composed for Clara during her midcareer transformation had fallen by the wayside in nineteenth-century concert life, then, his music and its canonic status remained central to her professional identity.

Epilogue

Nineteenth-century writings often spoke of reforming virtuosity once and for all, as in Schumann's proclamation of a Utopian "New Poetic Future," Herrmann Hirschbach's prophesies about a redemptive efflorescence of masterworks, and Eduard Hanslick's triumphal account of Vienna's "Artistic Renaissance" and its virtuoso "priests." Scholars often suggest that, around midcentury, the consolidation of the piano and orchestral canons settled important debates about virtuosity. This watershed did transform the frames in which audiences encountered virtuosity and the values that performers and composers strove to embody. In fact, though, the virtuosity discourse continued throughout the later nineteenth century and beyond, evolving alongside its participants' broader aesthetic and cultural concerns. Writers continued to debate distinctions between transcendent and superficial virtuosity, and ambitious performers and composers avidly courted the former distinction.

Without attempting a comprehensive account, I would like to sketch three ways in which Schumann figured in this later history: with a body of repertoire that was still emerging in the later nineteenth century, through the performer-composers with whom he collaborated during his last productive years, and as one of many individuals who laid the foundations for a larger ideological inheritance.

Schumannian Showpieces after Schumann

Several of Schumann's compositions only entered the concert repertory and the virtuosity discourse after his death. As I noted at the end of chapter 6, his 1830s piano cycles only became standard recital fare after Clara began programming them in the late 1850s. The Violin Concerto never served as a vehicle for Joseph Joachim. Instead, it became one of many exhibits in debates about Schumann's late works, in Joachim's correspondence and in twentieth- and twenty-first-century criticism and scholarship.[1]

The performance history of the *Études symphoniques* yielded many distinct reinterpretations of Schumannian virtuosity. In 1873, Clara allowed Simrock to publish the five variations Robert had composed for the *Fantaisies et finale* and left out of the *Études* (see chapter 3). Pianists began a tradition of incorporating these posthumous variations into their performances of the *Études*. Because pianists have developed different ways of ordering the posthumous and published variations, this tradition that at once revives posthumous music and gives pianists a rare opportunity to creatively recompose canonic repertoire. Their different orderings give virtuosic display different trajectories. Alfred Cortot's study edition of the *Études*, for example, suggests positioning the posthumous variations at regular intervals: because they are slower and more lyrical than the published ones, they stretch out the piece's drive to the finale and tone down its inexorable momentum. Maurizio Pollini, by contrast, recorded all five posthumous variations in the middle of the sequence, creating a valley of lyrical, at times quasi-improvisatory music flanked by steep crescendos.[2]

Schumann's Cello Concerto Op. 129 was a more substantial posthumously canonized work. He published it in 1854, but performances that he planned in Düsseldorf fell through. Ludwig Ebert gave what was most likely the first performance in Oldenburg in 1860. The concert was not widely publicized, and the work remained obscure. In 1867, the *Signale für die musikalische Welt* announced David Popper's Breslau performance as the premiere.[3]

As it entered the repertoire, the Cello Concerto became one more Schumann showpiece in which listeners heard a serious mode of solo performance—for some, serious to a fault. Whereas critics usually recognized that the Concert Allegro and violin Phantasie scripted crowd-pleasing displays, early reviews of the Cello Concerto held that the work subverted appealing spectacle to the point of austerity. The *Signale* account of Popper's performance described the concerto as rarefied in its appeal: "It is not a piece intended to have an effect in a large hall; but all the more will the connoisseur [*Kenner*] be gripped by its soundness." The reviewer emphasized the first movement's overall affect, writing that "an elegiac magic embraces the whole first movement" and that the solo in particular takes on a "melancholy color."[4] In 1855, violinist and composer Karl Böhmer had taken a more critical tone when reviewing the score for the *Neue Berliner Musikzeitung*. He also noted the mood (which he described as "serious, dignified quietude") and praised the structure: "The arrangement of the main ideas is clearer, more thoughtful, and more flowing [than in the Phantasie]." Much as he commended the composition, Böhmer also complained that it deprived the soloist of opportunities for stunning display. He wrote, "The invention of cantilenas and passagework is not as rhapsodic and melismatic as that of the Phantasie . . . so that the player cannot truly bring them or himself to fruition."[5]

In part, these qualities emerge from the way Schumann undercuts structural boundaries and veers away from brilliant passagework at unexpected junctures. The first movement's second theme, for example, never reaches a cadence and instead blends into the culminating display. At the seam between these sections, the cello combines an expressive leap of a seventh derived from the second theme with a triplet scale that anticipates the figuration to come. The display's triplet arpeggios momentarily slow for wide leaps and lyrical turns that transform gestures from the second theme. Only in the last four measures does the culminating display turn to a brilliant flow of scales. Even here, Schumann does not sustain this climax with a full tutti, nor does he strongly affirm the exposition's modulation from A minor to C major: on the final note of the cello's last flourish, the dominant of C major morphs chromatically into that of A minor, and the development begins at a sparsely orchestrated *piano*.

Other moments in the concerto similarly smooth over significant arrival points. The first movement's development springs two false recapitulations. Schumann harmonically masks the true recapitulation, which begins with two augmented-sixth chords and only reaches A minor once the theme's first phrase is well under way. Though the final movement ends with an outpouring of rapid figuration, the windup is gradual. The cadenza reaches a low point of velocity and brilliance, halting the momentum for double stops, wide leaps, and figuration that twists through embellishing nonharmonic tones. Over the course of thirty-four measures, triplet figuration coalesces into regularity, switches from repeated double-stops to arpeggios, and accelerates first into sixteenth notes and then into *schneller, fortissimo* triplets. Despite Böhmer's complaint, the Cello Concerto does not lack memorable themes and agile passagework. It does, however, lead the soloist and audience through moments of arrival that never receive climactic confirmation and through passagework that barely emerges from the emotive lyricism.[6]

The Virtuosity Debates and the Midcentury Factions

Rival midcentury musical factions used virtuoso performances, original showpieces, and writings about virtuosity to articulate their ideologies—Liszt and what became known as the New German School, and the Brahms–Joachim–Clara Schumann circle. Just as when Robert Schumann and Gottfried Wilhelm Fink clashed during the 1830s, approaches to virtuosity reflected larger aesthetic and cultural stances. In the later rivalry, critical debate and compositional self-positioning hinged on divergent responses to nineteenth-century historicism.

As we saw in chapter 6, Robert helped to shape Clara's and Joachim's careers while they were establishing themselves as paragons of *Werktreue*, musicians who cultivated what they considered a timeless tradition of instrumental music and often defined themselves against the New Germans. After Robert's death, they and their supporters continued to champion this ideology. One thinks of Hanslick's encomium to the virtuoso "priests," which conspicuously excluded Liszt and his students, or the Joachim biography by Johannes Moser and Joachim himself, which contrasted the violinist's supposed authenticity with Liszt's theatricality. Despite Liszt's gestures of support, Clara maintained her distance from him. In her private writings, she admired his playing but scorned his compositions. She wrote in her diary the day after Liszt's death in 1886:

> He was an eminent piano virtuoso, but as such a dangerous model for the young. Almost all emergent players imitate him, but they lack his spirit, genius, and grace, and therefore only a few great pure technicians and many caricatures arise. . . . For Liszt was a bad composer—in this regard, also pernicious for many . . . because his compositions lack the aforementioned qualities he possessed as a virtuoso; they are trivial, boring, and surely will completely depart from the world with his passing.[7]

The rivalry also played out in the professional interactions (or lack thereof) between these musicians. For example, Joachim and Clara were invited to perform at an 1870 Beethoven centennial concert in Vienna, but both declined because Liszt and Wagner had also been asked. In his letter to the committee, Joachim regretted that appearing alongside Liszt and Wagner, for him, would "mar the simple, noble greatness of Beethoven." Clara wrote to Joachim, "A Beethoven festival with Liszt and Wagner—that constricts my heart."[8]

The compositions Robert had written for or dedicated to Clara, Joachim, and Brahms were the first of many showpieces this circle cultivated, in which they framed virtuosity to match their ideology. To cite but one example: when Brahms gave his first piano recital in Vienna in 1862, he closed with his *Variations and Fugue on a Theme by Handel*, Op. 24. (He also presented the work to Clara Schumann as a birthday gift in 1861.) The *Variations* incorporate and reinterpret a range of historical allusions. By ending with a fugue, Brahms nodded to Beethoven's "Eroica" Variations, Op. 35, and "Diabelli" Variations, Op. 120. Like the two Beethoven fugues, Brahms manipulates his subject with learned contrapuntal procedures, in his case augmentation and inversion.[9] However, he foregrounded contrapuntal complexity to an even greater extent than either Beethoven work did. Both Beethoven sets continue past their fugues: the "Eroica" Variations ends by wreathing the theme in brilliant scales, and the "Diabelli" Variations concludes with a minuet variation and a crystalline, hushed coda. Brahms, by contrast, ends the *Handel Variations* with the double notes and ringing octaves of the fugue's final pedal point. Here, the fugue does not represent a penultimate treatment of the theme but the virtuosic culmination of the work. Brahms combined Beethoven allusion with a reach further into the musical past. He used the theme, unaltered, from the "Aria con Variazioni" from Handel's Suite in B-flat, HWV 434, and he scattered neo-Baroque variations throughout the piece. The ornaments in Variation 1 evoke Handel's, Variations 4 and 16 are canons, and Variation 19 is a *siciliano*.

The *Handel Variations* anticipate on the recital stage the exercise in compositional self-definition that shaped Brahms's Symphony No. 1, completed fifteen years later.[10] As Mark Evan Bonds has shown, the finale alludes to a Beethoven theme—the "Ode to Joy" from the Ninth Symphony—but suppresses it. As it goes on, the finale instead emphasizes complex motivic development and references to Mozart's "Jupiter" Symphony.[11] Granted, Brahms's symphony begs to be heard as a pointed rebuttal to Wagner's claims about the obsolescence of the instrumental symphony in the face of the *Gesamtkunstwerk*, whereas the *Handel Variations* does not invoke these genre-specific issues. Like the symphony, though, the showpiece aligns the composer-pianist with an eighteenth- and early nineteenth-century instrumental repertoire whose idioms he and his circle considered viable, and it revels in the more learned, esoteric corners of this tradition. Aesthetic debates were a timely issue for Brahms when he composed the *Variations*. In 1860, he and Joachim had written an essay against the New Germans. The editorial leaked to the press before they were finished collecting signatures, and the result embarrassingly bore only four names.

The New Germans advanced their own exemplars of transcendent virtuosity, notably Liszt himself. As I noted in chapter 5, scholars have shown how Liszt's Weimar piano works articulated his new compositional identity. Liszt's engagement with virtuosity continued into his post-Weimar decades, as did his supporters' polemics. In 1877, for example, Richard Pohl reviewed in the *Neue Zeitschrift* Liszt's performance for a meeting of the Allgemeine Deutsche Musikverein.[12] Pohl opened by regretting that some musicians insufficiently appreciated Liszt's accomplishments. In an obvious stab at the Brahms circle, he criticized those whose "classical outlook" has led only to "fruitless standstill" and "immortal boredom." On this occasion, Liszt performed two works for piano duo with his former student, Ingeborg von Bronsart—his *Concerto pathétique* and Saint-Saëns's *Variations sur un thème de Beethoven*, Op. 35. His solo numbers included Beethoven's Sonata Op. 31, no. 3, his own "Cantique d'Amour" from the *Harmonies poëtiques et religieuses*, and selections from his solo arrangement of Schubert's *Divertissement à la hongroise*. Pohl praised Liszt from various angles. On the duos, he wrote that to collaborate so impeccably on such short notice would have been impossible for any pianist who had not trained with Liszt. When he described Liszt's solo playing, he turned him into a victorious Icarus: "When he is bound by no collaboration with others, by no orchestra and by no chorus, when he can indulge himself completely free and unrestrained, he ascends like an eagle-king to the sun of art, soars alone and majestic over the small earth under him, and drinks that pure ether of music that is harmful to ordinary mortals."

Partisan critics made similar claims about Liszt's showpieces. For example, like Brahms's *Handel Variations*, Liszt's *Variations on a Motive by Bach* reinterprets a Baroque source. Composed in 1862 and published in 1865 (for organ) and 1875 (for piano), the *Variations* treats the lament-bass from the opening chorus of Bach's cantata, *Weinen, Klagen, Sorgen, Zagen*. (Liszt wrote the work shortly after the deaths of his daughter, Blandine, and son, Daniel.) The showpiece begins with a transcription of Bach's chorus but soon uses the passacaglia variations to unfurl a catalogue of Lisztian piano techniques. A slow section loosens the chaconne pattern and refracts the lament motive through thematic transformation. At the end of the *Variations*, Liszt drew upon his experience writing concert paraphrases and turned to the last movement of Bach's cantata, a setting of the chorale "Was Gott tut, das ist wohlgetan." An 1876 review in the Berlin music journal *Echo* continued the strand of Liszt reception that read sublimity into his virtuosity: "[The *Variations*] do not impart a languishing charm but drag us under the pounding thunder of an inexorable bass volcano with transcendental, grandiose sweep that follows an unfettered mass of tones into the spirit-realm." The reviewer extolled the *Variations'* combination of virtuosity and avant-garde structure. The piece represented the "triumphant *Glanzzeit* of the piano," and, in it, "The grand master of pianism and piano composition shows the necessity and delight of turning away from the laws of conventional architecture for those who do not regard astute dialectic as mere scholastic quibbling."[13]

The Virtuosity Discourse as Nineteenth-Century Inheritance

Well into the present day, ideas about superficial and serious virtuosity have remained an important lens through which musicians and listeners within the culture of Western "classical" music view and valorize their art. The virtuosity discourse has joined other persistent musical legacies of the nineteenth century: the heroic image of Beethoven, for example, or expectations of audience behavior at concerts.

Music journals in the late nineteenth and twentieth centuries continued to publish essays that made sweeping claims about virtuosity. They often employed rhetoric and voiced anxieties similar to those we have seen in writings by Schumann and his contemporaries: comparisons between virtuosos and circus performers, laments about public appetite for virtuosity, dichotomies between the sensuality of shallow virtuosity and the spirituality of high art, and exhortations for virtuosos to reject their own egotism and revere the musical masterwork. Meanwhile, other writers purported to defend virtuosity against what they considered a puritanical art-music establishment, only to propose their own hierarchies of virtuosos.[14]

For late twentieth- and early twenty-first-century audiences and musicians, the virtuosity discourse retains its political and cultural agendas, from the aspirational to the exclusionary. Concert pianists routinely promote themselves as musicians who possess superhuman technical skills but somehow transcend "mere" virtuosity, a capability they and their listeners might attribute to their extraordinary nuance, intellectual sophistication, grasp of musical structure, or devotion to more esoteric corners of the repertoire. For example, younger pianist Khatia Buniatishvili (b. 1987) makes such a claim with unusual directness on her promotional website: "Khatia prefers not to be regarded as a child prodigy: virtuosity for its own sake does not appeal to her."[15] The statement distinguishes Buniatishvili's current performances from her childhood achievements and, more broadly, from stereotypes about prodigies with astonishing technique but only nascent musical understanding. Marc-André Hamelin's website promotes his virtuosity by invoking different categories. A collection of press clippings includes a *Washington Post* review by Anne Midgette. In her account, technical mastery exists separately from expressive "profundity" to the point that a pianist who possesses both becomes a "crossover artist" (though Midgette avoids explicitly privileging either quality):

> Virtuoso pianists tend to be divided into two groups: those of supreme technical ability and those with a profound aptitude for expression. These two groups are often treated as if they were mutually exclusive, and critics are fond of exclaiming when a member of one group shows himself able to travel into the terrain of the other.

> The Canadian pianist Marc-André Hamelin is a prime example of this kind of crossover artist.[16]

Henry Kingsbury's (admittedly contentious) ethnography of an unnamed American conservatory notes that the music students he observed tended to regard technical mastery and "soul" as separate issues that they needed to navigate.[17]

Writers on virtuosity have also remained preoccupied with distinguishing between connoisseurs attuned to supposedly intellectual or otherwise inner ideals and less initiated listeners easily impressed with physical feats. The 1999 *NPR Guide to Building a Classical CD Collection* speaks with the voice of Eduard Krüger's Music Director when its cover promises that the reader will become a "better listener" by learning to distinguish "technical brilliance from emotional truth."[18] In a scathing 1990 article on Vladimir Horowitz, Joseph Horowitz opined that the pianist excelled most at "brains in the fingers" repertoire (such as Moritz Moszkowski's pyrotechnic miniatures). Though Vladimir Horowitz and his marketers had often attempted to reinvent his image by presenting him as a devotee of the classics and man of broad intellectual interests, Joseph Horowitz argues that his actual playing did not change. The critic blamed philistine American audiences. Whereas the upper echelons of Russian musical society had encouraged Vladimir Horowitz to develop an adventurous repertoire, he claims, moving to the United States had "doomed him to a career of maximum fame, fortune, and virtuosic display."[19]

I am not suggesting that Schumann and his contemporaries necessarily offer the key to these later episodes in the virtuosity discourse. Even during his lifetime, Schumann was one of many voices in the conversation about virtuosity, his music one act on a crowded nineteenth-century stage. Just as Schumann's approach to virtuosity adapted to different performers, genres, and facets of nineteenth-century musical aesthetics, the larger virtuosity discourse itself evolved—even if it retained some nineteenth-century rhetoric, anxieties, and ideologies.

Schumann's activities during the "Age of Virtuosity" do offer a rich view of the musical and intellectual ferment that gave questions about virtuosity unprecedented urgency and generated a diverse array of responses. He reveals the history of virtuosity as one in which musicians anxiously questioned what kind of social and aesthetic status they could attain as performers with extraordinary physical skills, as composers who scripted astonishing performative displays. In the face of this overriding concern, though, he invites us to be attuned to the delights, sensuousness, and immediacy of virtuoso performance as well as to aspirations about legitimacy and cultural prestige—even if this balancing act should leave us (as it often left Schumann) wondering how to mediate between these pleasures.

Notes

List of Endnote Abbreviations

AmZ	*Allgemeine musikalische Zeitung*
AmAW	*Allgemeiner musikalischer Anzeiger Wien*
Briefedition	Schumann, *Schumann Briefedition*
BNF	Schumann, *Robert Schumann's Briefe: Neue Folge*
Caecilia	*Caecilia: Algemeen Muzikaal Tijdschrift van Nederland*
GS	Schumann, *Gesammelte Schriften über Musik und Musiker*
Joachim Briefe	Joachim, *Briefe von und an Joseph Joachim*
Jugendbriefe	*Jugendbriefe von Robert Schumann*
NZfM	*Neue Zeitschrift für Musik*
Signale	*Signale für die musikalische Welt*
TB	Schumann, *Tagebücher*

Introduction: The Virtuosity Discourse

1. Schumann, "Antonio Bazzini," *GS*, 2:134.
2. Ibid., 2:134–135.
3. Nineteenth-century definitions of "virtuosity" differed from sixteenth- and seventeenth-century ones. During earlier periods, a "virtuoso" could be someone accomplished in any artistic or intellectual discipline. Among musicians, the term implied achievement as a composer and theorist along with achievement as a performer. By the nineteenth century, "virtuosity" referred mainly to performing ability on a particular instrument. For a concise survey of definitions, see Jander, "Virtuoso."
4. Hanslick, *Geschichte des Concertwesens in Wien*, 289–372.
5. See Schnapper, "Piano Variations," and Deaville, "Publishing Paraphrases and Creating Collectors."
6. Gooley, *Virtuoso Liszt*, 13 (which describes a "backlash"); Gooley, "Battle against Instrumental Virtuosity"; Gramit, *Cultivating Music*, 139 (which describes critics concerned about a "threat from within"); Wood, *Romanticism and Music Culture in Britain*, 1 (which coins the term "virtuosophobia").
7. For some recent examples, see Gooley, *Virtuoso Liszt* and "Battle against Instrumental Virtuosity"; Hamilton, *After the Golden Age*; Kawabata, *Paganini*; Klassen, *Clara Schumann*; Hunter, "To Play as if from the Soul"; Leppert, "Cultural Contradiction; Schnapper, *Henri Herz*; Wood, *Romanticism and Music Culture in Britain*. For two studies that do give considerable space to musical analysis, see Kregor, *Liszt as Transcriber* and Samson, *Virtuosity and the Musical Work*.
8. Gooley, *Virtuoso Liszt*, 13; Schnapper, *Henri Herz*, 14, 17, 87.
9. Stephen Lindeman's study of nineteenth-century piano concertos, for example, presents a richly contextualized formal analysis of Schumann's Piano Concerto Op. 54

and briefly describes the work as "devoid of formulaic or hollow virtuosity." Christoph-Hellmut Mahling persuasively argued that the Piano Concerto represented a response to Clara Wieck's Piano Concerto Op. 7. He summarized that, in the first movement of Robert's concerto, "the virtuoso element is indeed available, but downgraded to a means of representing musical objectives and not used in the foreground as a goal in and of itself." Neither author explains exactly how and why Schumann's concerto might manifest these qualities or whether audiences heard it that way. Lindeman, *Structural Novelty and Tradition*, 168; Mahling, "Das Klavierkonzert op. 54 von Robert Schumann," 150.

10. Plantinga, *Schumann as Critic*, 16, 23, 196–218.

11. Barthes, "Loving Schumann," 293.

12. Gay, *Naked Heart*, 33.

13. Landis, *Longing*, 97, 148.

14. Gooley, "Battle against Instrumental Virtuosity," 86–87; Koßmaly, "On Robert Schumann's Piano Compositions," 306–307.

15. Such an approach differs from some other recent essays on Schumannian virtuosity. Thomas Kabisch, for example, argues that the "Abegg" Variations redeem their virtuosity by incorporating it into a process of "becoming," which Kabisch derives from the twentieth-century philosopher Vladimir Jankélévitch. Matthias Hansen's study of the same piece argues that processes of motivic development set it far above comparable showpieces by Moscheles. My point is not that either of these scholars is necessarily wrong: both make revelatory points about the music. However, my own interest lies in contemporary contexts rather than transhistorical categories. Kabisch, "Schein, Sein, Werden"; Hansen, "Robert Schumanns 'Virtuosität.'"

16. Ernst Ortlepp, "Kunst," *Der Komet* 39 (September 26, 1834): 310. "Wir sind überzeugt, was ein Seb. Bach, was ein Beethoven, was ein Paganini in sich getragen, das ruht auch in Schumann."

17. "Ker.," "Concert Allegro mit Introduction," *Signale* 13, no. 41 (September 27, 1855): 321–322.

18. Of course, this book does not exhaust the topic of Schumann's virtuosity. I focus on genres and instruments that figured most prominently in the virtuosity discourse and on works whose reception most pointedly discussed virtuosity. There remains more to say, to cite but a few examples, about the Konzertstück for four horns, Op. 86, the unpublished *Konzertsatz* in D minor, and the role virtuosity plays in *Carnaval* and other piano cycles, the violin sonatas, or the Fantasie Op. 17. I have not attempted comprehensive, genre-specific surveys such as Claudia Macdonald has already made for Schumann's concertos and Damien Ehrhardt for the variations. Many of the virtuosos Schumann encountered beg for more attention than they have received, both here and in other scholarship. Even so, the cases I explore reveal some of the most formative and broadly significant episodes in Schumann's engagement with virtuosity.

19. Goehr, *Imaginary Museum*, esp. 232–234; Weber, *Great Transformation of Musical Taste*, esp. 235–251; Dahlhaus, *Nineteenth-Century Music*, 134–142; Hunter, "To Play as if from the Soul"; Samson, *Virtuosity and the Musical Work*, esp. 133–174; Trippett, "Après une Lecture de Liszt."

20. Marcello, "Il Teatro Alla Moda—Part I," esp. 388–403.

21. Applegate, "How German Is It?" 285–287; Gramit, *Cultivating Music*; Weber, *Music and the Middle Class*, 61–98.

22. Hoffmann, "Beethoven's Instrumental Music," 1193.

23. John Daverio, *Robert Schumann*, 89.

24. Schilling, "Virtuos," in *Encyclopädie der gesammten musikalischen Wissenschaften*, 7:783.

25. Felix Mendelssohn to Ignaz Moscheles, Berlin, 1833. *Felix Mendelssohn: Briefe*, 2:8.

26. August Kahlert, "Das Concertwesen der Gegenwart," *NZfM* 16, no. 27 (April 1, 1842): 105.

27. Gramit, *Cultivating Music*, 141.

28. Krüger's "Ueber Virtuosenunfug" appeared in issues 17 through 22 of the 1840 *NZfM*.

29. Gooley, "Battle against Instrumental Virtuosity," 88–94.

30. Pederson, "Romantic Music under Siege," 61–64.

31. Eduard Krüger, "Ueber Virtuosenunfug," *NZfM* 13, no. 21 (September 9, 1840): 82.

Part I. Schumann and the Piano Virtuosity of the 1830s

1. Schumann to Hummel, August 20, 1831, *BNF* 31; Theodore Töpken, manuscript transcribed in Burger, *Robert Schumann: Eine Lebenschronik*, 74.

2. See, for example, Samson, *Virtuosity and the Musical Work*, 19. Otto Biba applies the term to chamber and orchestral repertory in "Carl Czerny and Post-Classicism."

3. *Allgemeine musikalische Zeitung, mit besonderer Rücksicht auf den österreichischen Kaiserstaat* 5, no. 46 (June 9, 1821): 365–366.

4. Samson, *Virtuosity and the Musical Work*, 19.

5. See Gooley, "Battle against Instrumental Virtuosity," 97; Samson, *Chopin*, 35, 110–111.

6. Samson, *Virtuosity and the Musical Work*, 29–52.

7. Schnapper, "Piano Variations," 287.

8. Schumann, "II. Konzerte für Pianoforte mit Orchester," *GS*, 1:162.

9. Samson, *Chopin*, 121–125, 165–167; Rosen, *Romantic Generation*, 361–377.

1. Florestan among the Revelers: Postclassical Virtuosity and Schumann's Critique of Pleasure

1. By describing this music as "popular," I do not mean to suggest that it pervaded all social strata. It thrived within the middle class, a demographic with access to pianos and leisure time for instruction, playing, and listening (whether at home or in concert).

2. Plantinga, *Schumann as Critic*, 33–39.

3. Ibid., 32; Gooley, "Battle against Instrumental Virtuosity," 85–86.

4. On the last point, see Beiche, "Die *NZfM*."

5. Plantinga, *Schumann as Critic*, 34; Draheim, "Robert Schumann und Henri Herz," 165.

6. Samson, *Virtuosity and the Musical Work*, 19; Schnapper, "Piano Variations" 282–286; Watkins, *Metaphors of Depth*, 114–118.

7. Samson, *Virtuosity and the Musical Work*, 3; Samson, *Chopin*, 37.

8. Schumann, "Aus den kritischen Büchern der Davidsbündler," *GS*, 1:9. The original essay, which I quote here, contains several passages that differ from the later *Gesammelte Schriften*. *NZfM* 1, no. 19 (June 5, 1834): 73.

9. Kullak, *Die Ästhetik des Klavierspiels, 30.*

10. Wolfgang Amadeus to Leopold Mozart, December 28, 1782, in Spaethling, *Mozart's Letters, Mozart's Life*, 336–337.

11. On Schumann's engagement with Hummel, see Kroll, *Johann Nepomuk Hummel*, 275–290.

12. Friedrich Wieck to Johanna Christiana Schumann, Leipzig, 1830, in Eismann, *Robert Schumann*, 1:63.

13. Macdonald, *Robert Schumann and the Piano Concerto*, 52–56; Reiman, *Schumann's Piano Cycles*, 38.

14. Schumann, "Rondos für Pianoforte," and "Variationen für Pianoforte," *GS*, 1:241, 1:298.

15. Schumann, "Variationen für Pianoforte: Erster Gang," *GS*, 1:221. See also "H. Herz, zweites Concert mit Orchester," 1:154.

16. Schumann, "H. Herz, zweites Concert," 153.

17. Schumann, "Sigismund Thalberg, großes Concert mit Begleitung des Orchesters," *GS*, 1:153.

18. Schumann, "Sigism. Thalberg, Th. Döhler, J. Rosenhain," *GS*, 1:409.

19. *AmZ* 38, no. 33 (August 17, 1836): 544.

20. *AmZ* 37, no. 4 (January 28, 1835): 60.

21. Gottfried Wilhelm Fink, "Recension," *AmZ* 30 (April 9, 1828): 233–239. Translation adapted from Biba, "Carl Czerny and Post-Classicism," 15.

22. Fink, "Recension," 234.

23. Ibid., 235–236.

24. Gottfried Wilhelm Fink, "Bravourstücke für verschiendene Instrumente mit Orchesterbegleitung," *AmZ* 35, no. 33 (August 14, 1833): 533–539.

25. Ibid., 539.

26. Ibid., 534–535.

27. Wurst, *Fabricating Pleasure*, xiv.

28. "Ueber den Lokalkarakter der Hamburger, ihre Modebelustigungen und Zeitkürzigung," in *Journal des Luxus und der Moden*, abridged reprint ed., ed. Werner Schmidt (Leipzig: Leipzig, 1867–68) 2:253. Quoted in Wurst, *Fabricating Pleasure*, 62–63.

29. Wurst, *Fabricating Pleasure*, 67.

30. On these lines of argument, see ibid., 55–71.

31. Czerny, *Systematische Anleitung*, 75. Translations adapted from Mitchell, *Systematic Introduction*, 86.

32. Czerny, *School of Practical Composition*, 1:87.

33. Czerny, *Systematische Anleitung*, 75; Mitchell, *Systematic Introduction*, 87.

34. Fink, "Werke für das Pianoforte," *AmZ* 38, no. 30 (July 27, 1836): 489.

35. Fink, "Recensionen," *AmZ* 33, no. 1 (January 5, 1831): 7–12.

36. Fink, "Werke für das Pianoforte," *AmZ* 38, no. 29 (July 20, 1836): 471.

37. Czerny, *Von dem Vortrage*, 59.

38. Schnapper, "Piano Variations," 282–286. For one study emphasizing dramaturgical interpretations, see Suttoni, "Piano and Opera," 244–323.

39. Czerny, *School of Practical Composition*, 1:86.

40. See, for example, ibid., 1:21–28, 31.

41. Schnapper, *Henri Herz*, 158–162.

42. Czerny, *School of Practical Composition*, 1:87.

43. Liszt imitated this contrapuntal combination in his own *Réminiscences de "Norma."*

44. See Rink, *Chopin*, 3–5.

45. Studies of concerto forms have not standardized a term for this section of passagework, and those that have been used do not capture the construction and

significance of the closes in nineteenth-century concertos. Analyses of eighteenth-century piano concertos (such as Mozart's) often simply refer to these sections as closing themes. However, culminating displays in nineteenth-century concertos are not necessarily based on closing themes and may not even have a distinct thematic profile. James Hepokoski and Warren Darcy employ the term "display episode" and note that the passagework occurs after an exposition or recapitulation has already reached tonal closure. I prefer "culminating display" because it emphasizes that this section of the piece represents a climax—that it was an essential rather than a peripheral part of the form. Hepokoski and Darcy, *Elements of Sonata Theory*, 543–548.

46. Macdonald, *Robert Schumann and the Piano Concerto*, 24–34.

47. Other aspects of the Hummel suggest Mozart's influence. Hummel, for example, engages in formal punning when he deftly converts the second theme in the orchestral ritornello into a closing theme and, from there, into the primary theme of the solo exposition.

48. Schumann, "Anzeiger," *NZfM* 2, no. 44 (June 2, 1835): 178.

49. "Kalkbrenner": Kalk = "Lime," Brenner = "Burner." The Brenner Pass is a mountain pass through the Alps.

50. "Thalberg": Thal = "Valley," and Berg = "Mountain."

51. Schumann, "S. Thalberg, 12 Etüden," *GS*, 1:288–289.

52. "Grande Fantaisie et Variations . . . par S. Thalberg," *NZfM* 1, no. 2 (April 7, 1834): 6–7.

53. "Recensionen," *AmZ* 37, no. 29 (July 22, 1835): 470–471.

54. "XII Etudes pour le Piano," *AmZ* 39, no. 37 (September 13, 1837): 600–601.

55. *NZfM* 5, no. 20 (September 6, 1836): 79.

56. Schumann, "Variationen für Pianoforte: Dritter Gang," *GS*, 1:227.

57. Plantinga suggests that Schumann's admiration of Döhler's variations "betrays a kind of guilty fascination." I would propose, though, that Schumann's review does not suggest that he was reluctant to commend these passages. Rather, he differentiated between his estimation of Döhler's craft and inventiveness and his view of Döhler's overall aesthetic. *Schumann as Critic*, 203.

58. Schumann, "Variationen," *GS*, 1:228–229.

59. Schumann, "F. Kalkbrenner, viertes Concert," *GS*, 1:156. Macdonald, *Robert Schumann and the Piano Concerto*, 123–127.

60. Schumann, "F. Kalkbrenner," 156.

61. Ibid., 156.

62. On the aristocratic arena for the Liszt–Thalberg rivalry, see Gooley, *Virtuoso Liszt*, 7–8, 59–76.

63. Applegate, "Robert Schumann," 7–10.

64. Schumann, "Sigismund Thalberg, großes Concert," 153.

65. For two studies of this discourse, see Kallberg, *Chopin at the Boundaries*, 32–45, and Ellis, "Berlioz."

66. Discussions of amateur, female pianists usually note that piano playing was a display of accomplishment and marriageability. Gillen D'Arcy Wood has argued for a more multivalent understanding of the practice, noting that it could also serve as family and solitary entertainment. Wood, *Romanticism and Music Culture*, 153–157.

67. Czerny, *Briefe über den Unterricht*, 46.

68. Parakilas, "History of Lessons," 114–115.

69. Wieck, *Clavier und Gesang*, 13–15. Translation adapted from Wieck, *Piano and Song*, trans. Pleasants, 30–31.

70. Applegate, "Robert Schumann," 4, 12.

71. Erlin, *Necessary Luxuries*, for example, 1–4, 44–52. I would like to thank Dr. Erlin for sharing his book with me prior to its publication.

72. Gramit, *Cultivating Music*, for example, 13, 130–131, 145.

73. See, for example, Kallberg, *Chopin at the Boundaries*, 38–45.

74. Schumann, "Fastnachtsrede von Florestan," *GS*, 1:39.

75. Ibid., 42.

76. Schumann, "Etüden für das Pianoforte," *GS*, 1:392.

77. Schumann, "Sigism. Thalberg," *GS*, 1:410.

78. Ibid., 410.

79. Schumann, *TB*, 2:78.

80. Schumann, "Variationen für Pianoforte: Zweiter Gang," *GS*, 1:226.

81. Hanslick, *Geschichte des Concertwesens in Wien*, 331.

82. Schilling, "Thalberg, Sigismund," in *Encyclopädie*, 7:629.

2. Florestan's Wine, Clara Wieck's Spirit: Postclassical Virtuosity and Poetic Interiority

1. See Hepokoski, "Monumentality and Formal Processes," and Todd, "Piano Music Reformed," 205–210.

2. Daverio, *Robert Schumann*; Watkins, *Metaphors of Depth*, 86; Moßburger, "Poetische Harmonik."

3. Daverio, "Schumann's Systems," 50–54.

4. "Zur Eröffnung des Jahrganges 1835," *NZfM* (January 2, 1835): 2–4.

5. "Zur Eröffnung des Jahrganges 1835," *GS*, 1:38. Watkins has also noted the change of words. She interprets the 1835 address as a critique of "mechanical" approaches to musical form, an equally plausible reading. *Metaphors of Depth*, 92.

6. "Charakteristische Studien für das Pianoforte, *GS*, 1:362.

7. "Variationen für Pianoforte," *GS*, 1:224. All three elements appear on the first page of Benedict's variations.

8. Schumann, "Trios," *GS*, 1:179.

9. Watkins, *Metaphors of Depth*, 102.

10. Schumann, "Trios," *GS*, 1:179.

11. For three representative studies, see Daverio, "Schumann's Systems"; Reiman, *Schumann's Piano Cycles*; Perrey, *Schumann's Dichterliebe*.

12. Moßburger, "Poetische Harmonik," 194.

13. Robert Schumann, *Mottosammlung*. The collection includes quotations from Novalis, both Schlegel brothers, Goethe, Jean Paul, and numerous other sources. For more general discussions of the terms "prosaic" and "poetic" in German writings on music and literature, see Pederson, "Enlightened and Romantic German Music Criticism," 20–24; Danuser, *Musikalische Prosa*, 17–19. My account in this paragraph incorporates literary sources cited by both scholars.

14. Schumann could have read Novalis in one of the several editions of his works published in the late 1820s. Schumann, *Mottosammlung*, 500, 557. Novalis, "Anekdoten," in *Schriften* 2:573–574.

15. Novalis, *Das Allgemeine Brouillon* (1798–99), in *Schriften*, 3:312–313.

16. Goethe, "Stages of Man's Mind (1817)," 203.

17. Gay, *Naked Heart*.

18. Schumann, *TB*, 1:337.

19. "Sechs Lieder ohne Worte," *GS*, 1:98; "Die C-Dur Sinfonie von Schubert," *GS*, 1:464.

20. Gay, *Naked Heart*, 4.

21. Schumann, "12 Etüden für Pianoforte," *GS*, 1:254–255.

22. Jim Samson observes that Chopin's etudes frequently "blur the boundaries between such categories as melody, harmony, and figuration." Samson, *Chopin*, 122–124.

23. Schumann, "Ein Opus II," *AmZ* 33, no. 49 (December 7, 1831): 805–808. For the *Gesammelte Schriften* version, see *GS*, 1:5–7. I will cite from the *AmZ* text here.

24. See, for example, Pederson, "Enlightened and Romantic German Music Criticism," 83–84; Downes, "Kierkegaard," 272–276.

25. Schumann to Castelli, April 28, 1832, in *BNF*, 36.

26. Plantinga, *Schumann as Critic*, 35.

27. Schumann, "Ein Opus II."

28. Pederson, "Enlightened and Romantic German Music," 16–17, 81–84.

29. Samson, *Chopin*, 37–38; Rink, "Tonal Architecture," 82.

30. Mark Everist, "Speaking with the Supernatural," 117–118. Plantinga, *Schumann as Critic*, 227.

31. Quoted in Litzmann, *Clara Schumann*, 1:33–34.

32. Quoted in ibid., 1:27.

33. "Leipzig," *AmZ* 33, no. 48 (November 30, 1831): 796. It seems likely that Knorr was the namesake for the Julius of Schumann's review.

34. Wieck's review appeared in two German journals, *Caecilia* and *Der Komet*. I cite from the former. Friedrich Wieck, "'Là ci darem la mano' varié pour le pianoforte . . . par Frédéric Chopin," *Caecilia: Eine Zeitschrift für die musikalische Welt* 14, no. 55 (1832): 219–223. The *Komet* article appeared January, 1832.

35. Friedrich Wieck's and Schumann's similar programmatic readings and proximate completion dates beg the question of originality. It remains unclear whether Schumann's "Ein Opus II" used a program his teacher had already suggested, whether Wieck imitated his fanciful student, or whether their readings emerged simultaneously in conversations and lessons. One of Wieck's letters to his wife hints that Schumann's essay came first: on October 26, 1831, he wrote that he had sent the essay to Paris and that she could show it to Schumann, but that it "won't be as poetic as his." In any case, as I note below, Schumann and his teacher used *Don Giovanni* imagery for different rhetorical purposes. *Friedrich Wieck Briefe*, 36.

36. "'La ci darem la mano.' Varié pour le Pianoforte," *AmAW* 2, no. 32 (August 7, 1830): 125.

37. Quoted in Litzmann, *Clara Schumann*, 35.

38. "'Là ci darem la mano.' Varié pour le Pianof.," *AmZ* 33, no. 49 (December 7, 1831): 810.

39. *Iris im Gebiete der Tonkunst* 1, nos. 37 and 38 (November 5, 1830).

40. See, for example, her debut of the piece in Weimar on October 7, 1831, and her Frankfurt concert on January 25, 1832. Clara Schumann, Programmsammlung, 454 and 460.

41. Downes, "Kierkegaard," 272; Daverio, "Schumann's Systems," 54–55.

42. Wieck, "Là ci darem la mano," 222.

43. Ibid., 223.

44. Ibid., 221, Rellstab, *Iris*.

45. Schumann did not explain Florestan's seemingly offhand remark. He may have meant it simply as high praise. However, it might also refer to the essay's larger argument.

Florestan draws a sharp, perhaps intentionally exaggerated boundary between, on one hand, composers widely regarded as transcendent creators whose works evinced their own intellectual or spiritual involvement and, on the other, virtuosos specializing in performance and composition for a single instrument. Chopin, Florestan hints, had synthesized these two fields of accomplishment, the *geistig* and the visceral.

46. Downes, "Kierkegaard," 272.

47. Schumann, "Ein Opus II," 807.

48. Schumann—who by 1854 was a respected composer of large orchestral and choral works—might have omitted the detail to mask his early enthusiasm for popular pianism.

49. Samson, *Chopin*, 25–26.

50. Clara Schumann, Programmsammlung, 500 and 514.

51. Reiman, *Schumann's Piano Cycles*, 35–36.

52. Ibid., 21–24.

53. From Novalis, "Logologische Fragmente," in *Schriften*, 2:545.

54. Chopin to Titus Woychiechowski, December 12, 1831, in Chopin, *Selected Correspondence*, 99.

55. Schumann, "Ein Opus II," 807.

56. Ibid., 808. The imagery here differs slightly from the later *Gesammelte Schriften* version.

57. I would like to thank Thomas Synofzik, director of the Schumann Haus archive, for his transcription of Schumann's manuscript, on which mine is based, and for giving me permission to publish my translation. I would also like to thank Hanne Spence and Lynne Tatlock for some helpful discussions of the manuscript.

58. "Ohne mein Wissen hat ein mir unbekannter Sch[elm] die nachstehende Odeonnummerm zur Hälfte in einem früheren Jahrgang der allgemeinen musik[alischen] Zeitung abdrucken lassen, den eigentlichen kritischen Theil mithin zu meinem Verdruss vergessen." Schumann, "Odeon: Chopin."

59. Readers interested in the original German text should consult Synofzik, "'Eine Apotheose Mozarts' Ein unbekannter Entwurf zu Robert Schumanns Erstlingsrezension über Chopins Opus II," 24–52.

60. Schumann's script near the end of this sentence is virtually illegible. I would like to thank Thomas Synofzik for his suggestion that Schumann might have meant to write "Gleichnisse," which would yield the "parable" translation. Contextual evidence might support that reading—the sentence would then acknowledge the unusual, short-story format of the review. In any case, though the rest of the essay contains a few scratchings-out, Schumann's script is legible.

61. One wonders why Schumann did not include the epilogue in the *Neue Zeitschrift* or his *Gesammelte Schriften*. One possibility is that, by the time he was editing his own journal, Schumann had moved on to more extensive and ambitious critical endeavors, which he believed more rigorously and explicitly demonstrated his critical acumen. As I note below, he designed his Hiller review as such a defense.

62. Schumann to Fink, September 27, 1831, in *Jugendbriefe*, 154.

63. Schumann, "Ein Opus II," 809.

64. Macdonald, "Schumann's Piano Practice," 546–566.

65. Schumann, *TB*, 1:353–354. Translation adapted from Macdonald, "Schumann's Piano Practice," 546.

66. Klassen, *Clara Schumann*, 134–146.

67. The text of Schumann's review is reproduced in the cited edition of the *Gesammelte Schriften*. "Reminiszenzen aus Klara Wiecks letzten Konzerten in Leipzig," *GS*, 2:350. The aphorisms derived from the review and included in the original *Gesammelte Schriften* appear throughout "Aus Meisters Raros, Florestans, und Eusebius' Denk- und Dicht-Büchlein," *GS*, 1:17–36.

68. de Vries, *Die Pianistin*, 304–315.

69. "Wiek (oder Wieck), Clara," in Schilling, *Encyclopädie*, 7:861.

70. "Correspondenz," *NZfM* 2, no. 20 (March 10, 1835): 81.

71. Schumann, "Reminiszenzen," 350–351; "Denk- und Dichtbüchlein," 21.

72. Translation adapted from Kregor, *Liszt as Transcriber*, 133.

73. Clara Schumann, Programmsammlung, 465 and 466.

74. Schumann, "Reminiszenzen," 352.

75. "Wieck, Clara" in Schilling, 862.

76. "Clara Schumann in Wien," *Signale* 14, no. 5 (January): 46.

77. "Liszt in Wien," *NZfM* 8, no. 34 (April 27, 1838): 136.

78. Schumann, "Reminiszenzen," 351.

79. Goertzen, "Clara Wieck Schumann's Improvisations," 153–162.

80. Clara Schumann, Programmsammlung, 520.

81. Ibid., 489.

82. Schumann, "Soiréen für das Pianoforte," *GS*, 1:251.

83. "C.O.," "Deutschland," in Herlossohn, *Damen Conversations Lexikon*, 3:154.

84. *NZfM* 2, no. 1 (January 2, 1835): 3–4.

85. Schumann, "Ferdinand Hiller," *GS*, 1:43–44.

86. Ibid., 1:44–45.

87. Ibid., 1:45–46.

88. Ibid., 1:49.

89. Ibid., 1:51. The *Gesammelte Schriften* version is shorter than the *NZfM*, but the cited edition contains the full text in an endnote.

90. Ibid., 1:49–50.

91. Ibid., 1:48.

92. Macdonald, "Robert Schumann's F-Major Piano Concerto," 462–496.

93. Schumann's word for "shapes"—*Gestalten*—could connote specifically human figures. *TB*, 1:361.

94. Macdonald, *Robert Schumann and the Piano Concerto*, 40–41, 52–56, 60–61.

95. Schumann's latest revisions date from August 1831. The chronology makes a strong case that Macdonald's edition reflects what the composer played for Friedrich Wieck and his guests at the August 14 soiree. Macdonald acknowledges that because any autograph fair copies of the movement are now lost, her edition cannot claim to be a definitive text but rather the latest extant version (see "Robert Schumann's F-Major Piano Concerto," 13). Even so, the features of the recapitulation's culminating display that I point out here were present in Schumann's drafts of this section from the beginning of its genesis: the abrupt move to F-sharp minor, for example, the contrapuntal passagework, the chromatic progressions elaborated by sustained bass notes and treble arpeggios, the sustained augmented sixth, and the sudden snap back into the striding accompaniment. Even though Schumann changed some harmonic and figurational details as he revised, the drafts show that this trajectory was fundamental to his plan.

96. Macdonald, *Robert Schumann and the Piano Concerto*, 61–66.

3. Poetic Showpieces in the Cultivated Salon

1. Ferris, "Public Performance"; Anthony Newcomb, "Schumann and the Marketplace," 269.

2. For some broader studies of salon life and domestic musical traditions, see Atwood, *Parisian Worlds*, 101–136; Beci, *Musikalische Salons*; Ronyak, "Performing the Lied"; Weber, *Music and the Middle Class*, 36–69.

3. Gooley, "Battle against Instrumental Virtuosity," 79–82.

4. Eduard Krüger's "Ueber Virtuosenunfug" appeared in issues 17–22 of the 1840 *Neue Zeitschrift für Musik*.

5. Dahlhaus described the latter category as "pseudosalon music" characterized by "a deadly mixture of sentimental tunefulness and mechanical figuration." Dahlhaus, *Nineteenth-Century Music*, 147–148.

6. Kallberg, *Chopin at the Boundaries*, 32–45. On the image of salon music, see also Ellis, "Berlioz"; and Fellinger, "Die Begriffe *Salon*."

7. Robert Schumann, "Kürzere Stücke für Pianoforte," *NZfM* 15, no. 30 (October 12, 1841): 118; "Sigism. Thalberg, Th. Döhler, J. Rosenhain," *GS*, 1:409.

8. My purpose in this chapter is not to reconstruct nineteenth-century categories of salon music but to consider the broader significance of salon life for Schumann and the virtuosity discourse. On the former issue, see Fellinger, "Die Begriffe *Salon*," 134–141.

9. Borchard, "Opferaltäre der Musik," 30; Ralf Wehner, "Felix Mendelssohn Bartholdys Verhältnis," 64–69.

10. Ferris, "Public Performance," 361–381.

11. Schumann, "Duos," *GS*, 1:180–181.

12. Translation adapted from Ferris, "Public Performance," 373.

13. Schumann, "Adolph Henselt, zwölf Etüden," *GS*, 1:357.

14. "Adolph Henselt," *NZfM* 8, no. 2 (January 5, 1838): 8. Translation from Ferris, "Public Performance," 374.

15. Kaskel later became the Countess von Baudissin. For a biographical sketch, see Wenzel, "Sophie von Baudissin."

16. "Sara" [Sophie Kaskel], "Adolph Henselt," *NZfM* 7, no. 15 (August 22, 1837): 57–58.

17. Ibid.

18. Macdonald, "Schumann's Piano Practice," 530–534.

19. Robert Schumann, "J. F. [sic] Carus," *NZfM* 18, no. 7 (January 23, 1843): 27–28.

20. See, for example, *TB*, 1:152, 156, 337, 399.

21. Daverio, *Robert Schumann*, 58. Robert Schumann to Julius Schumann, February 11, 1830, Heidelberg, in Schumann, *Jugendbriefe*, 102–104.

22. Reiman, *Schumann's Piano Cycles*, 6–7, 37–47.

23. Gooley, "Schumann and the Agencies."

24. Jensen, *Die Davidsbündler*, 72.

25. Ibid., 73–75. Dörffel speculates that Schumann's style of playing might have derived from attempts to capture full organ textures using the pedal.

26. Robert Schumann to J. August Lemke, Leipzig, January 11, 1831. Schumann, *Briefe und Notizen Robert und Clara Schumanns*, 32.

27. See Köhler, "Ein Werk I"; Draheim, "Schumann und Chopin," 235.

28. Daverio, *Robert Schumann*, 66.

29. Ludwig Rellstab, "Thème sur le nom Abegg pp." *Iris* 3, no. 8 (February 24, 1832): 31.

30. Gottfried Wilhelm Fink, "Thème sur le nom 'Abegg,'" *AmZ* 35, no. 37 (September 11, 1833): 615.

31. Köhler, "Ein Werk I," 365–379; Hansen, "Robert Schumanns 'Virtuosität,'" 137.

32. Daverio, *Robert Schumann*, 68.

33. Gensel, "Henriette Voigt," 398; on games in Parisian salons, see Atwood, *Parisian Worlds*, 134.

34. Smart, "Parlor Games," 43–52.

35. Ronyak, "'Serious Play.'"

36. Rellstab, "Thème sur le nom Abegg," 31.

37. Schumann does add extra repetitions of the first half of the theme, so that we hear four times a section that the theme only presents twice.

38. Fink, "Thème sur le nom 'Abegg,'" 615.

39. Rellstab, "Thème sur le nom Abegg," 31.

40. Richter (Jean Paul), *Horn of Oberon*, 122 (emphasis added).

41. Daverio, "Schumann's Systems," 71–75; Reiman, *Schumann's Piano Cycles*, 15–17; Watkins, *Metaphors of Depth*, 98–113; Ferris, "'Was will dieses Grau'n bedeuten?'" 135–137.

42. Schumann, *TB*, 1:133.

43. Daverio, "Schumann's Systems," 72.

44. Ibid., 71–75; Reiman, *Schumann's Piano Cycles*, 15–17, 57, 116. For other studies of intermovement organization in the cycles, see Kaminsky, "Aspects of Harmony"; and Kramer, "*Carnaval*."

45. Hill, *Soul of Wit*, 91–94.

46. Siebert, *Der literarische Salon*, 254–264, 325.

47. Kabisch, "Musik in Salon," 114, 117.

48. Friedrich Schlegel, "Lyceums-Fragmente," in Schlegel, *Kritische Friedrich-Schlegel-Ausgabe*, 2:154.

49. Richter, *Horn of Oberon*, 120.

50. Schumann, *TB*, 2:90.

51. Schumann, "Aus Meister Raro's, Florestan's und Eusebius' Denk- und Dicht-büchlein," *GS*, 1:23.

52. Schlegel, "Lyceum-Fragmente" and "Ideen" in Schlegel, *Kritische Friedrich-Schlegel-Ausgabe* 2:158, 258.

53. Reiman, *Schumann's Piano Cycles*, 18–20.

54. Siebert, *Der literarische Salon,* 263.

55. Schlegel, "Athenäums-Fragmente," in *Kritische Friedrich-Schlegel-Ausgabe* 2:170.

56. Hill, *Soul of Wit*, 91.

57. Ronyak, "'Serious Play,'" 142–143, 148–153.

58. Gooley, "Schumann and the Agencies," 145–146.

59. Hoeckner, "Schumann and Romantic Distance."

60. Richter, *Horn of Oberon*, 61 (emphasis added).

61. Gensel, "Robert Schumann's Briefwechsel"; Gensel, "Henriette Voigt."

62. Wolfgang Boetticher, "Weitere Forschungen" and "Neue Materialien"; Robert Schumann, "Erinnerungen an eine Freundin," *GS*, 1:446–452. See also Bergmann and Gerber, "Voigt, Henriette."

63. See Daverio, *Robert Schumann*, 149–150.

64. My account of Voigt's biography draws from Gensel, "Henriette Voigt," and Bergmann and Gerber, "Voigt, Henriette."

65. Gensel, "Henriette Voigt," 398.

66. Boetticher, "Weitere Forschungen," 54–55; Boetticher, "Neue Materialien," 49.

67. Schumann, *TB*, 2:23, 27.

68. Schumann, "Erinnerungen," 446.

69. *NZfM* 11, no. 35 (October 29, 1839): 140.

70. Schumann, "Erinnerungen," 450.

71. Ibid., 446.

72. Felix Mendelssohn to Henriette Voigt, Düsseldorf, January 10, 1835, in Mendelssohn, *Acht Briefe*, 12.

73. Schumann, "Erinnerungen," 449.

74. Gensel, "Henriette Voigt," 395; Boetticher, "Neue Materialien," 52. Schumann to Henriette Voigt, August 22, 1834, Leipzig, *BNF*, 35.

75. Schumann, "Erinnerungen," 449.

76. Ibid., 451.

77. Ibid.

78. Boetticher, "Neue Materialien," 54.

79. Bergmann and Gerber, "Voigt, Henriette."

80. Gensel, "Robert Schumanns Briefwechsel," 271, 326–327; Daverio, *Robert Schumann*, 150.

81. Schumann, *TB*, 2:28.

82. Schumann, "Erinnerungen," 449.

83. Todd, *Mendelssohn*, 303.

84. Henriette Voigt to Robert Schumann, Leipzig, March 20, 1838, in Gensel, "Robert Schumann's Briefwechsel," 368.

85. Voigt to Schumann, Berlin, June 3, 1838, in ibid., 369.

86. Ibid.

87. Available in an edition and completion by Andreas Boyde. Robert Schumann, *Variationen über ein Thema von Schubert*.

88. Messing, *Schubert*, 1:12.

89. Schumann, "Variationen für Pianoforte: Dritter Gang," *GS*, 1:227–228.

90. I would like to thank Bertrand Federinov of the Bibliothèque du Musée Royale for sending me a copy of the Mariemont manuscript and Matthias Wendt of the Robert Schumann Forschungsstelle, Düsseldorf, for letting me study a copy of the Gesellschaft manuscript. Schumann, *Fantaisies et finale*. Ehrhardt, "La variation chez Robert Schumann," 2:758–794.

91. Studies of the *Études* list anywhere from three to five preliminary versions, each of which places a different selection of variations in a different order. These include: Schumann's autograph sketches for some of the etudes; the Mariemont manuscript (in which Schumann tried two different orderings before deciding on a third); the copyist's manuscript (in which the variations appear according to the final Mariemont ordering but, on the flyleaf, are listed in yet another); and the published 1837 version. Schumann reworked the *Études* for republication in 1852, eliminating two variations. See McCorkle, *Robert Schumann*, 56–59; Ehrhardt, "Les *Études symphoniques*," 293–294.

92. For completions of the unfinished variation, see Ehrhardt, "La variation chez Robert Schumann," 2:778–779; Warburton, "Some Performance Alternatives," 44–45.

93. Herttrich, "Preface," v.

94. Schilling, "Fricken, Ernestine v.," in *Encyclopädie*, 3:57. On von Fricken's life after 1836, see Bergmann, "Fricken, Ernestine von."

95. See, for example, Fuller-Maitland, *Schumann*, 53–54. For present-day acknowledgments, see Todd, "On Quotation," 81–82; McCorkle, *Robert Schumann*, 54; Böhme-Mehner, "Sinfonische Etüden für Klavier," 1:75.

96. Marston, *Schumann*, 36–37. On works that seem to allude to others but whose composers and critics did not acknowledge such connections, see Reynolds, *Motives for Allusion*.

97. My discussion employs J. Peter Burkholder's methodology for evaluating borrowings. He proposes that scholars address the composer's knowledge of the borrowed source, its structural role in the new composition, its conformity to established borrowing practices, and whether it has an apparent meaning or purpose. Burkholder, "Borrowing," 4:5–8.

98. Friedrich Wieck to Clementine Wieck, Magdeburg, February 3, 1834 [?], in Wieck, *Friedrich Wieck Briefe*, 48. See also Reich, *Clara Schumann*, 22.

99. Palmer, *Heinrich August Marschner*, 418. Schumann, "Theaterbüchlein (1847–1850)," *GS*, 2:160.

100. Schumann, "Aphorismen (II)," *GS*, 1:127–128.

101. Koβmaly's essay ran from the first to the twelfth issue of the *Zeitschrift*'s sixteenth volume.

102. Hanslick, "Der Templer und die Jüdin (1883)," in Hanslick, *Musikalisches Skizzenbuch*, 4:119.

103. Ibid., 125; Palmer, "Templer und die Jüdin," 688.

104. Writing variations and fantasies on themes from different sources—even combinations of original and borrowed themes—was an accepted practice during the nineteenth century.

105. For example, the aforementioned article by Todd gives this interpretation. Böhme-Mehner, though, acknowledges the chronological problem.

106. *NZfM* 16, no. 2 (January 4, 1842): 5–6 and 16, no. 3 (January 8, 1842): 9–10.

107. This is not to imply that Marschner insulated himself from French and Italian trends. Like other composers of German Romantic opera, his work incorporates many elements of these traditions. See Palmer, *Heinrich August Marschner*, 217–219.

108. For example, Gottfried Wilhelm Fink, "*Der Templer und die Jüdin*," *AmZ* 40 (October 6, 1830): 658.

109. For one discussion of German fascination with the Middle Ages, see Williamson, *Longing for Myth*, 74–92.

110. Quoted in Boetticher, *Robert Schumanns Klavierwerk*, 2:245.

4. Virtuosity and the Rhetoric of the Sublime

1. Rosen, *Romantic Generation*, 655.

2. "76," "Concert sans Orchestre pour le pianoforte," *AmAW* 19, no. 26 (July 29, 1837): 102. Ute Scholz identifies "76" as von Seyfried. "Schumanns Ausschnittsammlung *Zeitungsstimmen*," 156.

3. Ellis, "Liszt: the Romantic Artist," 6–8; Gooley, *Virtuoso Liszt*, 47; Leppert, "Cultural Contradiction," 254–268.

4. For examples of a more topic-based approach, see Webster, "The *Creation*," 64–92, and Wurth, *Musically Sublime*, which explores correspondences between theories of the sublime and compositional strategies in a range of repertoire.

5. Allanbrook, "Is the Sublime a Musical Topos?" 263–265.

6. See, for example, Rehding, *Music and Monumentality*, 3, 34–36; Taruskin, *Oxford History of Western Music*, 2:643–651, 656, 732–734, which emphasizes choral and symphonic works but also discusses Beethoven's Sonata Op. 111; Sisman, "Learned Style"; Webster, "The *Creation*"; Mathew, "Beethoven's Political Music."

7. Hoffmann, "Beethoven's Instrumental Music"; Christian Friedrich Michaelis, "The Beautiful and the Sublime in Music," in le Huray and Day, *Music and Aesthetics*, 289–291.

8. Bonds, "Symphony as Pindaric Ode," 139.

9. Ellis, "Berlioz," 29–30, 50–54.

10. Jean Paul (Richter), *Horn of Oberon*, 73–76; Schlegel, "Introduction," 245; Johann Gottfried von Herder, "Vom Hörbarer Erhabenen," in Schumann, *Dichtergarten für Musik*, 161–164. Schumann could have read Hoffmann's Beethoven essay in the author's *Kreisleriana*. Though Schumann surely encountered Kant's writings during his education and reading, Kant rarely appears in his diaries or collections of quotations.

11. Robert R. Clewis argues that Kant himself presents the sublime in these terms. Clewis, *Kantian Sublime*, 176–177, 184–186.

12. Schumann, "Fastnachtsrede von Florestan," *GS*, 1:40–41.

13. Schumann, "Abonnementkonzerte in Leipzig 1840–41," *GS*, 2:49–50.

14. Schumann, "Monument für Beethoven," *GS*, 1:131.

15. Schumann, "Fastnachtsrede," 41.

16. Ibid. Translation from Watkins, *Metaphors of Depth*, 102.

17. Philip Shaw, *Sublime*, 18.

18. Mathew, "Beethoven's Political Music"; Hibberd, "Cherubini."

19. Kant, *Critique of the Power of Judgment*, 148.

20. Christoph Friedrich Michaelis, "Einige Bemerkungen über das Erhabene der Musik," *Berlinische musikalische Zeitung* 1, no. 46 (1805): 180. Translation adapted from le Huray and Day, *Music and Aesthetics*, 290.

21. Gustav Schilling, "Erhaben und Erhabenheit," in Schilling, *Encyclopädie*, 2:615.

22. Burke, *Philosophical Enquiry*, 36–37, 122.

23. Rayman, *Kant on Sublimity*, 149.

24. Friedrich Schiller, "On the Sublime," in Schiller, *Naïve and Sentimental Poetry*, 202.

25. Battersby, *Gender and Genius*, 74–77.

26. Schumann, "Fastnachtsrede," 42.

27. Gooley, *Virtuoso Liszt*, 47; See also Ellis, "Liszt," 6–8; Leppert, "Cultural Contradiction," 254–268; Gooley, "Battle against Instrumental Virtuosity," 98–99.

28. Plantinga, *Schumann as Critic*, 216–217; Seibold, *Robert und Clara Schumann*, 1:89–90.

29. Schumann, "Etüden für das Pianoforte," *GS*, 1:442–443.

30. Ibid., 443.

31. Ibid.

32. Ibid., 444.

33. Schumann did criticize some aspects of Liszt's programming. He noted, for example, that he would rather have heard music by Chopin than the *Hexameron* and that Liszt's transcription of the scherzo and finale from Beethoven's Symphony No. 6 sounded too weak in the concert hall. However, Schumann's extravagant praise outweighs these criticisms. If anything, the minor quibbles accentuate the compliments: Schumann demonstrates to readers that he has retained his critical perspective and is not simply starstruck. Leon Plantinga has detected a note of reservation here "about the real issue—the music Liszt played," noting that Schumann only singled out the Weber *Konzertstück* and an unidentified Chopin etude for praise. I would argue, though, that this focus does not signal ambivalence. Schumann's review emphasized the effect of Liszt's performances rather than evaluating individual works. Seibold has similarly

noted Schumann's overall positive tone. Plantinga, *Schumann as Critic*, 217. Seibold, *Robert und Clara Schumann*, 1:136–137.

34. Schumann, "Franz Liszt," *GS*, 1:479.

35. Ibid., 480.

36. Gooley, *Virtuoso Liszt*, 99–105.

37. Schumann, "Franz Liszt," *GS*, 1:483. On Liszt's Napoleonic image and the *Konzertstück*, see Gooley, *Virtuoso Liszt*, 78–105.

38. Schumann to Clara Wieck, March 25, 1840, Leipzig, in Schuman and Schuman, *Clara und Robert Schumann Briefwechsel*, 3:1005.

39. Schumann to Clara Wieck, Leipzig, March 22, 1840, in ibid., 3:999–1000.

40. For one summary of these concerts, see Gooley, *Virtuoso Liszt*, 157–164.

41. Schumann, "Franz Liszt," *GS*, 1:481.

42. Schumann, "Franz Liszt," *GS*, 1:479, 481.

43. See, for example, Jean Paul, *Horn of Oberon*, 74.

44. On these connections, see Gooley, *Virtuoso Liszt*, 65–70.

45. Krebs, *Fantasy Pieces*, 31–39.

46. "76," "Concert," 102.

47. Schumann kept Seyfried's review in his collection of press clippings, and Wasielewski might have come across it while conversing with the composer and researching his book. Wasielewski, *Robert Schumann*, 154.

48. Roesner, "Schumann's 'Parallel' Forms," 268–273. My diagram incorporates some aspects of Roesner's analysis.

49. This movement defies classification among conventional formal paradigms for finales. Any search for a sonata form runs up against themes whose keys are nonnormative for second-theme groups and whose modulations do not stick. Although Roesner suggests a rondo form as a possible point of comparison, theme X only returns at the hinges of the parallel form, and transitions lead only to contrasting episodes. I am not arguing, however, that the finale contains a "failed" exposition or recapitulation in the sense James Hepokoski and Warren Darcy have used. The preparation and first appearance of theme Z does mark a significant juncture that banishes all hope for a normative exposition. (We might, at first hearing, suspect that Y is merely a digression within a first theme group.) However, Hepokoski's and Darcy's examples generally establish a formal paradigm and then diverge from it. By contrast, Schumann's finale never presents the defining gestures of a normative sonata or rondo form.

If there is "failure" in the *Concert* finale, it would occur in the disrupted themes themselves or, perhaps, in a listener's attempts to apply expectations of a rondo or sonata to a movement that develops into neither. It would be reasonable to speculate that a listener might have done so: sonata, rondo, or sonata-rondo finales were standard in early nineteenth-century sonatas such as Beethoven's and Weber's. Wasielewski's observation about the lack of a "second, calming subject" hints at such a frustrated hearing. Understanding the finale this way would increase its disorienting intensity: we would hear not just the destabilization of individual themes but the thwarting of formal expectations.

I would hesitate to present this reading as a definitive explanation for Schumann's design. Schumann and his contemporaries experimented with diverse structures for finales, and it remains unclear whether he intended this one to be heard in relation to sonata or rondo norms. In any case, the reception of the finale stresses its quality of overwhelming ferocity more than it does any such comparison. Hepokoski and Darcy, *Elements of Sonata Theory*, 177–179, 245–249. Roesner, "Schumann's Parallel Forms," 271.

50. "76," "Concert," 102.

51. Ibid., 101.

52. Roesner speculates that Schumann's publisher, Tobias Haslinger, might have pushed him to do so. "Autograph of Schumann's Piano Sonata," 103.

53. Tobias Haslinger to Schumann, Vienna, June 13, 1836, in *Briefedition* Series III, vol. 8, 184.

54. "76," "Concert," 102.

55. Schumann, "II. Konzerte für Pianoforte mit Orchester," in *GS*, 1:162.

56. Macdonald, *Robert Schumann and the Piano Concerto*, 155–160.

57. Schumann, "I. Moscheles," in *GS*, 1:114

58. Schumann, "Konzerte für Pianoforte," in *GS*, 1:387.

59. Ignaz Moscheles, quoted in Schumann, "Concerte für das Pianoforte," *NZfM* 6, no. 16 (February 24, 1837): 65.

60. Franz Liszt, "Compositions pour piano, de M. Robert Schumann," in Liszt, *Franz Liszt: Sämtliche Schriften*, 1:380–382.

61. Ibid., 382.

62. Ibid., 374.

63. Ibid.

64. Ibid., 382.

65. Schumann to Clara Wieck, Leipzig, November 29, 1837, in *Briefedition* Series III, vol. 8, 151. Schumann to Ernst A. Becker, Leipzig, December 11, 1839, in *BNF*, 174.

66. Wolfgang Boetticher provides some of Moscheles's original text in *Robert Schumanns Klavierwerke*, 3:15.

67. Though there is no extant evidence that Schumann asked Moscheles's permission, there is no evidence that Moscheles minded. The two composers kept corresponding after the remarks appeared, and none of their extant letters mentioned Schumann's handling of the "review."

68. Schumann, "Concerte," 65.

69. See Gooley, *Virtuoso Liszt*, 22–24.

70. See Gut's and Kleinertz's commentary in Liszt, *Franz Liszt: Sämtliche Schriften*, 471–472.

71. On the sublime in the "Eroica" and in Beethoven's heroic style more generally, see Burnham, *Beethoven Hero*, 149–150, and Naested, "How to Bring the Ocean." Hoffmann's essay emphasizes the Fifth Symphony, but its title refers to Beethoven's instrumental music in general.

72. Kregor, *Liszt as Transcriber*, 131–148.

73. Ernst Ortlepp, "Kunst," *Der Komet* 39 (September 26, 1834): 310–311. "Aber gewiß wird er auf seinem Wege ein ganz anderes Ziel erreichen als die Modecomposition, die keinen höhern Gedanken fassen als den Leuten jeden Bissen mundgerecht zu machen."

74. For an edition of the *Exercice*, see Michael J. Luebbe, "Robert Schumann's *Exercice*." On figurational resemblances between the Toccata and several Hummel pieces, see Kroll, *Johann Nepomuk Hummel*, 288–289.

75. On Schuncke's biography, see Cooper, *Robert Schumann's Closest "Jugendfreund."* I would like to thank the late Dr. Cooper for generously sharing many hard-to-find Schuncke scores with me.

76. Ludwig Schuncke, "Kalkbrenner, Variat. Brill. Sur une Mazourka de Chopin," *NZfM* 1, no. 14 (May 19, 1834): 55–56

77. "56," "Intermezzi per la pianoforte . . . Allegro . . . Toccata," *AmAW* 17, no. 39 (September 25, 1835): 154–155. The first Latin quotation is adapted from Horace's *Ars poetica*, the second from Virgil's eighth Eclogue.

78. Schumann, "Kapriccios und andere kurze Stücke," in *GS*, 1:193. "Franz Liszt," 480.

79. Daverio, *Robert Schumann*, 65.

80. Ortlepp, *Beethoven*.

81. For one foundational study of Beethoven's middle-period style and its association with the "heroic," see Burnham, *Beethoven Hero*.

82. Marston, "Schumann's Heroes," 52–53.

83. Schumann never wrote an essay on the "Eroica" comparable to his "Fast-nachtsrede" and "Monument" discussions of the Ninth and Fifth Symphonies. His reviews do, however, evince a strong familiarity with the work. In some cases, he pointed out resemblances between the "Eroica" and recent compositions, criticizing cases he found too derivative. See "Neue Symphonieen für Orchester," *GS*, 1:427, "Streichquartette," *GS*, 2:76.

84. Schumann, "VI Études de concert," *GS*, 1:213.

85. Marston, "Schumann's Heroes," 53.

86. Burnham, *Beethoven Hero*, 12–13.

87. Lester, "Robert Schumann and Sonata Forms," 197.

88. A. B. Marx, for example, described the "Eroica" opening as the "hero idea stepping forth after two forceful blows." Quoted in Thomas Sipe, "Interpreting Beethoven," 255. On openings in Beethoven's "heroic" style, see Burnham, *Beethoven Hero*, 32–45.

89. Burnham, *Beethoven Hero*, 18–24.

90. Ibid., 3–18.

91. Jean Paul, *Horn of Oberon*, 74.

92. Gottfried Wilhelm Fink, *AmZ* 36, no. 42 (October 15, 1834): 689–691.

93. Schumann, "Kapriccios," 193.

94. Furthermore, Leon Plantinga has suggested that specific passages in the Caprice evoke moments in Beethoven's Sonatas Op. 10, no. 1, Op. 27, no. 2, and Op. 53. *Schumann as Critic*, 259.

95. Ibid.; Cooper, *Schumann's Closest "Jugendfreund,"* 135; Draheim, "Preface," 4.

96. It seems unlikely that Schumann incorporated the Beethoven allusions after meeting Schuncke. Schumann later recorded that he had completed the Toccata around Michaelmas, and the two did not meet until December. As Luebbe notes, it is possible that he further revised the Toccata before the 1834 publication. However, no evidence documents such a revision, and Schumann had already developed a penchant for Beethoven citation well beforehand. "Robert Schumann's *Exercice*," 435.

97. Gooley, "Schumann and the Agencies," 143.

98. Carl Ferdinand Becker, "Florestan und Eusebius, Zwolf Etüden. (Etudes Symphoniques). Op. 13," *NZfM* 17, no. 14 (August 18, 1837): 50.

99. An 1839 review of Schumann's *Études* and *Concert sans orchestre* from the Prague journal *Ost und West* said of both, "Schumann turns the piano into an orchestra . . . Schumann wants symphonies for the piano." An 1856 review of Clara's performance of the *Études* (probably the later, 1852 version) attributed the title to their "fullness of tone." More recently, Jean-Pierre Bartoli has noted that the work emulates the textures of the "post-Beethovenian orchestra." "Ueber Robert Schumann's Compositionen," *Ost und West* 3, no. 21 (March 13, 1839): 84. *Abendblatt der Wiener Zeitung* 14, no. 14 (January 17, 1856): 53. Bartoli, "Les *Études symphoniques*," 79, 83.

100. See William Sterndale Bennett to Robert Schumann, Cambridge, August 26, 1837, in Boetticher, *Briefe und Gedichte*, 32–34.

101. Broyles, *Beethoven*, 93.

102. Hepokoski, "Monumentality," 244.

103. Hanslick, *Aus dem Tagebuch*, 344–345. For one discussion of Beethoven allusions in the concerto, see Hepokoski, "Monumentality," 221, 229.

Part II. Schumann's Virtuosity and the Culture of the Work Concept

1. Schumann, "Fragmente aus Leipzig," *GS*, 1:311.

2. Information about the season from the Gewandhaus Programmsammlung, Robert Schumann Haus, Zwickau.

3. For one foundational study of the work concept, see Goehr, *Imaginary Museum*. The work concept, though crucial to nineteenth-century aesthetics, did not necessarily originate then, and it shaped music in other traditions and historical contexts. See Talbot, *Musical Work*.

4. On the German corner of this movement, see Applegate, "How German Is It?" 286–289.

5. For one study of the flexibility of nineteenth-century piano performance, see Hamilton, *After the Golden Age*, 179–224.

6. Hunter, " 'To Play as if from the Soul,' " 384–387.

7. Samson, *Virtuosity and the Musical Work*, 148.

8. Trippett, "Après une Lecture de Liszt."

5. Steps to Parnassus? Schumann's Equivocal Work Concept

1. Samson, *Virtuosity and the Musical Work*, 75.

2. On Schumann's reinterpretations of Paganini's harmonies, see Plantinga, *Schumann as Critic*, 262. John Daverio's study of Schumann and Paganini discusses his Op. 3 transcriptions, and Harald Krebs's considers only Op. 10, no. 2 and the Op. 3 set. Daverio, "Il circolo magico." I would like to thank Claudia Macdonald for providing me with the unpublished English version of this paper. Krebs, *Fantasy Pieces*, 52, 69–70, 100–102.

3. Schumann, "Henri Vieuxtemps und Louis Lacombe," *GS*, 1:15." See also Schumann, *TB*, 1:173.

4. Schumann, *TB*, 1:342.

5. Schumann, "Aus Meisters Raro's, Florestan's und Eusebius' Denk- und Dicht-Büchlein," *GS*, 1:27.

6. Schumann, "Kapriccios und andere kurze Stücke," *GS*, 1:194.

7. Krebs identifies other influences, including Beethoven, Hummel, and Schubert. Schumann also developed metrically dissonant virtuosic pieces prior to encountering Paganini, as in sketches for the "Abegg" Variations or the *Exercice* version of the Toccata.

8. Daverio, "Il circolo magico," 53. Krebs, *Fantasy Pieces*, esp. 69–70.

9. Schumann, *TB*, 1:404.

10. Mai Kawabata explores these aspects of Paganini's image in *Paganini*, 26–75.

11. Gooley, "La Commedia del Violino," 373.

12. Daverio, "Il circolo magico," 42.

13. Gooley, "La Commedia del Violino."

14. Schumann, *TB*, 1:282–283.

15. Schumann, "IV Études de Concert," *GS*, 1:212.

16. Ibid.

17. Ibid., 212–213.

18. Plantinga, *Schumann as Critic*, 262.

19. Schumann, "VI Études de Concert," 213.

20. Wolfgang Seibold interprets the essay as largely critical in tone, citing several of its negative statements. My reading differs: Schumann, I would argue, was making a much more ambivalent statement about how one should evaluate the etudes to begin with. Seibold, *Robert und Clara Schumann*, 1:89–90.

21. Joseph Mainzer, "Aus Paris," *NZfM* 6, no. 46 (June 9, 1837): 185.

22. See Samson, *Virtuosity and the Musical Work*, 26–52.

23. Schumann, "Etüden für das Pianoforte," *GS*, 1:439–440.

24. Ibid.

25. Ibid., 439, 440.

26. Ibid., 440.

27. Ibid.

28. Eduard Krüger, "Ueber Virtuosenunfug," *NZfM* 13, no. 18 (August 29, 1840): 69–70.

29. Krüger, "Ueber Virtuosenunfug," *NZfM* 13, no. 20 (September 5, 1840): 78–79.

30. Krüger, "Ueber Virtuosenunfug," *NZfM* 13, no. 18: 69.

31. See Schumann's footnote to "Phistister und Antiphilister," *NZfM* 14, no. 43 (May 28, 1841): 174.

32. Heinrich Hirschbach, "Antiphiliströses," *NZfM* 13, no. 30 (October 10, 1840): 119.

33. See the aforementioned "Philister und Antiphilister."

34. Hirschbach, "Antiphiliströses," 120.

35. Eduard Krüger, "Odioses," *NZfM* 14, no. 33 (April 23, 1841): 133–134.

36. Eduard Krüger, "Das Virtuosenconcert," *NZfM* 14, no. 43 (May 28, 1841): 172.

37. Krüger, "Das Virtuosenconcert,"*NZfM* 14, no. 40 (May 17, 1841): 160.

38. Heinrich Hirschbach, "Vermischte Aufsätze von H. Hirschbach: Componist und Virtuos," *NZfM* 18, no. 30 (April 13, 1843): 119–120.

39. Johann Nepomuk Hummel to Schumann, May 24, 1832, in Boetticher, *Briefe und Gedichte*, 91. Gottfried Weber, in *Caecilia: Eine Zeitschrift für die musikalische Welt* 16, no. 62 (1834): 94–98. Koßmaly, "On Robert Schumann's Piano Compositions," 308. Daverio discusses perceptions of Schumann's 1830s piano music in "Schumann's Systems," 50–51.

40. My discussion of Schumann's midlife style is indebted to Julie Hedges Brown, "Higher Echoes of the Past."

41. "Leipzig," *AmZ* 45, no. 3 (January 18, 1843): 47. "Rescensionen," *AmZ* 46, no. 9 (February 28, 1844): 149. August Kahlert, "Robert Schumann: Quartett," *AmZ* 48, no. 28 (July 13, 1846): 472. "Nachrichten," *AmZ* 43, no. 16 (April 21, 1841): 330.

42. For an overview, see Thym, "Schumann."

43. Schumann, *TB*, 2:401.

44. See, for example, Anthony Newcomb's study of Schumann's revisions to the first movement of his Sonata Op. 22. "Schumann and the Marketplace," 286–291.

45. Daverio, *Robert Schumann*, 306, 323–325. Again, one can find precedents for these features before 1845: the closing double fugue of the Piano Quintet, for example, or the motivic transformations in the Symphony No. 4 (whose first version dates from 1841).

46. Gooley, "Schumann and the Agencies," 129.

47. Schumann, *TB*, 2:402.

48. On Schumann's revisions and the question of whether any of them can count as "definitive," see Newcomb, "Schumann and the Marketplace," 275–302.

49. Ehrhardt, "La variation chez Robert Schumann," 182.

50. Macdonald, *Robert Schumann and the Piano Concerto*, 223–246, 263–721; "'Mit einer eignen'"; Lindeman, *Structural Novelty and Tradition*, 141–172; Koch, *Das Klavierkonzert des 19. Jahrhunderts*, 230–238; Edler, "Große Form als thematische Dramaturgie," 163–179; Synofzik, "Ein Rückert-Kanon." For Schumann's essay that anticipates the structure of the *Phantasie*/first movement, see "I. Moscheles, fünftes Concert . . . Sechstes Concert," *GS*, 1:163.

51. Macdonald, "Konzert für Klavier und Orchester," 676; *Robert Schumann and the Piano Concerto*, 163; Lindeman, *Structural Novelty*, 139; Daverio, *Robert Schumann*, 237–238; Mahling, "Das Klavierkonzert op. 54 von Robert Schumann."

52. Liszt's two piano concertos feature unifying strategies similar to Robert's and Clara's. Liszt began working on both in the 1830s, but he did not publish his first until 1857 and his second until 1861. There is no evidence that Robert saw these works while Liszt was drafting them. In fact, Lindeman speculates that Liszt might have drawn upon Clara Wieck's Concerto Op. 7, which he could have heard when their paths crossed in Vienna. *Structural Novelty*, 139.

53. Friedrich Wieck, Leipzig, October 24, 1833, in *Friedrich Wieck Briefe*, 47; Robert Schumann to Friedrich Wieck, Zwickau, January 10, 1833, in Schumann, *Schumann Briefedition*, Series I, vol. 2, 60; Schumann to Clara Wieck, Leipzig, November 29, 1837, in *Briefedition* Series I, vol. 4, 151.

54. Brown, "Higher Echoes of the Past," 525–560; Bonds, *After Beethoven*, 131. Anthony Newcomb discusses other allusions in "Once More," 240, 245–246.

55. Daverio, *Robert Schumann*, 241; Mahling, "Das Klavierkonzert op. 54 von Robert Schumann," 150–151; Macdonald, "Konzert für Klavier und Orchester," 676. Mahling's argument does not include discussion of music—it relies on Robert's writings about Clara's concerto, the fact that Clara did not perform her piece during or after the 1840s, and, perhaps, the reader's familiarity with both works.

56. My discussion of Robert's reinterpretations emphasizes structure—the pathways that virtuosic display followed rather than the passagework itself. The two concertos use radically different styles of figuration. Whereas Clara's transitions and culminating displays use textures similar to Chopin or Hummel, Robert's first movement often relegates fast figuration to the piano's middle register and places it beneath lyrical upper voices.

57. Quoted in Klassen, *Clara Wieck-Schumann*, 114.

58. Ibid., 140.

59. Schumann, "Schwärmbriefe," *NZfM* 3, no. 46 (December 8, 1835): 182.

60. Ibid.

61. Schumann to Wieck, November 29, 1837.

62. See Macdonald, "Critical Perception," 24–37.

63. "Clara Wieck: erstes Concert," *AmaW* 10, no. 36 (September 16, 1838): 143. "Wiek, Clara," in Schilling, *Encyclopädie*, 6:862.

64. Macdonald, "Critical Perception," 31.

65. "'Là ci darem la mano' varié pour le pianoforte," *Caecilia: Eine Zeitschrift für die musikalische Welt* 14, no. 55 (1832): 223–224.

66. "Correspondenz," *NZfM* 2, no. 20 (March 10, 1835): 83.

67. Goertzen, "Clara Wieck Schumann's Improvisations," 153–162.

68. Claudia de Vries has noted that the transitions have a generally "improvisational effect." *Die Pianistin*, 167.

69. Macdonald describes both the second theme and the closing display as having "a wonderfully improvisatory quality"—echoing Clara's critics but taking a positive tone. "Critical Perception," 28.

70. See Appel, "Kritischer Bericht," 189–192. For a facsimile of the Mehner manuscript, see Robert Schumann, *Piano Concerto in A Minor*. The transition I discuss is on pages 24–30.

71. Edler, "Große Form als thematische Dramaturgie," 174.

72. The full sonata form was apparently a feature of the concerto from its beginnings as the *Phantasie*: it appears fully worked out and orchestrated in the Mehner manuscript.

73. Schumann, "II. Konzerte für Pianoforte mit Orchester," *GS*, 1:163.

74. Alfred Dörffel, "Robert Schumann, Op. 54," *NZfM* 26, no. 5 (January 15, 1847): 17–19. Brendel acknowledged that he contributed to the essay. See Appel, "Kritischer Bericht," 206.

75. Hanslick, *Aus dem Concert-Saal*, 182.

76. Macdonald, *Robert Schumann and the Piano Concerto*, 229; Edler, "Große Form als thematische Dramaturgie," 175.

77. Macdonald, *Robert Schumann and the Piano Concerto*, 266.

78. Gender surely influenced some of the differences in reception, but it is not the only explanation. After all, critics routinely criticized Robert's own 1830s piano works as incoherent or "subjective," and admiring accounts of his 1840s works describe his mastery and clarity as a new achievement. In any case, as I have argued, Robert courted these responses through the concerto's design.

79. "Aus Dresden," *AmZ* 47, no. 52 (December 31, 1845): 927. "Leipzig," *AmZ* 48, no. 1 (January 1846): 12. Julius Schladebach, *Dresdner Abendzeitung* 47, no. 52 (December 25, 1845): 927. Quoted in Appel, "Kritischer Bericht," 196–197.

80. "Robert Schumann," *Die Grenzboten* 9, sem. 2, vol. 1 (1850): 496.

81. Dörffel, "Robert Schumann, Opus 54," 17.

82. Ibid., 18.

83. *AmZ* 48, no. 1 (January 1846): 12.

84. Dörffel, "Robert Schumann, Op. 54," 18.

85. Hanslick, *Aus dem Concert-saal*, 183.

86. Macdonald, *Robert Schumann and the Piano Concerto*, 264.

87. Some current and nineteenth-century commentators classify the finale as a rondo or sonata-rondo, but the movement is in fact a sonata form. A rondo flavor does emerge when variants of the primary theme recur in the orchestra during the closing display and in the tutti sections before the development and coda.

6. Festivals of the Virtuoso Priesthood: Collaborating with Clara Schumann and Joseph Joachim

1. Hanslick, *Geschichte des Concertwesens in Wien*, 1:418

2. Hamilton, *After the Golden Age*, 228. Indeed, *Werktreue* was a powerful, contested idea precisely because it entailed perceived insight and reverence and did not merely hinge on interpretive literalism.

3. For one nuanced discussion, see Garratt, "Mendelssohn and the Rise."

4. These factions were not exclusive, and the debate ran alongside exchange and overlap. Brahms, for example, employed compositional techniques associated with Liszt and Wagner (sometimes reinterpreting and implicitly critiquing them). See, for example, Brodbeck, "Brahms, the Third Symphony."

5. Schumann, "Neue Bahnen," in *GS* 2:301.

6. Recent biographies that discuss late Schumann sympathetically include Daverio, *Robert Schumann*; Geck, *Robert Schumann*; and Worthen, *Robert Schumann*.

7. The nature of Robert Schumann's illness and the precise cause of his death have been loaded, much-discussed issues, with scholars and physicians proposing diagnoses. I would not presume to offer my own, or indeed to enter the debate at all. On the late works' reception, see Struck, *Die umstrittenen späten Instrumentalwerke*, e.g., 678–688.

8. For a fuller account, see Hirsch, "Segregating Sound," 55–56.

9. Struck, *Die unstrittenen späten Instrumentalwerke*; Struck, "Gewichtsverlagerungen."; Tunbridge, *Schumann's Late Style*, 116–129.

10. Clara Schumann, Clara Schumann Programmsammlung, 598, 620.

11. Many scholars have noted that Clara's programming shifted during the 1840s. See, for example, Reich, *Clara Schumann*, 254–255; Weber, *Great Transformation of Musical Taste*, 245–248; Pettler, "Clara Schumann's Recitals."

12. Clara Schumann Programmsammlung, 695.

13. See Gooley, *Virtuoso Liszt*, 179–181; Samson, *Chopin*, 285–288.

14. Whereas critics debated whether and which opera-based showpieces transcended superficial pleasure, a discourse of interiority was essential to the *Lied ohne Worte* genre. The textures, unadorned melodies, and occasional titles (*Volkslied*, for example) evoked intimate lied performance and German lieder poetry, and many contemporary critics wondered about unheard, ineffable texts behind the music. For one recent study, see Todd, "Mendelssohn's *Lieder ohne Worte*."

15. Clara first performed Mendelssohn's *Variations sériuses* on December 23, 1848. Schumann, Clara Schumann Programmsammlung, 716. On some occasions, she performed the Mendelssohn as a closer, sometimes in the interior of the program.

16. Todd, "Piano Music Reformed," 205–209.

17. Schumann, *TB*, 2:181. Translation adapted from Reich, *Clara Schumann*, 255. Clara's surviving correspondence does not indicate whether she had viewed Henselt's and Thalberg's music so negatively in the 1830s. Even if she did, she knew that other critics felt differently, having read reviews such as those I discussed in chapters 1–3.

18. Macdonald, *Robert Schumann and the Piano Concerto*, 275–277.

19. *Neue Musik Zeitung für Berlin* 1, no. 9 (March 3, 1847): 82.

20. "Tagebuch: Aus Leipzig," *Die Grenzboten* 3, Semester 2, vol. 2 (1844): 566.

21. Robert Schumann to Clara Wieck, Vienna, December 3, 1838, in Schumann, *Briefedition* Ser. 1, vol. 5, 145.

22. Liszt, "Clara Schumann," *NZfM* 41, no. 23 (December 1, 1854): 245–252. Scholars have debated the extent to which Liszt's partner, Princess Carolyne von Sayn-Wittgenstein, contributed to his midcentury writings. My discussion here does not consider this issue. Regardless of whether Sayn-Wittgenstein was involved with the "Clara Schumann" essay, it is more important for my argument that it appeared under Liszt's name.

23. Liszt, "Robert Schumann (1855)."

24. Deaville, "Making of a Myth," 190–194.

25. Liszt, "Clara Schumann," 246.

26. Ibid.

27. Hamilton, *After the Golden Age*, 79.

28. Liszt, "Clara Schumann," 250.

29. Ibid.

30. Quoted in Lossewa, "Marfa Sabinina," 223.

31. Liszt, "Clara Schumann," 251.

32. "Das 31. niederrheinische Musikfeste zu Düsseldorf," *Signale* 11, no. 24 (June, 1853): 187.

33. Garratt, *Music and Social Reform*, 89.

34. Otto Jahn, "Das Dreiunddreißigste niederrheinische Musikfest in Düsseldorf," in *Gesammelte Aufsätze über Musik*, 173–198. Porter, "New Public," 216.

35. Eichhorn, "Vom Volksfest," 14–25.

36. Appel, "Kritischer Bericht," 212.

37. Quoted in Litzmann, *Clara Schumann*, 2:133, 138.

38. *AmZ* 47, no. 52 (December 31, 1845): 927.

39. *Signale* 4, no. 2 (January, 1846): 9.

40. "Das 31. niederrheinische Musikfest," *Süddeutsche Musikzeitung* 2, no. 24 (June 13, 1853): 95; *Signale* 11, no. 24 (June 1853): 188; Ludwig Bischoff, "Das 31. niederrheinische Musikfest," *Rheinische Musik-Zeitung* 3, no. 154 (June 11, 1853): 1228.

41. *Signale* 11, no. 24 (June 1853): 185.

42. Porter, " New Public," 219–221; Eichhorn, "Vom Volksfest " 15–25.

43. Garratt, *Music and Social Reform*, 88–89.

44. Bischoff, "Das 31. niederrheinische Musikfeste," 1227.

45. *Signale* 8 (February 20, 1855): 66. During Robert's lifetime, Clara performed Opus 92 on February 14, 1850 (Leipzig), November 5, 1850 (Cologne), March 13, 1851 (Düsseldorf), and December 6, 1855 (Leipzig).

46. The Allegro Appassionato was not the only work Robert composed that stages his and Clara's public personae. Julie Hedges Brown, for example, has shown that the finale of the Piano Quartet alludes to Beethoven, Schubert, and one of the Novelettes Robert had written for Clara during their engagement. Brown argues that the play between Robert's "public" style and the Novelette (a work that held private meaning for the Schumanns) reflects the changing nature of their partnership during the early years of their marriage. By relegating the Novelette allusion to a lyrical interlude, Brown proposes, Robert might have hinted at his desire to gain public recognition in his own right and recognized that Clara was increasingly bound by private responsibilities to their family. My discussion here and elsewhere in this chapter considers the Schumanns' public images rather than their private negotiations, and the strategies I trace emphasize not only Clara's inextricable connection to Robert's work but also her power as its public exponent. Brown, "Higher Echoes of the Past," 545–560.

47. *NZfM* 32, no. 20 (March 5, 1850): 103.

48. *Signale* 13, no. 52 (December 13, 1855): 420.

49. Macdonald, *Robert Schumann and the Piano Concerto*, 281.

50. Meyer, *Style and Music*, 204–205, 323.

51. Interpreting the Introduction as part of the exposition does not normalize the form. Doing so would create second and third theme groups in vi and IV.

52. Daverio, *Robert Schumann*, 420.

53. *Signale* 8, no. 8 (February 20, 1850): 66.

54. See, for example, Maintz, *Franz Schubert*, as well as the studies by both Reiman and Brown that I have cited elsewhere.

55. Schumann, "Die C-dur-Sinfonie von Franz Schubert," *GS*, 1:461, 463.

56. Bonds, *After Beethoven*, 5–27, 117.

57. Gingerich, *Schubert's Beethoven Project*, 231.

58. Macdonald, *Robert Schumann and the Piano Concerto*, 271; Hanslick, *Geschichte der Concertwesen in Wien*, 1:338.

59. Schumann, Clara Schumann Programmsammlung, 767–778.

60. On the Schumanns' connections to the Netherlands and the planning of the tour, see Bodsch, Knechtges-Obrecht, and Nauhaus, *Enthusiasmus und Fackelzug*. Hugh Macdonald has described the Netherlands tour's logistics, everyday activities, and social encounters. *Music in 1853*, 172–180.

61. Clara Schumann to Marie von Lindeman, January 3, 1853, in Brunner, *Alltag und Künstlertum*, 204.

62. See Bodsch, Knechtges-Obrecht, and Nauhaus, *Enthusiasmus und Fackelzug*, 32.

63. *Caecilia* 10, no. 23 (December 1, 1853): 213–214. For their invaluable help with the Dutch translations in this chapter, I would like to thank Att and Robert McDowell (the former a translator, the latter a professor emeritus of mathematics at Washington University in Saint Louis). For daily papers that advertised the concerts, see, for example, *Nieuwe Amsterdamsche Courant* (November 28, 1853): 2 and *Utrechtsche Provinciale Stadts-Courant* (November 23, 1853): 3.

64. *Caecilia* 10, no. 22 (November 15, 1853): 208.

65. Schumann, *TB*, 2:441, 444, 446; *Caecilia* 11, no. 2 (January 1, 1854): 6.

66. *Caecilia* 10, no. 24 (December 15, 1853): 226.

67. Litzmann, *Clara Schumann*, 2:287.

68. Clara Schumann to Marie von Lindeman, January 3, 1853, 203.

69. Schumann, *TB*, 2:441, 444.

70. Ibid., 446; Bodsch, Knechtges-Obrecht, and Nauhaus, *Enthusiasmus und Fackelzug*, 66–85.

71. *Caecilia* 10, no. 24 (December 15, 1853): 225.

72. *Caecilia* 10, no. 23 (December 1, 1853): 214; ibid., no. 24 (December 15, 1853): 224.

73. *Signale* 12, no. 43 (October 26, 1854): 346. The article is a review of Clara's October 23, 1854, Leipzig concert.

74. *Caecilia* 10, no. 23 (December 1, 1853): 214; ibid., no. 24 (December 15, 1853): 225. Schumann, *TB*, 2:441–442.

75. November 26 (Utrecht), November 30 (The Hague), December 2 (Amsterdam).

76. Macdonald, *Robert Schumann and the Piano Concerto*, 296.

77. The construction of the entire first theme group hints at a Baroque concerto style—rather than presenting a single theme, it consists of short, sequentially repeated modules.

78. Draheim, "Konzertante Werke," 387.

79. Schumann's late works frequently employ Baroque styles and structures. Joseph Kerman, for example, heard traces of Baroque ritornello form in the first movement of the Violin Concerto and the Konzertstück for Four Horns Op. 86, and Michael Struck has argued that passagework in late Schumann often emulates *fortspinnung* by taking on motivic significance. Schumann also composed piano accompaniments for Bach solo violin and cello works in 1852 and 1853. Kerman, "The Concertos," 182, 191; Struck, "Gewichtsverlagerungen," 45–47.

80. Rosen, *Classical Style*, 448.

81. For example, Schumann and Schumann, *Clara und Robert Schumann Briefwechsel*, 3:915, 1129. Clara Schumann, Clara Schumann Programmsammlung 833, 836.

82. Sumner Lott, "At the Intersection," 266–269.

83. Struck has described "synthesizing coda themes" as a hallmark of late Schumann and divides them into "chorale style" and "lyrical" categories. My discussion here and elsewhere in this chapter considers a greater variety of compositional strategies. *Die umstrittenen späten Instrumentalwerke*, 591–595.

84. Ibid., 234.

85. Macdonald, *Robert Schumann and the Piano Concerto*, 296.

86. Rehding, *Music and Monumentality*, 5–8.

87. Meyer, *Style and Music*, 204–205, 209–210. See also Rehding, *Music and Monumentality*, 3–4.

88. Though Michael Struck has shown that the brass melody synthesizes rhythmic and motivic ideas from other parts of the work, these links are recondite. In its overall effect, the coda seems not to glorify a previously heard theme but to introduce a new melody that suddenly sweeps away the cadenza. *Die umstrittenen späten Instrumentalwerke*, 227.

89. *AmZ* 47, no. 47 (November 19, 1845): 838–839. I would like to acknowledge one useful repository of sources related to Joseph Joachim: Robert W. Eshbach's website devoted to the violinist. Eshbach includes a bibliography and a biography-in-progress, replete with links to concert reviews and other sources (and, for some, transcriptions and translations). Eshbach, *Joseph Joachim*.

90. "Joachim in Düsseldorf," *Zeitung für Norddeutschland: Hannoversche Morgenzeitung*, no. 1137 (May 22, 1853). Transcribed in Eshbach, *Joseph Joachim*.

91. *Süddeutsche Musik-Zeitung* 2, no. 24 (June 13, 1853): 95.

92. Robert's notes from 1849 show that he was planning on writing a piece for violin and orchestra. At that time, he might have designed it for Ferdinand David, concertmaster in Leipzig. However, he only began drafting the concerto and the Phantasie after meeting Joachim. See Struck, *Die umstrittenen späten Instrumentalwerke*, 241.

93. Joachim to Robert Schumann, Hanover, June 2, 1853, in *Joachim Briefe*, 1:59.

94. Robert Schumann to Joachim, Düsseldorf, June 8, 1853, in ibid., 1:62.

95. Robert Schumann to Joachim, Düsseldorf, October 7, 1853, in ibid., 1:84.

96. Robert Schumann to Joachim, Düsseldorf, September 14, 1853, in ibid., 1:77.

97. Joachim to Andreas Moser, Berlin, August 5, 1989, in ibid., 3:486–488.

98. Joachim to Clara Schumann, Paris, January 31, 1887, in ibid., 3:302; Joachim to Clara Schumann, Hannover, October 15, 1857, in ibid., 1:453 and October 21, 1857, in ibid., 1:454; Clara Schumann to Joachim, Munich, November 27, 1857, in ibid., 1:465–466.

99. Eighteenth-century concertos pause on a $V^{6/4}$ to signal a cadenza. Concertos by Schumann and his contemporaries, though, use a wider variety of harmonies for this purpose—what these junctures have in common is their rhetorical emphasis (a strong tutti and a dramatic pause, usually) and a signal for harmonic resolution. For example, Mendelssohn's Violin Concerto uses the dominant, Schumann's Piano Concerto a German augmented sixth, and the Phantasie the subdominant.

100. Tunbridge, *Schumann's Late Style*, 126.

101. Kapp, "Schumann als Violinkomponist," 19. Tunbridge has described the Beethoven as Schumann's model in more general terms. She notes that critics have tended to see Schumann's virtuosic writing for violin as flawed, and she speculates that this may be because Schumann used the Beethoven as his model. She describes the Beethoven as "magnificent and difficult" but "not a flashy showpiece." *Schumann's Late Style*, 116.

102. The Beethoven concerto is in D major, a standard "pastoral" key, and evokes a pastoral style at several points in its first movement. In this context, lyrical retreats might evoke specifically bucolic tranquility. By contrast, Robert's Violin Concerto is in D minor and makes no pastoral references. Plantinga, *Beethoven's Concertos*, 217–218.

103. Leistra-Jones, "Staging Authenticity." See also Moser, *Joseph Joachim*, 149–150.

104. *Süddeutsche Musik-Zeitung* 2, no. 3 (January 17, 1853): 11.

105. *Dwight's Journal of Music* 2, no. 11 (June, 18 1853): 86–87. Transcribed in Eshbach, *Joseph Joachim*.

106. *Times*, no. 21130 (June 1, 1852): 8. Transcribed in Eshbach, *Joseph Joachim*.

107. Leistra-Jones has argued that Brahms's Violin Concerto stages another aspect of Joachim's image: his ability to seem as though he was improvising a set composition. "Improvisational Idyll."

108. Robert Schumann to Joachim, Düsseldorf, February 8, 1854, in *Joachim Briefe*, 1:154.

109. Joachim to Robert Schumann, Hanover, November 17, 1854, in ibid., 1:228–229.

110. *Signale* 19 (January 19, 1854): 28.

111. Though Joseph Kerman described the theme as a polka—one of the dance crazes of the 1840s and 1850s—the movement is in common time rather than 2/4, and any resemblance to conventional polka rhythms is faint. Kerman, "The Concertos," 193.

112. Macdonald, *Robert Schumann and the Piano Concerto*, 300.

113. Discussing this style of music raises complex terminological issues. Shay Loya's recent study of the "Hungarian-Gypsy" tradition uses the term *verbunkos* for music in the style played by "Gypsy" bands and *style hongrois* to refer to evocations of *verbunkos* in Western concert music. Schumann's Phantasie fits the latter category. A more significant problem is that "Gypsy" is at best a misleading and at worst an offensive term for the Roma. And yet, describing it as "Romani music" would also be problematic, not least because the Roma cultivated folk music that differed from the "Gypsy" style. And, as Loya notes, performers in "Gypsy" ensembles were often but not always Roma. For purposes of this study, I use "Roma" when referring to the actual people and "Gypsy" (in scare quotes) when discussing the half-imaginary culture depicted in music, literature, and other media, as well as contemporary stereotypes about that culture. My wording is indebted to Loya, *Liszt's Transcultural Modernism*, xv, 60–61, and Locke, *Musical Exoticism*, 137.

114. Daverio, *Crossing Paths*, 214.

115. Brown, "Schumann and the *Style Hongrois*," 265–299.

116. On *hallgató*, see Bellman, *The* Style Hongrois, 102–105. Loya, *Liszt's Transcultural Modernism*, xvi, 79.

117. Bellman, *The* Style Hongrois, 92.

118. Loya, *Liszt's Transcultural Modernism*, 7.

119. To cite but one example: Liszt's 1859 *Des Bohémiens et leur musique en Hongrie* (On the Gypsies and Their Music in Hungary) makes the insulting claim that the Roma were attuned only to their "primary impulses" and that without "intelligent" Hungarian listeners, "Hungarian-Gypsy" music would have vanished. Ralph Locke discusses this passage in *Musical Exoticism*, 141.

120. The Mendelssohn reference is widely acknowledged, but its significance has gone unexplored. Kerman (who described the Phantasie as a shallow, ineffective work) even proposed that it showed one composer "misunderstanding" another. "The Concertos," 193. Daverio, *Robert Schumann*, 469; Draheim, "Konzertante Werke," 393.

121. Daverio, *Crossing Paths*, 239–242. Of course, Schumann and his contemporaries also tried to "elevate" popular styles other than the *style hongrois*—the waltzes in *Papillons*, for example, or the postclassical framework of the "Abegg" Variations.

122. "Confirmed classicists" might also refer to opponents of the New German School. Joachim to Liszt, January 9, 1854, in *Joachim Briefe*, 1:143.

123. Daverio, *Crossing Paths*, 230–239.

124. Joachim to Brahms, Hannover, October 15, 1861, in Moser, *Johannes Brahms im Briefwechsel*, 1:312 (emphasis added).

125. Joachim's statement invokes a trope common in German music criticism—that, when German composers employed other national styles, they somehow elevated them. He made a similar claim when favorably comparing Haydn to Dvořák in a letter to his nephew, cited in Eshbach, "Joachim's Youth," 569.

126. Borchard, *Stimme und Geige*, 127; Eshbach, "Joachim's Youth," 566–569.

127. Robert Schumann to Joachim, October 7, and November 21, 1853, *Joachim Briefe*, 1:84, 105.

128. On the latter point, see Borchard, *Stimme und Geige*, 132, and Eshbach, "Joachim's Youth," 569.

129. *NZfM* 61, no. 15 (April 9, 1875): 149.

130. Richard Pohl, "Zur Erinnerung an Robert Schumann," *NZfM* 45, no. 19 (October 31, 1856): 199.

131. Appel, Hermstrüwer, Nauhaus, and Bär, *Clara und Robert Schumann*, 120.

132. Schumann, Clara Schumann Programmsammlung, 836.

133. Reich, *Clara Schumann*, 241–245; de Vries, *Die Pianistin*, 282.

Epilogue

1. See, for example, Struck, *Die umstrittenen späten Instrumentalwerke*, 294–322, 331–366.

2. Cortot suggests the following order: I, PV1, II, III, IV, V, PV4, VI, VII, PV2, PV5, VIII, IX, PV3, X, XI, XII. Cortot, *Édition de Travail*. Pollini plays the posthumous variations in the order given in the critical edition and inserts them after Etude V. Maurizio Pollini, *Schumann–Pollini: Klavierkonzert, Symphonische Etüden, Arabeske* (1990), CD, Deutsche Gramophon 445 552-2.

3. On Ebert's performance, see Draheim, "Konzertante Werke" 139. *Signale* 26, no. 2 (January 1868): 23.

4. *Signale* 26, no. 2 (January 1868): 23.

5. *Neue Berliner Musikzeitung* 9, no. 3 (January 17, 1855): 17–18.

6. Claudia Macdonald has also noted the harmonic continuity and deceptive resolution. However, my interpretation differs from hers. She argues that the concerto downplays virtuosity in general, whereas I am suggesting a more subtle blurring of boundaries and subversion of expectations. *Robert Schumann and the Piano Concerto*, 290.

7. Quoted in Litzmann, *Clara Schumann*, 3:479.

8. Joachim to Franz Egger, Vienna May 21, 1870, and Clara Schuman to Joachim, Baden, June 13, 1870, in *Joachim Briefe*, 3:41–42.

9. Many accounts of the *Handel Variations* acknowledge these Beethoven links and chart Brahms's contrapuntal style. For example, Musgrave, *Music of Brahms*, 53–58, and Rink "Opposition and Integration," 85–89.

10. My argument resonates with Malcolm MacDonald's, who describes the *Variations* as a "manifesto" in line with Brahms's critique of the New Germans. *Brahms*, 178.

11. Bonds, *After Beethoven*, 148–170.

12. Richard Pohl, "Die 14. Tonkünstler-Versammlung des Allgemeinen Deutschen Musikvereins," *NZfM* 73, no. 28 (July 6, 1877): 285–287.

13. "Liszt, Franz, Variationen über das Motive von Bach," *Echo* 26 (1876): 95.

14. To cite but a few: William Apthorp, "The Virtuoso and the Public," *Musical World* (March 15, 1879): 167; J. N. Burk, "The Fetish of Virtuosity," *Musical Quarterly* 4, no. 2 (1918): 282–292; Florizel von Reuter, "Virtuosität," *Signale* 83, no. 20 (May 20, 1925): 815–817; Marc Pincherle, trans. Willis Wagar, "Virtuosity," *Musical Quarterly* 35, no. 2 (1949): 226–243.

15. Accessed January 9, 2014, http://www.khatiabuniatishvili.com.

16. Accessed January 8, 2014, http://www.marcandrehamelin.com.

17. Kingsbury, *Music, Talent, and Performance*, 136.

18. Libbey, *NPR Guide*.

19. Horowitz, "Letter from New York."

Bibliography

Other Sources

Allanbrook, Wye J. "Is the Sublime a Musical Topos?" *Eighteenth-Century Music* 7, no. 2 (2010): 263–279.

Appel, Bernhard R. "Kritischer Bericht." Robert Schumann, *Klavierkonzert a-Moll op. 54*, edited by Bernhard R. Appel, in *Robert Schumann Ausgabe*, ser. 1, Werkgruppe 2, vol. 1, 175–285. Mainz: Schott, 2003.

Appel, Bernhard R., Inge Hermstrüwer, Gerd Nauhaus, and Ute Bär, eds. *Clara und Robert Schumann: Zeitgenössische Porträts*. Düsseldorf: Droste, 1994.

Applegate, Celia. "How German Is It? Nationalism and the Idea of Serious Music in the Early Nineteenth Century." *19th-Century Music* 21, no. 3 (1998): 274–296.

———. "Robert Schumann and the Culture of German Nationhood." In Kok and Tunbridge, *Rethinking Schumann*, 3–14.

Atwood, William G. *The Parisian Worlds of Frédéric Chopin*. New Haven, CT: Yale University Press, 1999.

Barthes, Roland. "Loving Schumann." In *The Responsibility of Forms*, translated by Richard Howard, 293–298. New York: Hill and Wang, 1985.

Bartoli, Jean-Pierre. "Les Études symphoniques de Schumann: plaidoyer analytique pour le rejet des 'Variations posthumes.'" *Analyse musicale* 76 (1992): 76–86.

Battersby, Christine. *Gender and Genius*. Bloomington: Indiana University Press, 1989.

Beci, Veronika. *Musikalische Salons: Blütezeit einer Frauenkultur*. Düsseldorf: Artemis und Winkler, 2000.

Beiche, Michael. "Die *NZfM* im Vergleich mit der *Allgemeinen musikalischen Zeitung*." In *"Eine neue poetische Zeit": 175 Jahre Neue Zeitschrift für Musik*, Schumann Forschungen 14, edited by Michael Beiche and Armin Koch, 23–36. Mainz: Schott, 2013.

Bellman, Jonathan. *The Style Hongrois in the Music of Western Europe*. Boston: Northeastern University Press, 1993.

Bergmann, Hanna. "Fricken, Ernestine von." In Instrumentalistinnen-Lexikon, Sophie Drinker Institut für Musikwissenschaftliche Frauen- und Geschlechterforschung. Accessed March 15, 2013. www.sophie-drinker-institut.de.

Bergmann, Hanna, and Mirjam Gerber. "Voigt, Henriette." In Instrumentalistinnen-Lexikon, Sophie Drinker Institut für Musikwissenschaftliche Frauen- und Geschlechterforschung. Accessed March 15, 2013. www.sophie-drinker-institut.de.

Biba, Otto. "Carl Czerny and Post-Classicism." In *Beyond The Art of Finger Dexterity: Reassessing Carl Czerny*, edited by David Gramit, 11–22. Rochester, NY: University of Rochester Press, 2008.

Bodsch, Ingrid, Irmgard Knechtges-Obrecht, and Gerd Nauhaus, eds. *Enthusiasmus und Fackelzug: Robert und Clara Schumann in den Niederlanden*. Aachen: Shaker, 2010.

Boetticher, Wolfgang. "Neue Materialien zur Begegnung Robert Schumanns mit Henriette Voigt." In *Florilegium Musicologicum: Hellmut Federhofer zum 75. Geburtstag*, edited by Christoph-Hellmut Mahling, 45–56. Tutzing: Hans Schneider, 1988.

———. *Robert Schumanns Klavierwerke: Neue biographische und textkritische Untersuchungen*. 3 vols. Wilhelmshaven: Heinrichshofen, 1976.

———. "Weitere Forschungen an Dokumenten zum Leben und Schaffen Robert Schumanns." In *Robert Schumann—Ein romantisches Erbe in neuer Forschung: Acht Studien herausgegeben von der Robert-Schumann-Gesellschaft Düsseldorf*, 43–56. Mainz: Schott, 1984.

Boetticher, Wolfgang, ed. *Briefe und Gedichte aus dem Album Robert und Clara Schumanns*. Leipzig: VEB Deutscher Verlag für Musik.

Böhme-Mehner, Tatjana. "Sinfonische Etüden für Klavier, Op. 13." In *Robert Schumann: Interpretationen seiner Werke*, edited by Helmut Loos, 72–77. Laaber: Laaber, 2005.

Bonds, Mark Evan. *After Beethoven: Imperatives of Originality in the Symphony*. Cambridge, MA: Harvard University Press, 1996.

———. "The Symphony as Pindaric Ode." In *Haydn and his World*, edited by Elaine Sisman, 131–154. Princeton, NJ: Princeton University Press, 1997.

Borchard, Beatrix. "Opferaltäre der Musik." In *Fanny Hensel geb. Mendelssohn Bartholdy: Komponieren zwischen Gesellikeitsideal und romantischer Musikästhetik*, edited by Beatrix Borchard and Monika Schwarz-Danuser, 27–44. Stuttgart: J. B. Metzler, 1999.

———. *Stimme und Geige: Amalie und Joseph Joachim*. Vienna: Böhlau, 2005.

Brodbeck, David. "Brahms, the Third Symphony, and the New German School." In *Brahms and His World*, edited by Walter Frisch and Kevin C. Karnes, rev. ed., 95–116. Princeton, NJ: Princeton University Press, 2009.

Brown, Julie Hedges. "Higher Echoes of the Past in the Finale of Schumann's 1842 Piano Quartet." *Journal of the American Musicological Society* 57, no. 3 (2004): 511–564.

———. "Schumann and the *Style Hongrois*." In Kok and Tunbridge, *Rethinking Schumann*, 256–299.

Broyles, Michael. *Beethoven: The Emergence and Evolution of Beethoven's Heroic Style*. New York: Excelsior, 1987.

Brunner, Renate, ed. *Alltag und Künstlertum: Clara Schumann und ihre Dresdner Freundinnen Marie von Lindeman und Emilie Steffens*. Sinzig: Studio, 2005.

Burger, Ernst. *Robert Schumann: Eine Lebenschronik in Bildern und Dokumenten*. In collaboration with Gerd Nauhaus. Mainz: Schott Musik International, 1999.

Burke, Edmund. *A Philosophical Enquiry into the Origin of Our Ideas of the Sublime and Beautiful*. 1759. Edited by Adam Phillips. New York: Oxford University Press, 1990.

Burkholder, J. Peter. "Borrowing." In *The New Grove Dictionary of Music and Musicians*. 29 vols. 2nd ed. Edited by Stanley Sadie, 4:5–41. New York: Grove, 2001.

Burnham, Scott. *Beethoven Hero*. Princeton, NJ: Princeton University Press, 1995.

Chopin, Frédéric. *Selected Correspondence of Fryderyk Chopin*. Edited by Bronislaw Edward Sydow. Translated by Arthur Hedley. London: Heinemann, 1962.

Clewis, Robert R. *The Kantian Sublime and the Revelation of Freedom*. Cambridge: Cambridge University Press, 2009.

Cooper, Ruskin King. *Robert Schumann's Closest "Jugendfreund": Ludwig Schuncke (1810–1834) and His Piano Music*. Hamburg: Fischer, 1997.

Cortot, Alfred. *Édition de Travail des Oeuvres de Schumann: Op. 13 Études Symphonqiues en forme de Variations*. Paris: Salabert, 1948.

Czerny, Carl. *Briefe über den Unterricht auf dem Pianofote*. Vienna: Diabelli, 1839.

———. *School of Practical Composition*. Translated by John Bishop. London: R. Cocks, 1848.

———. *Systematische Anleitung zum Fantasieren auf dem Pianoforte*, Op. 200. Vienna: Diabelli, 1836. Translated and edited by Alice L. Mitchell. *A Systematic Introduction to Improvisation on the Pianoforte*. New York: Longman, 1983.

———. *Von dem Vortrage (1839): Dritter Teil aus* Vollständige theoretisch-practische Pianoforte-Schule, Op. 500. Reprint. Edited by Ulrich Mahlert. Wiesbaden: Breitkopf und Härtel, 1991.

Dahlhaus, Carl. *Nineteenth-Century Music*. Translated by J. Bradford Robinson. Berkeley: University of California Press, 1989.

Danuser, Hermann. *Musikalische Prosa*. Regensburg: Gustav Bosse, 1975.

Daverio, John. *Crossing Paths: Schubert, Schumann, and Brahms*. Oxford: Oxford University Press, 2002.

———. "Il circolo magico: Schumann e la musica di Paganini." In *Schumann, Brahms e l'Italia*. Atti dei convegni Lincei 165, 41–58. Translated by Michele Caniato. Rome: Accademia Nazionale dei Lincei, 2001.

———. *Robert Schumann: Herald of a New Poetic Age*. Oxford: Oxford University Press, 1997.

———. "Schumann's Systems of Musical Fragments and *Witz*." In *Nineteenth-Century Music and the German Romantic Ideology*, 49–88. New York: Schirmer, 1993.

Deaville, James. "The Making of a Myth: Liszt, the Press, and Virtuosity." In *New Light on Liszt and His Music: Essays in Honor of Alan Walker's 65th Birthday*, edited by Michael Saffle and James Deaville, 181–195. Stuyvesant, NY: Pendragon, 1997.

———. "Publishing Paraphrases and Creating Collectors: Friedrich Hofmeister, Franz Liszt, and the Technology of Popularity." In *Franz Liszt and His World*, edited by Christopher H. Gibbs and Dana Gooley, 255–291. Princeton, NJ: Princeton University Press, 2006.

de Vries, Claudia. *Die Pianistin Clara Wieck-Schumann: Interpretation im Spannungsfeld von Tradition und Individualität*. Schumann-Forschungen 5. Mainz: Schott, 1996.

Downes, Stephen. "Kierkegaard, a Kiss, and Schumann's 'Fantasie.'" *19th-Century Music* 22, no. 3 (1999): 268–280.

Draheim, Joachim. "Konzertante Werke." In *Schumann Handbuch*, edited by Ulrich Tadday, 376–399. Stuttgart: Bärenreiter, 2006.

———. "Preface." Sonata in G minor, Op. 3, by Ludwig Schuncke. Wiesbaden: Bretikopf und Härtel, 1986.

———. "Robert Schumann und Henri Herz." In *Robert Schumann und die französische Romantik*, Schumann Forschungen 6, edited by Ute Bär, 153–166. Mainz: Schott, 1997.

———. "Schumann und Chopin." In *Schumann Studien 3/4*. Edited by Gerd Nauhaus. Cologne: Studio, 1994.

Edler, Arnfried. "Große Form als thematische Dramaturgie: Überlegungen zum Kopfsatz von Schumanns Klavierkonzert a-Moll op. 54." In *Robert Schumann und die große Form*, edited by Bernd Sponheuer und Wolfram Steinbeck, 163–719. Frankfurt: Lang, 2009.

Ehrhardt, Damien. "La variation chez Robert Schumann: Forme et evolution." 2 vols. PhD diss., Université Paris-Sorbonne, 1997.

———. "Les *Études symphoniques* de Robert Schumann: Projet d'intégration des variations posthumes." *Revue de Musicologie* 78, no. 2 (1992): 289–306.

Eichhorn, Andreas. "Vom Volksfest zur 'musikalischen Prunkausstellung': Das Musikfest im 19. Jahrhundert als Forum bürgerlicher Selbstdarstellung." *Die Musikforschung* 52, no. 1 (1999): 5–28

Eismann, Georg. *Robert Schumann: Ein Quellenwerk*. Leipzig: Breitkopf und Härtel, 1956.

Ellis, Katharine. "Berlioz, the Sublime, and the *Broderie* Problem." In *Hector Berlioz: Miscellaneous Studies*, edited by Fulvia Morabito and Michela Niccolai, 29–59. Bologna: Ut Orpheus, 2005.

———. "Liszt, the Romantic Artist." In *The Cambridge Companion to Liszt*, edited by Kenneth Hamilton, 1–13. New York: Cambridge University Press, 2005.

Erlin, Matt. *Necessary Luxuries: Books, Literature, and the Culture of Consumption in Germany, 1770–1815*. Ithaca, NY: Cornell University Press, 2014.

Eshbach, Robert W. "Joachim's Youth: Joachim's Jewishness." *Musical Quarterly* 94, no. 4 (2011): 548–592.

———. *Joseph Joachim: Biography and Research*. Accessed Freburary 20, 2015. josephjoachim.com.

Everist, Mark. "Speaking with the Supernatural: E. T. A. Hoffmann, George Bernhard Shaw, and *Die Oper Aller Opern*." *Mozart-Jahrbuch* (2002): 115–134.

Fellinger, Imogen. "Die Begriffe *Salon* und *Salonmusik* in der Musikanschauung des 19. Jahrhunderts." In *Studien zur Trivialmusik des 19. Jahrhunderts*, edited by Carl Dahlhaus, 131–141. Regensburg: Gustav Bosse, 1967.

Ferris, David. "Public Performance and Private Understanding: Clara Wieck's Concerts in Berlin." *Journal of the American Musicological Society* 56, no. 2 (2003): 351–408.

———. "'Was will dieses Grau'n bedeuten?' Schumann's 'Zwielicht' and Daverio's 'Incomprehensibility Topos.'" *Journal of Musicology* 22, no. 1 (2005): 131–153.

Fuller-Maitland, J. A. *Schumann*. New York: Scribner, 1880.

Garratt, James. "Mendelssohn and the Rise of Musical Historicism." In *The Cambridge Companion to Mendelssohn*, edited by Peter Mercer-Taylor, 55–70. Cambridge: Cambridge University Press, 2004.

———. *Music, Culture and Social Reform in the Age of Wagner*. Cambridge: Cambridge University Press, 2010.

Gay, Peter. *The Naked Heart*. New York: Norton 1995.

Geck, Martin. *Robert Schumann: The Life and Work of a Romantic Composer*. Translated by Stewart Spencer. Chicago: University of Chicago Press, 2013.

Gensel, Julius. "Henriette Voigt: Erinnerguen aus dem Leipziger Musikleben zu Mendelssohns Zeit." *Die Grenzboten: Zeitschrift für Politik, Literatur, und Kunst* 68, no. 1 (1909): 393–400.

———. "Robert Schumann's Briefwechsel mit Henriette Voigt." *Die Grenzboten: Zeitschrift für Politik, Literatur, und Kunst* 51, no. 2 (1892): 269–277, 324–332, 368–375.

Gingerich, John M. *Schubert's Beethoven Project*. Cambridge: Cambridge University Press, 2014.

Goehr, Lydia. *The Imaginary Museum of Musical Works*. Rev. ed. New York: Oxford University Press, 2007.

Goertzen, Valerie Woodring. "Clara Wieck Schumann's Improvisations and Her 'Mosaics' of Small Forms." In *Beyond Notes: Improvisation in Western Music of the Eighteenth and Nineteenth Centuries*, edited by Rudolf Rasch, 153–162. Turnhout: Brepols, 2011.

Goethe, Johann Wolfgang von. "Stages of Man's Mind" (1817). In Goethe, *Essays on Art and Literature*, edited by John Gearey, translated by Ellen and Ernest H. von Nardorff, 203–204. Vol. 3, *Goethe: Collected Works*. New York: Suhrkamp, 1986.

Gooley, Dana. "The Battle against Instrumental Virtuosity in the Early Nineteenth Century." In *Franz Liszt and His World*, edited by Christopher H. Gibbs and Dana Gooley, 75–112. Princeton, NJ: Princeton University Press, 2006.

———. "La Commedia del Violino: Paganini's Comic Strains." *Musical Quarterly* 88, no. 3 (2005): 370–427.

———. "Schumann and the Agencies of Improvisation." In Kok and Tunbridge, *Rethinking Schumann*, 129–156.

———. *The Virtuoso Liszt*. Cambridge: Cambridge University Press, 2004.

Gramit, David. *Cultivating Music: The Aspirations, Interests, and Limits of German Musical Culture, 1770–1848*. Berkeley: University of California Press, 2002.

Hamilton, Kenneth. *After the Golden Age: Romantic Pianism and Modern Performance*. New York: Oxford University Press, 2008.

Hansen, Matthias. "Robert Schumanns 'Virtuosität': Anmerkungen zu den *Abegg-Variationen* und ihrem kompositorischen Umfeld." In *Musikalische Virtuosität*, edited by Heinz von Loesch, Ulrich Mahlert, and Peter Rummenhöller, 132–141. Mainz: Schott, 2004.

Hanslick, Eduard. *Aus dem Concert-Saal: Kritiken und Schilderungen*. Vienna: Wilhelm Braumüller, 1897.

———. *Aus dem Tagebuch eines Musikers*. 3rd ed. Berlin: Allgemeiner Verein für deutsche Litteratur, 1892.

———. *Geschichte des Concertwesens in Wien*. Vienna: Wilhelm Braumüller, 1869.

———. *Musikalisches Skizzenbuch: Neue Kritiken und Schilderungen*. 1888. Reprint, Farnborough: Gregg, 1971.

Hepokoski, James. "Monumentality and Formal Processes in the First Movement of Brahms's Piano Concerto No. 1 in D Minor, op. 15." In *Expressive Intersections in Brahms: Essays in Analysis and Meaning*, edited by Heather Platt and Peter H. Smith, 217–51. Bloomington: Indiana University Press, 2012.

Hepokoski, James, and Warren Darcy. *Elements of Sonata Theory*. Oxford: Oxford University Press, 2006.

Herlossohn, Carl, ed. *Damen Conversations Lexikon*. 10 vols. Leipzig: Volkmar, 1834–1838.

Herttrich, Ernst. "Preface." *Symphonische Etüden*, by Robert Schumann, edited by Ernst Herttrich. Munich: G. Henle, 2006.

Hibberd, Sarah. "Cherubini and the Revolutionary Sublime." *Cambridge Opera Journal* 24, no. 3 (2012): 293–318.

Hill, Carl. *The Soul of Wit: Joke Theory from Grimm to Freud*. Lincoln: University of Nebraska Press, 1993.

Hirsch, Lily E. "Segregating Sound: Robert Schumann in the Third Reich." In Kok and Tunbridge, *Rethinking Schumann*, 51–66.

Hoeckner, Berthold. "Schumann and Romantic Distance." *Journal of the American Musicological Society* 50, no. 1 (1997): 55–132.

Hoffmann, E. T. A. "Beethoven's Instrumental Music." 1813. In *Source Readings in Music History*, edited by Oliver Strunk, Leo Treitler et al., 1193–1197. New York: Norton, 1998.

Horowitz, Joseph. "Letter from New York: The Transformations of Vladimir Horowitz." *Musical Quarterly* 74, no. 4 (1990): 636–648.

Hunter, Mary. " 'To Play as if from the Soul of the Composer': The Idea of the Performer in Early Romantic Aesthetics." *Journal of the American Musicological Society* 58, no. 2 (2005): 357–398.

Jahn, Otto. *Gesammelte Aufsätze über Musik*. 2nd ed. Leipzig: Breitkopf und Härtel, 1867.

Jander, Owen. "Virtuoso." In *The New Grove Dictionary of Music and Musicians*. 29 vols. 2nd ed. Edited by Stanley Sadie, 26:789–790. New York: Grove, 2001.

Jensen, Gustav. *Die Davidsbündler: Aus Robert Schumann's Sturm-und-Drang Periode*. Leipzig: Breitkopf und Härtel, 1883.

Joachim, Joseph. *Briefe von und an Joseph Joachim*. Edited by Johannes Joachim and Andreas Moser. 3 vols. Berlin: Julius Bard, 1911–1913.

Kabisch, Thomas. "Musik in Salon: Konvention und Nuance." *Musiktheorie* 23, no. 2 (2008): 110–140.

———. "Schein, Sein, Werden: Anmerkungen zur instrumentalen Virtuosität bei Robert Schumann." *Musiktheorie* 21, no. 3 (2006): 195–208.

Kallberg, Jeffrey. *Chopin at the Boundaries: Sex, History, and Musical Genre*. Cambridge, MA: Harvard University Press, 1996.

Kaminsky, Peter. "Aspects of Harmony, Rhythm, and Form in Schumann's *Papillons*, *Carnaval*, and *Davidsbündlertänze*." PhD diss., Eastman School of Music, 1989.

Kant, Immanuel. *Critique of the Power of Judgment*. Edited by Paul Guyer. Translated by Paul Guyer and Eric Matthews. Cambridge: Cambridge University Press, 2000.

Kapp, Reinhard. "Schumann als Violinkomponist." In *Robert Schumann: das Spätwerk für Streicher*, edited by Andreas Meyer, 13–31. Mainz: Schott, 2012.

Kawabata, Mai. *Paganini: The "Demonic" Virtuoso*. Rochester, NY: Boydell, 2013.

Kerman, Joseph. "The Concertos." In *The Cambridge Companion to Schumann*, edited by Beate Perrey, 173–194. Cambridge: Cambridge University Press, 2007.

Kingsbury, Henry. *Music, Talent, and Performance: A Conservatory Cultural System*. Philadelphia: Temple University Press, 1988.

Klassen, Janina. *Clara Schumann: Musik und Öffentlichkeit*. Cologne: Böhlau, 2009.

———. *Clara Wieck-Schumann: Die Virtuosin als Komponistin*. Kassel: Bärenreiter, 1990.

Koch, Juan Martin. *Das Klavierkonzert des 19. Jahrhunderts und die Kategorie des Symphonischen*. Musik und Musikanschauung im 19. Jahrhundert 8. Sinzig: Studio, 2001.

Köhler, Hans Joachim. "Ein Werk I: Zur Genese der *Abegg-Variationen* op. 1 von Robert Schumann." In *Schumanniana Nova: Festschrift Gerd Nauhaus zum 60 Geburtstag*, edited by Bernhard R. Appel, Ute Bär, and Matthias Wendt, 363–386. Sinzig: Studio, 2002.

Kok, Roe-Min, and Laura Tunbridge, eds. *Rethinking Schumann*. Oxford: Oxford University Press, 2011.

Koßmaly, Carl. "On Robert Schumann's Piano Compositions." Translated by Susan Gillespie. In *Schumann and His World*, edited by R. Larry Todd, 303–316. Princeton, NJ: Princeton University Press, 1994.

Kramer, Lawrence. "*Carnaval*, Cross-Dressing, and the Woman in the Mirror." In *Musicology and Difference*, edited by Ruth Solie, 311–323. Berkeley: University of California Press, 1993.

Krebs, Harald. *Fantasy Pieces: Metrical Dissonance in the Music of Robert Schumann.* Oxford: Oxford University Press, 1999.

Kregor, Jonathan. *Liszt as Transcriber.* Cambridge: Cambridge University Press, 2010.

Kroll, Mark. *Johann Nepomuk Hummel: A Musician's Life and World.* Lanham, MD: Scarecrow, 2007.

Kullak, Adolph. *Die Ästhetik des Klavierspiels.* Berlin: J. Guttentag, 1861.

Landis, J. D. *Longing.* New York: Harcourt, 2000.

Le Huray, Peter, and James Day, trans. and ed. *Music and Aesthetics in the Eighteenth and Early-Nineteenth Centuries.* Cambridge: Cambridge University Press, 1981.

Leipzig Gewandhaus Programmsammlung. Robert Schumann Haus, Zwickau.

Leistra-Jones, Karen. "Improvisational Idyll: Joachim's 'Presence' and Brahms's Violin Concerto, op. 77." *19th-Century Music* 38, no. 3 (2015): 243–271.

———. "Staging Authenticity: Brahms, Joachim, and the Politics of *Werktreue* Performance." *Journal of the American Musicological Society* 66, no. 2 (2013): 397–436.

Leppert, Richard. "Cultural Contradiction, Idolatry, and the Piano Virtuoso: Franz Liszt." In *Piano Roles: Three Hundred Years of Life with the Piano,* edited by James Parakilas, 252–281. New Haven, CT: Yale University Press, 1999.

Lester, Joel. "Robert Schumann and Sonata Forms." *19th-Century Music* 18, no. 3 (1995): 189–210.

Libbey, Ted. *The NPR Guide to Building a Classical CD Collection.* 2nd ed. New York: Workman, 1999.

Lindeman, Stephen. *Structural Novelty and Tradition in the Early Romantic Piano Concerto.* Stuyvesant, NY: Pendragon, 1999.

Liszt, Franz. *Franz Liszt: Sämtliche Schriften.* Edited by Detlef Altenburg. Vol. 1, *Frühe Schriften.* Edited by Rainer Kleinertz with collaboration by Serge Gut. Wiesbaden: Brietkopf und Härtel, 2000.

———. "Robert Schumann (1855)." Translated by John Michael Cooper, Christopher Anderson, and R. Larry Todd, in *Robert Schumann and his World,* edited by R. Larry Todd, 338–361. Princeton, NJ: Princeton University Press, 1994.

Litzmann, Berthold. *Clara Schumann: Ein Künstlerleben.* 3 vols. Leipzig: Breitkopf und Härtel, 1920.

Locke, Ralph P. *Musical Exoticism: Images and Reflections.* Cambridge: Cambridge University Press, 2009.

Lossewa, Olga. "Marfa Sabinina und ihre Erinnerungen an Clara und Robert Schumann." In *Schumann Studien* 6, edited by Gerd Nauhaus, 195–224. Sinzig: Studio, 1997.

Loya, Shay. *Liszt's Transcultural Modernism and the Hungarian-Gypsy Tradition.* Rochester, NY: University of Rochester Press, 2011.

Luebbe, Michael J. "Robert Schumann's *Exercice pour le Pianoforte.*" In *Schumanniana Nova: Festschrift Gerd Neuhaus zum 60 Geburtstag,* edited by Bernhard R. Appel, Ute Bär, and Matthias Wendt, 423–448. Sinzig: Studio Verlag, 2002.

Macdonald, Claudia. "Critical Perception and the Woman Composer: The Early Reception of Piano Concertos by Clara Wieck Schumann and Amy Beach." *Current Musicology* 55 (1993): 24–55.

———. "Konzert für Klavier und Orchester by Clara Schumann; Janina Klassen (Review)." *Notes* 48, no. 2 (1991): 674–676.

———. "'Mit einer eignen außerordentlichen Composition': The Genesis of Schumann's Phantasie in A Minor." *Journal of Musicology* 13, no. 2 (1995): 240–259.

———. *Robert Schumann and the Piano Concerto.* New York: Routledge, 2005.

———. "Robert Schumann's F-Major Piano Concerto of 1831 as Reconstructed from his First Sketchbook: A History of Its Composition and Study of Its Musical Background." PhD diss., University of Chicago, 1986.

———. "Schumann's Piano Practice: Technical Mastery and Artistic Ideal." *Journal of Musicology* 19, no. 4 (2002): 527–563.

Macdonald, Hugh. *Music in 1853: The Biography of a Year.* Woodbridge: Boydell, 2012.

MacDonald, Malcolm. *Brahms.* New York: Schirmer, 1990.

Mahling, Christoph-Hellmut. "Das Klavierkonzert op. 54 von Robert Schumann: Eine Antwort auf das Klavierkonzert op. 7 von Clara Wieck?" In *Robert and Clara Schumann und die nationalen Musikkulturen des 19. Jahrhunderts,* Schumann Forschungen 9, edited by Matthias Wendt, 149–152. Mainz: Schott, 2005.

Maintz, Marie Louise. *Franz Schubert in der Rezeption Robert Schumanns.* Kassel: Bärenreiter, 1995.

Marcello, Benedetto. *Il teatro alla moda.* 1720. Translated by Reinhard Pauly. "Il Teatro Alla Moda—Part I." *Musical Quarterly* 34, no. 3 (1948): 371–403. "Il Teatro Alla Moda—Part II." *Musical Quarterly* 35, no. 1 (1949): 85–105.

Marston, Nicholas. *Schumann: Fantasie, Op. 17.* Cambridge: Cambridge University Press, 1992.

———. "Schumann's Heroes: Schubert, Beethoven, Bach." In *The Cambridge Companion to Schumann,* ed. Beate Perrey, 48–61. Cambridge: Cambridge University Press, 2007.

Mathew, Nicholas. "Beethoven's Political Music, the Handelian Sublime, and the Aesthetics of Prostration." *19th-Century Music* 33, no. 2 (2009): 110–150.

McCorkle, Margit. *Robert Schumann: Thematic-Bibliographic Catalogue of the Works.* Munich: Henle, 2003.

Mendelssohn, Felix. *Acht Briefe und ein Facsimile von Felix Mendelssohn Bartholdy.* 2nd ed. Leipzig: Friedrich Wilhelm Grunow, 1871.

———. *Felix Mendelssohn: Briefe.* 1863. Reprint, Potsdam: Berlin-Brandenburg, 1997.

Messing, Scott. *Schubert in the European Imagination.* 2 vols. Rochester, NY: University of Rochester Press, 2006.

Meyer, Leonard B. *Style and Music: Theory, History, and Ideology.* Philadelphia: University of Pennsylvania Press, 1989.

Moser, Andreas, ed. *Johannes Brahms im Briefwechsel mit Joseph Joachim.* 3rd ed. Berlin: Deutsche Brahms-Gesellschaft, 1921.

———. *Joseph Joachim: ein Lebensbild.* Berlin: Behr's, 1898.

Moßburger, Hubert. "Poetische Harmonik." In *Schumann Handbuch,* edited by Ulrich Tadday, 194–211. Stuttgart: Metzler and Kassel, 2006.

Musgrave, Michael. *The Music of Brahms.* London: Routledge and Kegan Paul, 1985.

Naested, Henrik. "How to Bring the Ocean into the Concert Hall: Beethoven's Third Symphony and the Aesthetics of the Sublime." *Danish Yearbook of Musicology* 31 (2003): 17–36.

Newcomb, Anthony. "Once More 'Between Absolute and Program Music': Schumann's Second Symphony." *19th-Century Music* 7, no. 3 (1984): 233–250.

———. "Schumann and the Marketplace: From Butterflies to *Hausmusik.*" In *Nineteenth-Century Piano Music,* ed. R. Larry Todd, 258–315. New York: Schirmer, 1990.

Novalis. *Schriften.* Edited by Richard Samuel, Hans Joachim Mähl, and Gerhard Schulz. Stuttgart: W. Kohlhammer, 1960.

Ortlepp, Ernst. *Beethoven: Eine phantastische Charakteristik.* Leipzig: Hartknoch, 1836.

Palmer, A. Dean. *Heinrich August Marschner, 1795–1861: His Life and Stage Works.* Ann Arbor, MI: UMI Research Press, 1978.

———. "Templer und die Jüdin, Der." In *The New Grove Dictionary of Opera*, edited by Stanley Sadie, 4:686–688. New York: Grove, 1992.

Parakilas, James. "A History of Lessons and Practicing." In *Piano Roles: Three Hundred Years of Life with the Piano*, edited by James Parakilas, 112–124. New Haven, CT: Yale University Press, 1999.

Pederson, Sanna. "Enlightened and Romantic German Music Criticism, 1800–1850." PhD diss., University of Pennsylvania, 1995.

———. "Romantic Music under Siege in 1848." In *Music Theory in the Age of Romanticism*, edited by Ian Bent, 57–76. Cambridge: Cambridge University Press, 1996.

Perrey, Beate. *Schumann's Dichterliebe and Early Romantic Poetics: Fragmentation of Desire*. Cambridge: Cambridge University Press, 2002.

Pettler, Pamela Susskind. "Clara Schumann's Recitals, 1832–50." *19th-Century Music* 4, no. 1 (1980): 70–76.

Plantinga, Leon. *Beethoven's Concertos: History, Style, Performance*. New York: Norton, 1999.

———. *Schumann as Critic*. New Haven, CT: Yale University Press, 1967.

Porter, Cecilia Hopkins. "The New Public and the Reordering of the Musical Establishment: The Lower Rhine Music Festivals, 1818–67." *19th-Century Music* 3, no. 3 (1980): 211–224.

Rayman, Joshua. *Kant on Sublimity and Morality*. Cardiff: University of Wales Press, 2012.

Rehding, Alexander. *Music and Monumentality: Commemoration and Wonderment in Nineteenth-Century Germany*. Oxford: Oxford University Press, 2009.

Reich, Nancy. *Clara Schumann: The Artist and the Woman*. Rev. ed. Ithaca, NY: Cornell University Press, 2001.

Reiman, Erika. *Schumann's Piano Cycles and the Novels of Jean Paul*. Rochester, NY: University of Rochester Press, 2004.

Reynolds, Christopher Alan. *Motives for Allusion: Context and Content in Nineteenth-Century Music*. Cambridge, MA: Harvard University Press, 2003.

Richter, Jean Paul Friedrich. *Horn of Oberon: Jean Paul Richter's School for Aesthetics*. Translated by Margaret R. Hale. Detroit, MI: Wayne State University Press, 1973.

Rink, John. *Chopin: The Piano Concertos*. Cambridge: Cambridge University Press, 1997.

———. "Opposition and Integration in the Piano Music." In *The Cambridge Companion to Brahms*, edited by Michael Musgrave, 79–97. Cambridge: Cambridge University Press, 1999.

———. "Tonal Architecture in the Early Music." In *The Cambridge Companion to Chopin*, edited by Jim Samson, 78–97. Cambridge: Cambridge University Press, 1992.

Roesner, Linda Correll. "The Autograph of Schumann's Piano Sonata in F Minor, Opus 14." *Musical Quarterly* 61, no. 1 (1975): 98–130.

———. "Schumann's 'Parallel' Forms." *19th-Century Music* 14, no. 3 (1991): 265–278

Ronyak, Jennifer. "Performing the Lied, Performing the Self: Singing Subjectivity in Germany, 1790–1832." PhD diss., Eastman School of Music, 2010.

———. "'Serious Play,' Performance, and the Lied: The Stägemann *Schöne Müllerin* Revisited." *19th-Century Music* 34, no. 2 (2010): 141–167

Rosen, Charles. *The Classical Style*. Exp. ed. New York: Norton, 1997.

———. *The Romantic Generation*. Cambridge, MA: Harvard University Press, 1995.

Samson, Jim. *Chopin*. Oxford: Oxford University Press, 1996.

———. "The Practice of Early-Nineteenth-Century Pianism." In Talbot, *The Musical Work*, 110–127.

———. *Virtuosity and the Musical Work: The* Transcendental Studies *of Liszt.* Cambridge: Cambridge University Press, 2003.

Schiller, Friedrich. *Naïve and Sentimental Poetry and On the Sublime.* Translated by Julias Elias. New York: Frederick Ungar, 1966.

Schilling, Gustav, ed. *Encyclopädie der gesammten musikalischen Wissenschaften oder Universal-Lexicon der Tonkunst.* 7 vols. Stuttgart: Köhler, 1835–1842.

Schlegel, August Wilhelm. *Kritische Schriften und Briefe.* Edited by Edgar Lohner. Stuttgart: W. Kohlhammer, 1964.

Schlegel, Friedrich. "Introduction to the *Transcendental Philosophy* (1800)." In *Theory as Practice: A Critical Anthology of Early German Romantic Writings,* edited by Jochen Schulte-Sasse et al., 244–267. Minneapolis: University of Minnesota Press, 1997.

———. *Kritische Friedrich-Schlegel-Ausgabe.* Edited by Hans Eichner. Munich: Ferdinand Schöningh, 1967.

Schnapper, Laure. *Henri Herz, magnat du piano.* Paris: École des hautes études en sciences sociales, 2011.

———. "Piano Variations in the First Half of the Nineteenth Century: An Industry?" Translated by Vivienne Hunt. In *Instrumental Music and the Industrial Revolution,* edited by Roberto Illiano and Luca Sala, 279–294. Lucca: Centro Studi Opera Omnia Luigi Boccherini-Onlus, 2010.

Scholz, Ute. "Schumanns Ausschnittsammlung *Zeitungsstimmen.*" In *"Eine neue poetische": 175 Jahre Neue Zeitschrift für Musik,* Schumann Forschungen 14, edited by Michael Beiche and Armin Koch, 145–186. Mainz: Schott, 2013.

Schumann, Clara. *Clara Schumann Programmsammlung.* Robert Schumann Haus. Zwickau.

Schumann, Clara, and Robert Schumann. *Clara und Robert Schumann Briefwechsel: Kritische gesamtausgabe.* 3 vols. Edited by Eva Weissweiler. Basel/Frankfurt: Stroemfeld/Roter Stern, 1984–2001.

Schumann, Robert. *Briefe und Notizen Robert und Clara Schumanns.* Edited by Siegfried Kross. 2nd ed. Bonn: Bouvier, 1982.

———. *Dichtergarten für Musik: Eine Anthologie für Freunde der Literatur und Musik.* Edited by Gerd Nauhaus and Ingrid Bodsch. Frankfurt: StadtMuseum Bonn und Stroemfeld, 2007.

———. "Ein Opus II: Entwurf zu Chopin Aufsatz." Zwi 17, 4871,V,2-A3. Robert Schumann Haus, Zwickau.

———. *Fantaisies et finale sur un thème de Mr. le Baron de Fricken.* Morlanwelz-Mariemont, Belgien, Bibliothèque du Musée Royale de Mariemont, 1132-c.

———. *Gesammelte Schriften über Musik und Musiker.* 1854. 5th ed. Edited by Martin Kreisig. Leipzig: Breitkopf und Härtel, 1914.

———. *Jugendbriefe von Robert Schumann.* Edited by Clara Schumann. 2nd ed. Leipzig: Breitkopf und Härtel, 1889.

———. *Mottosammlung: Übertragung, Kommentar, Einführung.* Edited by Leander Hotaki. Freiburg: Rombach, 1998.

———. Odeon: Chopin." Zwi 17, 4871,V,1-A3. Robert Schumann Haus, Zwickau.

———. *Piano Concerto in A Minor, Opus 54: Facsimile Reproduction of the Autograph Score.* Edited by Heinrich-Heine-Institut, Joseph A. Kruse, Akio Mayeda, and Bernhard R. Appel. Kassel: Bärenreiter, 1996.

———. *Robert Schumann's Briefe: Neue Folge.* Edited by Gustav Jansen. 2nd ed. Leipzig: Breitkopf und Härtel, 1904.

———. *Schumann Briefedition.* Edited by the Robert-Schumann-Haus, Zwickau, the Institut für Musikwissenschaft der Hochschule für Musik Carl Maria von Weber, Dresden, and the Robert-Schumann-Forschungsstelle, Düsseldorf, editorial direction by Thomas Synofzik and Michael Heinemann. Cologne: Dohr, 2008–.

———. *Tagebücher.* 3 vols. Edited by Georg Eismann and Gerd Nauhaus. Leipzig: VEB, 1971–1987.

———. *Variationen über ein Thema von Schubert.* Edited by Andreas Boyde. Leipzig: Hofmeister, 2000.

Shaw, Philip. *The Sublime.* New York: Routledge, 2006.

Siebert, Peter. *Der literarische Salon: Literatur und Geselligkeit zwischen Aufklärung und Vormärz.* Stuttgart: J. B. Metzler, 1993.

Seibold, Wolfgang. *Robert und Clara Schumann in ihren Beziehungen zu Franz Liszt.* 2 vols. Frankfurt: Peter Lang, 2005.

Sipe, Thomas. "Interpreting Beethoven: History, Aesthetics, and Critical Reception." PhD diss., University of Pennsylvania, 1992.

Sisman, Elaine. "Learned Style and the Rhetoric of the Sublime in the 'Jupiter' Symphony." In *Wolfgang Amadè Mozart: Essays on his Life and His Music,* edited by Stanley Sadie, 213–240. Oxford: Clarendon, 1996.

Smart, Mary Ann. "Parlor Games: Italian Music and Italian Politics in the Parisian Salon." *19th-Century Music* 34, no. 1 (2010): 39–60.

Spaethling, Robert, trans. and ed. *Mozart's Letters, Mozart's Life: Selected Letters.* New York: Norton, 2000.

Struck, Michael. *Die umstrittenen späten Instrumentalwerke Schumanns.* Hamburg: Karl Dieter Wagner, 1984.

———. "'Gewichtsverlagerungen': Robert Schumanns letzte Konzertkompositionen." In *Schumanns Werke: Text und Interpretation,* edited by Akio Mayeda and Klaus Wolfgang Niemöller, 43–52. Mainz: Schott, 1987.

Sumner Lott, Marie. "At the Intersection of Public and Private Musical Life: Brahms's Op. 51 String Quartets." *Journal of the Royal Musical Association* 137, no. 2 (2012): 243–305.

Suttoni, Charles. "Piano and Opera: A Study of the Piano Fantasies Written on Opera Tunes in the Romantic Era." PhD diss., New York University, 1973.

Synofzik, Thomas. "Ein Rückert-Kanon als Keimzelle zu Schumanns Klavierkonzert Op. 54." *Die Musikforschung* 58, no. 1 (2005): 28–32.

———. "'Eine Apotheose Mozarts' Ein unbekannter Entwurf zu Robert Schumanns Erstlingsrezension über Chopins Opus II." In *Correspondenz: Mitteilungen der Robert-Schumann-Gesellschaft E.V. Düsseldorf,* edited by Irmgard Knechtges-Obrecht (24–52). Aachen: Shaker, 2016.

Talbot, Michael, ed. *The Musical Work: Reality or Invention?* Liverpool: Liverpool University Press, 2000.

Taruskin, Richard. *The Oxford History of Western Music.* 5 vols. New York: Oxford University Press, 2005.

Thym, Jürgen. "Schumann in Brendel's *Neue Zeitschrift für Musik* from 1845 to 1856." In *Mendelssohn and Schumann: Essays on Their Music and Its Context,* edited by R. Larry Todd and Jon Finson, 21–36. Durham, NC: Duke University Press, 1984.

Todd, R. Larry. *Mendelssohn: A Life in Music.* New York: Oxford University Press, 2003.

———. "Mendelssohn's *Lieder ohne Worte* and the Limits of Musical Expression." In *Mendelssohn Perspectives*, edited by Nicole Grimes and Angela R. Mace, 197–214. Farnham: Ashgate, 2012.

———. "On Quotation in Schumann's Music." In *Schumann and His World*, ed. R. Larry Todd, 80–112. Princeton, NJ: Princeton University Press, 1994.

———. "Piano Music Reformed: The Case of Felix Mendelssohn Bartholdy." In *Nineteenth-Century Piano Music*, edited by R. Larry Todd, 178–220. 2nd ed. New York: Routledge, 2004.

Tovey, Donald Francis. *Essays in Musical Analysis*. Reprint edition. London: Oxford University Press, 1969.

Trippett, David. "Après une Lecture de Liszt: Virtuosity and Werktreue in the 'Dante' Sonata." *19th-Century Music* 32, no. 1 (2008): 52–93.

Tunbridge, Laura. *Schumann's Late Style*. Cambridge: Cambridge University Press, 2007.

Warburton, Thomas. "Some Performance Alternatives for Schumann's Opus 13." *Journal of the American Liszt Society* 31 (1992): 38–46.

Wasielewski, Wilhelm Joseph von. *Robert Schumann: Eine Biographie*. Dresden: Rudolph Kunze, 1858.

Watkins, Holly. *Metaphors of Depth in German Musical Thought*. Cambridge: Cambridge University Press, 2011.

Weber, William. *The Great Transformation of Musical Taste*. Cambridge: Cambridge University Press, 2008.

———. *Music and the Middle Class*. 2nd ed. Aldershot: Ashgate, 2004.

Webster, James. "The *Creation*, Haydn's Late Vocal Music, and the Musical Sublime." In *Haydn and his World*, edited by Elaine Sisman, 57–102. Princeton, NJ: Princeton University Press, 1997.

Wehner, Ralf. "Felix Mendelssohn Bartholdys Verhältnis zum musikalischen Salon seiner Zeit." In *Die Musikveranstaltung bei den Mendelssohns: Ein "musikalischer Salon?" Die Referate des Symposions am 2. September 2006 in Leipzig*, edited by Hans-Günter Klein, 61–70. Leipzig: Mendelssohn-Haus, 2006.

Wenzel, Silke. "Sophie von Baudissin." In *Musikvermittlung und Genderforschung: Musikerinnen-Lexikon und multimediale Präsentationen*, edited by Beatrix Borchard and administered by the Hochschule für Musik und Theater Hamburg. Accessed October 19, 2013. http://mugi.hfmt-hamburg.de.

Wieck, Friedrich. *Clavier und Gesang: Didaktisches und Polemisches* Leipzig: F. Whistling, 1853.

———. *Friedrich Wieck Briefe aus den Jahren 1830–1838*. Edited by Käthe Walch-Schumann. Cologne: Arno Volk, 1968.

———. *Piano and Song*. Translated by Henry Pleasants. Stuyvesant, NY: Pendragon, 1988.

Williamson, George S. *The Longing for Myth in Germany: Religion and Aesthetic Culture from Romanticism to Nietzsche*. Chicago: University of Chicago Press, 2004.

Wood, Gillen d'Arcy. *Romanticism and Music Culture in Britain, 1770–1840: Virtue and Virtuosity*. Cambridge: Cambridge University Press, 2010.

Worthen, John. *Robert Schumann: Life and Death of a Musician*. New Haven, CT: Yale University Press, 2007.

Wurst, Karin. *Fabricating Pleasure: Fashion, Entertainment, and Cultural Consumption in Germany, 1780–1830*. Detroit, MI: Wayne State University Press, 2005.

Wurth, Kiene Brillenburg. *Musically Sublime: Indeterminacy, Infinity, Irresolvability*. New York: Fordham University Press, 2009.

Index

Brahms, Johannes, works: Double Concerto Op. 102, 235, 236; Piano Concerto No. 1, Op. 15, 53, 153–154; Piano Quartet No. 1, Op. 25, 236; Piano Quartet No. 2, Op. 26, 235; Piano Sonata No. 1, Op. 1, 220; Symphony No. 1, 242; *Variations and Fugue on a Theme by Handel,* Op. 24, 242, 273n9, 274n10; Violin Concerto, 272n107

Brendel, Franz, 171, 188, 192–193, 237

"brilliant" style, 17–18, 20–21, 24–27, 30–31. *See also* Chopin, Frédéric; Czerny, Carl; Herz, Henri; postclassical virtuosity; Thalberg, Sigismond; variation sets

Bronsart, Ingeborg von, 243

Brown, Julie Hedges, 171, 176, 207, 228–229, 269n46

Broyles, Michael, 153

Bülow, Hans von, 235–236, 238

Buniatishvili, Khatia, 244

Burke, Edmund, 124, 129

Burkholder, J. Peter, 259n97

canon formation, 11–13, 53, 156, 195, 237–238; centrality in concert life, 221; Germanocentricity of, 199–200; Lower Rhine Music Festival, 204. *See also* Krüger, Eduard; neo-Baroque virtuosity; work concept

Carafa, Michele, 31

Carus, Agnes and Ernst August, 91, 100

Carus, Karl Erdmann, 91

Carus' salon, 91, 118. *See also* salon culture

Castelli, Ignaz, 58

chiaroscuro, 78, 79

Chopin, Frédéric, 20, 76, 82, 105; comment about "Ein Opus II," 68; and effect on Liszt, 167; and the "poetic," 39; postclassical virtuosity, 20. *See also* "brilliant" style; postclassical virtuosity

Chopin, Frédéric, works: Etude, Op. 25, no. 1 ("Aeolian Harp"), 57; Etudes, Opus 10, 79, *80, 81; Grand duo concertant sur des thèmes de "Robert le Diable,"* 88–89; nocturnes, 45; *Variations brillantes sur le rondeau favori de "Ludovic,"* Op. 12, 40–41; *Variations sur "Là ci darem la mano,"* Op. 2, 52, 58–63, *62–67,* 84–85, 100, 254n45 (*See also* "Ein Opus II"; the poetic)

chorales, 220, 243

Clewis, Robert R., 128, 260n11

codas, use of in symphonic tradition, 192. *See also* apotheosis codas; concertos

commodification of music, 13, 23–24. *See also* cultural consumption

Concert Allegro (Schumann). *See* Introduction and Concert Allegro Op. 134

concertos: culminating displays in, 37, 250–251n45; pleasurable qualities, 36–37; signal for cadenzas, 271n99; structural integration of, 174–175, 266n52. *See also* codas, use of in symphonic tradition; specific concertos

Concert sans orchestre, Op. 14 (Schumann), 134–145, *135, 138–141,* 263n99; borrowed theme in, 175; cadenza, 124, 125, *125,* 126; as a concerto, 142; dedication to Moscheles, 142–143; formal structure, 134, 136, *137,* 261n49; Liszt's review of, 144, 145; Moscheles's review of, 143–145, 262n67; reworking of, 173; virtuosic catastrophes in, 136, 138–142

Cooper, Ruskin King, 151

Cortot, Alfred, 240, 273n2

critiques of pleasure, 11, 22–24; cultural meanings in, 43–47; and rhetoric of luxury, aristocracy, and femininity, 37–43. *See also* Fink, Gottfried Wilhelm; the poetic; postclassical virtuosity

culminating displays, 34, 37, 250–251n45; Clara Schumann's piano concerto, 182, *183–185,* 266n56; description of, 37, 217, 250–251n45; in Kalkbrenner's Piano Concerto No. 4, Op. 127, 41, *42–43;* in Schumann's Introduction and Allegro Appasionato Op. 92, 207–210, 212; in Schumann's Introduction and Concert Allegro, 217, 218; in Schumann's piano concertos, 82–84, *83–84,* 182, 185–186, 189, 255n95; in Schumann's violin compositions, 227, 228, 231–235, 240–241. *See also* apotheosis codas; textures

cultural consumption, 28, 56; within culture of serious music, 197. *See also* commodification of music; pleasure

cultural nationalism. *See* German nationalism

cultural significance of the arts, 45, 46

culture of serious music, 3, 13–14, 52, 197. *See also* salon culture; virtuosity discourse; work concept

Czerny, Carl: career of, 25; comment in Voigt's diary, 108; on improvisation, 178; postclassical virtuosity, 20; Schumann critique of, 26; students of, 23; treatises on compositional and improvisational techniques, 29–30, 31, 34–37, 94, 178; as writer, 22–23; writings of, 94. *See also* "brilliant" style; improvisation and spontaneity; postclassical virtuosity

Czerny, Carl, works: Fink's analysis of fantasies, 27–28; Toccata Op. 92, 25

French Revolution, 129
Fricken, Baron Ignaz Freiherr von, 111, 122
Fricken, Ernestine von, 4, 105, 111, 116
Fricken, Madame le Baronne de, 111
Fries, Jakob, 44

Gade, Niels, 196
Garratt, James, 204
Gay, Peter, 56, 57
Geibel, Emanuel, 228, 231
gender and poetic interiority, 75–76
gender stereotypes, 44–45, 75–76, 88, 133–134, 201. *See also* women
Gensel, Julius, 104–105, 106
German nationalism, 11–12, 122, 156, 204–205; and music criticism, 44, 45. *See also* Lower Rhine Music Festival; the middle class; New German School
Gesammelte Schriften (Schumann), 54, 69, 72, 73, 197, 254n61. *See also* "Ein Opus II" (Schumann)
Gewandhaus. *See* Leipzig Gewandhaus
Gingerich, John, 211
Goertzen, Valerie Woodring, 76
Goethe, Johann Wolfgang von, 45, 55–56, 252n13
Gooley, Dana, 87, 101, 132, 151; "Battle against Instrumental Virtuosity," 7; on Liszt, 6, 131; on Paganini, 162
Gramit, David, 13, 46
Grillparzer, Franz, 75

hallgató style, 229, *229–230,* 231, 235. *See also* *style hongrois*
Hamelin, Marc-André, 244
Hamilton, Kenneth, 203
Hansen, Matthias, 93, 248n15
Hans Heiling (Marschner), 118, 121
Hanslick, Eduard, 49; "Age of Virtuosity," 2; on Brahm's Piano Concerto No. 1, Op. 15, 153–154; on *Der Templer* (Marschner), 121; on Schumann's Piano Concerto, Op. 54, 188, 193, 194; on the sublime, 153–154; "true priests of art," 195, 241; Vienna's "Artistic Renaissance," 239; on virtuosos, 53
Haslinger, Tobias, 60, 142, 262n52
Hausmann, Friedrich Christoph, 238
Heine, Heinrich, 41
Heller, Stephen, 196
Henselt, Adolph, 76, 89, 105; comment in Voigt's diary, 108; Kaskel review of, 90–91; and poetic interiority, 76
Henselt, Adolph, works: Andante and Allegro, Op. 3, 90; Etudes, Op. 2, 89, 90; Piano Concerto Op. 16, 205

Hepokoski, James, 153, 251n45, 261n49
Herder, Johann Gottfried von, 124, 128
Herlossohn, Carl, 77
the heroic, 125, 127, 132, 133. *See also* Beethoven, Ludwig van; Liszt, Franz; Toccata, Op. 7
Herttrich, Ernst, 111
Herz, Henri, 25, 122; Schumann critique of, 26. *See also* "brilliant" style; postclassical virtuosity
Herz, Henri, works: Concerto No. 1 in A Major, Op. 34, 26, 82; Piano Concerto No. 2, Op. 74, 27; *Variations de bravoure sur la romance de "Joseph,"* Op. 20, 75; variation sets, 20, 30–31; *Variations sur la cavatine favorite d "la Violette" de Carafa,* Op. 48, 25, 31–34, *32–33,* 59, 75
Hibberd, Sara, 129
Hill, Carl, 99, 100
Hiller, Ferdinand, 78, 204; Etudes, Op. 15, 45, 52, 77–80, *80–81. See also* the poetic
Hirschbach, Herrmann, 159, 239; "Antiphilistroses," 168–169; Krüger–Hirschbach debate, 168–170
historicism, 195–196, 220, 268n4. *See also* Netherlands tour
Hoeckner, Berthold, 103, 104
Hoffmann, E. T. A., 13, 56, 68, 106; essay on Beethoven's Fifth Symphony, 127, 128, 129–130, 260n10, 262n71; on the sublime, 128, 129. *See also* Beethoven, Ludwig van
Horowitz, Joseph, 245
Horowitz, Vladimir, 245
Hummel, Johann Nepomuk, 25; Schumann critique of, 26; on Schumann's *Papillons,* 170. *See also* postclassical virtuosity
Hummel, Johann Nepomuk, works: Etudes, Op. 125, 24–25; "Oberons Zauberhorn" Fantasy, Op. 116, 178; Piano Concerto No. 2 in A Minor, Op. 85, 17–18, *17, 18,* 20, 37, 251n47
"Hungarian-Gypsy Style." *See* *style hongrois*
Hünten, Franz, 20
Hunter, Mary, 157

ideal listener, 90–91. *See also* audiences, critiques of
ideal musical work, 159
Il teatro alla moda (Marcello), 13
improvisation and spontaneity, 30; and Schumann's style of improvisation, 91–92. *See also* Czerny, Carl; Schumann, Clara Wieck
L'incendio de Babilonia, 94
interiority. *See* the poetic
Introduction and Allegro Appassionato Op. 92 (Schumann), 196, 206–214; critiques of, 207,

290 *Index*

214; form and structure, 207, *208–210,*
212–214, *212–213;* influence of Schubert,
207, 210–211, 214
Introduction and Concert Allegro Op. 134
(Schumann), 9, *10,* 196, 214–215, 217–221,
219, 237
Iris im Gebiete der Tonkunst, 28, 61

Jahn, Otto, 204
Jean Paul, 4, 55, 68, 106, 252n13; and distance,
104; metaphor and Schumann's concept of
interiority, 55; on the sublime, 124, 128, 150;
and *Witz,* 98, 99, 100. *See also* the sublime;
Witz
Jensen, Gustav, 92
Joachim, Joseph, 53, 195; as authoritative
interpreter of canonic repertoire, 221;
compared to Liszt, 241; as paragon of
Werktreue, 221; as performer, 226–227,
272n107; and Schumann's Phantasie Op. 131,
221–223, 228, 231, 235–237, 236, 237; and
Schumann's Violin Concerto, 221–223, 226,
227–228, 236, 239, 271n92; and *style
hongrois,* 235–236; "true priest of art,"
195–197. *See also* Lower Rhine Music
Festival; virtuosos
Joachim, Joseph, works: Variations on an
Original Theme, Op. 10, 235; Violin
Concerto No. 2 in D Minor, Op. 11, 235, 237
Journal des Luxus und der Mode, 28–29, 56

Kabisch, Thomas, 99, 248n15
Kahlert, August, 171; "Das Concertwesen der
Gegenwart," 14
Kalkbrenner, Frédéric, 25, 251n49; and
postclassical virtuosity, 20; Schumann's
critique of, 133. *See also* postclassical
virtuosity
Kalkbrenner, Frédéric, works: Concerto No. 1,
Op. 61, 25; Piano Concerto No. 4, Op. 127,
41–43, *42–43;* Rondo "Le crainte et
l'espérance," Op. 131, 31, 36; *Variations
brillantes sur une mazourka de Chopin,*
Op. 120, 27, 146; *Variations sur un thème de
"La Straniera,"* Op. 123, 37–39
Kallberg, Jeffrey, 88
Kant, Immanuel, 124, 128, 129
"Kapellmeister Kreisler's Musical Sufferings"
(Hoffmann), 56
Kapp, Reinhard, 223
Kaskel, Sophie, 90–91, 256n15
Kerman, Joseph, 270n79, 272n111, 272n120
Khnopff, Fernand, 6
Kingsbury, Henry, 245

Kirchner, Theodor, 196
Klassen, Janina, 73, 177
Knorr, Julius, 60, 92, 253n33
Koch, Juan Martin, 174
Köhler, Hans Joachim, 93
Koßmaly, Carl, 7, 121, 122, 170–171
Krebs, Harald, 134, 161, 264n2 (chap5), 264n7
(chap5)
Kregor, Jonathan, 145–146
Krüger, Eduard, 87, 159; on the ideal performer,
53; "Ueber Virtuosenunfug," 14–15, 87, 168.
See also canon formation
Krüger-Hirschbach debate, 168–170
Kullak, Adolph, 25
"Kunst und Handwerk" (Goethe), 45

Landis, J. D., 6–7
Lapiński, Karol, 105
Leipzig Gewandhaus: Bazzini concert, 1–2;
Clara Schumann's collaboration with, 174,
186; conductors of, 78, 88; Joachim's
collaboration with, 222, 236; performance of
Beethoven's Fifth Symphony, 128; Schubert's
Ninth Symphony, 210; Schumanns'
Morgenunterhaltung, 171, 220; season of
1836–1837, 155; Voigt's participation with,
105–106
Leistra-Jones, Karen, 226, 272n107
Leppert, Richard, 131
Lester, Joel, 149
Lindeman, Stephen, 174, 247–248n9, 266n52
Liszt, Franz, 53, 154; efforts to build audiences
in Germany, 133; embodiment of the sublime,
125; essay on Clara Schumann, 5, 202–204,
268n22; his version of Weber's *Konzertstück,*
132; and Joseph Joachim, 237; Leipzig and
Dresden concerts, 125, 131–133, 154, 260n33;
"Lisztomania," 2; Liszt–Thalberg rivalry,
43–44, 145; d'Ortigue's biography, 166; as
performer, 74, 131, 154; piano concertos,
266n52; postclassical virtuosity, 20; on Roma,
272n119; on Schumann's *Concert sans
orchestre,* Op. 14, 142, 144, 145; shift from
performer to *Kapellmeister,* 157; Weimar
aesthetic, 157, 167, 202–203. *See also* the heroic;
Schumann, Robert, writings of; the sublime
Liszt, Franz, works: Beethoven symphony
transcriptions, 145–146; "Dante" Sonata, 157;
Étude en douze exercices, 21, 157, 166; *Études
d'exécution transcendante,* 157, 167; *Grandes
études,* 21, 131–132, 157, 166–167, 265n20
(*See also* work concept); Hungarian Rhapsody
No. 15, 235; *Réminiscences de "Norma,"*
250n43; *Variations on a Motive by Bach,* 243

Sabinina, Marfa, 203

salon culture, 20, 86, 122–123; aristocratic salons, 37–38, 43–44, 46; ciphers and *Witz*, 99–100; double image of salon music, 88–89, 256n5; and musical games, 93–94; Schumann's idealized salon, 88–89. *See also* "Abegg" Variations; Carus' salon; *Fantaisies et finale* (Schumann); the poetic; Voigt, Henriette; Witz (musical wit)

Samson, Jim: on Chopin, 18, 20, 59; on Liszt, 157, 167; postclassical music, 18, 20, 23, 24; virtuosity and work concept, 24, 159

Sayn-Wittgenstein, Princess Carolyne von, 268n22

Schiller, Friedrich, 124, 129–130, 151

Schilling, Gustav, 47; encyclopedia entry on Clara Wieck, 74, 75–76, 178; encyclopedia entry on Ernestine von Fricken, 116; encyclopedia entry on Thalberg, 49–50; on the sublime, 129; "Virtuos" (1838), 14, 47

Schladebach, Julius, 192

Schlegel, Friedrich, 98, 99, 100, 128, 129

Schlegel brothers, 252n13

Schnapper, Laure, 23

School of Practical Composition (Czerny), 30, 31

Schubert, Franz, works: *Divertissement à la hongroise*, 105, 228, 243; *Die schöne Müllerin*, 94; Symphony No. 9, 56, 207, 210–211, 214; waltzes, 68, 91, 109; "Wanderer" Fantasy, 178. *See also* Schumann, Robert, musical works: *Variationen über den "Sehnsuchtwalzer" von Franz Schubert*

Schumann, Clara Wieck, 4, 53; collaboration with Robert Schumann, 195–196, 198, 200–206, 269n46; concert programming, 59, 68, 76–77, 89, 198–201, 268n11, 268n17; as editor of Robert Schumann's works, 238; as the epitome of poetic performance, 73–77; on Liszt, 241–242; Liszt's essay on, 5, 202–204, 268n22; Lower Rhine Music Festival, 204–206; Netherlands tour (1853), 214–221; performance of Chopin's Variations, Op. 2, 60, 61, 68; Piano Concerto Op. 7 (*See* Piano Concerto Op. 7); the poetic in performance, 52; "team" programs, 200, 206–207; "true priest of art," 195–197, 198–206, 217; works of, 77, 118, 175, 176. *See also* improvisation and spontaneity; virtuosos

Schumann, Robert: change in compositional style, 160, 170–174, 177, 198, 201, 205, 265n45; collaboration with Clara and Joachim, 195–196, 198, 200–206, 269n46 (*See also* Introduction and Allegro Appassionato

Op. 92; Netherlands tour); in Düsseldorf, 197; fictional characters, 26 (*See also* Eusebius; Florestan; Raro); friendship with Henriette Voigt, 104–110; hand injury, 6–7; illness and his late works, 196, 197–198, 237, 268n7; inclusion in the canon, 237–238; Lower Rhine Music Festival, 204–206; *Morgenunterhaltung*, 171, 199–200, 220; musical career, 4–5; Netherlands tour (1853), 214–221; as pedagogue, 4, 78; as performer, 17, 25–26, 72–73, 82, 92; personal experience with Thalberg, 49; relationship with Fink, 52 (*See also Zeitung–Zeitschrift* rivalry); Schumann's idiosyncratic piano textures, 82–84, 92, 93, 101–104, 124; 1830s career change, 151; and *style hongrois*, 228–229; teachers, 4, 59, 82; and the virtuosity discourse, 5–7. *See also* "brilliant" style; culminating displays; textures

Schumann, Robert, musical works: *Ballscenen*, Op. 109, 228; *Carnaval*, Op. 9, 91, 98, 109, 111, 123, 161, 238, 248n18; Cello Concerto Op. 129, 240–241, 273n6; *Clavier Sonaten für die Jugend*, Op. 118, 228; *Concert sans orchestre*, Op. 14 (*See Concert sans orchestre*); *Davidsbündlertänze*, Op. 6, 92, 100, 108, 173; *Etüden in Form freier Variationen über ein Beethovensches Thema*, 147; *Études d'après les Caprices de Paganini*, Op. 3 (*See* Paganini transcriptions); *Études de concert d'après des caprices de Paganini*, Op. 10 (*See* Paganini transcriptions); *Études en forme des variations* (*See Études symphoniques*, Op. 13); *Études symphoniques*, Op. 13 (*See Études symphoniques*, Op. 13); *Exercice*, 151; Fantaisie, Op. 17, 103, 105, 118, 121, 147, 248n18; *Fantaisies et finale* (*See Fantaisies et finale*); *Fantasiestücke*, Op. 12, 56–57, 103, 105, 108; *Fest-Overture über das Rheinweinlied*, Op. 123, 204; Grand Sonata No. 3 (*See Concert sans orchestre*); Impromptus, 147, 175; Introduction and Allegro Appassionato Op. 92 (*See* Introduction and Allegro Appassionato Op. 92); Introduction and Concert Allegro Op. 134 (*See* Introduction and Concert Allegro); Konzertstück, Op. 86, 248n18; *Kreisleriana*, Op. 16, 56; *Liebesfrühling*, Op. 37 (with Clara Wieck Schumann), 176; *Lieder für die Jugend*, 228; *Nachtstücke*, Op. 23, 54; *Novelletten* Op. 21, 98; *Papillons*, Op. 2, 26, 91, 98, 103–104, 106, 170; *Phantasie*, 174, 178, 182; Phantasie Op. 131 (*See* Phantasie Op. 131); Piano Concerto in

F Major (unfinished), 26, 80–85, *83–84*, 91, 255n95; Piano Concerto Op. 54 (*See* Piano Concerto Op. 54); Piano Quartet Op. 47, 171, 176, 269n46; Piano Quintet Op. 44, 171, 200, 201, 229, 235; *VIII Polonaises,* 91; sonatas, 103, 106, 109, 134, 172, 175, 176; symphonies, 147, 171, 176, 178, 210; *Thème sur le nom "Abegg" varié,* Op. 1 (*See* "Abegg" Variations); Toccata, Op. 7 (*See* Toccata, Op. 7); *Variationen über den "Sehnsuchtwalzer" von Franz Schubert,* 109, *110* (*See also* Schubert, Franz); Violin Concerto (*See* Violin Concerto (Schumann))

Schumann, Robert, writings of: Bazzini review, 1–2, 3; on Beethoven, 128, 129, 130, 147, 263n83 (*See also* Beethoven, Ludwig van); on Brahms, 195–196, 237; on Clara Wieck's performances, 73–74, 75, 77; diary entries on new compositional style, 172–173; *Die Davidsbündler* articles (Schumann), 28, 70; "Erinnerungen an eine Freundin," 104, 106; fictional characters, 12 (*See also* Eusebius; Florestan; Raro); *Gesammelte Schriften,* 54, 58, 69, 72, 73, 249n8 (chap1), 254n61, 255n89; on Heinrich Marschner, 118, 121; Leipzig Parnassus review, 155–156, 194, 197; letter to Richard Pohl, 171–172; on Liszt, 147, 160, 260n33; on Liszt's *Grand études,* 160, 166–167; manifesto systematizing the poetic, 77–80; *Mottosammlung,* 45, 55, 252n13; "New Poetic Future," 239; New Year's address (1835), 54, 55, 77, 252n5; Novellettes, 269n46; "Odeon" essay, 70; on Paganini (*See* Paganini transcriptions); promotion of Liszt, 131–134 (*See also* the sublime); review of Hiller's etudes, 77–80; review of *Poesies musicales* (Müller), 88; sketch for *Die Wunderkinder,* 161. *See also* "Ein Opus II"; Liszt, Franz; *Neue Zeitschrift für Musik;* specific composer's names

the Schumannian poetic. *See* the poetic

Schuncke, Charles, 40

Schuncke, Ludwig: Schumann's friendship with, 104, 105; Schumann's Toccata, 126, 146; as virtuoso, 146–147, 161. *See also* virtuosos

Schuncke, Ludwig, works, 4, 20; Allegro Passionato Op. 6, 150–151; Caprice No. 2, Op. 10, 151, 263n94; Sonata Op. 3, 151; *Variations concertantes,* Op. 14, 109

Sechter, Simon, 34

Seibold, Wolfgang, 131, 260–261n33, 265n20

Seyfried, Ignaz von, 124, 134, 136, 142, 261n47

Shaw, Philip, 128

sheet-music market, 20

Siebert, Peter, 99, 100

Signale für die musikalische Welt: on Beethoven, 204; on Clara's performances, 205, 206–207, 217; on Joachim's performances, 228; on Lower Rhine Festival performances, 204, 205, 206; on Schumann's Cello Concerto, 240; on Schumann's Introduction and Concert Allegro Op. 134, 9, 15, 217

Smalt, Johannes Reinier, 215

Smart, Mary Ann, 94

Society for the Cultivation of Music, 215

Song of Love (film), 6

Sonntagsmusiken, 86, 88

Spohr, Ludwig, 61

Stägemann, Friedrich August and Elisabeth von, *Liederspiel,* 100

Stamaty, Camille, 105

Stockhausen, Julius, 195

Struck, Michael, 198, 220, 270n79, 271n83, 271n88

style hongrois, 228, 230–231, 235–236, 272n113, 273n121. See also *hallgató* style; *verbunkos* music

the sublime, 5, 11; as aesthetic experience, 124–125; rhetoric of, 126–131, 154. See also *Concert sans orchestre; Études symphoniques;* Jean Paul; Liszt, Franz; pleasure; Schumann, Robert, writings of: promotion of Liszt; Toccata, Op. 7

Sumner Lott, Marie, 220

Synofzik, Thomas, 174

A Systematic Introduction to Improvisation on the Pianoforte, op. 200 (Czerny), 30

Taubert, Wilhelm, 105; Piano Concerto No. 1, 175

Tausch, Julius, 204

Der Templer und die Jüdin (Marschner), 116, 118, *119–120,* 259n97

textures: "brilliant" style, 18, 24, 34; Clara Schumann's voicing, 74, 84–85, 263n99; lieder genre, 218, 268n14; Liszt's works, 21; orchestral, 152; postclassical showpieces, 94, 116; Robert Schumann's piano playing, 92, 256n25; to sustain listener's engagement, 34; three-handed technique, 21, 49; variation sets, 59, 61, 122. *See also* culminating displays

Thalberg, Sigismond, 21, 76, 251n50; postclassical virtuosity, 20; rivalry with Liszt, 43; Schumann's appreciation of, 48–51; Schumann's critique of, 37–40, 133, 134; three-handed technique, 21, 49. *See also* "brilliant" style; postclassical virtuosity

Thalberg, Sigismond, works: Andante Op. 32, 26; Caprice, Op. 15, 30; *Deux airs russes variés,* Op. 17, 49, *50–51,* 57; Etudes, Op. 26, 39; *Fantaisie sur des thèmes de "Moïse,"* Op. 33, 48, 49, 88; *Grande fantaisie et variations sur des motifs de "Norma,"* Op. 12, 34–36, *35–36,* 40; *Grand fantaisie sur "I Capuletti e Montechi,"* Op. 10, 39–40; Piano Concerto Op. 5, 44
three-handed technique, 21, 49
Toccata, Op. 7 (Schumann), 8–9, *9,* 124, 125, 126, 146–151, *148–149,* 172, 263n96. *See also* Beethoven, Ludwig van; the heroic
Töpken, Theodore, 17
transcendent interiority. *See* the poetic
Trippett, David, 157
Tunbridge, Laura, 223, 271n101

"Ueber Virtuosenunfug" (Krüger), 14–15, 87, 168

variation sets, 23, 30, 31–34, 71–72, 91, 94, 98; Schumann essay on, 40–41. *See also* "brilliant" style; commodification of music; specific works under Chopin, Czerny, Herz, Hummel, Kalkbrenner, Moscheles, Thalberg
verbunkos music, 228, 230, 272n113. See also *style hongrois*
Verhulst, Johannes, 215
Vieuxtemps, Henri, 160
Violin Concerto (Schumann), 196, 198, 221–222, *224–225,* 227–228, 239, 271n92, 272n102
virtuosity, definitions of, 2, 247n3
virtuosity discourse: anxiety about, 2–3, 12, 106–107; debates and musical factions, 241–243; Fink's analysis, 28; as German debate, 11–12; in the late nineteenth century and beyond, 239, 244–245; and the middle class, 13; nature of, 1–7; as revealed by showpieces, 8–11; Schumann's role in shaping, 7–8. *See also* the culture of serious music; neo-Baroque virtuosity; the poetic; the sublime; *Werktreue,* ideal of
virtuosos: compared to circus performers, 14, 107, 244; Krüger's image of the virtuoso, 14–15, 53, 168–170; prima donnas and castrati, 13; star virtuosos, 2, 11, 126–127; status and image of, 3; virtuoso "priests," 11,

195–197; and work concept, 168–169. *See also* entries for individual composer-performers
Voigt, Henriette, 5, 87, 94, 100, 104–110, 123. *See also* salon culture
Vorschule der Aesthetik (Jean Paul), 55, 98, 99, 104, 128, 150
de Vries, Claudia, 74, 238, 267n68

Wasielewski, Wilhelm Joseph von, 136, 261n47, 261n49
Watkins, Holly, 23, 54, 55, 252n5
Weber, Carl Maria von, 26; postclassical virtuosity, 20
Weber, Carl Maria von, works: *Aufforderung zum Tanze,* 26, 68, 91; *Der Freischütz,* 177; *Konzertstück,* Op. 79, 126, 132
Weber, Gottfried, 170, 178–179
Weber, William, 13
Werktreue, ideal of, 53, 156–157, 195, 198, 241–242, 267n2. *See also* Joachim, Joseph; Schumann, Clara Wieck; virtuosity discourse; work concept
Wieck, Clara. *See* Schumann, Clara Wieck
Wieck, Friedrich, 82; on Chopin's Variations, Op. 2, 60, 61, 253n35; *Clavier und Gesang,* 44–45; as manager of Clara's career, 8, 59–60; private soirees, 91; Schumann as student of, 25, 26. *See also* Schumann, Clara Wieck
Witz (musical wit), 98–100, 109. *See also* Jean Paul; salon culture
Witztheorie, 99, 117
women: and piano playing, 44–45, 251n66; and private performances of the salon, 87. *See also* Belleville, Anna Caroline de; Carus, Agnes; Fricken, Ernestine von; gender stereotypes; Kaskel, Sophie; luxury, aristocracy, and femininity; Schumann, Clara Wieck; Voigt, Henriette
Wood, Gillen d'Arcy, 44, 251n66
work concept, 11, 12, 157, 159; defined, 156, 264n3 (pt. II); Krüger–Hirschbach debate, 168–170. *See also* canon formation; Liszt, Franz, works: *Grandes études;* Paganini transcriptions
Wurst, Karin, 28, 29

Zeitung–Zeitschrift rivalry, 23; essays on Thalberg, 40. *See also* "Ein Opus II" (Schumann)

ALEXANDER STEFANIAK is Assistant Professor of Musicology at Washington University in Saint Louis.